Quantitative Reasoning in the Context of Energy and Environment

Quantitative Reasoning in the Context of Energy and Environment

Modeling Problems in the Real World

Robert Mayes
Georgia Southern University, USA

and

James Myers
University of Wyoming, USA

SENSE PUBLISHERS
ROTTERDAM/BOSTON/TAIPEI

A C.I.P. record for this book is available from the Library of Congress.

ISBN: 978-94-6209-525-0 (paperback)
ISBN: 978-94-6209-526-7 (hardback)
ISBN: 978-94-6209-527-4 (e-book)

Published by: Sense Publishers,
P.O. Box 21858,
3001 AW Rotterdam,
The Netherlands
https://www.sensepublishers.com/

Printed on acid-free paper

Book Cover Figures. Figure upper left: World Oil Production (Source: Association for the Study of Peak Oil and Gas. The Oil Conundrum. DAINA. 16 January 2011. ISBN 978-0-9644741-1-6). Figure upper right: Global Carbon Cycle (NASA/ GLOBE Carbon Cycle Project). Figure lower left: Atmospheric CO_2 (Source: U.S. Government NOAA Earth System Research Laboratory, March 2014). Figure lower right: Mountain Range. (Source: U.S. Fish and Wildlife Service. Alaska Peninsula National Wildlife Refuge).

CONTENTS

ACKNOWLEDGEMENTS

This work is the result of the QR STEM Project, a professional development program offered over three years to elementary, middle and secondary science and mathematics teachers in Wyoming. It is an accumulation of the work of many people which was recorded here by Robert Mayes and James Myers. First we would like to thank the many teachers who participated in the project, bringing their own inspiration to the modules they developed and implemented in classrooms. Second we want to thank all the faculty who provided workshops for the project: Mark Lyford, Alan Childs, Norm Shinkle, Tim Robinson, Pete Ellsworth, Jim Verley, Tim Slater, and Sylvia Parker. Supporting this cast were our graduate students Joel Pontius, Sarabdeep Singh, and Reshmi Nair. Finally we want to thank those you assisted us with the task of turning the QR STEM Project into QR STEM the book, including the thankless tasks of editing, reference checking, copyright chasing, and image finding.

RM would like to thank Rachel Walker and Franzi Peterson, graduate students who supported the effort. I want to give a special thanks to my wife Lori Mayes and son Mitchell Mayes who spent many nights at the dining room table pouring over the book. Without them and all of you this work would never have been completed.

JM acknowledges many long and fruitful discussions with Mark Lyford of the Life Sciences Program at the University of Wyoming over the course of this project. These discussions helped greatly in developing, testing, and refining the energy concepts presented in this book. My work was supported, in part, by National Science Foundation DUE 0737533. I owe a great debt to my wife Deborah whose support, encouragement, and assistance made it possible to get through the low points.

Robert Mayes

James Myers

QUANTITATIVE REASONING: CHANGING PRACTICE IN SCIENCE AND MATHEMATICS

Current State of Practice and New Direction

INTRODUCTION

In the summer of 2007 Jimm Myers, Mark Lyford, and I were working at the University of Wyoming on projects to improve secondary and post-secondary science and mathematics education. Jimm, a distinguished professor of Geology, was integrating real-world problem-based tasks into introductory level geology courses. Mark, Director of the Life Sciences program, was reinventing all lower division biology classes with the goal of actively engaging students in developing understanding of essential concepts. I was Director of the University of Wyoming Science and Mathematics Teaching Center (SMTC), which led professional development efforts for inservice science and mathematics programs across Wyoming. We had set as a goal for the SMTC to establish programs that would engage teachers in interdisciplinary STEM teaching around real-world challenges that were place-based. The three of us met that summer to discuss working together on a project that would integrate all of our efforts with the goal of providing innovative professional development for STEM teachers in Wyoming. The result of that meeting was the Quantitative Reasoning in Science, Technology, Engineering, and Mathematics (QR-STEM) project.

QR-STEM was launched in the meeting room of a tavern in Wapiti, Wyoming in the summer of 2008 with a group of 20 teachers. It was the most central location we could secure on the short notice provided by the state Mathematics and Science Partnership program that funded our effort. From these humble beginnings in a meeting room that also served as the square dance floor on weekends, we embarked on a three year journey to determine how to teach STEM that:

- was motivated by grand challenges in energy and environment;
- developed understanding of essential concepts in STEM beyond memorization of facts and mastery of skills;
- engaged students in studying global challenges addressed by STEM and how they impact the place in which they live;
- brought interdisciplinary lenses from biology, chemistry, earth sciences, physics, and mathematics to focus on important problems;
- enhanced quantitative reasoning in the sciences and mathematics.

QR STEM served 86 K-12 teachers over three years from 2008 to 2011, providing opportunities for teachers to improve both STEM content and pedagogical content knowledge and for us to develop and refine an approach to teaching STEM. We want to share with you in this volume the outcome of our work from QR STEM.

JUSTIFICATION

Preparing Students for Careers and Citizenship – Stakeholder Tools

What challenges exist for future generations of citizens? How do we educate the next generation to face such challenges? The National Academy of Sciences convened the Committee on Grand Challenges in Environmental Sciences to address the first question. The outcome was the report *Grand Challenges in Environmental Sciences* (National Academy Press, 2001), which identified eight grand challenges for which there is a need for significant infusion of research over the next two decades. Challenges such as:

- Biogeochemical cycles: understanding how human activity is perturbing the six nutrient cycles of carbon, oxygen, hydrogen, nitrogen, sulfur, and phosphorus which has impacts on climate change, CO_2 concentrations, acid rain, and chlorofluorocarbons (CFC);
- Biological diversity and ecosystem functioning: understanding the regulation and functional consequences of biological diversity which has impacts on rates of species extinction, threats to biological diversity, and controls on biological diversity;
- Hydrological forecasting: understanding and predicting changes in freshwater resources and the environment caused by floods, droughts, sedimentation, and contamination which threatens freshwater ecosystems.

The challenge for our education system is twofold. First, the education system must increase and then sustain a STEM pipeline of students to serve as the next generation of scientists, engineers, and mathematicians who will help research and solve such grand challenges. Second, and equally important, the education system must produce a scientifically literate citizenship that can make informed decisions about grand challenges. Economic, policy, and social issues will converge around the grand challenges forcing citizens to make decisions that will impact the future of their resources. These two desired outcomes will require that STEM education for all students will have deeper learning experiences facilitating the understanding and use of key scientific concepts to interpret, evaluate and solve real world problems. Scientific literacy and quantitative literacy are essential for both of these outcomes.

Scientific Literacy

The United States National Center for Educational Statistics (NAS, 1996) defines scientific literacy as the knowledge and understanding of scientific concepts and processes required for personal decision making, participation in civic and cultural affairs, and economic productivity. Another definition is provided by the National Science Education Standards:

> Scientific literacy means that a person can ask, find, or determine answers to questions derived from curiosity about everyday experiences. It means that a person has the ability to describe, explain, and predict natural phenomena. Scientific literacy entails being able to read with understanding articles about science in the popular press and to engage in social conversation about the validity of the conclusions. Scientific literacy implies that a person can identify scientific issues underlying national and local decisions and express positions that are scientifically and technologically informed. A literate citizen should be able to evaluate the quality of scientific information on the basis of its source and the methods used to generate it. Scientific literacy also implies the capacity to pose and evaluate arguments based on evidence and to apply conclusions from such arguments appropriately (National Science Education Standards, page 22).

Scientific literacy is one of the tenets of the QR STEM program. We believe it is essential for education to provide experiences that create both future scientists and scientifically literate citizens. But how does a teacher develop tasks that will elicit scientific literacy? What does it look like? What is the state of scientific literacy in the United States?

Let's begin with the last of these questions. The Program for International Student Assessment (PISA) is an international assessment measuring the performance of 15-year-olds in both science literacy and mathematics literacy every 3 years (Flesichman, Hopstock, Pelczar, & Shelley, 2010). PISA is coordinated by the Organization for Economic Cooperation and Development (OECD), an intergovernmental organization of 34 countries. Sixty countries and 5 other education systems participated as partners in PISA beginning in 2000. The U.S. sample consisted of 165 schools and 5,233 students. The fourth cycle of the assessment was given in 2009. On the science literacy scale the U.S. students scored 502, which was not significantly different from the OECD average of 501. The U.S. ranked 13th among the 34 OECD countries, tied with 12 other countries. Among all 64 countries taking PISA, the U.S. ranked 19th along with 13 other countries. Level 4 on the scientific literacy scale represents "the level at which students can complete higher order tasks such as selecting and integrating explanations from different disciplines of science or technology and linking those explanations directly to life situations" (U.S. Department of Education, 2010). For the U.S., 29% of students scored at or above this level. There was no significant difference between U.S. students and students in the other OECD countries that scored at the individual proficiency levels. U.S. students in 2009 outscored their 2006 PISA counterparts, but not by a significantly different margin. These findings indicate that there is work to be done in developing the scientific literacy of students in our schools.

It is easy to be sceptical about teaching students the STEM knowledge and understanding they will need to make informed decisions about socio-cultural-political issues. How can we know what issues will be important to them in the future? Or what new issues will arise? First scientific literacy is more than knowledge of science facts. We must avoid teaching STEM as isolated facts within set domains of knowledge, such as biology versus chemistry. A student who knows science as a collection of disconnected facts will not likely be able to recall the fact needed when deciding on whether or not to vote for legislation on climate change. In addition, the science knowledge they collected in high school may be out dated years later when needed even if they do recollect it. We need to develop the research skills that will allow our future citizens to research the problem, identify credible data, and make meaning of that data. So we need to focus on accessing knowledge not memorizing it.

Second, scientific literacy is not equivalent with teaching the scientific method. We need to avoid teaching science as if there is a single method of inquiry. *Taking Science to School* (Duschl, Schweingruber, & Shouse, 2007) calls to move learning towards literacy and modelling practices in the sciences. The National Research Council report identifies four proficiencies in science that all students should attain:

- Strand 1: Know, use, interpret scientific explanations of the natural world;
- Strand 2: Generate and evaluate scientific evidence and explanation;
- Strand 3: Understand the nature and development of scientific knowledge;
- Strand 4: Participate productively in scientific practices and discourse.

The four strands emphasize a move from science as inquiry to science practices rooted in model-building and model-refining, moving science out of its current silos of biology, chemistry, earth systems, and physics into a more integrated STEM approach focused on the application of science in real-world contexts. Science as model-building is defined as learning science as a process of building theories and models using evidence, checking them for internal consistency and coherence, and testing them empirically (Duschl, et al., 2007). We believe that modelling real-world problems will provide students with a richer more diverse perspective on what it means to do science. Science is not one way of thinking; it is many ways of thinking.

Third, scientific literacy is more than understanding the sociology of science: the notion of a community of scientists who are fallible, where there are multiple methods of doing science, and science ethics are debated. We need to engage students in the practice of doing science that they can relate to their world, not just instruct them on that practice. The National Research Council report *A Framework for K-12 Science Education: Practices, Crosscutting Concepts, and Core Ideas* (NRC, 2011) states that STEM disciplines permeate our lives and thus are central to meeting humanity's most pressing challenges. The report proposes three dimensions around which STEM education should be coordinated:

- Crosscutting concepts that unify the study of science through common application across science fields
- Scientific practices
- Core ideas in physical sciences, life sciences, earth and space sciences, technology, and the applications of science

Common to both NRC national reports is a focus on the interdisciplinary study of real-world problems that emphasize key STEM understandings and practices. In QR STEM we focus on engaging students in STEM through the exploration of real-world problems through an interdisciplinary lens.

A number of national science literacy projects have been undertaken including ocean (Ocean Literacy Network, 2011), atmosphere (UCAR, 2007), earth science (Earth Science Literacy Initiative, 2009), environmental (Pathways Project, 2012), climate (Climate Literacy Network, 2011), and energy literacy (Energy Literacy Project, 2011). A key component of developing the projects was the identification of 6 to 9 enduring understandings or essential principles within an area of science which a scientifically literate citizen should comprehend. The identification of enduring understandings that should drive the curriculum are supported by the Understanding by Design assessment framework, which we used as a framework for developing performance tasks in the QR STEM project.

Jimm Myers developed a model of literacies (Figure 1) which we used to guide the QR STEM project. Investigating the natural world through the application of science and scientific principles requires making sense of large amounts of data, assessing qualitatively the importance of different factors and performing simple calculations. These skills constitute the **fundamental literacies**. They are crucial to working in the real world as well as the scientific realm. These skills are important in nearly all professions, including the social sciences, humanities, and science, as well as in everyday activities such as selecting the best cell phone plan. It is likely that many of these skills were introduced at some point in a student's education. However, if they do not engage in using these skills within the context of science, they will not likely develop fluency in using the skills. Understanding and using scientific content requires mastering a series of **technical literacies**. Although some of them vary from one scientific discipline to another, other technical literacies are shared by a number of scientific disciplines. Unlike with the fundamental literacies, many individuals will have had limited, if any, experience with these types of skills. Yet, a quick perusal of any introductory science textbook will demonstrate clearly the importance of these literacies in understanding and applying scientific content. Combining the fundamental and technical literacies with scientific content produces **scientific understanding**, that is; the ability to use scientific knowledge in new settings and to draw correct inferences and conclusions from scientific reasoning. Most introductory science courses are designed to go only this far in their instruction. They assume students can apply what they have learned in the course to societal applications without further assistance. In addition, many assume students have mastered the two literacies or will learn them on their own during the course. They rarely provide systematic and meaningful practice with these critical tools.

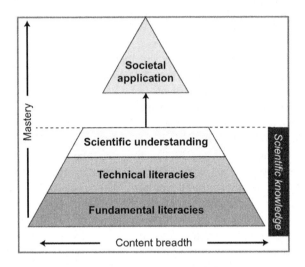

Figure 1. Literacies model.

Fundamental literacies consist of three abilities:

- Ability to read a table or interpret a graph or chart;
- Facility to make qualitative assessments;
- Aptitude to perform simple quantitative calculations correctly.

It is important to remember that these are filters for real-world data representation. This differs from their role in academic settings. Mastery of fundamental and technical literacies requires constant practice and application in a variety of contexts. Combined with scientific content, literacies produce scientific understanding. The barrier to literacies leading to scientific understanding is transfer – use of information/ skills of one domain in another domain (Robins, 1996). A liberal education is founded on the concept of transfer, but many students lack the ability to transfer knowledge between classes. Unfortunately many introductory science courses assume implicit transfer of science knowledge to the real-world, even though it is rare even for the best students. To facilitate classroom to real-world transfer, Myers and Massey (2008) defined **citizenship literacies**. These are the skills necessary to apply scientific understanding and knowledge to a variety of complex societal problems. Citizenship literacies are classified into critical thinking, understanding social context, and informed engagement. They are designed to help students connect science to real-world problems in a meaningful and effective way. These literacies enable them to be effective spokespersons.

Mathematical Literacy

A second tenet of the QR STEM program is mathematical literacy. The Expert Group for Mathematics of PISA provides the following definition.

> Mathematical literacy is an individual's capacity to identify and understand the role that mathematics plays in the world, to make well-founded judgments, and to engage in mathematics in ways that meet the needs of that individual's current and future life as a constructive, concerned and reflective citizen (OECD, 1999).

The ability to apply mathematics within a community of practice and as a citizen has received a great amount of attention in mathematics education over an extended period of time. It is not surprising then that this ability has been included in constructs that go by many names other than mathematical literacy which either overlap or even subsume one another. This ability is referred to as numeracy, number sense, quantitative literacy, contextualized mathematics, modelling, and quantitative reasoning, as well as mathematics literacy. These different names come with different definitions, including the following:

> Quantitative literacy involves sophisticated reasoning with elementary mathematics more than elementary reasoning with sophisticated mathematics (Steen 2004).

> Quantitative literacy is an aggregate of skills, knowledge, beliefs, dispositions, habits of mind, communication capabilities, and problem-solving skills that people need in order to engage effectively in quantitative situations arising in life and work (International Life Skills Survey 2000).

> Quantitative reasoning is the power and habit of mind to search out quantitative information, critique it, reflect upon it, and apply it in public, personal and professional life (National Numeracy Network 2011).

As with science literacy, the current status of mathematical literacy has been assessed by PISA (Fleischman, Hopstock, Pelczar, & Shelley, 2010). U.S. 15 year olds had an average score of 487 on the mathematics literacy scale, lower than the OECD average of 496. The U.S. ranked 18 out of 33 OECD counties, with scores not significantly different from 11 other countries. Only 5 countries had lower scores than the U.S. Among all 64 countries in the sample the U.S. ranked 24th, along with 12 other countries. A proficiency level of 4 indicates students can complete higher order tasks such as solving problems that involve visual and spatial reasoning in unfamiliar contexts and carrying out sequential processes (OECD 2004, p. 55). Twenty-seven percent of U.S. students scored at or above level 4, lower than 32% of students in OECD countries. Level 2 represents a baseline level of mathematics proficiency at which students begin to demonstrate literacy skills that enable them to actively use mathematics (OECD 2004, p. 55). While 23% of U.S. students scored at or below this level, this did not differ significantly from the other OECD countries. Finally, the U.S. mathematics literacy scores were higher in 2009 then 2006, but not significantly higher.

In the QR STEM Project we considered multiple conceptions of mathematical literacy in the context of energy and environment, and choose to use the term **Quantitative Reasoning within Context** (QRC). We incorporated into QRC the conception of the **act of quantification**, which we interpret as the fundamental mathematical process by which one moves from context to quantity and back to context. Thompson (2011) defines quantification as the process of conceptualizing an object and an attribute of it so that the attribute has a unit measure, and the attribute's measure entails a proportional relationship (linear, bi-linear, or multi-linear) with its unit. Quantification requires conceptualization and reconceptualization in relation to each other of the object being quantified, the attributes of that object, and the measure of the attribute. The aforementioned conception of science as modeling was also integrated into QRC.

In the seminal work *Mathematics and Democracy: The case for quantitative literacy,* Steen (2001) is clear that quantitative literacy is more than mathematics and statistics:

> Quantitative literacy is more a habit of mind, an approach to problems that employs and enhances both statistics and mathematics. Unlike statistics, which is primarily about uncertainty, numeracy is often about the logic of certainty. Unlike mathematics, which is primarily about a Platonic realm of abstract structures, numeracy is often anchored in data derived from and attached to the empirical world. (p. 5)

Shavelson (2008) in *Reflections on Quantitative Reasoning: An assessment perspective* seeks a definition of quantitative reasoning by exploring three approaches to the topic: psychometric (behavioral roots), cognitive (mental process roots), and situative (social-contextual roots). The psychometric tradition has reached a consensus that there is a QR factor, that is, performance on QR tests are distinguishable from performance on other mathematics tests. QR requires reasoning based on mathematical properties and relations, with a low demand on computation and high demand on reasoning with numbers, operations, and patterns. Situative researchers view QR within a community of practice:

> ...those individuals engaged in culturally relevant activities in which reasoning quantitatively is demanded and the various resources of the community would be brought to bear on those activities. They would view a person accomplished in QR as having the capacity to engage others in working together to think critically, reason analytically and to solve a problem. Cognitive abilities, from this perspective, reside in a community of practice. (Shavelson 2008, p. 8)

Table 1 from Shavelson (2007) contrasts mathematics and QR.

Table 1. Contrast of Mathematics with QR

Mathematics	Quantitative Reasoning
Power in abstraction	Real, authentic contexts
Power in generality	Specific, particular applications
Some context dependency	Heavy context dependency
Society independent	Society dependent
Apolitical	Political
Methods and algorithms	Ad hoc methods
Well-defined problems	Ill-defined problems
Approximation	Estimation is critical
Heavily disciplinary	Interdisciplinary
Problem solutions	Problem descriptions
Few opportunities to practice outside classroom	Many opportunities to practice outside the classroom
Predictable	Unpredictable

Source: Shavelson, R. J. (2008). Reflections on quantitative reasoning: An assessment perspective. Calculation vs. Context, 27.

Madison (2006) provides a situative definition of QR as carried out in real-life, authentic situations; its application is in the particular situation, one dependent upon context including socio-politics. QR problems are deeply contextualized, ill defined, open-ended, real-world tasks that require analysis, critical thinking, estimation, interdisciplinary approaches, and the capacity to communicate a solution, decision, or course of action clearly in writing.

The definition of QRC we used in the QR STEM Project draws on all of the above constructs as well as our own work on quantitative reasoning in the context of energy and environment.

Quantitative Reasoning in Context (QRC) is mathematics and statistics applied in real-life, authentic situations that impact an individual's life as a constructive, concerned, and reflective citizen. QRC problems are context dependent, interdisciplinary, open-ended tasks that require critical thinking and the capacity to communicate a course of action.

While acknowledging that QR does occur in abstract mathematical situations without real world context, our focus is on QR in context.

So what are the components of quantitative reasoning in context? Steen identifies components of quantitative literacy which citizens should acquire, including confidence with mathematics (numeracy, estimation), cultural appreciation of mathematics (nature and history), interpreting data, logical thinking, making decisions, using mathematics in context, number sense, practical computation skills, prerequisite knowledge of algebra, geometry, statistics, and symbol sense. The Mathematical Association of America (MAA 1998) includes interpreting models, using multiple representations (symbolic, visual, numeric, graphic), applying arithmetical, algebraic, geometric, and statistical methods, estimating to determine reasonableness, and recognizing limits of algorithmic methods. Jan de Lange (2001) enumerates what he calls competencies for mathematics literacy:

1. *Mathematical thinking and reasoning.* Posing questions characteristic of mathematics; knowing the kind of answers that mathematics offers, distinguishing among different kinds of statements; understanding and handling the extent and limits of mathematical concepts.
2. *Mathematical argumentation.* Knowing what proofs are; knowing how proofs differ from other forms of mathematical reasoning; following and assessing chains of arguments; having a feel for heuristics; creating and expressing mathematical arguments.
3. *Mathematical communication.* Expressing oneself in a variety of ways in oral, written, and other visual form; understanding someone else's work.
4. *Modeling.* Structuring the field to be modeled; translating reality into mathematical structures; interpreting mathematical models in terms of context or reality; working with models; validating models; reflecting, analyzing, and offering critiques of models or solutions; reflecting on the modeling process.
5. *Problem posing and solving.* Posing, formulating, defining, and solving problems in a variety of ways.
6. *Representation.* Decoding, encoding, translating, distinguishing between, and interpreting different forms of representations of mathematical objects and situations as well as understanding the relationship among different representations.
7. *Symbols.* Using symbolic, formal, and technical language and operations.
8. *Tools and technology.* Using aids and tools, including technology when appropriate.

In the early stages of QR STEM we began by conducting a curricular analysis of what mathematics and statistics were central to a study of science. Table 2 presents an updated version of essential QR processes based on our work on the National Science Foundation Pathways project.[1] These are quantitative tools that we found occurring with great regularity in energy and environment contexts.

We grouped the quantitative reasoning tools within four processes we believe are essential to QRC: quantification act, quantitative literacy, quantitative interpretation, and quantitative modeling. We will discuss each of the processes in more detail later.

While a collection of mathematical and statistical tools are necessary, it is not enough to memorize algorithms. QRC is difficult to teach and learn because, as Hughes Hallett posited in *Mathematics and Democracy,* it involves insight as well as algorithms (Hughes Hallet, 2001).

Such insight, Hughes Hallett noted, connotes an understanding of quantitative relationships and the ability to identify those relationships in an unfamiliar context; its acquisition involves reflection, judgment, and above all, experience. Yet current school curricula seldom emphasize insight and do little to actively support its development at any level. This is very unfortunate. The development of insight into mathematics should be actively supported, starting before children enter school (de Lange, 2001).

The Netherlands addressed concerns about algorithmic-based teaching by clustering the required mathematical competencies. For example clustering insight, reasoning, reflection, and generalization so that students viewed them as a connected set of tools, any of which could be drawn upon in an open-ended problem, rather than providing separate contexts for each of the four competencies. If mathematics were taught by engaging students in real-world, problem-based tasks that required the insight to select

Table 2. QR Processes

Quantification Act	Quantitative Literacy	Quantitative Interpretation	Quantitative Modeling
Variable Identification	*Numeracy*	*Math Representations*	*Logic*
Object Attribute Measure	Number Sense Small/Large Numbers Scientific Notation	Table/Graph Equation Statistical Displays	Syllogistic Logic
Communication	*Measurement*	*Science Diagrams*	*Problem Solving*
Force-dynamic Scientific Discourse Quantitative Discourse	Accuracy Precision Estimation Unit Analysis	Box Models Complex Systems	Problem Formulation Heuristics
Context	*Proportional Reasoning*	*Statistics/Probability*	*Models*
QR Avoidance Computation Driven Situative View	Fraction/Ratio Percent Rates/Change Proportions Dimensional Analysis	Randomness Risk Correlation Z-scores Confidence Intervals	Normal Distribution Regression Models Logistic Growth Simulations
Variation	*Basic Prob/Stats*	*Translation*	*Inference*
Causation Covariation	Empirical Probability Counting Central Tendency Spread	Compare Models Contrast Models	Making Inference Hypothesis Testing Practical Significance

the appropriate competencies to bring to bear on the problem, then perhaps the disparity between quantitative reasoning and mathematics would not be so great. Unfortunately the standard practice of teaching mathematics from a perspective of mastering algorithms in isolation from context has resulted in a gap that is large and by most unrecognized.

The gap is further expanded by the current silo nature of teaching mathematics and science. Mathematics is arranged in strands which are largely isolated from one another; silos of arithmetic, algebra, geometry, and the culminating calculus course are the standard. Science has its own silos of biology, chemistry, earth science and physics. Teaching mathematics or science in silos gives a misleading view of the subjects. Students move through the curriculum never seeing the connection between the subjects. The development of insight and intuition about how mathematics and science provide interdisciplinary lenses to solve real-world problems is precluded. It comes down to the philosophical view of what mathematics and science are. Are they pure theoretical abstraction? Or were their theories and concepts created to model phenomena in the natural and social world? We believe that for most persons the second case is the most essential. The silo approach does not reflect how mathematics or science is applied in the natural world. Real-world problems do not often align themselves along a single content strand, rather they call for interdisciplinary approaches. Steen (1990) and Freudenthal (1973) call for mathematics curricula to feature multiple parallel strands grounded in appropriate childhood experiences. As in the natural science literacy projects, mathematics educators have been seeking enduring understandings which could serve as a basis for such strands that are essential to the development of insight for mathematical literacy. Steen recommended five such enduring understandings: dimension, quantity, uncertainty, shape, and change. The OECD PISA mathematics expert group adapted these to create four phenomenological categories to describe the mathematics needed for literacy: quantity, space and shape, change and relationships, and uncertainty (OECD 2002). Definitions of these categories were provided by de Lange (2001) and are given below.

- *Quantity.* The overarching idea is a need for quantification to organize the world. Important aspects include an understanding of relative size, recognition of numerical patterns, and the ability to use numbers to represent quantifiable attributes of real-world objects (measures). Quantity deals with the processing and understanding of numbers that are represented to us in various ways. An important aspect of dealing with quantity is quantitative reasoning, whose essential components are developing and using number sense, representing numbers in various ways, understanding the meaning of operations, having a feel for the magnitude of numbers, writing and understanding mathematically elegant computations, doing mental arithmetic, and estimating.
- *Space and Shape.* Patterns are encountered everywhere around us: in spoken words, music, video, traffic, architecture, and art. Shapes can be regarded as patterns: houses, office buildings, bridges, starfish, snowflakes, town plans, cloverleaves, crystals, and shadows. Geometric patterns can serve as relatively simple models of many kinds of phenomena, and their study is desirable at all levels (Gru"nbaum

1985). In the study of shapes and constructions, we look for similarities and differences as we analyze the components of form and recognize shapes in different representations and different dimensions. The study of shapes is closely connected to the concept of "grasping space" (Freudenthal 1973)—learning to know, explore, and conquer, in order to live, breathe, and move with more understanding in the space in which we live. To achieve this, we must be able to understand the properties of objects and the relative positions of objects; we must be aware of how we see things and why we see them as we do; and we must learn to navigate through space and through constructions and shapes. This requires understanding the relationship between shapes and images (or visual representations) such as that between a real city and photographs and maps of the same city. It also includes understanding how three-dimensional objects can be represented in two dimensions, how shadows are formed and interpreted, and what perspective is and how it functions.

- *Change and Relationships.* Every natural phenomenon is a manifestation of change, and in the world around us a multitude of temporary and permanent relationships among phenomena are observed: organisms changing as they grow, the cycle of seasons, the ebb and flow of tides, cycles of unemployment, weather changes, stock exchange fluctuations. Some of these change processes can be modeled by straightforward mathematical functions: linear, exponential, periodic or logistic, discrete or continuous. But many relationships fall into different categories, and data analysis is often essential to determine the kind of relationship present. Mathematical relationships often take the shape of equations or inequalities, but relations of a more general nature (e.g., equivalence, divisibility) may appear as well. Functional thinking— that is, thinking in terms of and about relationships— is one of the fundamental disciplinary aims of the teaching of mathematics. Relationships can take a variety of different representations, including symbolic, algebraic, graphic, tabular, and geometric. As a result, translation between representations is often of key importance in dealing with mathematical situations.
- *Uncertainty.* Our information-driven society offers an abundance of data, often presented as accurate and scientific and with a degree of certainty. But in daily life we are confronted with uncertain election results, collapsing bridges, stock market crashes, unreliable weather forecasts, poor predictions of population growth, economic models that do not align, and many other demonstrations of the uncertainty of our world. Uncertainty is intended to suggest two related topics: data and chance, phenomena that are the subject of mathematical study in statistics and probability, respectively. Specific mathematical concepts and activities that are important in this area include collecting data, data analysis, data display and visualization, probability, and inference.

Source: De Lange, J. (2001). Mathematics for Literacy. In Madison, B. & Steen, A. (Eds). *Quantiative Literacy: Why numeracy matters for schools and colleges.* New Jersey: National Council on Education and Disciplines. Currently available through the Mathematics Association of America (MAA) at the following website: www.maa.org

In QR STEM we defined quantitative reasoning more broadly then the definition given under the quantity category. For us QRC includes the categories of quantity, change and relationship, and uncertainty. The space and shape category was not central to our conception of QRC, though the process of interpreting graphical representations certainly engages students in components of this category. Recall that our context for quantitative reasoning is science. The work of de Lange (2001) raises concerns about "confronting nonscience students with mathematics applications that need specific science literacy at a nonbasic level". The question is one of transfer and familiarity with the situation. Transfer of knowledge and understanding across domains is challenging. In fact research has shown that near transfer (between two domains which have strong structural and context similarity) is difficult and far transfer (between widely disparate domains with implicit structural similarity) is rare. One means of increasing the ability to transfer is to engage students in solving real-world open-ended problems in different contexts. Another is to use competency clusters. In QR STEM we strove to engage students in real-world situations derived from global challenges that were also relevant to them in their local place. Our goal was to have them function as scientifically literate citizens.

We have introduced a lot of terms related to mathematical literacy and quantitative reasoning. How do they interrelate? The answer to that question might well depend on who you ask. The work of de Lange (2001) provides a categorization of types of basic mathematics literacy (Figure 2) for students up to age 15 which gives some coherence to the web of relationships. But realize it is only one view and there are many. His categorization has the four enduring understandings on the lowest level

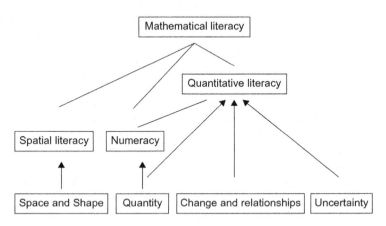

Figure 2. Web of Mathematics Literacy. Source: De Lange, J. (2001). Mathematics for Literacy. In Madison, B. & Steen, A. (Eds). Quantiative Literacy: Why numeracy matters for schools and colleges. New Jersey: National Council on Education and Disciplines. Currently available through the Mathematics Association of America (MAA) at the following website: https://www.maa.org/external_archive/QL/pgs75_89.pdf

relegated to three intermediate literacies: spatial literacy (understanding properties of objects, relative position of objects, visual perception, creation of 2D and 3D pathways, navigational practices), numeracy literacy (ability to handle numbers and data, evaluate numbers in context, mental processing and estimating in real-world contexts), and quantitative literacy. He then places mathematical literacy as the overarching literacy.

In the QR STEM project we place quantitative reasoning at the top tier in place of mathematical literacy (Figure 3). We follow de Lange (2001) in having quantitative literacy as one of the processes supporting QRC, but not in listing quantitative reasoning as a lower level component of quantity within quantitative literacy. We have three other processes (literacies) that we feel are essential to QRC: act of quantification, quantitative interpretation, and quantitative modeling. The act of quantification expands on elements of quantity in de Lange's model. We see this as the fundamental process of building a quantity with which one would reason. Quantitative modeling moves aspects of change and relationship as well as uncertainty out from under quantitative literacy. We feel Duschl's (2007) new emphases on science as modeling necessitates highlighting the process of modeling within QRC. Within modeling we place change and relationship aspects of function models, data analysis, and functional thinking. From uncertainty we take inference as an element of modeling. We include the process of quantitative interpretation as essential to being a scientifically literate citizen. When data or models are provided in support of a position on a real-world problem, an informed citizen needs to be able to interpret that model. Quantitative interpretation draws multiple representations and translation between representations from the change and relationships category,

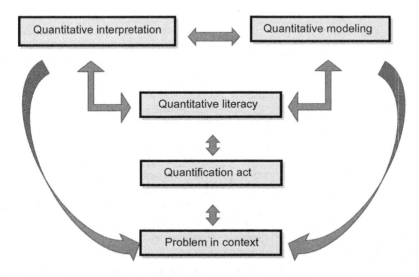

Figure 3. QRC Cycle. Source: Mayes, R., F.I. Peterson, & R. Bonilla 2013. Quantitative reasoning learning progressions for environmental science: Developing a framework. Numeracy 6: 1–28.

as well as probability, statistics (up to inference), data display and visualization from the uncertainty category. We will now expand on our discussion of the four QRC processes we have introduced.

Quantitative Reasoning in Context (QRC) has four key processes:

1. Act of Quantification: mathematical process of conceptualizing an object and an attribute of it so that the attribute has a unit measure, and the attribute's measure entails a proportional relationship (linear, bi-linear, or multi-linear) with its unit
2. Quantitative Literacy: use of fundamental mathematical concepts in sophisticated ways for the purpose of describing, comparing, manipulating, and drawing conclusions from variables developed in the act of quantification
3. Quantitative Interpretation: ability to use models to discover trends and make predictions, which is central to a person being a citizen scientist who can make informed decisions about issues impacting their communities
4. Quantitative Modeling: ability to create representations to explain a phenomena and revise them based on fit to reality

These processes interact within a quantitative reasoning cycle (Figure 3). When an individual reflects upon a real-life authentic situation that impacts their community or their personal life, they will likely begin reasoning about the situation using a qualitative science account of the phenomena. This qualitative account may be based only on a personal discourse (personal experiential theory of the world), rise to the level of including a school science discourse (acquired knowledge of science often without deep understanding), and perhaps progress to a full scientific discourse (science principles explain the phenomena). Even at the full scientific discourse level the individual may not have engaged in quantitative reasoning; in fact they may have actively avoided using QR. A quantitative account should be sought to provide data-driven support for the qualitative account and to provide evidence supporting conclusions.

Quantitative Act (QA). The quantitative reasoning cycle begins with the individual engaging in the *act of quantification* by identifying objects, their attributes, and assigning measures. Quantification provides variables that can be operated on mathematically or statistically. Second, depending on both the query of interest to the individual and the data they access, they engage in quantitative reasoning through one of the three processes of quantitative literacy, quantitative interpretation, or quantitative modeling. These three processes are interconnected and typically engaging in one requires elements of another. The output of QR is often a model that is then applied within the context of the situation to answer a question. The model may be a loosely connected set of relationships, a table, a graph, a science systems model, or even a mathematical function. This model will need to be tested against the real-world situation and probably modified, leading back to the need to further quantify, and so the cycle repeats.

Quantitative Literacy (QL) underlies both the interpretation and building of models. The variables resulting from quantification are operated on through QL, including such basics as performing computations, comparing, and estimating. QL is mostly arithmetic in nature, epitomizing the sophisticated use of basic mathematics. Within the quantitative literacy process we have identified four major components (Table 2) that underpin the sciences: numeracy, measurement, proportional reasoning, and descriptive statistics and basic probability. There is a great deal of variation in definitions of numeracy, from a mastery of arithmetic symbols and processes to being equivalent with quantitative literacy. We define numeracy as the ability to reason with numbers. Numeracy then is the logic and problem-solving aspect of QR on the arithmetic level. Numeracy includes having number sense, mastery of arithmetic processes (addition, subtraction, multiplication, and division), logic and reasoning with numbers, orders of magnitude, weights and measures. Number sense is defined as awareness and understanding about what numbers are, their relationships, their magnitude, the relative effect of operating on numbers, including the use of mental mathematics and estimation (Fennel and Landis 1994). Number sense includes the concepts of magnitude, ranking, comparison, measurement, rounding, degree of accuracy, and estimation. Measurement is of central importance to science, so it is separated out from numeracy in the framework as a second component of quantitative literacy which includes accuracy, precision, estimation, and measurement units. Proportional reasoning is often a major conceptual barrier to students, inhibiting their ability to reason quantitatively in science. Here we include pre-proportional reasoning skills such as an understanding of fraction, ratio, percent, and rates, all leading up to proportions. Basic probability and descriptive statistics are essential in data analysis in the sciences and require mostly arithmetic processes, so they are included as a fourth quantitative literacy component.

Quantitative Interpretation (QI) expands upon the use of arithmetic processes in QL to include more mathematically sophisticated algebraic, geometric, statistical, and calculus processes. The QL focus on discovering relationships between variables is supplanted in QI by interpreting models to explore trends and make predictions, a skill that is essential for the citizen scientist. We will use the term model in its broadest sense, certainly as much more than the typical mathematical interpretation of model as a function representing a situation. Our understanding of models includes any representation of data and data relationships which allows for interpreting a distinct case within context, exploring trends, drawing inferences, and making predictions. QI entails interpreting models represented as tables, graphs, statistical graphical displays, equations, and complex scientific diagrams, as well as being able to translate between models. It includes the ability to interpret data using probability (randomness, evaluating risks) and statistical analysis (normal distributions, correlation, causality, z-scores, confidence intervals). Algebraic techniques such as logarithms are included under QI since they are common in science and provide a means of interpreting very small or very large scales. QI at the most basic level is the ability to interpret the relationship between two variables; to interpret a model at a given instance or point. At the intermediate level it entails being able to identify trends, to interpret change. At the upper level it is the ability to make predictions through interpolation and extrapolation, to see correlations between data sets, to explain covariation between two variables, and to determine not only the direction but strength of association.

Quantitative Modeling (QM) is inexorably interconnected with quantitative interpretation, for surely when we create models we do so to interpret them. But QM extends QI by requiring the individual to create the model rather than interpret one that is given. We define QM as the act of model creation or model generation, while acknowledging that constructed thinking about or with a model is an essential process in model building. We assign this act of constructed thinking about or with models to QI. It could be argued that a citizen will not often create their own models, but extending existing models to answer new questions and understanding how models are created are essential to quantitative reasoning. QM requires a high level of reasoning, including logical thinking, problem solving, hypothesis testing, and caution in making over generalizations. QM engages individuals in formulating problems, developing linear, power, exponential, multivariate, and simulation models, and creating table, graph and even scientific diagram models. QM includes statistical hypothesis testing and understanding practical significance. Duschl's (2007) view of science as model building and model testing is underpinned by the ability to quantitatively model a phenomenon.

Above we have provide an overview of what quantitative reasoning in context (QRC) is and established a framework for it. For those wanting a more detailed review of the literature grounding the QRC framework see the appendix at the end of Chapter 1. In this appendix we expound upon the four key processes of QA, QL, QI, and QM, as well as support for QR within a context.

Engagement

A central issue in STEM education is how we engage students in the sciences and mathematics. Too many of our students leave the STEM pipeline, losing interest in science and mathematics that does not appear to relate in a meaningful way to their lives. The admonition from students of "When will I ever use this stuff?" is an outcome of not engaging them in real-world, place-based STEM tasks. However, de Lange (OECD, 2002) has raised concerns about having science serve as a context for quantitative reasoning. He discusses the concept of situation, which he defines as "the part of the student's world in which a certain problem is embedded". The distance of a situation from the student's personal life and interest is important to engagement.

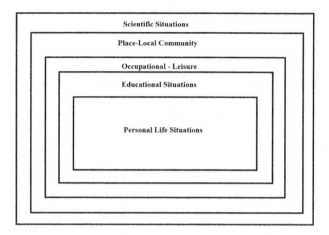

Figure 4. Engagement Situation Distance. Visual of work from Steen, L.A. (Ed.). (2001). Mathematics and democracy: The case for quantitative literacy. Princeton, NJ: The Woodrow Wilson National Fellowship Foundation, The National Council on Education and the Disciplines.

Steen (2001) developed a list of expressions of numeracy which can be used to create a categorization of distance from interest (Figure 4). The closer the distance from the student's personal life situation the more they will be engaged. Personal life situation includes things like games, sports, economic decisions, relationships, and health. Educational situation relates to understanding the role of mathematics in society, school activities, and the role of mathematics in other classes. Occupational and leisure situation involves understandings such as reasoning, understanding data, using statistics, finances, taxes, risks, rates, samples, scheduling, geometric patterns, budgets, and visualizations. Place and local community situations include citizens making intelligent decisions, evaluating conclusions, gather data and making inferences, and adopting a critical attitude. Scientific situations are the farthest removed from the personal life situation and so are by this model the hardest to motivate. However, this does not mean it cannot be done; just that it is a complex task with great potential awards.

We believe that to engage students in scientific situations you must select tasks that have global implications playing out in local place. Get students to think globally and act locally. Grand challenges in science identified by the National Research Council can serve as a source of global problems. Problem-based learning approaches provide a pedagogy for focusing instruction on real-world problems. Engaging students in global challenges is only half the story. Global challenges ensure that the student sees the critical importance of STEM in their future. However, such grand scales may overwhelm some students causing them to ask "What has this got to do with me and my community?" The global challenge needs to be tied to local place to ensure that students see the connection to their lives. This is key to engagement of the student in STEM. In QR STEM we focused on place-based pedagogy as a means of addressing these concerns.

Problem-based learning is a "learner-centered approach that empowers learners to conduct research, integrate theory and practice, and apply knowledge and skills to develop a viable solution to a defined problem." (Savery, 2006, p. 9). Long-term retention, skill development, and student and teacher satisfaction have been found to be benefits of problem-based learning when compared with traditional forms of instruction (Strobel & van Barneveld, 2009). Statistically significant gains in achievement have been observed for middle school science students experiencing science in a problem-based learning format (Williams, Pedersen, & Liu, 1998). The Jasper Woodbury series (CTGV, 1992) is an example of a problem-based mathematics curriculum for students in fifth grade and above. The CTGV (1992) reports improved student ability to solve word problems, plan to solve complex problems, and enhanced attitudes regarding mathematics when compared to students in the non-Jasper sections of the course. Inquiry-based instruction is closely aligned with problem-based learning (Savery, 2006, p. 16). Recently, it has been observed that lessons planned using an inquiry-based approach incorporating technology increased the higher-order thinking skills and technology use required in the lessons (Polly, 2011).

Place-based education that uses the environment as an integrating context for learning results in students who score higher on standardized tests in reading, writing, mathematics, science and social studies (Lieberman & Hoody, 1998; Bartosh, 2003; SEER 2000; NEETF, 2000). Other results from these studies indicate that students improve overall GPA, stay in school longer, and receive higher than average scholarship awards. Ernst and Monroe (2004) found that students in place-based programs significantly raised critical thinking skills. These positive outcomes are likely due to increased achievement motivation (Athman & Monroe, 2004), reduced discipline and classroom management problems (Falco, 2004; Lieberman & Hoody, 1998; NEETF, 2000; SEER, 2000), improved attendance (SEER, 2000), and more responsible behavior in school and community (Bartosh, 2003). The more exposure students have to place-based environmental education the more they report attachment to place, civic engagement, and environmental stewardship (Duffin et al., 2004). The American Institute for Research (2005) found that at-risk sixth graders engaged in place-based education significantly raised their science scores and improved problem solving and motivation to learn. Science from a model-building perspective is best achieved through integrated, interdisciplinary STEM instruction that incorporates place-based (Smith & Sobel, 2010) and problem-based pedagogies (Edelson & Reiser, 2006).

Inadequacies of Current Approach

Current pedagogical practices as embodied in the No Child Left Behind (NCLB) law typically assumes (1) that there is a single established body of mathematical and science skills that will prepare students to face the grand challenges of the 21st century, and (2) that those skills can be assessed on standardized tests. We believe based on the National Research Council (NRC) report, *Taking Science to School* (NRC, 2007), and our own research, that the NCLB view does not capture the complexity and interdisciplinarity of the curricula or assessment practices needed for developing scientifically literate citizens. We identified flaws in the current approach to STEM education that need to be addressed.

First, the science and mathematics curricula are too focused on coverage of facts and algorithms. We need to reduce the number of topics taught by identifying a limited set of enduring understandings that are essential to being able to apply science in real-world contexts. Enduring understandings are the big ideas in STEM that make it worth studying. We will discuss the concept of enduring understandings in more detail when we explore using the Understanding by Design assessment framework as a means of developing tasks.

Second, we need to teach science and mathematics within real-world contexts that are socially critical (for example the 8 grand challenges in environmental science). Learning mathematics and science in context should not be reserved for assessing skills already mastered. Real-world applications should be used as a context within which the learning of STEM facts and algorithms take place, along with the development of deeper understanding.

Third, we need to motivate our students to stay engaged in STEM and see the importance of it to them as both citizens and as a possible future career path. This is where place-based and problem-based pedagogies come into play. We can move a science situation into a community or personal life situation by relating global challenges to the student's local place.

Fourth, we need to improve student's critical thinking skills. Providing open-ended real-world tasks will engage students in problem formulation, which includes phrasing appropriate important questions within the science context, determining methods to study the problem, and selecting the correct tools from their STEM tool box. Having the students present their conclusions to others in addition to the teachers promotes the development of communication and collaborative problem solving.

Fifth, we need to be more interdisciplinary in our teaching. Real-world problems are seldom restricted to one area of STEM, rather they require collaborative efforts across disciplines. Quantitative reasoning provides a strong integrating factor for science if we require students to provide date-based defense of their decisions. Curriculum, instruction and assessment models need to break out of codified abstract sequences in school science and mathematics, sequences such as algebra, geometry, more algebra, pre-calculus in mathematics, or biology, chemistry, earth sciences, and physics in science.

QR STEM APPROACH

In QR STEM we took the approach of redesigning science and mathematics teaching by using quantitative reasoning as an integrating factor in teaching the sciences through real-world applications in energy and environment. Our approach was interdisciplinary, with science informed through quantitative reasoning and mathematics enriched through science context. We invited middle school and high school science and mathematics teachers to join interdisciplinary professional learning communities. In these communities the teachers selected real-world STEM topics within the broad areas of energy and environment for which they developed interdisciplinary curriculum modules. The framework for developing the modules was Understanding by Design (UbD) (Wiggins & McTighe, 2005), which required teachers to complete the backward design process:

- Stage 1: Identify desired results
- Stage 2: Determine acceptable evidence
- Stage 3: Plan learning experiences and instruction

The teachers were supported by experts in energy, environment, science education, mathematics education, and place-based education to create tasks that were based in global grand challenges but tied to their local region or community. QR STEM Symposia (Table 3) engaged teachers in professional development that emphasized increasing content knowledge in the science and mathematics of energy and environment; exploring quantitative reasoning processes including the act of quantification, quantitative literacy, quantitative interpretation, and quantitative modeling; exploring alternative pedagogical strategies including place-based and problem-based pedagogies; and applying the Understanding by Design framework to create performance tasks which anchored their curriculum modules. Once developed

Table 3. QR STEM Professional Development

	Symposium 0	Symposium 1	Symposium 2	Symposium 3	Review	Report
	Introductory Symposium	Transportation Symposium	Electricity Symposium	Climate Change Symposium	Peer Task Review	Post Task Report
Context	Energy Environment Overview	Energy in Transportation	Energy in Electricity	Environment Impacts		
QR	Quantitative Reasoning Overview	Quantitative Literacy	Quantitative Interpretation	Quantitative Modeling		
UbD	Understanding by Design Overview	Stage 1 Desired Results	Stage 2 Acceptable Evidence	Stage 3 Learning Experiences		
Pedagogy	Diverse Pedagogies	Teaching for Understanding	Place-based Pedagogy	Problem-based Pedagogy		

the modules were implemented by the teachers in their classrooms, engaging both the science and mathematics teachers in shared learning goals. To explore the impact of the modules on both teacher practice and student learning, the teachers engaged in lesson study and action research. The lesson study was based in the shared implementation of the module by the learning community. The learning community met on a regular basis with a science education faculty to discuss implementation and impact issues. The action research provided evidence of change in teacher practice and student learning. Teachers reported out findings to their peers in the program and the university faculty mentors.

Grand Challenges

To address the inadequacies in science and mathematics teaching and learning listed in the Inadequacies in Current Approach section, we began by focusing on authentic real-world problems identified by experts as being challenges for the next generation. We found the National Academy of Sciences report *Grand Challenges in Environmental Sciences* (NRC, 2001) to be a great resource in this regard. A committee of environmental scientists identified eight grand challenges in environmental science. Recall that a grand challenge is compelling for intellectual and practical reasons, offers potential for major breakthroughs on the basis of recent developments in science and technology, and is feasible given current capabilities and serious infusion of resources (2001, p2). These challenges fit our goals of having real-world socially significant science and mathematics applications that were interdisciplinary and could be related to one's place. The eight grand challenges are biogeochemical cycles, biological diversity and ecosystem functioning, climate variability, hydrological forecasting, infectious disease and environment, institutions and resource use, land-use dynamics, and reinventing the use of materials. You can find the report at http://www.nap.edu/catalog/9975.html. The QR STEM project was conducted in Wyoming, where energy production and environmental protection are paramount. So we selected the first four grand challenges as a focus for the project. Let's look at some of these challenges to gain some insight into how they can be used as a focus for middle and high school performance tasks.

The biogeochemical cycles grand challenge is to further our understanding of how Earth's major biogeochemical cycles are being perturbed by human activities. There are six nutrient elements: carbon, oxygen, hydrogen, nitrogen, sulfur, and phosphorus. Perturbation of these cycles is associated with climate change, greenhouse gases, carbon dioxide cycle, acid rain, and holes in the ozone. These are problems we hear about in the news all the time. The biological diversity and ecosystem functioning grand challenge is to understand the regulation and functional consequences of biological diversity. Problems stemming from this challenge are the increased rate of species extinction, threats to biodiversity, and controls on biological diversity. Finally, the hydrological forecasting grand challenge is to understand and predict changes in freshwater resources and the environment caused by flooding, droughts, sedimentation, and contamination. Concerns related to this challenge are the rapidly increasing consumption of freshwater by humans, threats to freshwater ecosystems, social and environmental impacts of floods and droughts, and consequences of water contamination.

With such variety it is easy to see how these grand challenges are ones that impact every community and citizen. It is, of course, impractical to cover them all in one science class, so the professional learning communities selected one on which they would focus. For purposes of improved student engagement, we worked with the teachers to select a challenge that was relevant to their home region. Restricting the science areas to energy and environment sharpened the focus for the professional learning communities, making it more likely they would find a common focus. Indeed, the first year of the project we did not restrict science area and found it very difficult to bring the teachers together around a common theme. While energy and environment worked well for Wyoming, they may not for your place. Selection of an appropriate science area for your region is an essential first step.

The grand challenges are inherently interdisciplinary. Try addressing one of them without viewing the problem from the perspective of biology, chemistry, earth sciences or physics. You simply don't get a complete picture of the problem. In addition the grand challenges are awash in data and modeling, providing an excellent opportunity to integrate quantitative reasoning into the performance task. Quantitative reasoning is the gateway to interdisciplinary mathematics and science teaching, because of the nature of discourse in science. Discourse is a general way of thinking and manner of talking about the world. We acquire our primary discourse through our personal relationships, home, and family. Secondary discourse we acquire through school and work. For a naïve student their science discourse is force dynamic, based in the student's theory of the world. They explain the world in terms of actors and enablers. The events of the world are caused by actors in accord with their ability, for example humans have more ability than animals. Actors have needs and events are the fulfillment of those needs. Students on this level describe the world in terms of objects and events rather than scientific explanations (Mohan, Chen, & Anderson, 2009).

> ...learners perceive a world where macroscopic events are the result of different natural tendencies. Living things grow and move, dead things decay or rot away, and flames consume their fuel. Thus, students .... reason using models that invoke notions of natural tendency and vitalism (p 684).

We found that students at this level avoid quantitative accounts. They prefer to offer qualitative accounts based on their experience. Students move from this level to the school science level. Our goal is to have students use scientific discourse rather than informal or school accounts.

In scientific discourse there is a hierarchy of dynamic systems at different scales and fundamental scientific principles govern the system. For example...

> there is a focus on chemical processes that connect systems (generation, transformation, and oxidation of organic carbon). These processes occur as

matter transformations at the atomic-molecular scale (e.g., photosynthesis, combustion) and are manifested at the macroscopic scale as growth, weight loss, decay, or burning (Mohan, 2009, p 684).

We believe that students at the level of scientific discourse require quantitative reasoning to provide data-based accounts supporting their conclusions.

Understanding by Design

Once the grand challenges were selected, we used the Understanding by Design (UbD) framework to guide development of performance tasks to anchor the curriculum module. We wanted to move the instruction from teaching for knowledge to teaching for understanding. Though we often claim as teachers to be after understanding, we may not adequately understand our goal. We asked teachers in QR STEM to provide examples of what constitutes evidence of student knowledge versus understanding. They worked in their professional learning communities to fill in the chart for the Knowledge versus Understanding Task (Figure 5). We then asked them to share their indicators with the whole group. This always precipitated a lively discussion among the teachers. Try this on your own before you read on.

What is the difference between knowledge and understanding? List in the left column below student behaviors that indicate the student has knowledge. In the right column list student behaviors that indicate the student understands.	
Knowledge	Understanding

Figure 5. Knowledge versus Understanding Task.

Knowledge is often rote, such as providing a definition or running through the steps of a process or algorithm. Understanding is fluid, transferable to new contexts, and transformable into new theories. If you understand then you can explain, apply in real-world contexts, and provide insight. Understanding is inherently more difficult to measure than knowledge. We are often satisfied with signs of apparent understanding, such as performing an algorithm in mathematics or implementing the scientific process in science, but find that student misconceptions are persistent and recurring even when they know their facts. Attempts to teach and assess for understanding must answer three questions (Wiggins & McTighe, 2005):

- If correct answers can offer inadequate or misleading evidence of understanding, or if good test results can hide misunderstanding, then what is genuine understanding?
- How does genuine understanding manifest itself?

- How can assessment and curriculum design more effectively and reliably reveal genuine understanding?

At this point we asked the professional learning communities to write a definition of understanding. They shared their definition with the other communities, debating and refining until the entire group had reached consensus on a definition. The teachers would come up with most if not all of the upper levels of Bloom's Taxonomy (Bloom, 1956) as characteristics of what it means to understand. A revised version of Bloom's Taxonomy is provided in Figure 6. The only level of Bloom's Taxonomy we would not consider understanding is remembering.

Teachers are usually familiar with Bloom's Taxonomy, so to provide a different lens through which to view understanding we introduced the Six Facets of Understanding developed by Wiggins and McTighe (2005). The six facets represent the ability to perform (explain, interpret, and apply) and the ability to gain insight (perspective, empathize, and self-knowledge). The first three facets represent performances one with understanding can do. If you understand, then you can explain by providing a thorough, supported, and justifiable account of phenomena, facts, and definition. The explain facet is theoretical and encompasses "Can I explain *why?*" The interpret facet includes the ability to tell meaningful stories, offer apt translations, and provide revealing historical or personal dimension to ideas and events. The interpret facet is personal and addresses "*What* does it mean to me?" The apply facet is the ability to effectively use and adapt what one knows in diverse contexts. The apply facet is pragmatic answering "*How* can I use it?" How do the three abilities to perform relate to the levels of Bloom's Taxonomy? The apply facet is analogous to level 3 of the taxonomy. The explain facet certainly relates strongly with level 2 of the taxonomy, understanding, but it also includes elements of analyzing, evaluating, and creating to explain why. The interpret facet departs in fundamental ways from Bloom's Taxonomy by focusing on affective rather than cognitive attributes of understanding.

1. Remembering Retrieving, recognizing, and recalling relevant knowledge from long-term memory, eg. find out, learn terms, facts, methods, procedures, concepts

2. Understanding Constructing meaning from oral, written, and graphic messages through interpreting, exemplifying, classifying, summarizing, inferring, comparing, and explaining. Understand uses and implications of terms, facts, methods, procedures, concepts

3. Applying Carrying out or using a procedure through executing, or implementing. Make use of, apply practice theory, solve problems, use information in new situations

4. Analyzing Breaking material into constituent parts, determining how the parts relate to one another and to an overall structure or purpose through differentiating, organizing, and attributing. Take concepts apart, break them down, analyze structure, recognize assumptions and poor logic, evaluate relevancy

5. Evaluating Making judgments based on criteria and standards through checking and critiquing. Set standards, judge using standards, evidence, rubrics, accept or reject on basis of criteria

6. Creating Putting elements together to form a coherent or functional whole; reorganizing elements into a new pattern or structure through generating, planning, or producing. Put things together; bring together various parts; write theme, present speech, plan experiment, put information together in a new & creative way

Figure 6. Bloom's Revised Taxonomy. Source: Anderson, L.W., & Krathwohl (Eds.). (2001). A Taxonomy for Learning, Teaching, and Assessing: A Revision of Bloom's Taxonomy of Educational Objectives. New York: Longman.

Wiggins and McTighe make the point that even innovative instructional approaches often focus on ability to perform, while ignoring ability to gain insight. The final three facets of understanding relate to the ability to gain insight. The perspective facet is the ability to see alternative points of view; literally the ability to see the big picture. The perspective facet is dispassionate asking "Whose point of view?" The empathize facet is the ability to find value in what others might find odd, alien, or implausible; to perceive sensitivity on the bases of prior direct experience. The empathize facet is passionate asking "What are you feeling?" Finally the self-knowledge facet is the ability to perceive personal style, prejudices, projections, and habits of mind that both shape and impede one's own understanding. Possessing this facet means you are aware of what you do not understand. The self-knowledge facet is introspective, asking "What are my prejudices?" The three insight facets may at first seem to be of less importance when exploring science and mathematics, which are naively viewed as impartial and unbiased. However, when we base our tasks in real-world problems and socio-political-ethical considerations become a central issue, then insight is essential to understanding.

Teaching for understanding is one of the central tenets of the QR STEM program. To understand understanding we examine findings from cognitive science research. Transfer is essential to learning, underlying the ability to apply facts and skills in novel situations. Near transfer to situations that have similar structure is difficult for students, far transfer to situations that have deeper structural similarities is extremely unlikely without explicit instruction. Students must learn to recognize patterns in problems; to see the structure of a problem behind the context and determine the mathematical and scientific tools that can be used to solve them. UbD proposes that at the basis of transfer lay enduring understandings:

> Enduring understandings are specific inferences based on big ideas that have lasting value beyond the classroom.....In thinking about enduring understandings for a unit or course, teachers are encouraged to ask, "What do we want students to understand and be able to use several years from now, after they have forgotten the details?" (Wiggins and McTighe, 2005, p. 342)

An enduring understanding has withstood the test of time and existed across cultures, becoming an essential component of science or mathematics. The UbD distinguishing features of understanding are:

- An understanding is an important inference, drawn from the experience of experts, stated as a specific and useful generalization.
- An understanding refers to transferable, big ideas having enduring value beyond a specific topic.
- An understanding involves abstract, counterintuitive, and easily misunderstood ideas.

- An understanding is best acquired by "uncovering (developed inductively, coconstructed by learners) and "doing" the subject (using ideas in realistic settings with real-world applications).
- An understanding summarizes important strategic principles in skill areas. (Wiggins & McTighe, 2005, p. 128-129).

In addition to transfer, metacognition is an important cognitive science conception that is central to developing understanding. Metacognition is literally thinking about thinking. Metacognition is higher order thinking that allows us to control our thinking processes. Cognitive science has identified three components to metacognition. Self-assessment is the metacognitive ability to assess one's own progress towards a solution. Self-awareness is the ability to know what you know and don't know, that is, to judge accurately our own level of skill or knowledge in a specific area. These are monitoring processes for thinking, involving decisions that assist in identifying the task, checking on progress on the task, evaluating that progress, and predicting the outcome of that progress. Self-regulation is the ability to control your learning, to step back from a problem and assess where you are and where you need to go. Regulation processes involve allocating resources to the task, determining a plan of attack for the task, and setting the intensity of work to be done on the task. These metacognitive skills are essential to the development of understanding. Without them we are doomed to experience the three pathologies of mislearning: amnesia (we forget), fantasia (we don't understand that we don't understand), and inertia (we are unable to use what we learn) (Wiggins & McTighe, 2005).

To develop tasks that stimulate understanding, Wiggins and McTighe (2005) created the Backward Design Process. In QR STEM, this process was the basis of our work with teachers in developing integrated STEM performance tasks. Backward design can be thought of as purposeful task analysis. Given a task to be accomplished, how does one get there? It can also be thought of as planned coaching. What kinds of lessons and practices are needed to master key performances? A typical instructional design is to begin with the text, a favorite lesson, or time honored activity, then derive targeted goals and standards. Backward design begins with the desired result, perhaps a standard, then derives the curriculum based on evidence of learning. UbD calls for the teacher to think like an assessor. This requires them to begin with a question and operationalize goals or standards in terms of assessment. To accomplish this UbD proposes three stages (Figure 7).

In Stage 1 we identify the desired results. The desired results may arise from district goals, state or national content standards, or school curriculum expectations. There is more content in science and mathematics than can be covered in a course, so we are obliged to make choices. UbD proposes that the choices should be made through identifying and focusing on enduring understandings. What should a student know, understand, and be able to do? What is worthy of understanding? What enduring understandings are desired?

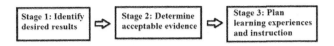

Figure 7. UbD Stages of Backward Design. Source: Wiggins, G. P. and McTighe, J. A. (2005). Understanding by Design. Alexandra, VI: Association for Supervision and Curriculum Development.

Stage 2 is to determine acceptable evidence that the desired result has been obtained. Think like an assessor by considering up front how you will determine if students have attained the desired understanding. Consider a range of assessment methods to collect the evidence, such as performance tasks to measure understanding, traditional assessments including quizzes and tests to assess essential knowledge and skills contributing to performance, self-assessment by students, and peer-assessment.

Stage 3 is to plan learning experiences and instruction. Note that the specifics of instructional planning occur after the desired results and assessments are identified, which is what makes it a backwards design. Ask questions such as the following: What enabling knowledge and skills will students need to perform effectively and achieve desired results? What activities will equip students with the needed knowledge and skills? What will need to be taught and coached, and how should it best be taught, in light of performance goals? What materials and resources are best suited to accomplish these goals? Is the overall design coherent and effective?

SUMMARY

QR STEM engaged professional learning communities of science and mathematics teachers in the Understanding by Design Backward Design Process. UbD was the framework used to develop performance tasks within the context of energy and environment. We had several professional development goals for our project. First, we wanted to demonstrate the connection between science and mathematics. We motivated this connection by addressing real-world grand challenges in STEM. Science and mathematics teachers collaborated on development of interdisciplinary units that engaged students by relating the grand challenge to their local place and community. Quantitative reasoning was a central focus of the project, serving as an integrating factor for mathematics in the sciences. Second, we sought to embed the science and mathematics within real-world contexts to motivate students and demonstrate the utility of STEM in their worlds. This was also aided by the grand challenges focus and place-based, problem-based pedagogies. Third, we aspired to increase both the content knowledge and pedagogical content knowledge of the teachers. STEM content focused on grand challenges of energy and environment. The nexus of energy and environment was an essential component of the project.

For example, there are a number of ways to increase available energy for the world including increased oil production, nuclear power, wind power, and solar power. Each of these sources of energy has positives and negatives, including the impact of each source on the environment. QR STEM strove to have teachers view the challenges through multiple science lenses including biology, chemistry, earth systems, and physics. Every grand challenge was addressed from all four science areas. Mathematics was addressed through quantitative reasoning, putting the focus on interdisciplinary science and mathematics. Quantitative reasoning concepts included the act of quantification within a science context, quantitative literacy as a tool to explore relationships and build models, quantitative interpretation of science models to develop scientifically literate citizens, and quantitative modeling to allow building and testing models within place. Pedagogical content knowledge in science and mathematics was incorporated into the teaching and learning of science content. QR STEM faculty engaged teachers in performance tasks for energy, environment, and quantitative reasoning, modeling the UbD framework, and teaching for understanding. Faculty demonstrated how to teach QR and science that was motivated by grand challenges, but related to place. Fourth we required that teaching for understanding STEM be the focus of the units being developed, not just mastery of knowledge. Faculty modeled the use of Understanding by Design in the development of performance tasks for teachers. Central to the development of units was identification of big ideas in science and mathematics from the areas of energy and environment. Fifth we desired the development of scientifically literate citizens who can make informed decisions about socio-political-economic issues that impact their place and the world. This was the desired outcome of the units developed by the professional learning communities for their students. We also wanted to assess the impact of QR STEM on teacher practice and student learning. To do this we required teachers to conduct action research in their classrooms on the impact of the unit on their students. The professional learning communities presented their findings to the QR STEM community, thus engaging in a meta-level performance task on practice.

The intent of this chapter was to provide the teacher and teacher professional developer with a theoretical framework for the QR STEM project. This framework provides support from the literature for the elements included in the project, such as teaching for understanding and quantitative literacy. Chapter 2 will provide specific examples from QR STEM of the entire process of interdisciplinary performance task development and evaluation.

REFERENCES

Adúriz-Bravo, A. (2012). A 'semantic' view of scientific models for science education. *Science and Education, 21*, 1–19. doi: 10.1007/s11191-011-9431-7

American Education Reach Out. (2010). *AERO Mathematics curriculum framework: K-8 standards and performance indicators*. Retrieved from http://www.projectaero.org/aero_standards/mathematicsframework/AEROMathematicsCurriculumFramework.pdf

American Institute for Research. (2005). *Adoption: Exploring the Initiation of ComprehensiveSchool Reform Models.* Presentation at American Educational Research Association, Montreal.
Athman, J., & Monroe, M. (2004). The effects of environment-based education on students' achievement motivation. *Journal of Interpretation Research, 9*(1), 9–25.
Bartosh, O. (2003). *Environmental education: Improving student achievement.* Doctoral dissertation, Evergreen State College.
Bloom, B. S. (Ed.). (1956). *Taxonomy of educational objectives, the classification of educational goals – Handbook I: Cognitive domain.* New York, NY: McKay.
Bennett, J. O., & Briggs, W. L. (2008). *Using and understanding mathematics: A quantitative reasoning approach,* Fourth Edition. Reading, MA: Pearson Addison Wesley.
Briggs, W. L. (2004). What mathematics should all college students know? In R. Gillman (Ed.), *Current practices in quantitative literacy* (pp. 17–19). Washington, DC: Mathematical Association of America.
Carlson, M., Jacobs, S., Coe, E., Larsen, S., & Hsu, E. (2002). Applying covariational reasoning while modeling dynamic events: A framework and a study. *Journal for Research in Mathematics Education, 33,* 352–378.
Clase, K. L., Gundlach, E., & Pelaez, N. J. (2010). Calibrated peer review for computer-assisted learning of biological research competencies. *Biochemistry and Molecular Biology Education, 3,* 290–295.
Clement, J., Lochhead, J., & Monk, G. S. (1981). Translation difficulties in learning mathematics. *The American Mathematical Monthly, 88,* 286–290.
Climate Literacy Network. (2011). *Climate literacy: The essential principles of climate science.* United States Global Change Research Program. March 2009. www. globalchange.gov
Cognition and Technology Group at Vanderbilt. (1992). The Jasper experiment: An exploration of issues in learning and instructional design. *Educational Technology Research and Development, 40*(1), 65–80.
Corcoran, T., Mosher, F. A., & Rogat, A. (2009). *Learning Progressions in Science: An Evidence-Based Approach to Reform.* CPRE Research Report# RR-63. Consortium for Policy Research in Education.
de Lange, J. (2001). *Quantitative literacy: Why numeracy matters for schools and colleges.* B. Madison, & A. Steen (Eds). Princeton, NJ: Woodrow Wilson National Fellowship Foundation.
Delgado, C., Stevens, S. Y., Shin, N., Yunker, M., & Krajcik, J. (2007). *The development of students' conception of size.* Paper presented at the National Association for Research in Science Teaching Conference, New Orleans, LA.
Dingman, S.W., & Madison, B. L. (2010). Quantitative reasoning in the contemporary world, 1: The course and its challenges. *Numeracy, 3,* Article 4.
Doerr, H., & English, L. (2003). A modeling perspective on students' mathematical reasoning about data. *Journal for Research in Mathematics Education, 34,* 110–136.
Duffin, M., Powers, A., & Tremblay, G. (2004). *Place-based Education Evaluation Collaborative (PEEC): Report on cross-program research and other program evaluation activities 2003–2004.* PEER Associates.
Duschl, R. A., Schweingruber, H. A., & Shouse, A. W. (Eds.). (2007). *Taking science to school: Learning and teaching science in grades K-8.* Washington, D.C.: National Academies Press.
Earth Science Literacy Initiative. (2009). *Earth science literacy principles.* http://www.earthscienceliteracy.org/
Edelson, D. C., & Reiser, B. J. (2006). Making authentic practices accessible to learners: Design challenges and strategies. In R. K. Sawyer (Ed.), *The cambridge handbook of the learning sciences* (pp. 335–354). New York, NY: Cambridge University Press.
Eggert, S., & Bögeholz, S. (2009). *Students' use of decision-making strategies with regard to socioscientific issues: An application of the rasch partial credit model.* Wiley Periodicals. Wiley InterScience online. Retrieved from www.interscience.wiley.com
Energy Literacy Project. (2011). Office of Energy Efficiency and Renewable Energy. http://energy.gov
Ernst, J., & Monroe, M. (2004). The effects of environment based education on students' critical thinking skills and disposition toward critical thinking. *Environmental Education Research, 10*(4), 507–522.
Falco, Edward. (2004). *Environment-based education: Improving attitudes and academics for adolescents.* Columbia, SC: South Carolina Department of Education.

CHAPTER 1

Fennel, F., & Landis, T. E. (1994). Number sense and operation sense. In C. A. Thornton & N. S. Bley (Eds.), *Windows of opportunity: Mathematics for students with special needs* (pp. 187–203). Reston, VA: National Council of Teachers of Mathematics.

Fleischman, H. L., Hopstock, P. J., Pelczar, M. P., & Shelley, B. E. (2010). *Highlights from PISA 2009: performance of US 15-year-old students in reading, mathematics, and science literacy in an international context.* (NCES 2011–004). National Center for Education Statistics.

Freudenthal, H. (1973). *Mathematics as an educational task.* Dordrecht: D. Reidel.

Friel, S., Curcio, F., & Bright, G. (2001). Making sense of graphs: Critical factors influencing comprehension and instructional implications. *Journal for Research in Mathematics Education, 32,* 124–158.

Gibson, R., Callison, C., & Zillmann, D. (2011). Quantitative literacy and affective reactivity in processing statistical information and case histories in the news. *Media Psychology, 14,* 96–120.

Grünbaum, B. (1985). Geometry strikes again. *Mathematics Magazine, 58,* 12–17.

Hastings, A., Arzberger, P., Bolker, B., Collins, S., Iyes, A. R., Johnson, N. A., & Palmer, M. (2005). Quantitative bioscience for the 21st century. *BioScience, 55,* 511–517.

Hughes-Hallett, D. (2001). Achieving numeracy: The challenge of implementation. In L. A. Steen (Ed.), *Mathematics and democracy: The case for quantitative literacy* (pp. 93–98). USA: The National Council on Education and the Disciplines.

Hunter, C. M., Caswell, H., Runge, M. C., Regehr, E. V., Amstrup, S. C., & Stirling, I. (2010). Climate change threatens polar bear populations: a stochastic demographic analysis. *Ecology, 91*(10), 2883–2897.

International Life Skills Survey (ILSS). (2000). *Policy research initiative.* Statistics. Canada.

Izsák, A. (2003). "We want a statement that is always true": Criteria for good algebraic representations and the development of modeling knowledge. *Journal for Research in Mathematics Education, 34,* 191–227.

Jones, G., Taylor, A., & Broadwell, B. (2009). Estimating linear size and scale: Body rulers. *International Journal of Science Education, 31,* 1495–1509.

Karplus, R., Pulos, S., & Stage, E. K. (1983). Early adolescents' proportional reasoning on 'rate' problems. *Educational Studies in Mathematics, 14,* 219–233.

Koedinger, K., & Nathan, M. (2004). The real story behind story problems: Effects of representations on quantitative reasoning. *The Journal of the Learning Sciences, 13,* 129–164.

Langkamp, G., & Hull, J. (2007). *Quantitative reasoning and the environment: Mathematical modeling in context.* Upper Saddle River, NJ: Pearson Education.

Lehrer, R., Schauble, L., Carpenter, S., & Penner, D. (2000). The interrelated development of inscriptions and conceptual understanding. In P. Cobb, E. Yackel, & K. McClain (Eds.), *Symbolizing and communicating in mathematics classrooms: Perspectives on discourse, tools, and instructional design* (pp. 325–360). Mahwah, NJ: Lawrence Erlbaum Associates.

Lehrer, R., & Schauble, L. (2004). Modeling natural variation through distribution. *American Educational Research Journal, 41,* 635–679.

Lesh, R. (2006). Modeling students' modeling abilities: The teaching and learning of complex systems in education. *The Journal of the Learning Sciences, 15,* 45–52.

Lesh, R., Middleton, J., Caylor, E., & Gupta, S. (2008). A science need: Designing tasks to engage students in modeling complex data. *Educational Studies in Mathematics, 68,* 113–130.

Lesh, R., Post, T., & Behr, M. (1988). Proportional reasoning. *Number concepts and operations in the middle grades, 2,* 93–118.

Lieberman, G. A., & Hoody, L. L. (1998). *Closing the achievement gap: Using the environment as an integrating context for learning.* San Diego: State Education and Environment Roundtable.

Liu, M., Williams, D., & Pedersen, S. (2002). Alien Rescue: A problem-based hypermedia learning environment for middle school science. *Journal of Educational Technology Systems, 30*(3), 255–270.

Lobato, J., & Siebert, D. (2002) Quantitative reasoning in a reconceived view of transfer. *Journal of Mathematical Behavior, 21,* 87–116.

Logan, T., & Greenlees, J. (2008). Standardised assessment in mathematics: The tale of two items. In M. Goos, R. Brown, & K. Makar (Eds.), *Navigating currents and charting directions: Proceedings of the 31st annual conference of the Mathematics Education Research Group of Australia* (pp. 655–658). Brisbane, Australia: Mathematics Education Research Group of Australia.

32

Lowrie, T., & Diezmann, C. M. (2009). National numeracy tests: A graphic tells a thousand words. *Australian Journal of Education, 53*, 141–158.

Madison, B. L. (2006). Pedagogical challenges of quantitative literacy. In *Proceedings of the joint statistical meetings* (pp. 2323–2328). Alexandria, VA: American Statistical Association.

Madison, B. L., & Steen, L. A. (Eds.). (2003). *Quantitative literacy: Why numeracy matters for schools and colleges.* Princeton, NJ: National Council on Education and the Disciplines.

Mathematics Association of America. (1998). *Quantitative reasoning for college graduates: A complement to the standards.* Retrieved from http://www.maa.org/past/ql/ql_toc.html

Matthews, M. (2007). Models in science and in science education: An introduction. *Science and Education, 16*, 647–652. doi: 10.1007/s11191-007-9089-3

Mohan, L., Chen, J., & Anderson, C. W. (2009). Developing a multi-year learning progression for carbon cycling in socio-ecological systems. *Journal of Research in Science Teaching, 46*, 675–698.

Moore, K. C., Carlson, M. P., & Oehrtman, M. (2009). The role of quantitative reasoning in solving applied precalculus problems. In *Twelfth Annual Special Interest Group of the Mathematical Association of America on Research in undergraduate mathematics education (SIGMAA on RUME) conference.* Raleigh, NC: North Carolina State University.

Myers, J. D., & Massey, G. (2008). Understanding earth resources: What's sociology got to do with it? *Research in Social Problems and Public Policy, 16*, 73–98.

NAS. (1996). *National Assessment of Educational Progress: Science Framework.* National Center for Educational Statistics. Retrieve from http://necs.ed.gov

National Numeracy Network (NNN). (2011). *What is numeracy/QL/QR?* Retrieved from http://serc.carleton.edu/nnn/resources/index.html

National Research Council (NRC). (2001). *Grand challenges in environmental sciences.* Washington, DC: National Academy Press.

NRC (2007). See Duschl reference.

National Research Council (NRC). (2011). *A framework for K-12 science education: Practices, crosscutting concepts, and core ideas.* Washington, DC: National Academy Press.

National Research Council (1996). *National Science Education Standards.* Washington, DC: The National Academies Press.

The National Environmental Education & Training Foundation (NEETF), & North American Association for Environmental Education (NAAEE). (2000). *Environment-based education: Creating high performance schools and students.* Washington, DC: NEETF.

Ocean Literacy: The Essential Principles of Ocean Sciences K-12. (2005, June). *Pamphlet resulting from the 2-week on-line workshop on ocean literacy through science standards.* National Geographic Society, National Oceanic and Atmospheric Administration, Center for Ocean Sciences Education Excellence, National Marine Educators Association, College of Exploration.

Oehrtman, M. C., Carlson, M. P., & Thompson, P. W. (2008). Foundational reasoning abilities that promote coherence in students' understandings of function. In M. P. Carlson & C. Rasmussen (Eds.), *Making the connection: Research and practice in undergraduate mathematics* (pp. 27–42). Washington, DC: Mathematical Association of America.

Organization for Economic Cooperation and Development (OECD). (1999). *Measuring student knowledge and skills: A new framework for assessment.* Paris, France: OECD.

Organization for Economic Cooperation and Development (OECD). (2000). *Programme for International Student Assessment (PISA).* Paris, France: OECD.

Organization for Economic Cooperation and Development (OECD). (2002). *OECD Annual Report.* Paris, France: OECD.

Organization for Economic Cooperation and Development (OECD). (2004). *PISA 2003 Technical Report.* Paris, France: OECD.

Pathways Project. (2012). National Science Foundation project. http://pathwaysproject.kbs.msu.edu

Piaget, J., & Beth, E. (1966). *Mathematical epistemology and psychology.* Dordrecht, Netherlands: D. Reidel.

Polly, D., & Hannafin, M. J. (2011). Examining how learner-centered professional development influences teachers' espoused and enacted practices. *The Journal of Educational Research, 104*(2), 120–130.

Robins, D. Spink, A., & Goodrum, A. (1996). Elicitation behavior during mediated information retrieval. *Information Processing and Management, 34*(2–3), 257–273.

Rode, K. D., Amstrup, S. C., & Regehr, E. V. (2010). Reduced body size and cub recruitment in polar bears associated with sea ice decline. *Ecological Applications, 20*, 768–782.

Savery, J. R. (2006). Overview of problem-based learning: Definitions and distinctions. *Interdisciplinary Journal of Problem-based Learning, 1*(1), 3.

Schwartz, D. L., & Martin, T. (2004). Inventing to prepare for future learning: The hidden efficiency of encouraging original student production in statistics instruction. *Cognition and Instruction, 22*, 129–184.

Schwarz, C. V., Reiser, B. J., Davis, E. A., Kenyon, L., Archer, A., Fortus, D., Shwartz, Y., Hug, B., & Krajcik, J. (2009). Developing a learning progression for scientific modeling: Making scientific modeling accessible and meaningful for learners. *Journal of Research in Science Teaching, 46*, 632–654.

State Education and Environment Roundtable. (2000). California student assessment project: The effects of environment-based education on student achievement. Retrieved November 25, 2003, from http://www.seer.org/pages/csap.pdf

Shavelson, R. J. (2008). Reflections on quantitative reasoning: An assessment perspective. In B. L. Madison & L. A. Steen (Eds.), *Calculation vs. context: Quantitative literacy and its implications for teacher education* (pp. 22–47). Washington, DC: Mathematical Association of America.

Smith, G. A., & Sobel, D. (2010). *Place- and community-based education in schools (Sociocultural, political, and historical studies in education)*. New York, NY: Routledge.

Smith III, J., & Thompson P. W. (2007). Quantitative reasoning and the development of algebraic reasoning. In J. J. Kaput, D. W. Carraher, & M. L. Blanton (Eds.), *Algebra in the early grades* (pp. 95–132). New York, NY: Lawrence Erlbaum Associates.

Speth, E. B., Momsen, J. L., Moyerbrailean, G. A., Ebert-May, D., Long, T. M., Wyse, S., & Linton, D. (2010). 1, 2, 3, 4: Infusing quantitative literacy into introductory biology. *CBE-Life Sciences Education, 9*, 323–332.

Steen, L. A. (Ed.). (1990). *On the shoulders of giants: New approaches to numeracy*. Washington, DC: National Academy Press.

Steen, L. A. (Ed.). (2001). *Mathematics and democracy: The case for quantitative literacy*. Princeton, NJ: The Woodrow Wilson National Fellowship Foundation, The National Council on Education and the Disciplines.

Steen, L. A. (2004). *Achieving quantitative literacy: An urgent challenge for higher education*. Washington, DC: Mathematical Association of America.

Strobel, J., & van Barneveld, A. (2009). When is PBL more effective? A meta-synthesis of metaanalyses comparing PBL to conventional classrooms. *Interdisciplinary Journal of Problem-based Learning, 3*(1), 4.

Stroud, M. J., & Schwartz, N. H. (2010). Summoning prior knowledge through metaphorical graphics: An example in chemistry instruction. *Journal of Educational Research, 103*, 351–366.

Svoboda, J., & Passmore, C. (2011). The strategies of modeling in biology education. *Science and Education*, 1–24. doi: 10.1007/s11191-011-9425-5

Taylor, A. R., & Jones, M. G. (2009). Proportional reasoning ability and concepts of scale: Surface area to volume relationships in science. *International Journal of Science Education, 31*, 1231–1247.

Thompson, P. W. (1994). The development of the concept of speed and its relationship to the concepts of rate. In G. Harel & J. Confrey (Eds.), *The development of multiplicative reasoning in the learning of mathematics* (pp. 181–234). Albany, NY: SUNY Press.

Thompson, P. W. (1999). *Some remarks on conventions and representations*. Cuernavaca, Mexico: Panel for the PMENA XXI Working Group on Representations.

Thompson, P. W. (2002). Didactic objects and didactic models in radical constructivism. In K. Gravemeijer, R. Lehrer, B. van Oers, & L. Verschaffel (Eds.), *Symbolizing, modeling, and tool use in mathematics education* (pp. 191–212). Dordrecht, Netherlands: Kluwer.

Thompson, P. W. (2011). Quantitative reasoning and mathematical modeling. In L. L. Hatfield, S. Chamberlain, & S. Belbase (Eds.), *New perspectives and directions for collaborative research in mathematics education* (pp. 33–57). Laramie, WY: University of Wyoming.

Thompson, P. W., & Saldanha, L. A. (2003). Fractions and multiplicative reasoning. In J.Kilpatrick, G. Martin &D. Schifter (Eds.), *Research companion to the principles and standards for school mathematics* (pp. 95–114). Reston, VA: National Council of Teachers of Mathematics.

UCAR Trenberth, K. E., & Asrar, G. R. (2007). Challeges and opportunities in water cycle research: WCRP contributions. *Surveys in Geophysics, 27*(3). Springer.

U.S. Department of Education. (2010). See Fleischman, Hopstock, Pelczar and Shelley.

Verschaffel, L., De Corte, E., & Vierstraete, H. (1999). Upper elementary school pupils' difficulties in modeling and solving nonstandard additive word problems involving ordinal numbers. *Journal for Research in Mathematics Education, 30,* 265–285.

Wiggins, G. P., & McTighe, J. A. (2005). *Understanding by design*. Ascd.

Wilkins, J. L. (2000). Preparing for the 21st century: The status of quantitative literacy in the United States. *School Science and Mathematics, 100,* 405–418.

Wiser, M., & Smith, C. (2009). How does cognitive development inform the choice of core ideas in the physical sciences? Commissioned paper for National Research Council. Committee on Core Ideas in Science, Washington, DC.

Zahner, D., & Corter, J. (2010). The process of probability problem solving: Use of external visual representations. *Mathematical Thinking and Learning, 12,* 177–204.

RESEARCH SUPPORTING QR FRAMEWORK

This appendix provides a more detailed review of the literature grounding the QRC framework.

Act of Quantification

An underlying cognitive attribute of QR is the process of quantification, which serves as a process underpinning QL, QI, and QM. Recall that Thompson (2010) defines quantification as the process of conceptualizing an object and an attribute of it so that the attribute has a unit measure, and the attribute's measure entails a proportional relationship (linear, bi-linear, or multi-linear) with its unit. But what does quantification look like?

Thompson and Saldanha (2003) provided an example of quantification as a root of quantitative reasoning by considering the question: What is torque and how might one quantify it? The object one conceives of as torque is a system involving turning something around a fixed point that behaves differently the farther from the fixed point you are. The attribute of that object is the "amount of twist", as in the case of recognizing it takes more strength to hold a pail of water farther from our body then closer. The measure of torque associated with this attribute is more complicated, since the measure must take into account simultaneously the distance that a force is applied from the fixed end, the amount of force being applied, and that amount of twistiness is proportional to each of these components. Quantification is known to be a significant component in modeling and has been found to be difficult for students (Thompson 2011). Thompson just completed a National Science Foundation funded research project, Project Pathways: Opening Routes to Math and Science Success for all Students, examining the professional development of secondary mathematics teachers. The project clearly showed the importance of teachers having a productive image of good student reasoning, including an image of how their actions can influence student thinking.

The act of quantification is the conceptualization process in which quantities are assigned to attributes, with properties and relationships formed among them. This process does not focus on a numerical solution, rather on the conceptual process of solving a given problem. Thompson (2011) provided evidence of the act of quantification within a science context with an 8th grade class of students by addressing how they might measure the explosiveness of a grain silo. Collectively the students were quantifying the problem by first thinking that an explosion occurs when flames burn fast and other knowledge they recalled from science regarding oxidation. The students then started to discuss volume of grain dust in relation to surface area exposed, eventually concluding that they need a unit measure of dust surface area per dust volume per silo volume as a way to measure explosiveness. This process required students to quantify the problem by conceptualizing attributes and how they would measure it (Thompson 2011).

Part of the conceptualization process of the act of quantification is the ability to conceive of the problem mentally through an image. A study conducted by Moore, Carlson and Oehrtman (2009) shows the necessity of a correct mental image in order to quantify the problem and create relationships between the attributes. The study conducted with pre-calculus students showed that when students undergo the process of quantification, they create mental images using drawings or physical objects to represent a given problem. Once students were able to create the correct image, they were able to create correct formulas for solving a given problem. On the other hand, without this mental model, the students found no meaning in the formulas (Moore et al. 2009).

The ability to quantify the problem is necessary if students are to find meaning in numerical computations rather than memorizing formulas which they never derived. Smith III and Thompson (2007) give examples of this process by comparing a numerical solution to a given problem with a quantitative or conceptual solution. Consider the following problem: A father will be 38 years old at some point when he will also be 3 times as old as his daughter, who is currently 7 years old. How old he is right now? The act of quantification takes problems such as this and emphasizes mathematical reasoning when solving problems by focusing on quantities and relationships among them (Smith and Thompson 2007). In this case, the difference between the two people's ages and the ratio of how many times older the father is than the daughter would be the relationships of focus. Having created these quantities and their relationships, students are able to develop a conceptual understanding of the given problem, and in turn use mathematical concepts to solve the problem. These conceptual ideas create a support for using algebra as a tool for problem solving.

An important aspect of quantification is covariational reasoning, which is defined as "cognitive activities involved in coordinating two varying quantities while attending to the ways in which they change in relation to each other" (Carlson et al. 2002, 354). Lobato and Siebert (2002) conducted a teaching experiment in a course on linear functions and slopes in which they closely studied the progress of one particular student. The focus was on a wheelchair ramp problem where the students were questioned regarding the steepness of the ramp. In particular, Lobato and Siebert believed that focusing on slope as a calculation to determine steepness would cause some loss in potential transfer of knowledge, rather the focus should be on slope as a ratio of two varying quantities measuring some attribute; that is on covariation. The student first believed that height was the only determining factor of steepness. After some probing from the interviewer, the student was able to accept that length also influenced the steepness of the ramp, but the student could not vary the height and length of the ramp independently. However, by the end of the teaching experiment, the student was able to construct a ratio between the height and length. This is an example of the development of covarying quantities. It is important to take note that when the student was asked if he had learned about slope, he responded that it is rise over run, however he did not interpret slope to be a measure of steepness of the ramp. This indicates that the attributes of the object must first be determined and a relationship formed between the attributes, before measurement is performed.

An earlier case study by Thompson (1994) also showed the obstacle students have in understanding proportional reasoning or ratio due to lacking an understanding of covariational reasoning. The student in Thompson's study thought of time as an implicit quantity with respect to distance, in a given speed problem. Just as in the Lobato and Seibert study, the student was not able to see two quantities of equal stature in the beginning of the teaching experiment. However, in both cases, the students were able to create the ratio by the end of the experiment by first acknowledging two explicit quantities. In this case the student acknowledged time as an explicit quantity and in turn created the ratio. The traditional teaching of speed as distance divided by time does not allow for the development of the concept of speed as a ratio and has little relevance to the understanding of speed (Thompson 1994).

Quantitative Literacy

We propose four components of QL related to science: numeracy, measurement, proportional reasoning, and descriptive statistics/basic probability. Science requires students to work with very large and very small numbers, a numeracy skill. Putting these numbers in perspective is a challenge for students. For example the diameter of a hydrogen nucleus is approximately 0.000000000000001 meter while the total energy consumption in the United States is 100,000,000,000,000,000,000 joules. Scientific notation is used to represent small and large numbers in a format that is easier to comprehend and easier to perform operations upon: hydrogen nucleus is 1 x 10^{-15} meters and U.S. energy consumption is 1 x 10^{20} joules. This facilitates issues of order of magnitude or powers of 10 in science, such as U.S. energy consumption being 35 orders of magnitude of a hydrogen nucleus. It also leads to the need to do arithmetic operations with powers of 10, such as multiplying powers of 10 by adding the powers. Science is replete with extremely small and large numbers which are often incomprehensible to students. Three techniques for bringing numbers into perspective are estimation, comparisons, and scaling (Bennett and Briggs 2008).

The sciences require careful comprehensive measurement of quantities such as distance, area, volume, discharge (1 acre-foot per day), mass, density, force, pressure, work, moment, energy, power, and heat. Some quantities are measured directly (i.e. length in meters or feet, weight in Newtons or pounds, and temperature in Celsius, Fahrenheit, or Kelvin) using a variety of tools such as rulers, scales, inclinometers, spectrometers, and fluorometers, while others are measured indirectly or are calculated from other measures (i.e. area, volume, stream discharge (volume/ time), density (mass/volume), force (mass x acceleration), pressure (force/area), work (force x distance), and power (work/time)). Fundamental characteristics of measure are accuracy (how close the measurement is to the actual value), precision (how refined the measure is), and error (Langkamp and Hull 2007). Error in a measure can be calculated as an absolute error or absolute change (measured value – true value) or relative error or relative change (ratio of absolute error/true value). Estimation of measures, especially those that are calculated, provides an independent check on the calculations. Wiser and Smith (2009) conjecture a learning progression in which students move from a conception of felt weight to quantifying weight as measured by a scale. This progression requires understanding the quantitative nature of measure. They propose that students move from measuring weight and volume to an understanding of density by graphing weight as a function of volume.

Proportional reasoning encompasses complex cognitive abilities which include both mathematical and psychological dimensions. It requires a significant conceptual shift from concrete operational to formal operational levels of thought (Piaget and Beth 1966). It has been proposed as a major barrier to students' development of mathematical understanding, as well as negatively impacting the development of scientific understanding. Its pivotal position in science is as the most common form of structural similarity, a critical aspect of recognizing similar patterns in two different contexts. In addition, proportional reasoning underpins many of the QL components, including measurement, numeracy, and dimensional analysis. Proportional reasoning is a "form of mathematical reasoning that involves a sense of co-variation and of multiple comparisons, and the ability to mentally store and process several pieces of information" (Lesh et al. 1988). Lesh, Post, and Behr consider the essential characteristic of proportional reasoning to involve reasoning about the holistic relationship between two rational expressions (fractions, quotients, rates, and ratios). Proportional reasoning is not the ability to employ the cross multiplication algorithm, in fact rote use of this algorithm often replaces such reasoning. Early phases in proportional reasoning involve additive reasoning ($A - B = C - D$) and multiplicative reasoning ($A \times B = C \times D$). Traditional proportional reasoning involves relationships of the type $A/B = C/D$, where one of the values is unknown. Karplus et al. (1983) views proportional reasoning as a linear relationship between variables such as $y = mx$, where the y-intercept is 0. Proportional reasoning requires students to first understand fraction a/b, which at the most basic level is interpreted by students as comparing the part (numerator a) to the whole (denominator b) for like quantities. This basic concept of fraction underpins one notion of percentage as comparing part-to-whole. This is also an example of using a percentage to describe change. Taylor and Jones (2009) conducted a study with middle school students on their proportional reasoning abilities. The students attended a summer camp in which they participated in activities on surface area to volume applications. As a result, Taylor and Jones found that there is a significant correlation between proportional reasoning abilities and surface area to volume relationships. The study shows that there may also be a relationship between proportional reasoning and the scaling concept in science.

Ratio represents a relationship between two different quantities, focusing on part-to-part comparisons. Students must attain the conception of ratio before being able to set up equivalent ratios, one of the fundamental conceptions of proportional reasoning. The student can use the concept of ratio and multiplication to perform dimensional analysis in science. Dimensional analysis is the tracking of units when performing calculations or performing unit conversion. Performing dimensional analysis requires the student to understand ratios. Literally a student can track the calculations they need to perform by tracking the units. Other examples of ratios in science include parts per thousand or million, conversion factors such as $1000 \text{ cm}^3/1$ liter, and normalizing data. Percentage is a fraction or ratio represented as a part of a 100. Percentages can compare part-to-whole which is a representation of the fraction conception. Percentages can also compare part-to-part for like quantities, which is a representation of the ratio conception. Another use of percentages in science is making comparisons between a comparison value and a reference value using the percentage difference formula.

Students develop conceptions of rate of change separate from ratio, with the most basic conception of change that of a constant rate found in linear models. This change is represented by the slope of the line. Many students may conceive of change as being univariate at first, that is, they will take the difference of two occurrences of one variable without accounting for the change in a second. Slope is bivariate in nature, it takes into account the change in one variable with respect to another. This is the covariational conception discussed in the act of quantification section above.

A proportion is the equivalence between two ratios: $a/b = c/d$. Many students can manipulate proportions to find the missing value, as in $2/5 = x/10$, however this may indicate only rote use of the cross multiplying algorithm. True proportional reasoning requires a perception of structural similarity; a conception of n times as many. If a student reduces $A/B = C/D$ to $P = C/D$ when solving, then they are not using possible structural relationships but are solving using algebra without regard to structure. At a higher level of proportional reasoning a student moves from a conception of proportional reasoning as equivalent ratios to a conception of linear direct variation $y=kx$. Science contexts for proportional reasoning are often in the linear direct variation form. In addition students may extend this to indirect variation $y=k/x$. This requires an understanding of the underlying algebraic concepts of equivalence, variable, and transformations (structural similarity and invariance).

Probability is the chance of occurrence of an event, with the theoretical probability defined as: $P(e)=$(number of successful outcomes of event)/(total number of possible outcomes). Earth systems cannot be manipulated like dice to determine a theoretical probability. Often scientists can only estimate the probability through observations of the system. Empirical (experimental) probability is determining a probability based on observations or experiments. A probability is always between 0 and 1, so the probability of an event not occurring is $1 - P(e)$. For example if the probability of having a flood is 26%, then the probability of not having a major flood in a given year is 1 - 0.26 = 0.74 or 74%. Odds for an event are the ratio between the event occurring and the event not occurring. The odds of having a major flood in a given year are $(P(e))/(1-P(e))=0.26/0.74$ or the odds are about 1 in 3. There are more complicated probability problems such as conditional probability with dependent or independent events which are of use in science. Computing experimental probabilities requires counting the occurrence of events. Combinatorial techniques allow one to count without listing all the events. Some basic counting principles are the multiplication principle, the pigeonhole principle, permutations, and combinations. These methods are based in arithmetic principals, but quickly lead to the use of exponential and factorial principles. Theoretical probability may not often be used in science where the focus is on analyzing observed data, so no more will be said about these counting principles at this time.

Descriptive statistics allow us to summarize and describe data. The fundamental descriptive statistics are measures of the center of a distribution and measures of the spread in a distribution. Measures of central tendency include the mean, median, and mode. The mean is the sum of all the values divided by the number of values, while the mode is the most frequently occurring value. The mode is not often used in analyzing scientific data. The mean and median values for a data set can differ significantly, so it does make a difference what measure of central tendency is reported.

Intrinsically tied to measures of central tendency is the concept of variation, which measures how much the data are spread out. The simplest measure of variation is the range which is the difference between the largest and smallest values in the data set. While easy to calculate the range can be misleading, since one outlier can make it appear the data set is more spread than it is. To avoid this one can use quartiles (values that divide the data set into quarters) and the 5 number summary: lowest value, lower quartile, median, upper quartile, and highest value.

The most commonly used measure of variation is standard deviation, which measures the average distance of all data values from their mean. So we find the deviation which is the distance of a value from the mean, square the deviation so that positive and negative deviations don't cancel out when adding them which could conceal spread, and take the average of all deviations by summing them and dividing by one less than the total number of data values (this is an adjustment for working with a sample rather than a population). The result is called variance. But variance is in squared units and our original data is not squared, so we square root the variance to get standard deviation, which is in the same units as the original data. By Chebyshev's Rule for any set of data at least 75% of the data lie within 2 standard deviations of the mean and at least 89% of the data lie within 3 standard deviations of the mean. Any data value that lays 3 or more standard deviations from the mean is called an outlier and it is common practice to discard them from the data set.

The majority of what we have discussed to this point as elements of QL belong to the realm of number and arithmetic, only variation requires algebraic operations of taking roots or powers. So we see the meaning of Steen's admonition (Steen 2004) that QL is sophisticated reasoning with elementary mathematics. Other basic statistics that are used in science crossover from arithmetic to algebra such as z-scores (number of standard deviations a data point lay above or below the mean) and confidence intervals. However, it is amazing what one can do with arithmetic if they can but reason with it within a context.

So QL is the ability to use fundamental mathematical concepts in context and it plays an important role in today's modern society. The media, workplace, and our everyday lives have been filled with quantitative data. It is imperative that everyone be able to interpret and use the data presented to them to make informed decisions (Steen 2001; Madison and Steen 2003; Steen 2004). According to the Quantitative Literacy Design Team, "Most U.S. students leave high school with quantitative skills far below what they need to live well in today's society (Steen 2001, 1)." Data from the Third International Mathematics and Science Study (TIMMS) revealed that students in the U.S. performed relatively low compared to other countries in their mathematical skills. However, the same students responded that they enjoy mathematics and are confident in their performance (Wilkins 2000).

Numeracy, which in our case is the ability to reason with numbers, is the key to understanding data in our current society. Understanding requires more than formulas, rather it requires the ability to reason and think quantitatively (Steen 2001). Wilkins extends the definition of QL to one who is willing to "engage in situations that require a functional level of quantitative reasoning" (Wilkins 2000, 408). Unfortunately, many students lack QL skills due to a shallow coverage of these concepts in schools, a focus on college prep, and a narrow curriculum with the singular goal of calculus as the culminating experience. Many of the fundamental QL skills such as measurement, geometry, data analysis and probability do not get much time in the curriculum (Madison 2003).

The fundamental mathematical concepts necessary for non-calculus track students is addressed by Briggs (2004). Based on a study he conducted on a group of non-calculus track undergraduate students fulfilling general education requirements, Briggs found that the fundamental mathematical knowledge needed were logical thinking skills, estimation, statistical literacy, and financial mathematical knowledge. Students find it difficult to attain these skills as they often do not see the connection between the mathematical knowledge they acquire and applications to their daily lives. QL must be made compelling to students by showing them examples of how it impacts their lives, which are filled with quantitative information (Briggs 2004). According to Madison, "Many students do not believe that mathematics has very much to do with their everyday lives" (Madison 2006, 2325).

A study by Jones, Taylor, and Broadwell (2009) was done on the sense of scale and estimation using the body as a measurement tool. Using the body as a ruler allowed students to better visualize a measure and become more accurate in estimation. Consequently, students who had a better understanding of proportional reasoning gave more accurate values of estimation. Proportional reasoning is positively correlated with applying scale and estimation in real world problems. So proportional reasoning can be an obstacle for students in their understanding of concepts in science. Students' sense of scale was also studied by Delgado, Stevens, Shni, Yungker, and Krajcik (2007), who examined students' understanding of how big one object is compared to another, and the objects' absolute size.

Madison (2006) presents a pedagogical challenge related to QL: students have been taught for many years in traditional mathematics classrooms so their habits and attitudes can become obstacles. Thompson (1994) and Lobato and Seibert (2002) showed that teaching students formulas, such as slope is rise over run or speed is distance divided by time, does not provide students with the understanding to apply these concepts. In order for students to accept that they should understand a concept, they must be engaged. In this case they should be engaged in the material to a greater extent than in a traditional mathematics classroom (Madison 2006; Dingman and Madison 2010). Some positive outcomes have arisen in the studies done by Dingman and Madison. They concluded, "One of the positive changes we have seen is the modest shift in the students' views regarding the relevance of the mathematics in their everyday life. By placing the mathematical and statistical topics in real-world contexts, the connections to their life are much more real and apparent than their past experiences in learning mathematics (Dingman and Madison 2010, 6)."

Quantitative Interpretation

Quantitative interpretation is the ability to use models to make predictions and determine trends. Due to the fact that a model can take various forms (e.g. tables, graphs, statistical graphical displays, equations, or complex scientific diagrams) issues can arise in two different senses. First, the interpretation of a model can be challenging for students, especially if the model has multiple variables embedded within it. Second, the translation between models representing the same content can be difficult for students. For example, given a table and a graph of the same data, students can struggle to see the relationship between the two different representations. Understanding the multitude of representations available is important for organizing, synthesizing, explaining, and displaying data, which in turn is essential for being a citizen scientist.

The American Education Reach Out (AERO) organization states that "Representations are necessary to students' understanding of mathematical concepts and relationships" (2010, 11). Early understanding of multiple representations is important for students to progress mathematically (Schwartz and Martin 2004; Zahner and Corter 2010). Zahner and Corter (2010) propose in their model that students pass through four stages when problem solving. Stage 2 is mathematical problem representation. According to their model, to reach level 3 and 4, students must pass through this stage first. Therefore, the inability to interpret and represent a problem could be a barrier to student problem solving.

Representations take on numerous forms, from graphs and tables to equations and written text. They also vary in popularity. For example, Lowrie and Diezmann (2009) found maps are a type of representation that has increased in popularity recently. Maps are one representation that requires a certain amount of "decoding" (Logan and Greenlees 2008; Lowrie and Diezmann 2009), which can be very challenging for students. They argue that students can encounter difficulties when trying to separate graphical features from other demands posed by the task, such as linguistic knowledge and mathematical knowledge.

Examining multiple representations is important when discussing learning because often graphical representations and text appear side-by-side. Stroud and Schwartz (2010) base their study of metaphoric graphics in chemistry instruction on the notion of the redundancy effect. This occurs when students become overwhelmed with the amount of information presented as "text-based content" and it interferes with student learning (Stroud and Schwartz 2010). Thus, knowing how students read, interpret, and process simultaneous representations when learning content is important to consider when developing learning progressions and planning instruction (Clement et al. 1981). When more than one representation is presented side-by-side, it is important for the student to make meaning of each representation and draw connections among the different representations.

When asked to classify mathematical problems according to their difficulty many would argue that story problems are among the most difficult for students to solve. According to a study conducted by Koedinger and Nathan (2004) this may not always be the case. They divide the problem-solving process into two phases, a comprehension and a solution phase (Koedinger and Nathan 2004). During the comprehension phase the type of problem representation chosen plays a vital role for the students' understanding as well as their problem solving strategies. Koedinger and Nathan (2004) discovered in their study that students showed fewer difficulties concerning story word problems than with symbolic problems, such as equations, when the language and context used are accessible to them.

Friel, Curcio, and Bright (2001) investigated the comprehension of statistical graphs. They identified four categories influencing graph comprehension: purpose for using a graph, characteristics of the tasks, characteristics of the discipline, and the characteristics of graph readers. According to Friel et.al., a vital component of graph comprehension is understanding that there are three areas of graph perception, namely "visual decoding, judgment task, and context" (Friel et al. 2001, p. 152). All three components need to be adequately addressed to ensure improved graph comprehension. This is supported by the study conducted by Zahner and Corter (2010). They call for further research to enhance teachers' understanding of how students comprehend graphs, which in turn can result in new instructional strategies.

Thompson has conducted several studies on representation (Thompson 1994, 1999, 2002; Thompson and Saldanha 2000; Oerthman et al. 2008). Thompson (1994, p. 53) found that "any problem typology suffers this same deficiency, namely that any given situation can be conceived in a multitude of ways". During his teaching experiment he discovered that a model can easily be interpreted or viewed in different ways, which emphasizes the subjective character of interpretation. Furthermore, Thompson (1999) discovered that even after spending a significant amount of time in groups working on an interpretation of a specific point on a graph, students' individual answers showed internal incoherence. Even after groups came to consensus on the meaning of a point on a graph, when asked to write down an answer individually the responses differed from their group work; such that more internal incoherence was noted and a large portion of students could not even state an answer. Thompson (1999) concluded that even though the students had reached an agreement on one interpretation within their groups, it did not necessarily mean that each student had reached the same interpretation internally. "[W]hat individuals understand may be expressed as something stable in the way they interact, but the extent to which interaction-as-stable-pattern reflects individuals' understandings may be uncertain at best" (1999, p. 6). This indicates the difficulties of assessing students' understanding and poses problems when interpreting students' answers in terms of whether or not the student has reached an understanding of a model or not. Thompson and Saldanha (2000) also studied the role of representations in the field of statistics and probability. They found that student misunderstandings in this area arise as early as elementary school and can be reduced through exposing students more to statistics and probability in early years of school.

Quantitative Modeling

Quantitative modeling (QM) is the ability to create representations to explain phenomena. It requires extensive logical thinking and reasoning for an individual to produce a model. QM includes formulating problems, finding best fit linear, power, and exponential function models, setting up simulation models, and creating table, graph and scientific diagram models.

The seminal research done by Schwarz, Reiser, Davis, Kenyon, Acher, Fortus, Shwartz, Hug, and Krajcik (2009) in the Modeling Designs for Learning Science (MoDeLS) project defines scientific modeling as elements of practice including constructing, using, evaluating, and revising scientific models, and the metaknowledge that guides and motivates the practice. They developed a learning progression for modeling. The Consortium for Policy Research in Education (CPRE) report, *Learning Progressions in Science: An Evidence-based Approach to Reform* (Corcoran et al. 2009) defines a learning progression as a set of "empirically grounded and testable hypotheses about how students' understanding of, and ability to use, core scientific concepts and explanations and related scientific practices grow and become more sophisticated over time, with appropriate instruction" (p. 8). The learning progression for scientific modeling has two dimensions:

- scientific models as tools for predicting and explaining
- models change as understanding improves

Their learning progression for science modeling is unique in that the primary focus is a scientific process rather than a scientific concept, which is at the core of most science learning progressions. The modeling progression is focused on upper elementary and middle school grades. Students moved along the learning progression from illustrative to explanatory models, developing increasingly sophisticated views of the explanatory nature of models, and developing more nuanced reasons to revise models.

Lesh (2006), in a paper on students' modeling abilities, calls for a deep understanding of complex systems which are becoming more and more prominent in the 21st century. This refers to nearly any attempt at modeling real world phenomena. Students need to know how to focus on the most important processes they want to model, as well as strategies of modeling. Lesh (2006) differentiates between three different kinds of complex systems which can be very challenging for students to understand: real world systems, conceptual systems, and models describing and explaining students modeling abilities (Lesh 2006). The components of each system are defined and labeled, but they derive their meaning by being part of the system and can therefore not be investigated individually. According to Lesh (2006) mathematics includes the learning of sets of rules to the same degree as it includes the ability to model real world situations (Lesh 2006). This idea of enhancing the design of tasks that engage students in complex modeling is exemplified in a study by Lesh, Middleton, Caylor, and Gupta (2008). They introduce the idea of model-eliciting activities (MEA) to enhance students' modeling abilities. Their MEA intend to make students' thinking explicit around the use and creation of models.

Thompson's (2011) approach to quantitative modeling focuses on the act of quantification, especially concerning dynamic situations, and quantitative covariation. He defines two aspects that are essential when using mathematics to model dynamic situations. First, students need to understand the quantities themselves and visualize that their images include values that vary. Second, students need to form a representation of the "object made by uniting those quantities in thought and maintaining that unit while also maintaining a dynamic image of the situation in which it is embedded" (Thompson 2011, p. 27).

QM plays a major role in the sciences (Adúriz-Bravo 2012; Lehrer et al. 2000; Matthews 2007; Svoboda and Passmore 2011) and modeling in science needs to be taught in a dynamic manner. Scientists develop, use, and revise their models in a cyclic process. This process should be accessible for students so they understand the dynamic nature of science. Additionally, there is a need for an emphasis on argumentation in science for which mathematical reasoning skills are a prerequisite. Matthews (2007) describes the process as beginning with observations of real objects, which then need to be conveyed linguistically in some way. Within this step is where quantitative reasoning takes place. This conveyed information, or model, is set within a discourse and can now be scientifically debated. The final step is the revision of the model, then the cycle starts over again. Adúriz-Bravo (2012) describes this process with the words: "inventing, applying, refining, and learning models (Adúriz-Bravo 2012, p. 16). Another study which supports the importance of modeling for students was conducted by Lehrer and colleagues (2000). They investigated two situations where children learn through design in elementary school. Most important for education by design are the tasks, tools, and representations. The basic idea is to align classroom activities to how scientists in the real world work. It begins with a problem (task) which needs to be specified and should lead to the construction of a working model. This model needs to be tested and if needed re-designed. Finally, students need to elaborate the important ideas behind their model and data. Their classroom implementations also demonstrated how important it is to connect new material to children's existing knowledge. Children's previous knowledge needs to be assessed by teachers before introducing new tasks.

Doerr and English (2003) investigated how instructional tasks can enhance students' modeling abilities in two middle school classrooms, one in Australia and one in the USA. Their instructional tasks were different from traditional textbook problems and addressed "the creation of ranked quantities, operations and transformations on those ranks, and, finally, the generation of relationships between and among quantities to define descriptive and explanatory relationships" (Doerr and English 2003, p. 131). They provided instruction, which differed from the traditional way of simply guiding students through specific problem solving strategies, enabling them to develop their own ways of approaching, refining, and expanding their thinking about problems. Their results showed that after students were exposed to the novel instruction, they were capable of defining their own quantities (ranks) and operating on those quantities to build a basis for interpreting and revising their models. Additionally, they discovered that since students approached problems with a variety of different models, the communication about and translations between models was facilitated.

Issues with modeling abilities can begin in elementary school as indicated by Verschaffel, De Corte, and Vierstraete (1999). They investigated upper elementary students' modeling ability concerning addition and subtraction problems and discovered many student difficulties. According to them, the majority of students' difficulties are due to the superficial and traditional teaching approaches which focus simply on the process, but do not discuss the appropriateness and relevance of the operation within a context. Students tend to move straight to manipulating with the numbers of a given problem without having checked if their operations make sense contextually. This indicates, as in the study above, that one key to improving students' modeling abilities is through changing instructional strategies.

Lehrer and Schauble (2004) also discovered the need for improving instructional strategies. Their study explored upper elementary students' thinking in the context of natural distribution. Students worked with data to model plant growth. The main emphasis during instruction was placed on investigations carried out by the students. The students developed different models in order to draw inferences about plant growth as well as make predictions for the future. In addition, their understanding of influencing factors, such as light or fertilizer, was enhanced and the effects were incorporated in the models. This study demonstrated how important it is for students to construct their own models of real world phenomena, allowing them to draw inferences and to reach a deeper understanding.

One of the most difficult types of modeling for students is algebraic modeling. In a case study conducted by Izsák (2003) on how students go about modeling a physical device, he discovered that students can develop a set of skills that allows them to construct, evaluate and test their developed equations. This set of skills results from a combination of students' prior common knowledge and carefully guided student-based instruction. The students were able to develop a linear system of equations, evaluate it by plugging in values, and discuss and revise it in collaboration with each other. Hence, algebraic modeling can be mastered by students with the appropriate guidance, but it is not common in current classroom practice.

Thompson (2002) also focused on the role of instructors and how their teaching can be enhanced. He introduced the concept of didactic models, which "is for instructors and instructional designers what they intend students will understand and how that understanding might develop" (Thompson 2002, p. 212). Thompson's didactic models can be compared to the idea of a learning trajectory; they are intended to provide a path indicating how understanding might develop. The major difference is that Thompson's didactic model shows a "clear separation between descriptions of instructional sequences and descriptions of what students are to understand" (Thompson 2002, p. 213).

To instantiate science as modeling in the classroom, we must move from direct instruction of STEM as a collection of facts to be mastered and a narrow hypothesis testing view of scientific inquiry, toward curriculum, instruction and assessment models that embrace the four proficiency strands in *Taking Science to School* (Duschl, Schweingruber, & Shouse, 2007). Science teaching would be driven by science as model-building and refinement. This reformulation of curriculum, instruction and assessment proposes a significant change in the current teaching and learning of STEM, which is within the purview of the schools. It will require a significant shift in both student and teacher expectations in the classroom. Science from a model-building perspective is best achieved through integrated, interdisciplinary STEM instruction that incorporates place-based (Smith and Sobel 2010) and problem-based pedagogies (Edelson and Reiser 2006). Engaging students in real-world problems will require them to bring to bear knowledge and understandings from multiple subject areas, including biology, chemistry, earth systems science, physics, mathematics, and statistics. Building models and testing them will push both the teachers and students capabilities. There is a need to study the potential for students to engage in model-building and testing, establishing trajectories of student development though the creation of learning progressions which can assist teachers in tracking student formative development, and eventually to the construction of professional development programs. The theoretical foundations and pathways so established will guide the creation of developmentally appropriate performance tasks that will provide students with experiences that further their understanding of key concepts across STEM.

QR in Context

A keystone of our definition of quantitative reasoning is that it occurs within a real-world context. The importance of quantitative reasoning in context, especially within the context of science as mentioned above, is supported by research (Clase et al. 2010; Eggert and Bögeholz 2009; Gibson et al. 2011; Hastings et al. 2005; Speth et al. 2010).

A study that links environmental sciences to quantitative reasoning was performed by Eggert and Bögeholz (2009). This quantitative study asked students to make informed decisions in regards to the environment and sustainability by means of quantitative reasoning. A pencil-and-paper test focusing on the students' decision making competence was taken by 370 students. Another 83 students took the test with additional items addressing their verbal skills. The results of their study support the claim that "the first 2 years at secondary school seem to be crucial for fostering decision-making competence with respect to the use of decision-making strategies" (Eggert and Bögeholz 2009, p. 249).

Speth and colleagues (2010) investigated the importance of quantitative reasoning in a large-enrollment Introductory Biology course at a research university by means of formative and summative assessments. The results of their pre-intervention assessments showed that students were experiencing great difficulties with modeling via graphs and interpreting the information within the context. Their intervention throughout the course led to a significant gain in the students' abilities as well as a better understanding of the science being taught. According to this study quantitative reasoning needs to be incorporated throughout the entire curriculum and quantitative thinking should become "an intrinsic component in the construction of scientific knowledge" (Speth et al. 2010, p. 331).

Hastings and colleagues (2005) research also supports the importance of quantitative reasoning skills in the field of biological sciences. They illustrate five examples of quantitative reasoning in environmental biology, such as evolution of virulence, community ecology of disease, management of renewable resources, large-scale and global ecology, and scaling from individuals to ecosystems (Hastings et al. 2005). They define three major themes that are essential for quantitative biology: spatial and temporal variability, statistical integration of theory and data, and the problem of scaling. Stochastics, for example, plays a crucial role for investigating population development. In conclusion, Hastings and colleagues (2005) suggest that quantitative reasoning and modeling support biologists by clarifying environmental challenges and providing a deeper insight. The important role of stochastics in biology is also underlined by two studies investigating the connection between the development of polar bear cubs and the decline of sea ice, as well as the influence of climate change on polar bear populations (Rode et al. 2010; Hunter et al. 2010).

A study conducted by Clase and colleagues (2010) based on the importance of quantitative reasoning in biology calls for a change in teaching biology. Calibrated Peer Review (CPR), a web-based program, was foundational to the teaching method in an undergraduate class at a large land-grant research university. CPR assignments included several quantitative aspects including models and graphs, and students were asked to make causal conclusions and graph relationships. Their results indicate an increase in students' understanding after fulfilling the CPR assignments over one semester (Clase et al. 2010).

Gibson and colleagues (2011) investigated the effect of using statistical representations taken from case studies and news reports on a group of undergraduates with varying quantitative reasoning skills. Students with greater ability in arithmetic skills achieved more accurate results on a QR computer-based test. The test provided students with articles from which they were asked to extract and assess the numerical information in terms of the underlying content, and give estimations of, for example, ratios. They also found that students with lower ability arithmetic skills are "more attentive to, and affectively more engaged by, personalized information provided by detailed case reports" (Gibson et al. 2011, p. 114).

PEDAGOGICAL FRAMEWORK: A PATHWAY TO CITIZENSHIP PREPARATION

Professional Development Workshop

INTRODUCTION

In Chapter 1 we provided a framework for our work in QR STEM. In this chapter we walk through the process of collaborating with teachers in developing a unit driven by a performance task with a focus on the context of energy and environment. We have selected the very broad areas of energy and environment as fields from which to select topics. This choice was driven by our desire to make a connection to the state of Wyoming where QR STEM was conducted. I now live in Georgia, a very different region from Wyoming. If I was selecting STEM areas for Georgia I could still certainly focus on energy and environment, these are issues of concern to everyone. But the environmental focus might be ocean and pine forest in my region, rather than mountain and dry plains in Wyoming. If I was down the coast a bit in Florida near the NASA Space Center, then perhaps I would change areas completely and focus on space science. The point is to relate the area of STEM to your local region. But keep the topic broad enough that both teachers and students have freedom to select big ideas that relate to their region, so they can generate questions about that big idea in which they have a personal and place stake.

SETTING THE STAGE

Establish a Topic

In QR STEM we choose the topic areas of energy and environment since the interaction of these two is of strong state and regional interest. Wyoming produced over 432 million tons of low sulphur coal in 2009 alone and has massive coal reserves of 68.7 billion tons, making it the third largest state coal reserve (Figure 1). Wyoming production accounts for 40% of the coal produced in the United States. Wyoming coal is used to generate electricity in 38 states (Figure 2). While coal is the iconic energy resource in Wyoming, there are also large reserves of oil (53.1 million barrels produced in 2010), natural gas (2,517 trillion cubic feet produced in 2010), Uranium, plentiful solar energy with an abundance of sunny days in a dry climate.

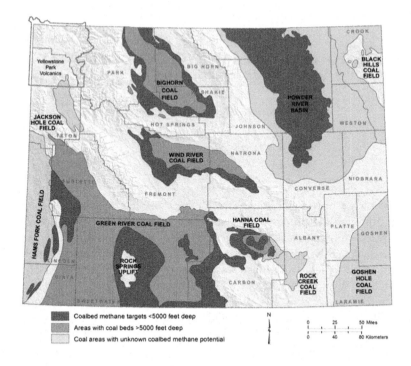

Figure 1. Wyoming Coal Reserves. Source: Glass, G.B. (1997). Coal geology of Wyoming State Geological Survey (WSGS, 2014). WSGS, 2014, Coalbed methane target map: Wyoming State Geological Survey, (Modified from Jones and De Bruin 1990), www.wsgs. uwyo.edu/Research/Energy/Oil-Gas/CBM.aspx (accessed 2014).

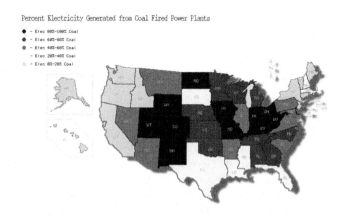

Figure 2. Electricity generated from coal. Source: U.S. Energy Information Administration (2007).

Figure 3a. Sunset uranium mine, Wyoming. Source: U.S. Department of Interior (2003).
Figure 3b. Oil wells near Teapot Dome, Wyoming Source EPA (Boyd Norton 1973). Figure 3c.
Solar Panels in the west. Source: U.S. Fish and Wildlife Service (2013). Figure 3d. Wind
turbine field in the west. Source: U.S. Fish and Wildlife Service (Winchell Jouhua, 2013).

While energy is the most important economic sector in Wyoming, the state has long prided itself on pristine air and mountain beauty, if not the cold winters that keep the population sparse. Wyoming tourism generated $2.6 billion in 2010, with visitors coming to see mountains, hunt on its plains, and fish in its streams (Figure 4). So there is a balance, a nexus, between energy and environment that makes it a regional grand challenge in Wyoming.

Figure 4. Grand Tetons, Wyoming. Source: Daniel Mayer (2006).

Establish the STEM-Societal Connection

With our overall topic of the nexus of energy and environment in place, Mark engaged the professional learning communities in a conversation about the import of the topic. He began by having the teachers consider their personal reliance on energy by asking:

How much energy do you use each day?
How much energy did you use to get to here today?

How much energy would you have used each day back in 1869?

How much impact do you have on the environment currently versus 1869?

Our mode of transportation has changed significantly across history, from walking, to the beast and wheel, and now the combustion engine (Figure 5). With this convenience has come an increased impact on the environment. The yen and yang of energy and environment is an understanding that we want to develop in students. We have choices to make and those choices have consequences.

Figure 5. Transportation: Yesterday versus today. Figure 5a. Mormon emigrants. Source: National Archives and Records Administration (War Department 1789). Figure 5b. Hummer H1 in the river.

The sources of energy and its level of consumption have changed over time. Figure 6 provides data on the history of energy in the United States. The primary source of energy before 1850 was wood. By around 1885 coal overtook the burning of wood as the primary energy source and with it came the soot plagued city of London. Still coal was king until around 1950 when petroleum became the most used energy resource. While petroleum remains the most used energy resource today, we see a diversification of energy resources in the 20th century. The age of petroleum has seen us take to the air, but it has also resulted in increased carbon dioxide emissions resulting in global climate change. Again there are benefits and consequences.

It is also important to understand that not all energy is created equal, that is, different resources are more practical for different needs. We don't burn coal to fuel planes for example. The United States energy flow diagrams in Figure 7 illustrate how certain energy resources serve specific needs. The flow diagrams provide an excellent example of why quantitative reasoning is so important for the understanding of science. Complex science models such as the flow diagrams are common and can be difficult to interpret for a student or even an adult citizen. First, these models often embed quantitative data within the pictorial representation, for instance the simpler flow model provides measures in quads of the amount of production and consumption of energy. What is a quad you might ask? A quad is a measure of energy, with 1 quad equaling 10^{15} Btu. So what is a Btu? Well more on measurement units in science

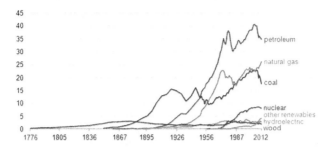

Figure 6. U.S. Energy History. Source: U.S. Energy Information Administration (2012).

in later chapters where the science and quantitative reasoning conceptions will be explored in detail. The point is that without some knowledge of the unit measure the flow model is difficult to interpret. This is an example of the need for students to be able to perform the act of quantification. Second, the science models present extensive interrelated information within a pictorial representation. Sorting out the details can be challenging. For example, the more complex flow diagram in Figure 8 is providing information not only on imports and exports, but on energy sources (fossil fuels, nuclear, renewable) and quads of energy consumed by different users (residential, commercial, industrial, and transportation). Third comparing science models from different sources can be challenging. Compare the model for energy flow in Figure 7 with Figure 8 and consider the variance in the measured values. Students often find a difference in values very disconcerting, such as the Figure 7 model having a natural gas supply of 24.63 quads and the Figure 8 model listing it as 23.37 quads. Students fail to question the authority providing the data or that data values are approximations and may vary. Instead they attempt to provide qualitative explanations for the differences, such as the measures being taken at different times or in different locations.

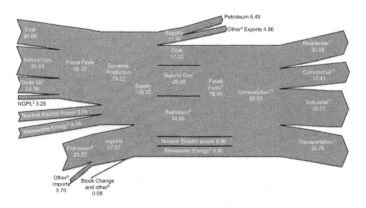

Figure 7. U.S. Energy Flow in Quadrillion Btu for 2012. Source: U.S. Energy Information Administration, Annual Energy Review (2012).

A question raised by the unused and useful energy categories in the second energy flow model in Figure 8 is energy efficiency, an important issue if one is examining energy use. We can relate efficiency to students on a more personal level. For example, estimate the amount of energy lost in lighting a bulb in your house. Do you have a number in mind? Ok now examine the energy efficiency model in Figure 9. The teachers in the QR STEM project were surprised to find that only 2% of the energy sent from the power plant to light the bulb were used to actually produce light. Such non-intuitive concepts provide excellent topics to pursue in a unit on understanding energy. From a quantitative reasoning perspective, notice that no unit measure is provided for energy in the efficiency model. Why not? In this model the focus is on a generic amount used, 100 units could be watts or megawatts. Such calculations with unitless measures are difficult for some students to grasp.

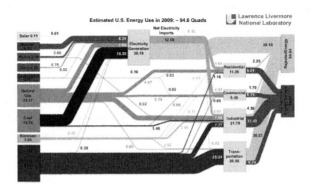

Figure 8. U.S. Energy Flow alternative model. Source: Lawrence Livermore National Laboratory and Department of Energy (2009).

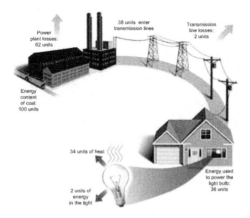

Figure 9. Energy efficiency. Source: National Academies (2008).

One of the central societal concerns for energy is simple, is there enough? This raises important issues of consumption and supply. The leading petroleum and electrical consumers are the industrialized nations and the United States is at the top in consumption (Figure 10). China and India energy consumption is on a sharp rise as they strive for their own version of the American dream. Quantitative representations such as the traditional coordinate plane graph for petroleum consumption and the scatter plot statistical display for electricity consumption allow us to explore trends in energy use. The electrical consumption model provides clear data on the have's and have not's on our planet by relating usage to the human development index. To understand this representation at a deeper level we must quantify the variable of human development index so we understand its attributes and measure. This provides yet another example of the importance of quantitative reasoning in the sciences.

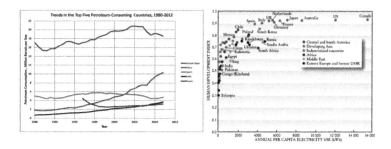

Figure 10. Top oil and electricity consuming countries. Figure 10a. Top oil consuming countries. Source: U.S. EIA (Plazak, 2013). Figure 10b. Electricity consumption by countries. Source: Physics Today, adapted from Lawrence Livermore National Laboratories (Pasternak, 2000).

We asked teachers to consider the question, "Will there be an energy crisis in the future?" To answer this question we must consider the economic variables of supply and demand. Let's begin with demand. The demand for all energy resources is on the rise and projections indicate that will not change in the near future (Figure 11). We also see from the model on the right that the majority of coal is used to produce the commodity of electricity. The energy by fuel type graph embeds the variable of percent of total share (right most axis) in a more traditional two dimensional graph of time by amount. While this type of embedding is not uncommon in science models, it is not common in mathematics and raises potential quantitative reasoning problems for students.

The next question for teachers was, "What is driving the increase in demand for energy?" The answer is rising populations and a push by undeveloped countries to become industrialized (Figure 12). World population is rising at ever increasing rates, with the increase from 1 to 2 billion taking 30 years (growth rate of 1/30 or approximately 33.3 million a year), while the increase from 2 to 3 billion took only 14 years (1/14 or 71.4 million a year). Compare this to the growth rate of

166.7 million a year to move from 5 to 6 billion. The growth is faster in Asia and Africa where there are more undeveloped countries with increasing appetites for energy Figure 13). Quantitatively it is important to see that not only is the population increasing, but it is increasing at increasing rates. Students need to understand the difference between linear growth and exponential growth to see the problem this causes for supply of energy.

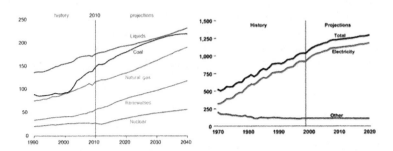

Figure 11a. Energy use by fuel type with projections measured in Btu. Source: EIA (2013). Figure 11b. Energy use by fuel type with projections as measured in Btu (left) and coal consumption for electricity in short tons (right). Source: EIA, Quarterly Coal Report (1998). Projections are extension of data in EIA report.

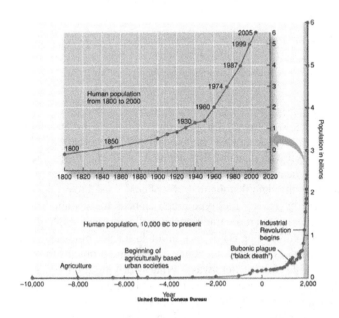

Figure 12. World population growth industrialization. Source: United States Census Bureau.

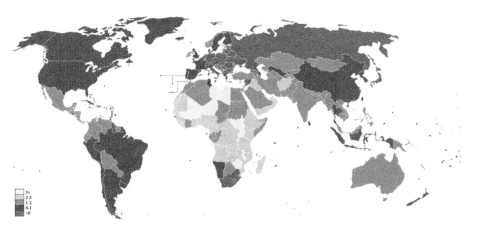

Figure 13. Population growth rates by region.

The fact that petroleum, coal, and natural gas are non-renewable resources begs the question, "When will we run out?" How long do we have to solve the problem with alternative energy sources? Rather than think of when we will fully deplete an energy resource, make a guess as to when we will no longer be able produce the supply to meet the demand. This is called the peak and indicates when we will have shortages if we do not come up with alternative sources. So take a guess as to the year we will reach peak oil? What about peak coal? Do you have a number in mind? Figure 14 and 15 provide multiple models predicting peak oil and peak coal. Most projections have peak oil occurring between 2010 and 2020. All but the most optimistic projections have the peak occurring by 2040. Peak coal is predicted to occur around 2020 and begin a steep decline by 2060. From a quantitative reasoning perspective students need to understand that these models are based on estimates of potential oil and coal reserves. Models of complex situations like the peak of oil and coal are at best educated guesses. Supply may be underestimated due to undiscovered reserves not being included. Demand may decrease due to the use of renewable alternative energy resources such as solar and wind. Part of becoming an informed citizen capable of making data-based decisions about complex grand challenges such as energy supply is understanding that models have error and may even be manipulated to support a certain view point.

An enduring understanding of energy is that the fossil fuel era will decline. It must, since the supply is not infinite and we are using it at an incredible rate. Figure 16 presents a model of the rise and fall of the fossil fuel era. This does not mean that electricity and modern transportation has to stop, just that we have to find other ways to power them in a post fossil fuel era.

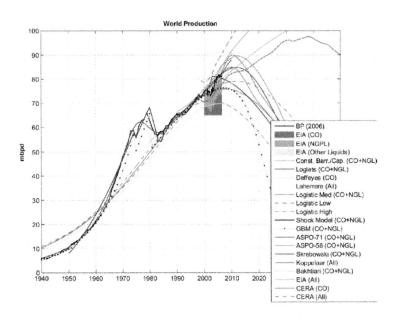

Figure 14. World Oil Production (Source: Association for the Study of Peak Oil and Gas. The Oil Conundrum. DAINA. 16 January 2011. ISBN 978-0-9644741-1-6).

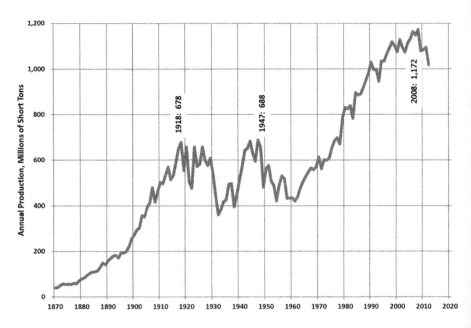

Figure 15. Peak coal in United States.

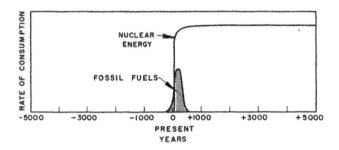

Figure 16. Fossil Fuel Era. Relative magnitudes of possible fossil fuel and nuclear energy consumption. Source: Nuclear Energy and the Fossil Fuels (Hubbert, 1956).

We must be careful about presenting the energy picture as an "end of days" scenario. Consider the case of Thomas Malthus who wrote about the pending disaster of population growth exceeding food supply. He determined that the human population was increasing at an exponential rate, but the food supply was not, so there was a pending crisis (Figure 17). In his own words, "The power of population is so superior to the power of the earth to produce substance for man, that premature death must in some shape or other visit the human race" (in *An Essay on the Principle of Population*, 1798). This was written in the late 18th century, yet here we are today with abundant food (at least in industrialized countries). So where did Malthus go wrong? He wrote his thesis on the dawn of an agricultural revolution which he did not foresee. The mechanization of agriculture after World War II and the Green Revolution (a series of research, development, and technology initiatives between 1940 and 1970) substantially increased crop yields. We cannot foresee future technological and research advances that may impact a pending energy crisis. In any case, we want our students to be aware of the approaching post-fossil fuel era so they can deal with the grand challenges presented by it.

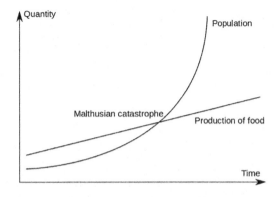

Figure 17. Malthus' basic peak food model. Source: Malthusa (1798).

There will be many challenges in the post-fossil fuel era. First energy sources have best fits to particular energy sectors (Figure 18). For example, coal, which generates 22.8% of energy, is used primarily in generating electric power and not in transportation. So loss of coal presents different challenges then loss of nuclear power. Second, as conventional reservoirs are depleted we turn to unconventional reservoirs which are more expensive to produce (this is called EROEI - energy returned on energy invested) and have decreasing energy density (amount of energy stored per unit volume). Figure 19 provides a hydrocarbon recovery model of this relationship. From a quantitative reasoning viewpoint Figure 19 does not provide quantitative data directly, but does indicate relationships between multiple variables which are being measured. Understanding relationships between variables through their attributes is essential to quantifying variables for use in models. The hidden quantitative values in Figure 19 include measures of energy density. For example gas shales and tar sands are future reservoirs that have a low EROEI. Third, to fill the energy gap caused by depleted fossil fuel reservoirs we will have to use a diverse energy resources portfolio. Possible post-fossil fuel era energy resources include nuclear power, wind energy, solar energy, biofuels, and hydrogen. However each of these comes at a cost to the environment, as does the retrieval of replacement fossil fuel reservoirs such as shale gas and oil sands. The million dollar question is "What should our future energy portfolio look like?"

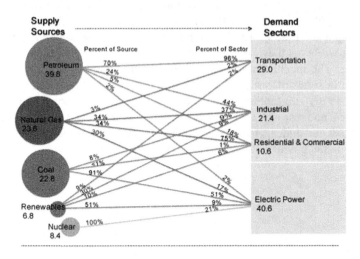

Figure 18. Energy sources and sectors. Source: EIA Annual Energy Review (2007).

Mark then asked the teachers about the energy-environment nexus: every choice we make about energy has an impact on environment. In the fossil-fuel era, the burning of petroleum products has been connected to an increase in atmospheric carbon dioxide (Figure 20). Carbon dioxide acts as a greenhouse gas which is believed to play a major role in global climate change and is a major source of ocean acidification

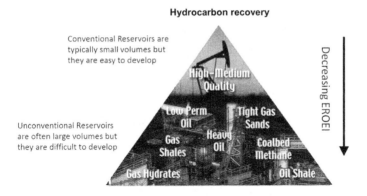

Figure 19. Resource Triangle. Source: How Technology Tranfer Will Expand the Development of Unconventional Gas, Worldwide, Holditch & Ayers (2006).

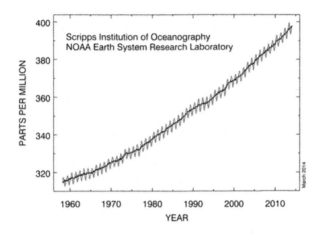

Figure 20. Atmospheric CO_2 (Source: U.S. Government NOAA Earth System Research Laboratory (March 2014)).

which poses a threat to ocean food chains (Figure 21). From a quantitative reasoning perspective, the atmospheric carbon dioxide model overlays a cyclic data cycle on an underlying increasing trend. Such fluxes in data can confuse students, causing short term phenomena like annual cycles to distract them from the long term increase in carbon dioxide over the past 40 years. We hear this in students arguments against the increasing trend, "Sure is a cold day, so much for global warming." This is a question of scale, which is an important underlying quantitative concept in science. Scale in science varies from extremely small (microscopic/atomic/ millisecond) to vast (landscape/global/eons), but we live and experience the world on a macroscopic scale (measurable and observable with the naked eye).

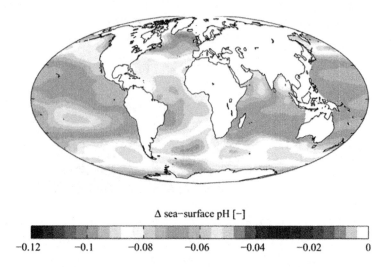

Δ sea–surface pH [−]

−0.12   −0.1   −0.08   −0.06   −0.04   −0.02   0

Figure 21. Ocean Acidification – estimated change in sea surface pH from the pre-industrial period (1700s) to the present day (1990s). Change is caused by invasion of anthropogenic CO2. Source: Global Ocean Data Analysis Project and World Ocean Atlas (2007).

A counter argument to concerns about the increase in carbon dioxide is supported by viewing the problem on a scale of eons. Figure 22 presents data on atmospheric carbon dioxide from 450 years ago to now. We can quantitatively interpret the trends in the graph as naturally occurring cycles. The argument has been made that we are just in a natural cycle of carbon dioxide change. These arguments are excellent examples of the importance of the quantitative concept of scale in science.

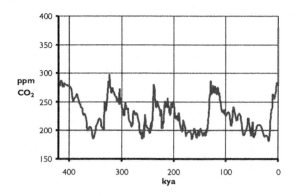

Figure 22. Flux in atmospheric carbon dioxide during the past 417,000 years (kya = one thousand years ago). Source: U.S. Department of Energy, Trends a Compendium of Data on Global Change (2003).

An important aspect of building models in science is identifying the variable quantities that impact the phenomena of interest. The variables serve as the building blocks for the model. When the teachers were asked "What are the components making up global fossil carbon emissions?" they immediately responded with petroleum (gas) and coal. After some thought, they added natural gas to the mix. But the teachers did not account for the role that cement production plays in global carbon emissions (Figure 23). The quantification act is essential to extracting mathematical information from the context of science. It begins with identifying objects within the context (i.e. cement production), assigning attributes to the object (cement production involves a chemical conversion when limestone $CaCO_3$ is converted to lime CaO which releases carbon dioxide; cement is used in construction across the globe), and determining a measure (million metric tons of carbon per year).

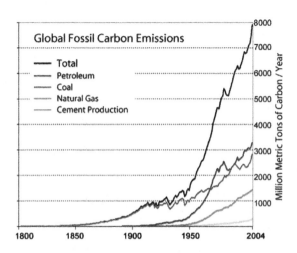

Figure 23. Global fossil carbon emissions. Source: United States Department of Energy (2007). Figure by Mark Thorpe.

A tenet of the QR STEM project is that students should not only engage in understanding grand challenges in energy and environment, but should propose solutions to the challenges which they communicate to peers and experts. Both the future energy portfolio and carbon dioxide dilemma allow students to explore multiple solution scenarios through stabilization wedge games. These games can serve as the key performance task of a unit which assesses understanding of complex energy and environment issues. As an example let's use the Stabilization Wedge Game for Carbon Dioxide Emissions. Set the stage for the game with the following article from S. Pacala and R. Socolow:

Humanity already possesses the fundamental scientific, technical, and industrial know-how to solve the carbon and climate problem for the next half-century.

67

A portfolio of technologies now exists to meet the world's energy needs over the next 50 years and limit atmospheric CO_2 to a trajectory that avoids a doubling of the preindustrial concentration. Every element in this portfolio has passed beyond the laboratory bench and demonstration project; many are already implemented somewhere at full industrial scale. Although no element is a credible candidate for doing the entire job (or even half the job) by itself, the portfolio as a whole is large enough that not every element has to be used.

The goal of the game is to stabilize carbon dioxide emissions at the level in 2005, about 7 billion tons of carbon emitted per year. In Figure 24, a scenario for stabilization is represented as a stabilization triangle. We cannot stabilize the carbon dioxide emissions by using only one strategy, we will need to choose from energy conservation strategies, fossil-fuel based strategies, nuclear energy, and renewable energy and biostorage strategies. Figure 25 provides the wedges which the students will select from to fill the stabilization triangle.

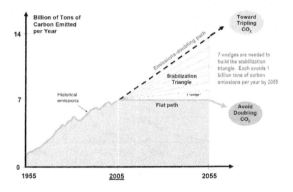

Figure 24. Stabilization wedges and triangles. Source: Carbon Mitigation Initiative, Princeton Environmental Institute (Hotinski, 2011).

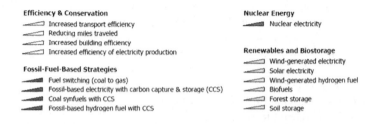

Figure 25. Stabilization wedges. Source: Carbon Mitigation Initiative, Princeton Environmental Institute (Hotinski, 2011).

Students must defend their choice of wedges and there are many constraints on each wedge, for example the efficiency in carbon dioxide reduction by fuel type (Figure 26) and the development of lithium batteries for hybrid cars (Figure 27).

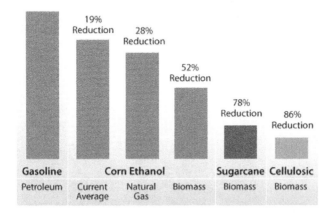

Figure 26. Fuel gas emissions reductions. Source: U.S. Department of Energy, Alternative Fuels Data Center, Life cycle energy and greenhouse gas emission impacts of different corn ethanol plant types (2007).

Figure 27. Lithium battery car – Tesla Roadster.

Balancing energy and environment is complex, but their inextricable tie to a myriad of social parameters (e.ge. politics, health, economics) makes this a mind bending task. We want students to be aware of the complexity of the energy and environment question, so as future citizens they can make more informed decisions. Figure 28 indicates the complexity of the energy and environment nexus and provides yet another interesting science model showing the endless variety of representations used to display information. Quantitative reasoning includes the capacity to interpret models which embed variables (using size of circle to represent magnitude of impact), a skill that is essential for a scientifically and quantitatively literate society.

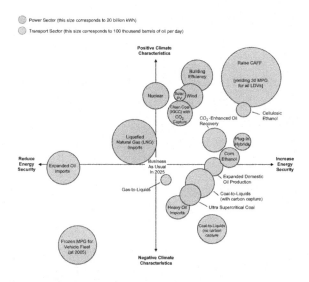

Figure 28. Energy and environment impact of power sector and transportation sector.
Source: World Resources Institute, Climate and Energy Security Impacts and Tradeoffs in
2025 www.wri.org (April 2008).

At this point Jimm, our energy expert, provided the teachers with a primary energy sources chart (PES provided in Figure 29, completed version in Figure 30) and asked the teachers to fill it in to the best of their ability. After the teachers had worked on the chart for a period of time, Jim asked "What is the basic scientific principal in this table that is the important take home point?" The answer, energy is simply converted from one form to another. All modern industrialized societies do is convert energy from one form to another and in the process capture some small fraction of that energy to do something useful, e.g. move a car, light a room, produce cement. Also note how many energy sources can be traced back to the sun, especially fossil fuels which are stored energy from the sun. So fossil fuels are the solar battery that humankind has not yet been able to devise.

Modern industrialized societies use a variety of *primary energy sources (PES)*, including: oil, natural gas, coal, nuclear, etc. Different PES represent different types of energy. For example, wind energy harnesses, in fact, the kinetic energy of moving air. Thus, the primary energy type of wind is kinetic energy. The kinetic energy of the wind is, in turn, produced by the radiant (solar) energy that heats the atmosphere. Thus, the primary energy type of wind is kinetic energy, its secondary energy type is radiant (solar) energy and ultimately it is derived from nuclear fusion (see row in table below). Different PES are traded in different units and their energy densities expressed via a wide combinations of units. Armed with this knowledge, please complete the table below to the best of your ability.

energy source	energy type			physical state	trading units	energy density units
	primary	secondary	tertiary			
				conventional		
oil						
natural gas						
coal						
nuclear						
				renewables		
hydroelectric						
solar						
wind	kinetic	solar	nuclear fusion	gas	kW-hr	
tidal						
biomass						
biofuels						
				alternative/unconventional		
oil sand						
geothermal						

Figure 29. Primary energy sources (PES) chart. Source: Jim Myers (2014).

energy source	energy type			physical state	trading units	energy density units
	primary	secondary	tertiary			
				conventional		
oil	chemical	solar	nuclear fusion	liquid	bbl tonnes	Btu/bbl, Btu/tonne
natural gas	chemical	solar	nuclear fusion	gas	ft^3, thousand ft^3 (tcf), million ft^3 (MMcf), trillion ft^3 (Tcf)	Btu/ft^3, Btu/tcf Btu/MMcf, Btu/Tcf
coal	chemical	solar	nuclear fusion	solid	tons tonnes	Btu/lb, Btu/t, Btu/tonne
nuclear	mass	nuclear fusion		solid	lbs U_3O_8	Btu/lb
				renewables		
hydroelectric	kinetic	potential	solar	liquid	kW-hr	-
solar	radiant	nuclear fusion		-	kW-hr	-
wind	kinetic	solar	nuclear fusion	gas	kW-hr	-
tidal	kinetic	gravitational		liquid	kW-hr	-
biomass	chemical	solar	nuclear fusion	solid	lb, t	Btu/lb, Btu/t
biofuels	chemical	solar	nuclear fusion	liquid	gal, L	Btu/bbl, Btu/gal
				alternative/unconventional		
oil sand	chemical	radiant	nuclear fusion	semi-solid	bbl, gallons	Btu/bbl, Btu/gal
geothermal	thermal	solar		-	kW-hr	

Figure 30. Primary energy sources (PES) chart (completed). Source: Jim Myers (2014).

Discussions about energy policy involve a large number of ***primary energy sources (PES)*** such as petroleum, natural gas, liquefied natural gas (LNG), coal, nuclear, wind, etc.; a bewildering array of units in which fuels are traded and sold; and another variable set of units used to express the energy contained in a given mass or volume of fuel, e.g. energy density. At the same time, the various primary energy sources are characterized by very different physical states, e.g. solid, liquid and gas. While such a difference may appear trivial, it in fact has profound implications for what types of

71

tasks each type of PES is best suited for. Thus, they place important constraints on any possible fuel switching. This array of units and primary energy sources are routinely encountered in virtually all media articles that discuss various energy policies. To contribute meaningfully to the nation's energy debate, students and citizens must be familiar with these terms and the basic energy science behind them.

Energy science is interdisciplinary, requiring the integration of biology, chemistry, earth science, physics and mathematics. It includes subject areas that are absent in most science course sequences, such as thermodynamics. It also uses a language in which everyday words have special meanings, such as heat, work and energy, which is a potential source of confusion for students (Solomon, 1983). In addition, it is essential to discuss energy within a real-world context. Consider the political debates concerning domestic petroleum drilling. An informed voter needs to know something about the context of petroleum production to make a wise decision. Jimm had teachers consider the following questions:

- What is the average daily oil production for Saudi Arabia versus the United States? Answer: 10.4×10^6 barrels per day versus 6.9×10^6
- How many barrels of oil does Saudi Arabia produce each year versus the United States? Answer: 37.9×10^9 versus 2.58×10^9 barrels
- What was the daily production rate for an average well in Saudi Arabia in 1998 versus the United States? Answer: 5,140 barrels per day versus 11 barrels per day
- Estimate the number of producing wells in Saudi Arabia versus the United States? Answer 2,023 wells versus 627,272 wells in the United States, if you include stripper wells that produce less than 10 barrels per day then the U.S. number goes up to 1,239,418.

Figure 31. U.S. and Saudi Arabia oil fields. Figure 31a. Greensburg Oil Field, Louisianna (Paul Heinrich, March 2008). Figure 31b: Highways are clearly visible leading from the capital west to the Dukhan oil fields, of Saudi Arabia. Source: NASA (2012).

It is evident that the United States is already tapping out oil reserves and is still not nearly matching the output of Saudi Arabia. These simple facts give an entirely different perspective on "drill, baby, drill".

Our goal for the overview of energy and environment was to convince the teachers and you that this is a timely and relevant topic for our students. It is a topic that the next generation will be wrestling with in the future, so it is worthy of study with a goal to develop understanding. It is a topic which is imbued with quantitative reasoning in science and requires a multidisciplinary approach. Finally energy and environment is a topic which connects science and society. These are all components we want the topic we choose for the unit to possess.

GRAND CHALLENGES

Relate Topic to Grand Challenges

Supplying the energy needed to support an expanding human population with a rising standard of living, while maintaining human and natural systems, is an increasingly difficult yet necessary task. Consequently, many individuals and organizations list energy as one of the grand challenges threatening humankind's future. Yet, few of the general public actually understand what a grand challenge is and why they are important. Before we discuss the energy grand challenge from an educational perspective, we want to set briefly the grand challenges in a larger context. The German mathematician David Hilbert published a list of 23 unsolved mathematically problems in 1901 (Hilbert, 1901). The publication of this list challenged the mathematical community to solve these problems. Over a century later, Hilbert's list has become the inspiration for the *grand challenges*. In a report on environmental sciences, the NRC (2001) defined grand challenges as "…major scientific tasks that are compelling for both intellectual and practical reasons, that offer potential for major breakthroughs on the basis of recent developments in science and technology, and that are feasible given current capabilities, and a serious infusion of resources." In another NRC report, *Creating a Disaster Resilient America* (NRC, 2005), grand challenges were defined as "…fundamental problems in S & T (science and technology) whose solution can be advanced by coordinated and sustained investments in research, education, communication, and application of knowledge and technology."

In the last two decades, the concept of grand challenges has permeated the scientific, engineering, technological, medical and social science communities. A partial list of disciplines or research areas in which grand challenges have been identified include: engineering (NAE, 2008), the chemical industry (NRC, 2005a), disaster mitigation (NRC, 2005b), global health (Varmus et al., 2003), environmental sciences (NRC, 2001), Earth and environmental sciences (Zoback, 2001), Earth system science (Schellnhuber and Sahagian, 2002; Steffen et al., 2004), and geosciences and energy (DePaolo and Orr, 2007). In his presidential address to the AAAS (American Association for the Advancement of Science) in 2006, Omenn also identified a series of grand challenges in science and engineering, multidisciplinary research, and public understanding and decision making.

Grand challenges are calls to spur progress toward solving important societal and environmental problems across a variety of disciplines. They are useful for establishing future research and funding priorities in various disciplines. Although difficult to define precisely, grand challenges share some common characteristics which include: a social relevance; the likelihood of significant economic impact; the ability to be solved in a reasonable time span, the need for a multidisciplinary approach; and the investment of significant resources to solve, both human and fiscal. A large number of grand challenge lists cite water, environmental change, land use modification, resource utilization /depletion, and energy as particularly pressing grand challenges facing humanity.

Despite the obvious importance of the various grand challenges, many, including us, would argue that energy is one of the most important grand challenges facing humankind today. Energy is characterized not by a single challenge, but several. These challenges are many, complex, and multifaceted. They vary in scale from local to regional to national. Now with an expanding global population, energy's grand challenges have attained global and hence international scale. At the broadest level, the challenges of energy can be grouped into three areas:

- supply – physical availability of primary energy sources;
- access – the inability/ability of nations to acquire the energy sources they need because of political conditions;
- environmental impact – changes in the natural world due to exploration, production and use.

For the last 150 years, environmental impact was mostly local in scope, at most expanding to a regional scale. For example, pollution in the Niger Delta of Nigeria has been for the most part of local concern. Now, with the importance of climate change the focus has changed to the global scale. Unfortunately, these issues are not isolated. Rather, they are closely related and solutions to one are likely to have impacts in the other areas.

The historical approach to solving an energy issue has been to consider only the energy science (ES), technology (T) and economics (E). This approach has produced solutions that have not always been the most just. They have often adversely impacted local populations and severely impacted the environment. If the energy grand challenge is multifaceted, then its solutions should be as well. In addition, solutions are more sustainable, equitable and effective when additional perspectives are considered, including energy context (EC), environment (EN), social institutions (SI), culture (C), politics (P), etc. These perspectives are usually only considered when there is excess wealth. An energy solution function might look like:

$$ESol = f(ES, T, E, EC, EN, SI, C, P,...)$$

where all the variables and their interaction with each other are considered.

Technology is a key variable in the energy solution function. Technology indicates what is physically possible and is increasingly important as we move from the fossil fuel era and look for new energy sources in the future. For example, debates about wind and solar energy hinge on technology components, as does a switch to green energy solutions such as biofuels. Discussions about what is technologically feasible and what is not are critical if we are to make a successful transition from fossil fuels to new sources of energy. We didn't get it right for nuclear energy, as was evidenced by nuclear disasters such as those in Japan. We can't afford to make similar mistakes with green energy. Energy instruction must be multi-dimensional, including development of both deeper content and context. Energy science and technology are critical to the discussion and are unique to the subject area. Social context is necessary to connect with students and is strongly influenced by the teacher's own interest in energy and environment. In addition, pedagogy must facilitate transfer of classroom knowledge to real-world problems. We must develop student's scientific literacy, ability to handle uncertainty and ambiguity, critical thinking, and problem solving, as well as developing specialized skills such as reading maps. Finally, we must improve students' quantitative reasoning ability.

PLACE-BASED LENSE

Relate Grand Challenges to Place

Relating the chosen STEM topic to grand challenges gives the instructional unit immediate legitimacy in the eyes of both teachers and students. Who isn't impacted by the energy and environment grand challenges identified above? The next issue after legitimacy is engagement. We need to ensure that both teachers and students will be engaged in the grand challenge. This is where the place-based pedagogy is important. We want to tie the grand challenge to the place in which the student lives. Recall the engagement situation distance we discussed in Chapter 1 (Chapter 1, Figure 4). Scientific situations are at the furthest distance from personal life situations, meaning engagement may be an issue. Grand challenges are compelling, but also lie at the outer reaches of engagement situation distance. Students may proclaim, "What does this have to do with me?" when world issues are the focus. So we bring the grand challenge closer to home by asking the teacher and student to think globally and act locally. What impact does the grand challenge have on your community, for your future occupational prospects, and for your personal life situation?

The economics, environmental, social and other perspectives of energy solutions are determined by social context. For example, petroleum production has had vastly different impacts in Norway and Nigeria. Production of Nigeria's hydrocarbon reserves has produced many negative social, political, economic and environmental impacts. The vast wealth flowing into the country has funded massive corruption, inequitable distribution of wealth and pitted various ethnic factions against each other for a share of the petrowealth. Political unrest has characterized the Niger Delta where various groups routinely capture foreign and domestic oil workers and hold them for ransom. Acts of vandalism and terrorism against the country's oil infrastructure has produced serious environmental damage as well as loss of life. In addition, lax environmental laws and their enforcement have resulted in significant damage to the wetlands of the delta. In contrast, in Norway the discovery of the oil and gas fields of the North Sea has been an economic boon for the country. Production from the fields has made Norway one of the world's biggest exporters of oil and gas. The country has protected its environment with strict laws. For example, they have required the sequestration of carbon dioxide produced from natural gas production at Sliepner, the first such operation in the world. In addition to carefully guarding their environment as well as social and political institutions, Norway has set aside a portion of its hydrocarbon wealth for future generations. Few would argue against the overall good that has resulted from hydrocarbon production in this nation.

A key variable in the energy solution function is social context. Social context provides the relevancy for science. Context is provided by addressing topical issues in the news and varying scope from local to international (Figure 32). Context introduces different viewpoints and perspectives, as well as providing a connection to students' lives.

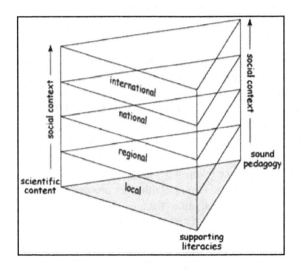

Figure 32. Social context in science. Source: Jimm Myers (2014).

QR STEM SYMPOSIA DRIVERS

Narrow the Focus from Grand Challenges to Topics

The grand challenge of energy and environment is a very broad topic. It is important to narrow the focus and eventually identify enduring understandings that we want students to develop. We began narrowing the topic by identifying three specific aspects of energy and environment that dramatically impact every U.S. citizen: transportation, electricity, and climate change (Figure 33). These three aspects served as the science content focus for the three summer QR STEM symposia. For each aspect we demonstrated the multidisciplinary nature of the topic by considering it through the lenses of biology, chemistry, earth science and physics. In addition, we used a variety of activities within each of these scientific disciplines to explicitly demonstrate the link between STEM topics and quantitative reasoning. At the same time, these activities were designed to illustrate the complexity and richness of the energy and environment grand challenge.

Figure 33. Three aspects of energy and environment driving QR STEM symposia.
Figure 33a. Transportation: traffic at night. Source: Sebastian Grunwald (2012).
Figure 33b. Electricity: wind turbine field in the west. Source: U.S. Fish and Wildlife Service
(Winchell Jouhua, 2013). Figure 33c. Climate Change: projected change in annual mean
surface air temperature. Source: NOAA Geophysical Fluid Dynamics Laboratory.

Transportation

Modern societies are highly dependent upon transportation. We value our ability to move rapidly around our cities, states and the nation. At the same time, transportation moves our goods and makes a modern economy possible. Transportation is also a major source of environmental impact and is threatened by a decreasing global petroleum supply. As societies have evolved, transportation has becoming increasingly important. In Medieval times, an individual might spend an entire lifetime within five miles of their birth. Now, we think nothing of jetting off to Las Vegas for a weekend. Our major complaint about flying from North America or Europe is the duration of the flight, never reflecting on how much of an adventure such a journey would have been even a hundred years ago. Figure 34 indicates how transportation has grown as a major component of energy consumption. The U.S. Energy Flow diagram (Figure 35) indicates that of the 101 quads of energy used in the U.S., 29 quads or about 25% is used for transportation. Transportation is almost entirely dependent upon liquid fuels, primarily petroleum. This is because liquid fuel is easy to carry, utilize, and carries high energy in a small mass.

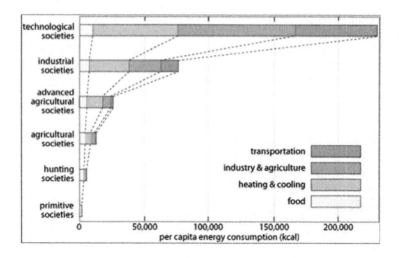

Figure 34. Fueling transportation over time. Source: Scientific American, The Flow of Energy in an Industrial Society (Cook, Sept. 1971).

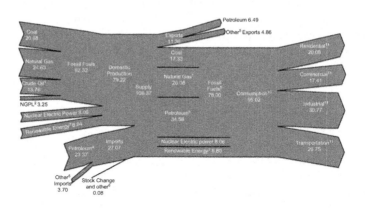

Figure 35. U.S. Energy Flow in Quadrillion Btu for 2012. Source: U.S. Energy Information Administration, Annual Energy Review (2012).

Of the primary energy sources, petroleum supplies 96% of the energy for transportation, representing nearly 70% of all petroleum consumption in the U.S. (Figure 36). Increasingly, there is worry about the availability of petroleum supplies. This is commonly expressed as Peak Oil (Figure 37), the point in the petroleum production curve where the maximum production is obtained. After this time, production continually falls. At the same time, demand is expected to continue to grow. The increasing divergence between demand and supply has led some to speculate about fundamental changes in how modern societies will function. Others have suggested we can easily wean ourselves from petroleum by simply growing our fuel. Yet, the difference in energy density of petroleum derived fuels versus those generated from bio materials (Figure 38) suggests this might be difficult. At the same time, the switch of crop land to fuel crops raises serious concerns for food supply in poorer nations.

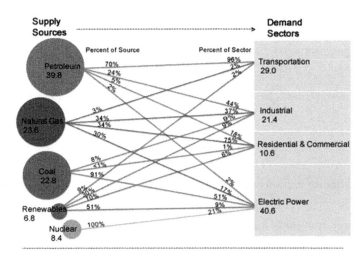

Figure 36. Energy sources and sectors. Source: EIA Annual Energy Review (2007).

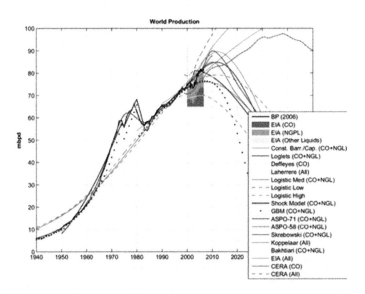

Figure 37. World Oil Production (Source: Association for the Study of Peak Oil and Gas. The Oil Conundrum. DAINA. 16 January 2011. ISBN 978-0-9644741-1-6).

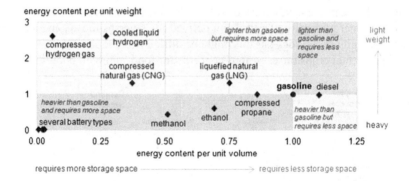

Figure 38. Energy density – Why are petroleum-based fuels so great? Source: U.S. Energy Information Administration (Feb. 2013).

The energy transportation topics explored with teachers in the QR STEM symposia included:

- Sustaining Transportation;
- Earth Science: Petroleum and Peak Oil – A look at the world's most valuable commodity;
- Physics: Thermodynamics and Heat Engines;
- Chemistry: Combustion;
- Biology: Biomass to Liquids – Our energy future.

Quantitative reasoning was integrated throughout the topics. Earth Science incorporated QR in a discussion of Arctic National Wildlife Refuge (ANWR) oil drilling impact. Physics focused on QR through home heating. Chemistry explored QR through heat of combustion, gas carbon footprint, and stoichiometry, while Biology integrated QR into discussions of ethanol, biofuels, CO_2, and water use in biofuel production.

Electricity

Electricity is another energy commodity that is critical to modern societies. Unlike coal, petroleum, and nuclear, electricity is not an energy source. It, like hydrogen, is an energy carrier. In just over a hundred years, electricity has changed industrialized societies. It can power the smallest electrical motors to operate car windows to large, electric-arc furnaces to produce steel. Unlike the primary energy sources, it can be generated in one place and consumed hundreds or thousands of miles away. Societies which have access to and consume more electricity correspond to those with a higher human development index (Figure 39). Put simply, those with a higher quality of life use more electricity.

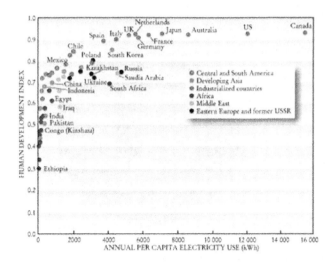

Figure 39. Electricity consumption by countries. Source: Physics Today, adapted from Lawrence Livermore National Laboratories (Pasternak, 2000).

U.S. economic growth is linked to increased use of electricity. Using 1986 as a base year, electricity use and Gross Domestic Product (GDP) followed similar trends through 2007 (Figure 40). A wide variety of fuels are used to generate electricity (Figure 41). The majority of electricity, 71.7%, is generated using fossil fuels, so fossil fuel prices have a big impact on the cost of electricity. Diversifying fuels for generation of electricity protects against shortages, price fluctuations, and change in regulatory policies.

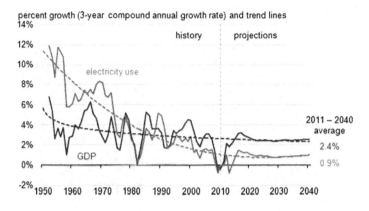

Figure 40. Electricity use and economic growth. Source: U.S. Energy Information Administration, Today in Energy (Mar. 2013).

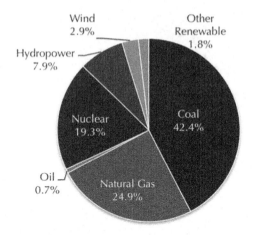

Figure 41. Electricity power generation by fuel type. Source: Energy Information Administration (EIA), Monthly Energy Review (May 2013).

The electric power industry must meet the demands of consumers, which are considerable. The industry has to address three types of loads: base load, intermediate load, and peak load. These loads vary by season with winter heating and summer cooling, as well as have daily variation (Figure 42). Generation of electricity must meet these varying demands, so it is important to have different types of plants

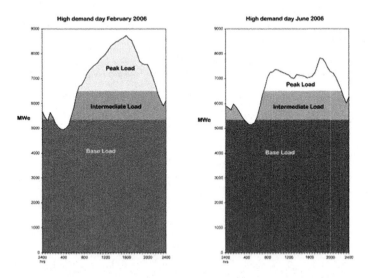

Figure 42. Electric load variation for a typical working day in Victoria, Australia for summer and winter day. Source: World Nuclear Association (Mar. 2012).

using different types of fuels. So what fuels should be used and what is the impact of burning those fuels on the environment? These are important questions. While electric use has continued to rise, advances in technology have reduced harmful emissions of sulfur and nitrogen oxides (Figure 43).

The electrical energy topics explored with teachers in the QR STEM symposia included:

- Electricity Powering Modern Societies;
- Earth Science: Coal and Electricity – Kicking a habit;
- Physics: Solar Electricity;
- Chemistry: Nuclear Power – Poised for revival?
- Biology: Wind and Electricity – A new habit?

Quantitative reasoning was integrated throughout the topics. Earth Science incorporated QR in a discussion of fuel consumption and plant design, SO_x, NO_x, and CO_2 emissions. Physics focused on QR through the Stirling engine. Biology integrated QR into discussions of increasing U.S. wind generated electricity.

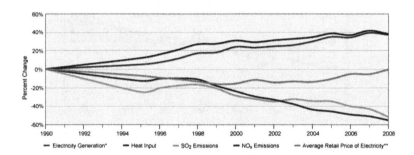

Figure 43. Trends in electricity generation and emissions. Source: Energy Information Administration and EPA (2009).

Climate Change

Energy and environment are inexorably linked. Decisions that we make on energy impact our environment in numerous ways. We focused on the impact on climate change. Surface air temperatures across the planet are changing and advanced models have been developed to predict future change (Figure 44). There is irrefutable proof that our climate is changing (Figure 45) with rising global air temperatures, but disagreement on what is driving the change. Many scientists believe that the rise in carbon dioxide in the Earth's atmosphere is driven in part by our extensive burning of fossil fuels (Figure 46). Carbon dioxide is a greenhouse gas which is trapping the sun's heat, with potentially devastating results for the environment – melting ice caps, sea water rise, and agricultural impacts (Figure 47).

83

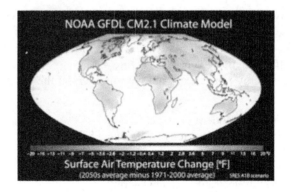

Figure 44. Climate Change: projected change in annual mean surface air temperature. Source: NOAA Geophysical Fluid Dynamics Laboratory.

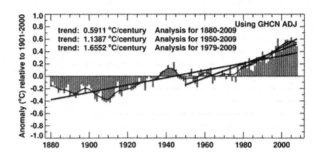

Figure 45. Global mean temperature change. Source: NOAA National Climate Data Center analysis.

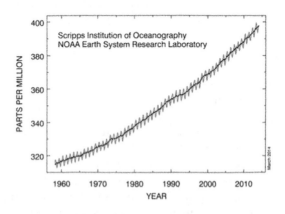

Figure 46. Atmospheric CO2 (Source: U.S. Government NOAA Earth System Research Laboratory (March 2014)).

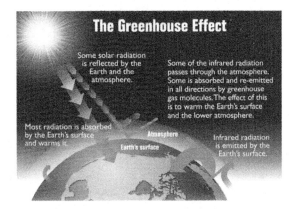

Figure 47. Greenhouse effect. Source: Environmental Protection Agency, Climate Change Indicators in the United States (Dec. 2012).

To understand the increase in carbon dioxide in the atmosphere students need to know and be able to interpret representations of the carbon cycle. Figure 48 is a box model of the carbon cycle. It indicates reservoirs where carbon is stored, such as in fossil fuel or the ocean, and flows between those reservoirs. For example, the deep ocean stores 38,100 units of carbon, with 100 units flowing to the shallow ocean and 91.6 units returning from the shallow ocean to the deep ocean. Note that more units of carbon flow from the atmosphere (92 units) to the ocean then from the ocean to the atmosphere (90 units), making the ocean a sink for carbon from the atmosphere. Also note that the biosphere and pedosphere return to the atmosphere the same combined amount that the atmosphere sends to them, 121.3 units. So nature appears to be in balance, that is, until you observe that fossil fuels are emitting 5.5 units of carbon into the atmosphere. The carbon from burning fossil fuels is accumulating in the atmosphere.

While there have always been fluctuations in the amount of carbon in the atmosphere as well as in global temperatures, long term temperature data from multiple modes of collecting data indicate that we are at a 1,000 year high global temperature (Figure 49). In the age of burning fossil fuels, the rate of change is greater than it has ever been (Figure 50).

The climate change topics explored with teachers in the QR STEM symposia included:

- Climate Change overview;
- Earth Science: Coal and Electricity – Kicking a habit;
- Physics: Climate Change Physics;
- Chemistry: The Carbon Cycle;
- Earth Science: Living in a Carbon-constrained World – Geological Carbon Sequestration;
- Biology: Living in a Carbon-constrained World – Biological Sequestration.

85

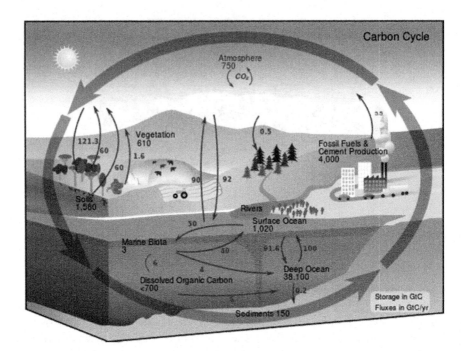

Figure 48. Carbon cycle model. Source: NASA Earth Observatory (May 2008).

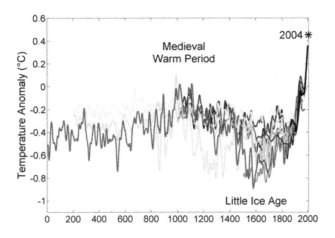

Figure 49. Temperature data from multiple models for reconstruction. Source: Global Warming Art project (Robert Rohde, 2005).

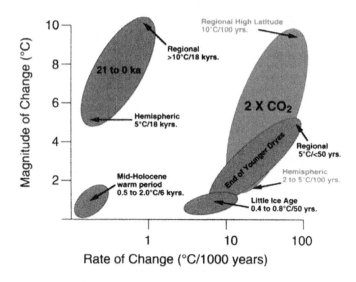

Figure 50. Rate of change in temperature. Source: Jackson, S.T. and J.T. Overpeck. 2000. Responses of plant populations and communities to environmental changes of the Late Quaternary. Paleobiology 26 (Supplement):194–220.

Quantitative reasoning was integrated throughout the topics. Earth Science incorporated QR in a discussion of estimating the cost of sequestration. Physics focused on QR through albedo. Biology integrated QR into discussions of rangeland carbon sequestration monitoring. Chemistry integrated QR through a discussion of carbon cycle stocks and fluxes as modeled by box models.

In the future U.S. citizens will face grand challenges in energy and environment. National surveys indicate they are ill-prepared for debates on these challenges. To better prepare citizens for the debate we must take an integrated approach to teaching about energy. It is essential of course to increase their knowledge about energy, but we must also address areas of energy science, technology, energy in context, and multiple perspectives within the social context such as economic, political, and legal. If we want citizens to make data-based scientifically informed decisions, then quantitative reasoning is an essential skill. Examine the many examples given in this chapter. These examples indicate the great variety of representations that are used to present information in the areas of energy and environment: statistical displays such as bar graphs and pie charts, flow diagrams, box models, graphs, scatterplots, tables, and equations. Informed citizens need to be capable of interpreting these models (quantitative interpretation) by identifying variables and their attributes (quantitative act), relating the variables to each other (quantitative literacy), and understanding how models are created (quantitative modeling) so they understand the strengths and limitations of models.

PRE-ASSESSING TEACHER UNDERSTANDING

Following the overview of energy and environment, the teachers were given an overview of quantitative reasoning in science contexts. Here we have introduced QR in some detail in Chapter 1 and have integrated our overview discussion of QR into the energy and environment overview. The purpose of the QR overview was to familiarize the science and mathematics teachers with the quantitative reasoning processes of quantitative act, quantitative literacy, quantitative interpretation, and quantitative modeling. We found the science teachers to be concerned about how to integrate the mathematical and statistical ideas into their current teaching. Some also had concerns about the mathematics content and many about their level of understanding of energy science. The mathematics teachers were concerned about their level of understanding of the science and their ability to use science as a context for teaching the mathematics they need to cover. These are common concerns and potential barriers to interdisciplinary teaching and learning. A central focus of QR STEM was to overcome the content and interdisciplinary barriers. We now continue with our discussion of how to collaborate with teachers on the development of interdisciplinary units in energy and environment.

Energy, Environment, and QR Preconceptions

The National Council of Supervisors of Mathematics recommendations on providing high quality professional development require collaboration with school leaders and teachers across three interconnected program components: diagnoses, design and implementation, and evaluation (Table 1). These three components are essential if professional development is to produce well-defined changes in teaching practice and student achievement. QR STEM addressed as many of the recommendations as possible within constraints of the project. The highlighted cells in the table were all addressed by our project.

Early and late in the project, assessments of teacher energy content knowledge (Handout 1) and quantitative reasoning content knowledge (Handout 2) were given. NOTE that all handouts are provided at the end of the chapter. Teacher attitude about QR was assessed with a survey (Handout 3). Teachers were asked to complete a standards worksheet both as individuals and as professional learning communities in order to tie their work on the QR STEM project to their classroom teaching (Handout 4). Evaluation of the overall impact of the project was conducted using the Concerns-Based Adoption Model (CBAM). CBAM identifies and provides ways to assess seven stages of concern (Table 2) (Hord, Rutherford, Huling-Austin, & Hall, 1987). These stages have major implications for professional development including attending to where people are and addressing questions they are asking when they are asking them, the importance of paying attention to implementation over an extended period of time, and the difficulty of changing the routine of practice (Loucks-Horsley, 1996). The CBAM assessments included workshop journal entries by teachers, the 3C inventory (Handout 5), UbD/

Table 1. Quality Professional Development

Diagnoses	Design	Implementation	Evaluation
Identify and agree upon the instructional problem to solve	Decide what intervention strategies are appropriate	Decide how strategies will be introduced	Ascertain what's working and look back on what worked
Survey teachers	Focus on specific content knowledge and related pedagogical content knowledge	Provide continuous training for all teacher leaders	Gather data for assessing and improving program's impact on target teaching practice
Teacher focus groups	Directly connect to classroom materials that students are using	Provide time and support necessary for teachers to gain skill and confidence in using materials	Establish attribution to improved student learning using appropriate performance assessments
Observe classroom instruction	Embody a clearly articulated theory of adult learning	Provide experiences that deepen both content and pedagogical content knowledge	Participating teachers gather before-and-after data on student understanding of a specific concept or procedure
Assess teacher content knowledge	Whole school or whole district participation	Permit modeling of the strategies with students while teachers observe	Teachers should observe and evaluate lessons taught to students by a PD leader
Examine student data	Sustain focus over time	Model and encourage teacher-pair instructional coaching	Teacher pairs should engage in peer teaching and discuss their observations
	Allow for practice, peer coaching, and follow-up	Provide time for teachers to share results of their experiences	PD providers use structured observation protocols to measure quality of teacher's use of strategies and materials
		Specific roles for administrators' in PD so they know what teachers are doing	

*Table 2. Concerns Based Model expressions of concerns about an innovation
(Hord & Hall et. al. 1987)*

Stage of Concern	Expression of Concern
6. Refocusing	I have some ideas about something that would work even better.
5. Collaboration	How can I relate what I am doing to what others are doing?
4. Consequence	How is my use affecting learners? How can I refine it to have more impact?
3. Management	I seem to be spending all my time getting materials ready.
2. Personal	How will using it affect me?
1. Informational	I would like to know more about it.
0. Awareness	I am not concerned about it.

QR implementation matrix (Handout 6), and the authentic assessment implementation matrix (Handout 7). In addition data from the Wyoming state assessment of educational progress were used to inform project impact. The content assessments were given as both pretest and posttest. The CBAM assessments were given multiple times throughout the project to determine concerns about implementation.

QR STEM SYMPOSIUM OUTLINE

Our goal is to provide both a resource for teachers interested in quantitative reasoning within the nexus of energy and environment and to provide professional development leaders with a plan for engaging STEM teachers in interdisciplinary STEM teacher practice. So we will take a moment here to describe how we setup the professional development workshops. In Chapter 1, Table 3 we provided an overview of the QR STEM professional development broken down into four symposia and two follow-up report sessions. Here we provide more detail on the professional development structure.

The agenda for symposia 0, 1, 2, and 3 are provided in Figures 51 through 54. They provide a detailed outline of the symposia. The first QR STEM Symposium was an introduction to the project and became known as Symposium 0 (Figure 51). The primary purpose of this short day and half symposium was to set the stage for work on increasing teacher content knowledge in the areas of energy science and environmental science, increasing teacher quantitative reasoning ability, introducing teachers to place-based education and problem-based learning,

	Friday (5-21-10)		Saturday (5-22-10)
4:00-5:00	Housing Check In	7:15	Northwest College Cafeteria open until 7:45
5:00	QR STEM Project Introduction (Bob) • Effective Professional Development	8:00	QR STEM Preassessment (Bob, Jimm, Mark)
6:00	STEM Energy and Environment Overture (Mark & Jimm) • Working Dinner served in Classroom at 6:30	9:00	QR STEM Energy and Environment Jimm, Mark, Norm, Allan • Electricity • Transportation • Climate Change
7:00	Quantitative Reasoning Overture • Mathematics (Bob) • Statistics	10:00	Teacher Work Session (John, Michael) • Standards Connections – Individual • Standards Connections- Group work
8:00	UbD: Teaching for Understanding (Bob)	11:30	PAWS Data Review: (Pete & Joel) • Connecting QR & EE to PAWS/Standards • Establish PLC
9:00	Day 1 Evaluation • QR STEM Survey • E&E Survey	12:00	Working lunch served in classroom
		1:00	PLC Work Session (All) • STEM Energy and Environment Identify enduring understandings
		2:00	Teacher Report out (Pete) • E&E – Standards Connection
			Day 2 Evaluation (Pete) CBAM
			Note: The computer system on campus is PC only. Please bring a thumb drive with your information or your own computer and projector.

QR STEM Symposium
May 21-22 2010
Powell, Wyoming
Northwest College (Science-Math Room 104)

Figure 51. QR STEM project Symposium 0 agenda.

and using the Understanding by Design framework to create a performance task to be implemented in their classrooms. We provided an overview of energy and environmental science, which was presented above in this chapter; an overview of quantitative reasoning which was presented in chapter 1; and a brief introduction to Understanding by Design which was summarized in chapter 1. At Symposium 0 we established interdisciplinary professional learning communities (PLC) of 4 to 5 teachers, requiring that each community had at least one mathematics teacher and one science teacher. While the teachers were given the option of self-selecting which PLC they would join, we encouraged teachers within a school district to form a PLC so they would have support within their school. We discussed with the PLCs how energy science, environmental science, and quantitative reasoning addressed current national and state science standards and mathematics standards. It was important to

QR STEM Symposium I — June 10-12 — Laramie, Wyoming		
June 10	**June 11**	**June 12**
	Session 2: STEM-UbD-QR	Session 4: STEM & QR Statistics
	8:00-9:30 Petroleum & Peak Oil: A Look at the World's Most Valuable Commodity (Myers) 9:30-10:30 Peak Oil • UbD Exercise (Enduring Understanding) • QR Exercise: Assessing ANWR's Oil Impact 10:30-10:45 Break 10:45-12:00 UbD Essential Questions (Ellsworth, Mahoney, Bernhisel) • PLC Exploration of Enduring Understanding • Essential Questions • PLC Planning Time	8:00-9:30 Combustion: Producing Heat from Chemical Energy (Childs) 9:30-10:30 Combustion • UbD Exercise • QR Exercise: Heats of combustion, gas' carbon footprint, stoichiometry 10:30-10:45 Break 10:45-12:00 QL Statistics (Mayes and Robinson) • Central Tendency • Spread
Working Dinner 6:00	Lunch 12:00-1:00	Lunch 12:00-1:00
Session 1: UbD- Science Overview 5:00-6:00 Preassessment Makeup for first timers 5:00-5:30 Welcome • Debrief PLCs on Enduring Understanding and Energy Science Activity (Mayes-Myers) 5:30-6:00 QR STEM PLC • QR assessment discussion (Mayes) PLC: Integrate new members (Ellsworth) 6:00-7:30 Understanding by Design Stage 1 Enduring Understanding (Mayes) • Overview of UbD • Characteristics of Enduring Understandings • QR Enduring Understandings 7:30-7:45 Break 7:45-9:00 Science Overview • Sustaining Transportation (Lyford)	Session 3: STEM & QR MATH 1:00-2:30 Thermodynamics and Heat Engines: Powering Transportation (Shinkle) 2:30-3:30 Thermo Engines • UbD Exercise • QR Exercise: Home Heating 3:30-3:45 Break 3:45-5:00 QL Mathematics (Mayes and Robinson) • Numeracy – small & large numbers • Proportional reasoning • Dimensional analysis • Scientific Notation 5:00-6:00 Place-Based (Parker)	Session 5: STEM & UbD 1:00-2:30 Biomass to Liquids – Our Energy Future? (Lyford) 2:30-3:30 Biofuels • UbD Exercise • QR Exercise: Ethanol, biofuels and CO_2, biofuels and water 3:30-4:30 PLC Work Session (Ellsworth, Mahoney, Bernhisel) • PLC work on essential questions leading to lesson/unit focus • Identify focus for performance tasks 4:30-4:45 Journaling (Ellsworth)
	Dinner on your own	

Figure 52. QR STEM project Symposium 1 agenda.

establish that introducing energy, environment, and QR into their classrooms did not have to be an add-on. Teachers are very conscious of the extensive amount of material they are already required to cover in their classes. We needed to assure them that these topics could be integrated into their required curriculum. We finished the symposium by having the PLCs brainstorm on science and mathematics enduring understandings they would like to develop a performance task around.

QR STEM Symposium 2 July 15-17 Riverton, Wyoming		
July 15	July 16	July 17
Session 1: UbD Review & Science Overview	Session 2: STEM-UbD	Session 4: STEM & QR Statistics
5:00-5:10 Welcome & Orientation	7:00 Breakfast at Hotel	7:00 Breakfast at Hotel
5:10-6:10 QR STEM Stage 1 (Ellsworth, Pontius) • PLC Stage 1 share out • 6 PLC each have 10 minutes to share Stage 1	8:00-10:00 Electricity (Childs) • Coal 10:00-10:30 Coal • UbD Exercise (performance tasks) • QR Exercise	8:00-10:00 Electricity (Shinkle) • Solar Thermal 10:00-10:30 Solar Thermal • UbD Exercise • QR Exercise
6:00 Working Dinner- Campus	10:30-10:45 Break	10:30-10:45 Break
6:10-7:15 Science Overview (Myers) • Electricity - Powering Modern Societies 7:15-7:30 Break	10:45-12:00 UbD Performance Task (Mayes) • GRASPS – Performance Task Creation • (If time) Rubrics • (If time) Reliability & Validity	10:45-12:00 QL Math & Statistics (Mayes, Robinson) • Statistical correlation • Causality • Sampling Bias • Graphical Representations
7:30-8:45 Understanding by Design (Mayes) Stage 2 Assessing Understanding • Think like an Assessor • Continuum of Assessment • Performance Task focus • 6 Facets – Performance Task creation		QL Mathematics (Mayes) • Interpreting models – tables, graphs, formulas • Logarithmic scales • Moving between representations • Review of QR Assessment Problems 5-10
	12:00-1:00 Lunch – Campus	12:00-1:00 Lunch – Campus
	Session 3: STEM & QR MATH 1:00-2:30 Place-Based (Parker) 2:30-2:45 Break 2:45-4:45 Electricity (Myers) • Nuclear • UbD Exercise • QR Exercise 4:45-5:15 Electricity •	Session 5: STEM & UbD 1:00-3:00 Electricity (Lyford) • Wind (Field Trip?) 3:00-3:30 Wind • UbD Exercise • QR Exercise 3:30-3:45 Break 3:45-4:45 PLC (Teacher Work Time) • PLC work on Stage 2 • Brief share out on Stage 2 4:45-5:00 Journaling (Ellsworth)
	6:30-8:00 Dinner at Hotel Catered	

Figure 53. QR STEM project Symposium 2 agenda.

Symposium 1, 2, and 3 were all two and half days in duration, each being hosted in a different area of the state. It is important to take professional development to the school district region as well as having the teachers come to the university site to access science facilities. Each of these symposia began with a debrief of tasks from the previous symposium. For Symposium 1 (Figure 52) the teachers debriefed on what enduring understandings they were considering as drivers for the performance task they were to create. The remainder of the first night session was split between an emersion of teachers in Stage 1 of Understanding by Design (UbD): Enduring Understanding, and an overview of the energy topic for the symposium which was

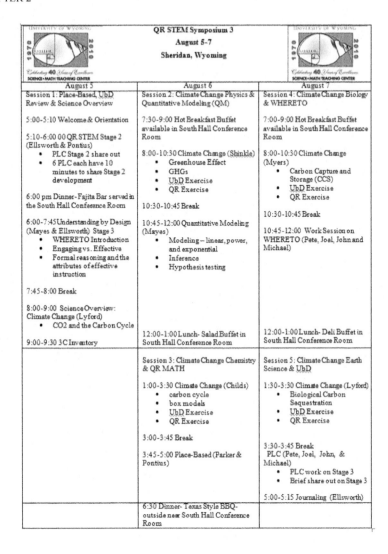

Figure 54. QR STEM project Symposium 3 agenda.

transportation. We will present later in this chapter a detailed example of working with teachers on stage 1 through stage 3 of developing their performance task. The energy and environmental science content explorations will be laid out in the science content chapters. On the second day of Symposium 1, we began with an interactive presentation on transportation from an Earth Science perspective: Petroleum and Peak Oil - A look at the world's most valuable commodity. We then had teachers return to the UbD performance task development by extending the enduring understanding into essential questions. The afternoon session kicked off with transportation from a physics perspective: Thermodynamics and Heat Engines – Powering transportation. The second day finished with a discussion of the quantitative literacy component of QR. We will provide a more detailed discussion of QR aspects of the program in the QR chapter. The third day began with a chemistry perspective on transportation: Combustion – Producing heat from chemical energy. We then extended the discussion of quantitative literacy with a focus on statistical representations. The afternoon of the third day began with a biology perspective on transportation: Biomass to Liquids – Our energy future? Symposium 1 concluded with a professional learning community work session focused on development of enduring understandings and essential questions for the performance task.

Each of the symposia were separated by a month, providing time for the professional learning communities to work on the stage development of their performance task. We established an online chat session for teachers to share ideas and ask questions in the interim. This allowed us to keep the conversation on development of the performance task active. At the end of each symposium, the teachers were assigned a specific task to complete by the start of the next symposium. For Symposium 1, the task was to complete Stage 1 of the UbD performance task development, including identifying enduring understandings and writing essential questions related to the understanding. Professional learning communities were required to report out on the task in the debrief sessions that started the next symposium.

Symposium 2 (Figure 53) began with a share out by the professional learning communities on UbD Stage 1 of their performance task. Each community presented their enduring understanding and essential questions to their peers and the QR STEM university faculty. Constructive criticism and supportive comments were provided yielding feedback for improving the performance task.

Following this, an overview of the second energy-environment topic was given: Electricity Powering Modern Societies. The first evening finished by engaging the teachers in UbD Stage 2: Assessing Understanding. The professional learning communities explored a continuum of assessment methods, being encouraged to build a variety of assessments from simple closed form to an open-ended performance task into their units. The UbD six facets of understanding were introduced as a means of eliciting assessments that engage students in a broad array of understanding. The second day began with a view of electricity from the perspective of chemistry with a focus on coal. The teachers were then introduced to a second approach to creating performance tasks that assess and engage students called GRASPS. GRASPS embeds the tasks in context and roles, increasing the engagement of students. An example of using GRASP is provided in the detailed discussion of performance task development below. The afternoon session introduced the teachers to place-based education, furthering the conversation about how to engage students by embedding the problem within the students' community or place. The second day finished with an Earth Science perspective on electricity generated through nuclear power. The final day started with a physics perspective on electricity generated via solar or thermal power. This was followed by a presentation on quantitative interpretation of science models.

The afternoon returned to electricity, but this time from the perspective of biology and wind energy. Symposium 2 closed with a professional learning community working session focused on developing Stage 2 of their performance task.

Symposium 3 (Figure 54) followed a similar schedule as Symposium 1 and 2. We began the first night with a report out by the professional learning communities on development of Stage 2 of their performance task, again receiving feedback from both peers and QR STEM faculty. The teachers were then introduced to UbD Stage 3: Plan Learning Experiences and Instruction. The teachers explored the UbD process of WHERETO which focuses on identifying instructional approaches and planning instruction. This is where curriculum development is undertaken, after identifying the outcomes (enduring understandings) and how they will be assessed. This was followed by an overview of the environmental topic of climate change. The second day began with the physics perspective on climate change: Greenhouse Effect. We then discussed the third component of QR, quantitative modeling. The afternoon introduced a chemistry perspective on climate change: Carbon Cycle. This was followed by a session on problem-based learning as a component of place-based education. The third day began with an Earth Sciences perspective of climate change: Carbon Capture and Storage. This was followed by a professional learning community working session on UbD Stage 3 WHERETO development of the performance task. After lunch a biology perspective of climate change was provided: Biological Sequestration. The final session was another working session for the teachers on UbD Stage 3.

This completed the summer performance task development seminars. The teachers participated in content knowledge development through extended explorations of energy and environmental issues related to transportation, electricity, and climate change. They had explored three components of quantitative reasoning: quantitative literacy, quantitative interpretation, and quantitative modeling. They had progressed through the three stages of Understanding by Design performance task development. In so doing, they had explored diverse pedagogies including teaching for understanding, place-based education, and problem-based learning. So armed, the professional learning communities were commissioned to finalize an energy and environment unit incorporating quantitative reasoning. The unit was to be taught by the teachers to one of their classes in the spring semester of the following school year. To facilitate the implementation of the unit we held two additional symposiums. The first was the QR STEM Peer Review Symposium held in October following the summer symposiums. The purpose of this symposium was to have the professional learning communities present the entire unit to their fellow QR STEM participant teachers and the QR STEM faculty. Teachers and faculty were provided an UbD Performance Task Rubric (Figure 55) to use in evaluating the tasks presented.

Another goal of this symposium was to introduce teachers to the concept of Action Research. We requested that the teachers conduct an informal action research study on the impact of their unit on their students learning and their teaching practice. We engaged the teachers in the four steps of practical action research identified

Criteria	Emerging	Developing	Proficient	Exemplary
I. Performance Task Development				
Template Does the 6 page UbD template provide the foundation for a performance task that is engaging and targets meaningful understanding?	1. Misconception of enduring understanding 2. Ineffective essential questions 3. Limited use of a variety of assessment strategies 4. Poor quality performance task 5. Unclear implementation plan, impossible to follow 6. Unclear what WHERETO elements are present in the learning plan	1. Partial or incomplete conception of enduring understanding 2. Moderately effective essential questions 3. Moderate use of a variety of assessment strategies 4. Partial or incomplete performance task 5. Lacks clear implementation plan, difficult to follow 6. Lacks clear WHERETO elements in learning plan	1. Substantial conception of enduring understanding 2. Generally effective essential questions 3. Frequent use of a variety of assessment strategies 4. Substantial performance task 5. Generally clear implementation plan 6. WHERETO elements are generally clear in the learning plan	1. Thorough and complete conception of enduring understanding 2. Highly effective essential questions 3. Consistent use of a variety of assessment strategies 4. Thorough and complete performance task 5. Exceptionally clear implementation plan 6. WHERETO elements are exceptionally clear in the learning plan
Curriculum Are the materials developed for the performance tasks of sufficient detail and quality to implement the unit?	1. Performance task is ineffective in engaging students (GRASPS design elements) 2. Performance task is ineffective at eliciting student understanding at multiple levels (6 Facets design element) 3. One type of assessment task is dominant 4. Ineffective at determining student's conception of enduring understanding	1. Performance task is somewhat effective in engaging students (GRASPS design elements) 2. Performance task is somewhat effective at eliciting student understanding at multiple levels (6 Facets design element) 3. Lacks variety across continuum of assessment tasks 4. Somewhat effective at determining student's conception of enduring understanding	1. Performance task is generally effective in engaging students (GRASPS design elements) 2. Performance task is generally effective at eliciting student understanding at multiple levels (6 Facets design element) 3. Multiple types of assessment across continuum of assessment tasks 4. Generally effective at determining student's conception of enduring understanding	1. Performance task is highly effective in engaging students (GRASPS design elements) 2. Performance task is highly effective at eliciting student understanding at multiple levels (6 Facets design element) 3. Exceptional variety across continuum of assessment tasks 4. Highly effective at determining student's conception of enduring understanding
II. Performance Task Evaluation/Presentation				
Action Research Is evidence provided of impact on student understanding and engagement?	1. Student data provided an unclear picture of student conception of the enduring understanding 2. Literature provided no evidence supporting the performance task development	1. Student data lacked clarity with respect to student conception of the enduring understanding 2. Literature provided weak evidence supporting the performance task development	1. Student data provided a generally clear picture of student conception of the enduring understanding 2. Literature provided moderate evidence supporting the performance task development	1. Student data provided an exceptionally clear picture of student conception of the enduring understanding 2. Literature provided strong evidence supporting the performance task development
Presentation Was the project presentation well organized and engaging?	1. The presentation was ineffective in that: there was little evidence of prior planning, practice, and consideration of audience; or presentation was unclear and confusing 2. The active participation task was ineffective	1. The presentation was somewhat effective in that: there was some problems with clarity, thoroughness and delivery; unclear whether audience, context, and purpose were considered 2. The active participation task was somewhat effective	1. The presentation was generally effective in that: ideas where presented in a clear, and through manner, showing awareness of the audience, context, and purpose 2. The active participation task was generally effective	1. The presentation was highly effective in that: ideas where presented in an engaging, clear, and through manner, mindful of the audience, context, and purpose 2. The active participation task was highly effective

Figure 55. Understanding by Design Performance Task Rubric.

Figure 56. Action research spiral. Source: Action Research: A Guide for the Teacher Researcher (5th Edition) (Geoffrey Mills, 2013).

Criteria	Emerging	Developing	Proficient	Exemplary
I. Unit and Performance Task Development				
Unit/Performance Task Is the enduring understanding and organization of the performance task clear?	1. Unclear enduring understanding 2. Ineffective essential questions 3. Limited use of a variety of assessment strategies in unit 4. Poor quality performance task	1. Partial or incomplete conception of enduring understanding 2. Moderately effective essential questions 3. Moderate use of a variety of assessment strategies in unit 4. Partial or incomplete performance task	1. Substantial conception of enduring understanding 2. Generally effective essential questions 3. Frequent use of a variety of assessment strategies in unit 4. Substantial performance task	1. Thorough and complete conception of enduring understanding 2. Highly effective essential questions 3. Consistent use of a variety of assessment strategies in unit 4. Thorough and complete performance task
Curriculum Are the materials developed for the performance tasks of sufficient quality to engage students and elicit enduring understanding?	1. Performance task is ineffective in engaging students (GRASPS design elements) 2. Performance task is ineffective at eliciting student understanding at multiple levels (6 Facets design element) 3. Ineffective at determining student's conception of enduring understanding	1. Performance task is somewhat effective in engaging students (GRASPS design elements) 2. Performance task is somewhat effective at eliciting student understanding at multiple levels (6 Facets design element) 3. Somewhat effective at determining student's conception of enduring understanding	1. Performance task is generally effective in engaging students (GRASPS design elements) 2. Performance task is generally effective at eliciting student understanding at multiple levels (6 Facets design element) 3. Generally effective at determining student's conception of enduring understanding	1. Performance task is highly effective in engaging students (GRASPS design elements) 2. Performance task is highly effective at eliciting student understanding at multiple levels (6 Facets design element) 3. Highly effective at determining student's conception of enduring understanding
II. Performance Task Impact				
Student Impact What was the impact on student understanding and engagement?	1. Student data provided an unclear picture of student conception of the enduring understanding 2. Performance task was ineffective at engaging students	1. Student data lacked clarity with respect to student conception of the enduring understanding 2. Performance task was somewhat effective at engaging students	1. Student data provided a generally clear picture of student conception of the enduring understanding 2. Performance task was generally effective at engaging students	1. Student data provided an exceptionally clear picture of student conception of the enduring understanding 2. Performance task was highly effective at engaging students
Teacher Impact What was the impact on teacher practice?	1. No evidence was provided of change in teacher practice	1. Limited evidence was provided of change in teacher practice, weakly connected to teaching of performance task	1. Teacher provided evidence of change in teacher practice which was moderately connected to performance task	1. Teacher provided clear evidence of change in teacher practice
III. Quality of Presentation				
Presentation Was the project presentation well organized and engaging?	1. The presentation was ineffective in that: there was little evidence of prior planning, practice, and consideration of audience; or presentation was unclear and confusing	1. The presentation was somewhat effective in that: there was some problems with clarity, thoroughness and delivery; unclear whether audience, context, and purpose were considered	1. The presentation was generally effective in that: ideas where presented in a clear, and through manner, showing awareness of the audience, context, and purpose	1. The presentation was highly effective in that: ideas where presented in an engaging, clear, and through manner, mindful of the audience, context, and purpose

Figure 57. QR STEM Final Project Presentation Rubric.

in Figure 56. The area of focus was identified as impact of the project. They were asked to collect data using the assessments in their performance tasks and report student learning outcomes. We requested them to select a small sample of students to interview on how they felt about the approach and what they believed they learned. The analysis and interpretation of the data was to involve only simple descriptive statistics, correlations, or t-tests for quantitative data. The analysis of qualitative data was a simplified version of Grounded Theory with a focus on identifying trends. Teachers were also to provide a self-reflection on the impact of the project on their teaching practice.

A final symposium was held the following April to provide the professional learning communities the opportunity to report out on the implementation of the unit. As in the Peer Review Symposium, the teacher's QR STEM project peers and faculty were the expert body to which the professional learning community reported. A QR STEM Final Project Presentation Rubric (Figure 57) was provided for the review. Each professional learning community received the rubric in advance of the symposium to guide their preparation for the presentation.

The other goal of the final symposium was to explore the development of a capstone course for the State of Wyoming Success Curriculum. The Success Curriculum determined what courses a high school student had to complete to be eligible for the state supported scholarship program. It included four years of science courses and four years of mathematics courses. We proposed an interdisciplinary STEM course with a context of energy and environment. A course which would stress the development of quantitative reasoning, science literacy, and mathematics literacy. We engaged in a dialogue with teachers about what such a course would look like and the barriers to implementing it in their school district. We asked three focus questions:

- What would be the key elements of a QR STEM capstone course?
- What are the barriers to implementing such a course and how can they be overcome?
- Who is the audience for such a course? Can it be a course that reignites student interest in STEM?

While we had excellent conversations on this topic with the teachers, the course was never implemented. We believe that moving students out of STEM taught in silos to an interdisciplinary, problem-based, place-based approach is the right course of action. We must engage students in real-world STEM if we want to increase those interested in being the next generation of scientists, technologists, engineers, and mathematicians.

REFERENCES

DePaolo, D. J., Orr, F. M., Benson, S. M., Celia, M., Felmy, A., Nagy, K. L., & Saarni, M.(2007). *Basic research needs for geosciences: Facilitating 21st century energy systems*. DOESC (USDOE Office of Science (SC)).

Hilbert, D. (1901). Mathematische probleme. *Archiv der Mathematik und Physik, 3*(1), 44–63.

Hord, S., Rutherford, W., Huling-Austin, S., & Hall, G. (1987). *Taking charge of change*. Alexandria, VA: Association for Supervision and Curriculum Development.

Loucks-Horsley, S. (1996). Professional development for science education: A critical and immediate challenge In R. W. Bybee (Ed.), *National standards and the science curriculum: Challenges, opportunities, and recommendations* (pp. 83–95). Dubuque , IA: Kendall/Hunt.

National Research Council (NRC). (2001). *Grand challenges in environmental sciences*. Washington, DC: National Academy Press.

NAE, Sheppard, S. D., Pellegrino, J. W., & Olds, B. M. (2008). On becoming a 21st century engineer. *Journal of Engineering Education, 97*(3), 231–234.

National Research Council (NRC). (2001). *Grand challenges in environmental sciences*. Washington, DC: National Academy Press.

NRC. (2005a). *Sustainability in the Chemical Industry: Grand Challenges and Research Needs*. NAS/NRC Board on Chemical Sciences and Technology Workshop, 2005; www.nap.edu/catalog. php?record_id=11437.

NRC (2005b). Mileti, D. S., & Gailus, J. L. (2005). Sustainable development and hazards mitigation in the United States: disasters by design revisited. *Mitigation and Adaptation Strategies for Global Change, 10*(3), 491–504.

NRC, Roundtable, D. (2005). *Creating a Disaster resilient America: Grand challenges in science and technology: Summary of a workshop.* National Academies Press.

Pacala, S., & Socolow, R. (2004). Stabilization wedges: Solving the climate problem for the next 50 years with current technologies. *Science, 305*(5686), 968–972.

Sahagian, D., & Schellnhuber, J. (2002). Global Change Newsletter. *International Geosphere-Biosphere Programme, 50,* 7–10.

Steffen, W., Sanderson, A., Tyson, P. D., Jäger, J., Matson, P. A., Moore III, B., Oldfield, F., Richardson, K., Schellnhuber, H. J., Turner, B. L., & Wasson II, R. J. (2004). *Global change and the Earth System. A planet under pressure.* Berlin: Springer Verlag.

Solomon, J. (1983). Learning about energy: How pupils think in two domains. *European Journal of Science Education, 5*(1), 49–59.

Varmus, H., Klausner, E., Zerhouni, T., Acharya, A., Daar, S., & Singer, P. A. (2003). Grand challenges in global health. *Science, 1*(302), 398–399.

Zoback, M. L. (2001). Grand challenges in earth and environmental sciences: science, stewardship, and service for the twenty-first century. *GSA Today, 41.*

ENERGY AND ENVIRONMENT
WORKSHOP HANDOUTS

The following handouts were used with teachers to support the introductory workshop for the QR STEM project.

HANDOUT 1: ENERGY CONTENT ASSESSMENT

Modern industrialized societies use a variety of primary energy sources (PES) including: oil, natural gas, coal, and nuclear. Different PES represent different types of energy. For example, wind energy harnesses the kinetic energy of moving air. Thus the primary energy type of wind is kinetic energy. The kinetic energy of the wind is, in turn, produced by the radiant (solar) energy that heats the atmosphere. Thus the secondary energy type of wind is radiant energy, which is ultimately derived from nuclear fusion. Different PES are traded in different units and their energy densities expressed via a vide combination of units. Armed with this knowledge, please complete the table below to the best of your ability.

energy source	energy type			physical state	trading units	energy density units
	primary	secondary	tertiary			
				conventional		
oil						
natural gas						
coal						
nuclear						
				renewables		
hydroelectric						
solar						
wind	kinetic	solar	nuclear fusion	gas	kW-hr	
tidal						
biomass						
biofuels						
				alternative/unconventional		
oil sand						
geothermal						

HANDOUT 2: QUANTITATIVE REASONING ASSESSMENT

The purpose of this assessment is to gather base-line data on your QR understanding. Please do your best to respond to each item, supporting your work with written comments on how you approached the problem. The questions are labeled to indicate three components of quantitative reasoning (QL literacy, QI interpretation, and QM modeling). QR requires a context and therefore is by necessity interdisciplinary. The context for QR here is energy and environment, which integrates the disciplines of biology, chemistry, earth science, physics, mathematics, and statistics.

Personnel Identification Number: _____

1. QL Numeracy: It is estimated that the average person drinks 3 10 ounce glasses of water a day. The U.S. population is on the order of 300 million people. Provide an estimate of how much water U.S. citizens drink in a year.
2. 2. QL Measurement: A small well in a rural village produces 3.5 gallons per minute. What is this discharge in meter^3/hour? You may need some of the following unit conversions: 1 cubic meter = 264 gallons = 35 cubic feet and 1 cubic centimeter = 0.03 fluid ounces.
3. QL Proportional Reasoning: A capture-recapture method is used to determine the size of the rat population on an island. A sample of 250 rats is captured and tagged. They are released and allowed to mix back into the population. Sometime later a random sample of 500 rats is taken, and 21 are tagged. Estimate the total rat population.
4. QL Prob/Stats: E-waste is caused by the disposal of electronic products. Cathode ray tubes (CRT) from computer monitors and televisions contain lead that can leach into ground water. The table below provides data on leachable lead for 36 models of CRTs. Find the median and discuss the process of finding the mean, which is 18.7 mg/L. An environmentalist wants to strengthen their point about the dangers of lead, which measure of central tendency would they use and why?

Year Made	CRT Maker	Lead (mg/L)	Year Made	CRT Maker	Lead (mg/L)	Year Made	CRT Maker	Lead (mg/L)
90	Clinton	1.0	93	Toshiba	3.2	94	Zenith	21.5
84	Matsushita	1.0	84	Matsushita	3.5	77	Zenith	21.9
85	Matsushita	1.0	84	Sharp	4.4	87	NEC	26.6
87	Matsushita	1.0	98	Samsung	6.1	96	Orion	33.1
89	Samsung	1.0	95	Samsung	6.9	85	Sharp	35.2
86	Phillips	1.0	98	Chunghwa	9.1	92	Phillips	41.5
84	Goldstar	1.5	89	Panasonic	9.4	84	Quasar	43.5

(*Continued*)

(Continued)

Year Made	CRT Maker	Lead (mg/L)	Year Made	CRT Maker	Lead (mg/L)	Year Made	CRT Maker	Lead (mg/L)
94	Sharp	1.5	97	Toshiba	10.6	92	Toshiba	54.1
94	Zenith	1.6	87	NEC	10.7	85	Toshiba	54.5
97	Toshiba	2.2	98	Samsung	15.4	93	Panasonic	57.2
97	KCH	2.3	92	Chunghwa	19.3	89	Samsung	60.8
91	Chunghwa	2.8	97	Chunghwa	21.3	89	Hitachi	85.6

5. QI Interpretation: Given the E-waste table in problem 4, use Excel to create the scatter plot of the data, and confirm the best fit line to the data is with $R^2 = 0.006$. What can you say about predicting the year the monitor was made based on lead level? Defend your conclusion using the table, graph, and/or linear model.
6. QI Statistics: The correlation between the lead in the monitors and the year the monitor was made is -0.08. What does the correlation being negative tell you about the relationship between lead and year? What does the small value of the correlation tell you about this relationship?
7. QM Modeling: Glaciers store water that is used in irrigation. The table below provides data on recent changes in length of the Rainbow Glacier on Mt. Baker in Washington State. Position refers to the location of the glacier's leading edge, as compared to its 1985 position. The scatter plot provides a graph of the data with 1985 as year 0. Determine a linear model for the data and use it to predict the length of the glacier in 2010 if it was 3,750 meters long in 1950. NOTE: an estimate of the model is sufficient. Explain how you arrived at your model.

Year	Position	Year	Position	Year	Position	Year	Position
1985	0	1989	-44	1993	-96	1997	n/a
1986	-11	1990	-55	1994	-116	1998	-201
1987	-22	1991	-60	1995	-137	1999	-241
1988	-33	1992	-75	1996	-161	2000	-246

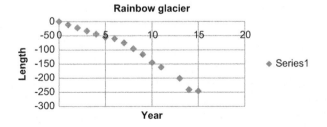

103

HANDOUT 3: QUANTITATIVE REASONING ATTITUDE SURVEY

General Instructions: The purpose of this survey is to explore attitudes teachers have towards mathematics and its relevance outside of the classroom. This is an anonymous survey. Please answer the questions to the best of your ability and knowledge. Please give only one answer to each question. THANK YOU FOR PARTICIPATING! (Based on Portland State University QL Survey, Assessment Resource Network)

Personnel Identification Number: _____

Section A: Attitude towards Quantitative Literacy (QL)

Quantitative Literacy: Mathematical skills that students use in the context of communicating ideas, either receiving information, providing information or making and communicating conclusions from data.

Indicate the extent to which you agree or disagree.	*Strongly Disagree*	*Disagree*	*Neutral*	*Agree*	*Strongly Agree*
1 Quantitative literacy (QL) is important to my area of teaching.					
2 I understand what quantitative literacy means.					
3 QL is important in my daily activities.					
4 I find myself applying QL in courses outside of my area of teaching.					
5 Having QL skills is important for a persons career.					
6 I have a good attitude towards math.					

Section B: Cultural Appreciation

Indicate the extent to which you agree or disagree.	Strongly Disagree	Disagree	Neutral	Agree	Strongly Agree
1 Math is important.					
2 Math plays an important role in science.					
3 Math plays an important role in technology.					
4 Math helps me to make sense of current events.					
5 I am aware of the origins of mathematics.					

Section C: Confidence with Mathematics

Indicate the extent to which you agree or disagree.	Strongly Disagree	Disagree	Neutral	Agree	Strongly Agree
1 I am comfortable taking math classes.					
2 Math scares me.					
3 I can use math as a communication tool.					
4 I recognize that math skills are important outside of "math classes."					
5 I routinely use mental estimates to interpret information.					
6 I enjoy math.					
7 I often take courses that contain a lot of math.					
8 I am comfortable with quantitative ideas.					
9 I am at ease in applying quantitative methods.					
10 I have good intuition about the meaning of numbers.					
11 I am confident about my estimating skills.					

Section D: Logical Thinking and Reasoning

Indicate the extent to which you agree or disagree.	Strongly Disagree	Disagree	Neutral	Agree	Strongly Agree
1 I am comfortable reading graphs.					
2 I am comfortable reading maps.					
3 I often use math to evaluate statistical information.					
4 I use math to evaluate the validity of poll results (e.g., political polls).					
5 I frequently question numerical information (e.g., graphs, tables, charts,) from various sources.					
6 I am confident in my ability to construct a logical argument.					

Section E: Prerequisite Knowledge and Symbol Sense

Indicate the extent to which you agree or disagree.	Strongly Disagree	Disagree	Neutral	Agree	Strongly Agree
1 I am confident using Excel or other statistical software.					
2 I am confident reading proofs.					
3 I enjoy writing proofs.					
4 I can interpret math proofs easily.					

Section F: Statistical Knowledge

Indicate the extent to which you agree or disagree.	Strongly Disagree	Disagree	Neutral	Agree	Strongly Agree
1 I am comfortable with statistics.					
2 I understand what the term data means.					
3 I am able to use data to interpret the validity of information.					
4 I am confident in my ability to use visual displays to interpret differences in data distributions.					

(Continued)

(Continued)

Indicate the extent to which you agree or disagree.	Strongly Disagree	Disagree	Neutral	Agree	Strongly Agree
5 I can use statistics as a tool to compare differences between populations.					
6 I am able to think about information in terms of numbers for the purpose of supporting claims.					

HANDOUT 4: STEM WITHIN ENERGY

We want teachers to consider the interdisciplinary STEM nature of energy topics. Thinking as an individual, a teacher, and a citizen, complete the table below by identifying the scientific, quantitative reasoning, and context themes important for each issue listed. Try to make sure each discipline column has roughly the same number of entries. To start, complete your own worksheet. Next work in groups to complete a group worksheet with the same information.

	Physics	Chemistry	Earth Sciences	Biology	QR	Context
Transportation						
Electricity						
Climate Change						
Energy & Environment						

HANDOUT 5: CBAM ASSESSMENT

CBAM stands for Concerns Based Adoption Model. Teachers considering and experiencing change evolve in the types of questions they ask and use of the innovation. We want to know where you stand with respect to seven stages of concern which are common when considering an innovation: awareness, informational, personal, management, consequence, collaboration, and refocusing. Using a scale of 1 to 10 described below, enter your level of concern for each item in the table.

Using a scale of 1 to 10 described below, enter your level of **concern** for each item in the table.

1 ◄- ►10

a low level of concern, i.e. comfortable proceeding with implementation or more learning

A high level of concern, i.e. many worries and doubts make proceeding with implementation or more learning overwhelming

		Rating
1	When it comes to implementing **instructional performance tasks**, my level of **concern** is ...	
2	When it comes to designing and implementing **authentic assessments**, my level of **concern** is ...	

Using a scale of 1 to 10 described below, enter your level of **confidence** for each item in the table.

1 ◄- ► 10

a low level of confidence, i.e. need much more guidance and/or new learning before implementing

a high level of confidence, i.e. comfortable proceeding with implemtation independently

		Rating
3	When it comes to implementing **instructional performance tasks**, my level of **confidence** is ...	
4	When it comes to designing and implementing **authentic assessments**, my level of **confidence** is ...	

Using a scale of 1 to 10 described below, enter your level of **commitment** for each item in the table.

1 ◄- ► 10

a low level of commitment, i.e. not sure I'll really make it happen, even if I think it's a good idea or know how to do it

a high level of commitment, i.e. I'll try to make it happen no matter what

		Rating
5	When it comes to implementing **instructional performance tasks**, my level of **commitment** is ...	
6	When it comes to designing and implementing **authentic assessments**, my level of **commitment** is ...	

HANDOUT 6: QUANTITATIVE REASONING IMPLEMENTATION MATRIX

The following matrices were used to measure teacher change in implementing QR STEM in their classrooms.

Quantitative Reasoning Implementation Matrix   Spring 2011   Cohort 4

PIN: _____

Mark the box next to the abbreviation for the description that most closely matches 1) your practice before participating in the Quantitative Reasoning project and 2) your current classroom practice after participation. If your rating has not changed, please remark the same rating rather than leaving the then column blank. Consider evidence provided in your student work to guide your ratings.

Category:	GETTING STARTED	EMERGING	EXPERIENCED	ADVANCED
Quantitative Reasoning across STEM disciplines	• develop quantitative literacy skills, such as numeracy, number sense, percents, dimensional analysis and estimation as it is included in the adopted curriculum and • rarely or never interpret or create models.	My instruction provides opportunities for students to... • begin to develop quantitative reasoning skills by applying numeracy, number sense, percents, dimensional analysis and estimation to interpret and draw inferences from graphs, tables, formulas and textual representations and • occasionally practice quantitative reasoning above and beyond the adopted curriculum and • occasionally create models and problems generated from a prescribed data set.	• consistently engage quantitative reasoning by interpreting and drawing inferences from age-appropriate complex models and problems, requiring more than a rote application of rules and consistently create models and problems based on both prescribed data sets and student generated/collected data and • apply quantitative reasoning in contexts which involve more than one STEM discipline.	• consistently engage in analyzing complex models and provide plausible defenses for interpretations • create, explain and defend original models and problems from student generated/collected data which requires the integration of content from more than one STEM discipline.
THEN ☐☐☐☐ NOW ☐☐☐☐ GS EM EX AD				
Applying UbD Components*	• apply one or more components of the UbD approach in lesson design and instruction but not in a connected and systematic manner	In designing instruction to maximize student learning, I ... • intentionally apply some components of the UbD approach in lesson design somewhat struggling with the mechanics of implementation resulting in varying degrees of quality	• systematically and consistently apply the components of the UbD approach in lesson design for a variety of selected content in my discipline.	• systematically and consistently apply components in my instructional decision-making and judiciously adapt it to enhance or improve my instructional effectiveness.
THEN ☐☐☐☐ NOW ☐☐☐☐ GS EM EX AD				

*Components the UbD approach: 1) creating essential questions from enduring learnings 2) creating instructional performance tasks using GRASPS 3) teaching for deep conceptual understanding 4) use the six facets of understanding as a guide in lesson and assessment design

Regarding three specific elements of teaching for conceptual understanding and transfer…			
Identifying Enduring Understandings and Essential Questions THEN NOW ☐ ☐ GS ☐ ☐ EM ☐ ☐ EX ☐ ☐ AD	• Most of the questions generated in my lesson design generally focus on discrete facts and skills and have a correct answer.	• Some of the questions generated in my lesson design focus on the larger principles and processes of my discipline, but many remain focused on discrete facts and skills	• I identify enduring learnings and essential questions for lessons and units which • lead to in-depth understanding of content that is transferable beyond the scope of a particular unit and has lasting value beyond the classroom • are open-ended and deliberately thought-provoking and lead to other questions. • represent big ideas and processes at the heart of the discipline.	• In addition to the experienced criteria, I identify enduring learnings and essential questions that consistently address the six facets of understanding.
Designing the instructional Performance Task THEN NOW ☐ ☐ GS ☐ ☐ EM ☐ ☐ EX ☐ ☐ AD	My instructional activities are designed to apply discrete skills and facts within the context of routine problems. They may be engaging but do not yield evidence that students can transfer their knowledge and skills to other contexts.	I design instructional performance tasks which are engaging and yield a product but focus on discrete facts and skills rather than complex principles and processes of my discipline.	I design instructional performance tasks which • are highly engaging, • encourage students to put everything together in the context of open-ended, nonroutine issues or problems, and • require students to integrate complete a complex product	In addition to the experiencd criteria, I design instructional performance tasks which • encourage innovation and application of personal judgment
Applying Six Facets of Understanding* THEN NOW ☐ ☐ GS ☐ ☐ EM ☐ ☐ EX ☐ ☐ AD	When I design lessons I don't intentionally address any of the six facets or I consider them but I am not yet gathering any evidence in student work of deep conceptual understanding of complex content.	I occasionally design lessons which intentionally address several of the six facets. These lessons occasionally yield evidence in student work of deep conceptual understanding of complex content.	I consistently and intentionally design lessons addressing most of the six facets of understanding. These lessons frequently yield evidence in student work of deep conceptual understanding of complex content.	The six facets of understanding systematically guide my lesson and assessment design and I revise instruction based on the evidence of deep conceptual instruction of complex content yielded in student work.

* Refer the Six Facets of Understanding Rubric. (Wiggins and McTee), to reflect on your ratings.

HANDOUT 7: AUTHENTIC ASSESSMENT IMPLEMENTATION MATRIX

Authentic Assessment Implementation Matrix   Spring 2011 Cohort 4

PIN: 4 _____

For each category, consider which description most closely portrays 1) your practice before participating in the Institute and 2) your classroom now.

| Designing and Evaluating Authentic Assessments | When it comes to CHECKING FOR ALIGNMENT, I... | | Then _____ Now _____ |
Getting Started (1)	Emerging (2)	Experienced (3)	Advanced (4)
• don't make it a priority because I am confident that I know my content which means my classroom assessments are bound to be well aligned to standards and my instruction. • leave checking the alignment of commercial assessments or external local or state assessments to the experts.	• assume the assessments I have written for use in my classroom are fairly well aligned. However, if my students don't perform well, I'm not always sure the test or task measured what it was meant to measure. • have questioned the alignment that some published materials claim exists in the supporting tests provided with the instructional materials I use. • have asked questions about how well our local district assessments and state tests are aligned to our standards.	• follow an intentional process, such as task analysis, to check for alignment between my classroom assessments and my curriculum • would not use the supporting tests provided by publishing companies without doing my own alignment check. • reconsider my alignment logic before drawing conclusions about student performance, when my students don't do as well as I expected on a newly designed classroom assessment • have explored on my own or participated with others in alignment studies regarding our local district and state assessments. • evaluate assessments for their potential to uncover misconceptions about content • distinguish between assessment items which capture knowledge or have the potential to reveal deep conceptual understanding	• can explain the process of aligning assessment to instruction and curriculum to others with confidence. • can lead colleagues in reviewing and revising assessments for alignment with confidence. • question and analyze local district/state and other external assessments for alignment and defend my positions with confidence.
		When it comes to IMPLEMENTING authentic assessments, I	Then _____ Now _____
• don't have the time to develop them or am not convinced they are a match for my curriculum	• mostly rely on other forms of assessment but am interested in reviewing authentic alternatives for my content • have concerns about how authentic assessments can be used fairly and consistently	• have developed and used some authentic assessments in my classroom successfully • differentiate between the tasks I design to engage students in instruction and the tasks I design to assess what students know and can do independently • design scoring mechanisms to fairly and consistently evaluate performance on authentic assessments	• use the student work returned from authentic assessments to inform my instruction and revise the assessment

HANDOUT 2 SOLUTIONS

Quantitative Reasoning Teacher Assessment

1. QL Numeracy: It is estimated that the average person drinks 3 10 ounce glasses of water a day. The U.S. population is on the order of 300 million people. Provide an estimate of how much water U.S. citizens drink in a year.

Solution: Estimate that an average person drinks 3 10oz glasses of water a day. There are 365 days in a year, and the U.S. population is on the order 300 million or 3×10^8. So an estimate of water drunk is: $\frac{30\ oz}{1\ day} \times \frac{365\ day}{1\ year} \times 3 \times 10^8 = 3.285 \times 10^{12}$ oz/ year. There is approximately 0.3381 oz in a milliliter so an average person drinks 9.716×10^{12} mL/year. The metric prefaces are another numeracy skill that students must master for science, for example there are 1000 mL in a liter so 9.716×10^9 L/ year.

2. QL Measurement: A small well in a rural village produces 3.5 gallons per minute. What is this discharge in meter³/hour? You may need some of the following unit conversions: 1 cubic meter = 264 gallons = 35 cubic feet and 1 cubic centimeter = 0.03 fluid ounces.

Solution: Calculated measures such as discharge can be represented in different units which students may be more familiar with. This also relates to dimensional analysis.

$$\frac{3.5\ gal}{1\ min} \times \frac{60\ min}{1\ hr} \times \frac{1\ m^3}{264.172\ gal} = \frac{0.795\ m^3}{1\ hr}$$

3. QL Proportional Reasoning: A capture-recapture method is used to determine the size of the rat population on an island. A sample of 250 rats is captured and tagged. They are released and allowed to mix back into the population. Sometime later a random sample of 500 rats is taken, and 21 are tagged. Estimate the total rat population.

Solution: A student may simply set up a proportion of tagged to total in the sample and tagged to total in the population. $\frac{21\ tag}{500\ total\ sample} = \frac{250\ tag}{x\ total\ population}$ which using the cross multiplication algorithm gives $21x = 250 \times 500$ so the population is about 5,952 rats. However such rote use of the cross multiplication algorithm may not indicate they are using proportional reasoning. To understand why the capture-recapture method works requires the student to use proportional reasoning. They understand that the population is about 24 times as much as the tagged rats and that this holds no matter how many rats are tagged in the original capture.

4. QL Prob/Stats: E-waste is caused by the disposal of electronic products. Cathode ray tubes (CRT) from computer monitors and televisions contain lead that can leach into ground water. The table below provides data on leachable lead for 36 models of CRTs. Find the median and discuss the process of finding the mean, which is 18.7 mg/L. An environmentalist wants to strengthen their point about the dangers of lead, which measure of central tendency would they use and why?

Solution: The *median* is the middle number when the data are arranged in ascending order. If there are an even number of data values then the median is the average of the two middle numbers. There are 36 data values so we average the 18th and 19th value: $\dfrac{9.1+9.4}{2} = 9.25$. The *mean* is the sum of all the values divided by the number of values: $\overline{x} = \dfrac{\sum values}{36} = \dfrac{673.3}{36} = 18.7$. The *mode* is the most frequently occurring value, which is 1.0. The mode is not often used in analyzing environmental data. Notice that the mean and median values differ significantly, so it does make a difference what measure of central tendency is reported. The CRT makers may report the median to argue that the amount of lead is not as high, while an environmental group would report the mean.

5. QI Interpretation: Given the E-waste table in problem 4, the scatter plot of the data, and the best fit line to the data $y = -0.02l + 90.73$ with $R^2 = 0.006$, what can you say about predicting the year the monitor was made based on lead level? Defend your conclusion using the table, graph, and/or linear model.

Solution: The R^2 values is very low, meaning that little of the variation is being explained by the model. So the model is not a good one from which to make predictions. If you ignore this fact and use the model anyway you can draw some very cautious conclusions. The slope of the line is negative but very small, so there is a slight downward trend indicating a slight reduction in lead for newer monitors. But it is important to note that the change is not significant.

6. QI Statistics: The correlation between the lead in the monitors and the year the monitor was made is -0.08. What does the correlation being negative tell you about the relationship between lead and year? What does the small value of the correlation tell you about this relationship?

Solution: The low correlation indicates that there is little relationship between year and lead. The negative value indicates that the lead is less for later years, but again not by much.

7. QM Modeling: Glaciers store water that is used in irrigation. The table below provides data on recent changes in length of the Rainbow Glacier on Mt. Baker in Washington State. Position refers to the location of the glacier's leading edge, as

compared to its 1985 position. The scatter plot provides a graph of the data with 1985 as year 0. Determine a linear model for the data and use it to predict the length of the glacier in 2010 if it was 3,750 meters long in 1950. NOTE: an estimate of the model is sufficient. Explain how you arrived at your model.

Solution: The intent was for them to estimate a line of best fit. The best way to do this is find the center of the data by calculating the mean of year and length (7.2, -100.4). The teachers could estimate a point they feel centers the data. This point acts as a pivot for the line of best fit, which they can estimate by rotating the line pinned by this point. The exact line of best fit is $y = -16.82x + 20.73$ with an R^2 of 0.966. The estimated line of fit will vary from this, but a negative slope between -10 to -20 and a y-intercept between 10 and 30 would indicate a good attempt at estimating a line of best fit. Whatever line of fit they provide, they should take 2010 – 1985 = 25 years and substitute this into their line to get an estimate of length. In the exact line of fit this would give $y = -16.82(25) + 20.73 = -399.77$ meters. While this gives how much the glacier receded, the actual length is the length at a given time minus the amount the glacier has receded. In 1950 the length was 3,750 meters. Between 1950 and 1985 if it was receding at the same rate the glacier was $y = -16.82(-35)+20.73 = 609.43$ meters longer in 1950. So the total recession from 1950 to 2010 was -609.43+-399.77 = -1009.2 meters. Subtracting from the length in 1950 gives 3750-1009.2 = 2,740.8 meters long in 2010.

ENERGY AND ENVIRONMENT PERFORMANCE TASK

We have presented an overview of the QR STEM project so STEM professional development leaders and teachers reading this have a sense of the big picture, including our goals, methods, and expected outcomes. We now turn to providing a detailed discussion of leading teachers in developing a performance task within the context of energy and environment using the Understanding by Design assessment framework (Wiggins and McTighe, 2005). STEM content will be integrated throughout the development, but the indepth discussion of energy and environment science will be provided in the science chapters. Here we focus on a specific performance task development as an exemplar for the process. We had 86 K-12 science and mathematics teachers creating performance tasks over the three years of the project. We will draw on our experiences with the teachers over the entire project to present what we found to be the best practices in engaging teachers in this type of work. We will walk you through the three Understanding by Design stages much as we did with the teachers. Imagine the variation in designs, questions, barriers, creativity, and interest that we encountered across the multiple professional learning communities in the QR STEM project, for each case was unique in its own right. We will tell the story through one exemplar, which is based on real cases but combines the experiences of many of the teachers in the project.

Understanding by Design Stage 1:

Enduring Understandings and Essential Questions

One of the central tenets of the QR STEM project was to have teachers teach for understanding. The Understanding by Design (UbD) framework supports this central tenet and we extensively used their approach and Design Handbook activities as we worked with teachers on developing an energy and environment unit. Changing teaching strategies requires a supportive community, so we established norms for the teachers and university faculty to follow so that teachers would be comfortable struggling with new approaches:

- Open-mindedness: be willing to test out new ideas and consider how barriers to them can be overcome;
- Curiosity: bring a positive attitude to exploring new methods of teaching;
- Discovery: we can all learn so be willing to try new approaches;

- Sincerity: when providing critique make it about the work not the person and present it in a way that is supportive not degrading;
- Brevity: allow everyone in the community to speak, don't dominate the time allowed;
- Engagement: all community members need to put their shoulder to the wheel, engage in all tasks you are given;
- Connections: the communities are interdisciplinary with varying expertise allowing everyone to make new connections.

Since teaching for understanding was our goal, we asked teachers to carefully consider the difference for teaching for knowledge versus teaching for understanding. We played a clip from an old Ma and Pa Kettle movie (Figure 1) where a banker is attempting to explain to the couple how profits for a venture will be shared. We asked teachers to listen to the short clip considering the banker as a teacher and Ma and Pa as his confused students. They were to identify what good qualities of teaching the banker displayed and why he failed to change the Kettle's unique style of doing mathematics. We asked them the following questions:

- Was the banker a good teacher? What characteristics of good teaching did he display?
- What are common teaching design errors you saw in the clip? Was the teaching activity-focused with the intent to engage but without a focused understanding as an outcome? Was the teaching coverage-focused with the intent of covering material without concern to understanding?

The banker presented four different arguments to Ma and Pa for why his method of calculating the split was correct, each of which were debunked by erroneous methods. So the banker provided multiple representations, gave clear explanations, and was patient with his students; but all to no avail. He failed to sway Ma and Pa because he ignored their misunderstandings about place value and arithmetic operations. In short, he never addressed their understanding. This is not uncommon in teacher practice. We present information with the hope that students will emulate our methods, ignoring their prior experience and the understandings they bring to the classroom. The banker provided knowledge, which can be rote and based in student experience and belief. Understanding is fluid, transferable to new contexts, transformable into new theories, and requires insight.

Figure 1. Ma and Pa Kettle do math (http://www.youtube.com/watch?v=X0aPKvNl9ek).

If understanding is our goal, how do we assess for it? We played another clip for teachers from Minds of Our Own (1997) which was produced by the Harvard-Smithsonian Center for Astrophysics. The clip came from Lessons from Thin Air (http://www.learner.org/resources/series26.html) which focused on the concept of photosynthesis (Figure 2). In one scene from the clip a middle school science student is handed a piece of wood and asked where it comes from? This student had just completed several lessons on photosynthesis which included hands-on laboratories. Yet despite being one of the best students in the class he could not explain where the log came from. We asked the teachers why the student did not develop an understanding of photosynthesis that allowed him to relate it the creation of the log? The student had mastered the components of the formula for photosynthesis and could correctly state it, but he did not relate this knowledge to the world in which he lived. He had knowledge, but not understanding.

Figure 2. Lessons from Thin Air. Minds of Our Own (1997) produced by the Harvard-Smithsonian Center for Astrophysics. Use with permission from the Annenberg Learner website (http://www.learner.org/resources/series26.html). All rights reserved.

We asked the teachers to think like assessors and break out of the conventional design for creating lessons. UbD identifies the conventional lesson design as having three stages. In Stage 1 of conventional design the teacher identifies the desired results or objectives of the lesson. In Stage 2 of conventional design the teacher plans the learning activity without considering how the activity or task will assess the students understanding. In Stage 3 of conventional design the teacher assesses the student, with the assessment developed after the lesson is completed. This leads to potential disconnect between the lesson and the assessment. This traditional lesson design is driven by the pressure of covering material and often leads to one of two teaching design errors. First there is Coverage-focused Teaching in which the goal is primarily to cover material, resulting in rote learning of a myriad of facts but not understanding. Second there is Activity-focused Teaching in which the teacher locates and enacts tasks that are meant to engage and even entertain students, but the tasks are not sufficiently tied to students developing understanding. We wanted to engage teachers in developing a performance task using the UbD Backward Design process (Figure 3). In backward design stages 2 and 3 of the conventional design are flipped, with the teacher thinking like an assessor. Once the desired results are determined (Stage 1 Backward Design), the teacher determines how to assess the desired results so she has evidence of the student's understanding (Stage 2 Backward Design), only then does the teacher plan the learning activity (Stage 3 Backward Design).

Stage 1 of the backward design process engages the teachers in identifying four key components that clarify the desired result (Figure 4). The teachers need to **establish goals** for the unit. These goals should be tied to national standards, state standards, school district program objectives, and agreed upon learner outcomes. The teachers need to identify **enduring understandings**, these are the big ideas we want students to take away from the unit and be able to apply in other settings. The teachers need to develop **essential questions**, which are questions that are open-ended, provocative, and engaging. These questions will guide the students' inquiry, helping them to uncover and discover big ideas. Finally, the teacher needs to determine what **knowledge and skills** will be required to achieve the enduring understanding. In QR STEM Symposium 1, the professional learning communities worked on identifying and creating these four components for their energy and environment unit.

Evidence of Understanding

- Think like an assessor
  - Conventional Design
    - Stage 1 ⟶ Stage 3 ⟶ Stage 2
  - Assessor (Backward) Design
    - Stage 1 ⟶ Stage 2 ⟶ Stage 3

  - Stage 1: Desired results – enduring idea
  - Stage 2: Evidence – assessment tasks
  - Stage 3: Learning Plan - activity

Figure 3. Understanding by Design backward design compared to conventional design. Wiggins, G. & McTighe, J.(2005). Understanding by Design, Association for Supervision and Curriculum Development.

The Understanding by Design Handbook provides a number of excellent design templates and design tools for developing a unit. They include graphic organizers that support teachers in thinking about how to teach for understanding. We selected a subset of these design tools to guide our teachers' creation of their energy and environment units. The first UbD design template we use was the Stage 1 – Identify Desired Results design template (Chapter 3 Appendix: Figure 16).

We had already narrowed the topic for the QR STEM project from all STEM content to energy and environment integrating quantitative reasoning (mathematics and

Stage 1: Desired Results
-- 4 categories

- Established Goals (G)
  - National, state, local, professional standards, program objectives, learner outcomes
- Enduring Understandings (U)
  - What we want students to come to understand about the big ideas
- Essential Questions (Q)
  - Open-ended provocative questions designed to guide student inquiry and focus on uncovering big ideas
- Knowledge and Skills (KS)
  - Discrete objectives students are to know and be able to do

Figure 4. Understanding by Design four categories for desired results. Wiggins, G. & McTighe, J.(2005). Understanding by Design, Association for Supervision and Curriculum Development.

statistics). While we were interested in developing interdisciplinary STEM units that teachers would implement in their classrooms, we learned from our first QR STEM cohort that a lack of science focus led to such diverse ideas we had difficulty managing the creative process. By the fourth cohort of teachers we had narrowed the topic even further to the energy and environment topics of transportation, electricity, and climate change. These are still very broad topics, allowing the PLCs plenty of latitude to make the topic relevant to their classrooms and their students' community (place-based).

We promised an exemplar for the development of an energy and environment unit, which tracks our teachers through the UbD framework. So we introduce here our exemplar unit and use it to explicate the process the teachers engaged in throughout the QR STEM project. We will call our fictitious professional learning community the PLC Cowboys, since we had all the real learning communities name themselves. The PLC Cowboys are typical of the many real PLCs we had throughout the QR STEM project, consisting of four teachers: a high school biology teacher, high school chemistry teacher, high school mathematics teacher, and a middle school science teacher. They are evenly represented by gender, two male and two female. After listening to the Symposium 0 overviews on energy, environment, and quantitative reasoning, and discussing with each other areas of personnel interest, they selected the topic of *population and its impact on energy and environment.* The PLC Cowboys presented their topic to the QR STEM teachers and faculty at the opening debrief session of Symposium 1. The feedback from their peers and the faculty indicated the topic had great promise for integrating QR into science and weaving each of the four science areas into the unit. In addition the topic held promise for inclusion of a strong social relevance component, which would support future discussions of making the unit place-based.

The PLC Cowboys now turned to the Identify Desired Results template to begin refining their topic through identifying enduring understandings supported by essential questions. They examined the NSTA National Science Standards (1996) and the NCTM National Mathematics Standards (2000), as well as the Wyoming State Standards for Science and Mathematics, to determine how they could relate the topic of population impact on energy and environment to required school district and state outcomes. The PLC Cowboys felt the unit could address elements of the following standards:

- NSTA Science Standard: Unifying Concepts and Processes including systems, order, and organization; evidence, models, and explanation; change, constancy, and measurement;
- NSTA Science Standard: Earth and Space Science including energy in the earth system; geochemical cycles;
- NSTA Science Standard: Science as Inquiry;
- NSTA Science Standard: Science and Technology including abilities of technology and understanding about science and technology;
- NSTA Science Standard: Physical Science including chemical reactions; conservation of energy; Interactions of energy and matter;
- NSTA Science Standard: Social Perspectives including population growth; natural resources; environmental quality; natural and human induced hazards; science and technology in local, national, and global challenges;
- NSTA Science Standard: Life Science including interdependence of organisms; matter, energy, and organization in living systems;
- NCTM Standard: Number and Operations including proportional reasoning; sense of large and small numbers; estimation and reasonableness of results;
- NCTM Standard: Algebra including generalizing patterns; interpret representations of functions; model and solve problems in context; analyze rates of change from graphical and numeric data;
- NCTM Standard: Geometry including use geometric ideas to solve problems in, and gain insight into, other disciplines;
- NCTM Standard: Measurement including making decisions about units and scales that are appropriate for problem situations involving measurement; understand metric measurement; analyze precision, accuracy, and approximate error in measurement situations; use unit analysis to check measurement computations;
- NCTM Standard: Data Analysis and Probability including formulate and design studies; use appropriate statistical representations; compute basic statistics; understand central tendency and spread; display and interpret bivariate data; identify trends in bivariate data; determine functions that model data.

Note the focus on identifying interdisciplinary standards that promote integration of biology, chemistry, earth science, physics, mathematics, and statistics. Interdisciplinary approaches were strongly encouraged by the project faculty. In Stage 1 we want the teachers to cast a wide net with respect to possible standards that could be met. This list of standards, while extensive at this point, will be refined throughout the unit development.

While the teachers had little difficulty identifying the established goals based on national and state standards, they struggled with identifying the enduring understandings. In many cases the teachers struggled with the distinction between knowledge and understanding with respect to the potential big ideas of the unit. For example, the PLC Cowboys chemistry teacher identified memorizing the periodic table as an enduring understanding, while the PLC Cowboys mathematics teacher wanted correctly substituting into the quadratic formula to be an enduring understanding. Both of these are knowledge not understandings. Considerable effort and extended discussion was needed to move some PLCs from knowledge to understanding outcomes.

Enduring understandings are the big ideas that anchor a unit and establish the rationale for it. Enduring understandings are concepts that are transferable to other venues, including connecting sections in a chapter, connecting chapters in a text, and connecting classes across subject areas leading to interdisciplinary approaches. It is the enduring understandings that make a topic worth studying, for they are the things that students will find useful later in life. If students can memorize it, then they can "Google" it. We need students who know what to do with the knowledge within a real-world context. To help elicit a deeper look at enduring understandings, we had the teachers use two UbD design tools: Structure of Knowledge tool and the Clarifying Content Priorities tool. First we had them work through the UbD Structure of Knowledge design tool (Chapter 3 Appendix: Figure 17). The purpose of this tool was to assist the PLCs in distinguishing between knowledge and enduring understandings. The Structure of Knowledge design tool can be seen as a funnel separating out the knowledge and understanding as you pass through it (i.e. top down) or as a cup to be filled up building on each subsequent level (i.e. bottom up).

The first level of the Structure of Knowledge tool asks teachers to identify factual knowledge and discrete skills related to the concept. Facts are declarative in nature; the foundation for understanding. Facts require apprehension, while understanding requires comprehension (Dewey, 1933). Facts are accepted truths upon which a theory is built. While essential for understanding, facts do not transfer to new settings. Skills are procedural in nature; they are algorithms or processes for doing things with facts. Skills are often discrete procedures that can be enacted without deep understanding of why the process works. Consider for example a student's ability to use the quadratic formula or state the formula for photosynthesis. This is a skill. Understanding comes with knowing when to apply the skill to solve a problem. Developing skills should be a means to a larger end, preparing the student to apply it in a real-world situation for example. Skills have limited transfer to new situations. The PLC Cowboys discussed facts and skills that underpin their topic of population and its impact on energy and environment. They found it difficult to get too specific on facts and skills without further clarification of the enduring understanding. Certainly the concept of population growth would require mastery of large numbers, exponential equations, and graphing. Facts about energy use and consumption, as well as environmental impacts of energy use would also be necessary. Many of the PLCs found it easier to start at the bottom with the principles and generalizations and work their way up the funnel. The process is not linear; teachers should skip around as they move up and down the Structure of Knowledge.

The second level of the Structure of Knowledge is the Big Ideas, which includes transferable concepts and complex processes. Concepts like factual knowledge are declarative in nature, however concepts differ from facts in that they are abstract mental constructs which are transferable across topics and contexts. Concepts are often associated in our memory with words or short phrases which evoke complex connections and understandings. Complex processes like discrete skills are procedural in nature, but processes differ from skills in that they are complex combinations of skills that are transferable within and across disciplines. The PLC Cowboys topic includes the transferable concepts of exponential growth in population, complex adaptive systems and sustainability in environment, and resource allocation in energy. Their topic elicits the processes of scientific literacy and quantitative reasoning, both of which require a complex combination of skills to accomplish the result of making informed data-based decisions about grand challenge issues in energy and environment. Consider for example the extensive collection of models provided for energy and environment in our prior discussions. These models include a variety of representations such as tables, equations, graphs, and box models. Quantitative interpretation of these models within the real-world context requires a broad array of mathematical skills which must be coordinated to determine trends, make predictions, and transfer across representations when comparing or contrasting models.

The third level of the Structure of Knowledge is principles and generalizations. These constitute the understandings we want students to take from the unit. Principles and generalizations are abstractions linking two or more concepts. They are transferable to new situations, providing a means to make sense of facts, skills, concepts and processes. The UbD Structure of Knowledge task asks teachers to state the understanding as a full-sentence statement articulating the principle or generalization that we want learners to come to understand. This understanding should be an unobvious and important inference needing uncovering.

The understanding for the PLC Cowboys unit is based on the IPAT equation for environmental impact. In the early 1970s, Erlich and Holdren identified three factors that created environmental impact and expressed the relationship in the following formula:

$$I = PAT$$

where I is environmental impact, P is population, A is affluence, and T is technology (Chertow, 2001). The simplicity of the model makes it a popular choice among scholars as a starting point for investigating the complex interactions of population, economic growth, and technological development with environmental impact. Some dire predictions have been made about the future of the environment of our planet. The world population (P) is increasing despite global efforts to control growth. The common desire to improve quality of life (A) means that affluence is also an increasing quantity in the equation. The explosion in gross domestic product (GDP) in India and China as they strive to reach the level of affluence in Europe and the United States is an example of the affluence variable. With two of the three quantities increasing we are left to ask, in the words of Ausubel (1996), "Can technology spare the earth?" In the emerging industrial ecology view, technology can compensate for environmental impact of not only more population, but a more affluent population. However technology is also a source of pollution and therefore has negative as well as positive environmental impacts. The combustion engine has freed us to travel faster and further, but the burning of fossil fuels has impacted climate change. Modern agricultural methods have allowed us to avoid the pending starvation of mankind foretold by Malthus, but pesticides and fertilizer are major environmental concerns. The PLC Cowboys wanted students to understand the complex interaction of population, affluence, technology, and environment. They felt they could narrow the topic by focusing on one or more of the energy and environment topics which they heard discussed in the QR STEM project: transportation, electricity, and climate change. For example, the unit could focus on the growing demand for energy to power transportation or to produce electricity, and the consequences of energy choices on climate change. The PLC Cowboys arrived at the following statement of an understanding for the unit.

> The principle we want students to come to understand is: There is a complex global interaction between increasing demands for energy supporting transportation and electricity for an increasing population with desires to be more affluent, and maintaining environmental quality. Technology plays a central role in addressing this conflict between energy and environment.

The PLC Cowboy's discussion around completing the Structure of Knowledge design element provides an initial proposal for the unit. The process is not linear, it is iterative. The PLC Cowboys will make many adjustments to this scheme as they move forward planning their unit.

The stage of identifying enduring understandings is central to the development of a unit that will focus on teaching for understanding. So we asked the PLCs to complete a second UbD design tool task focused on enduring understandings, the Clarifying Content Priorities design tool (Chapter 3 Appendix: Figure 18). We found this tool to be very popular with the QR STEM teachers. In fact, many used this tool in place of using the Structure of Knowledge design tool.

The Clarifying Content Priorities design tool consists of three concentric rings representing different levels of priority for unit content. The complement of the rings, that is the background field outside all three rings, represents the field of all possible content, topics, skills, and resources related to the topic of interest. In the information age in which we live with the explosive growth of new STEM knowledge it is not possible to address all content, even when restricted to energy and environment as the QR STEM project proposes. No matter what the content area, there is so much information that teachers are obliged to make choices. Even the chemistry or mathematics teacher with a coverage-focused approach to teaching, who plows through the entire book so everything is covered, is making choices. He is simply deferring the choice of content to the author of the book. The outer ring represents what is worth being familiar with. The unit will expose the students to broad brush knowledge, which extends the enduring understanding to related areas, but will not require mastery of this content. The PLC Cowboys will relate the history behind the concept of IPAT, including a chronology of development and names of key players, but this will be peripheral to the enduring understanding. The unit may also relate IPAT to other economic or social contexts beyond energy and environment that demonstrate the complexity of the issue, such as consumer consumption and demand, but without an expectation that these issues will be mastered. Assessment of content worth being familiar with would be through at most selected-response and constructed response items on quizzes and tests. They would not serve as the focus for open-ended performance tasks.

The middle ring represents content which is important to know and do. Mastery of this content is a prerequisite for success in accomplishing key performances that indicate understanding. The middle ring includes important knowledge that is the foundation of the enduring understanding. Knowledge includes facts, concepts, and principles underlying the enduring understanding. The PLC Cowboys identified important knowledge as including linear and exponential growth, sampling, concept of affluence and technology, energy resources, and environmental quality. Important skills are also included in this content priority, such as being able to implement processes, strategies, and methods. The PLC Cowboys unit will require students to use mathematical and statistical models in the context of energy and environment, interpret data representations, apply statistical process in analyzing data, and practice scientific literacy and quantitative reasoning. Important knowledge and skills are assessed using both selected-response and constructed response items which may be incorporated into more open-ended performance tasks targeting enduring understandings.

The inner most ring of the Clarifying Content Priorities design tool contains the big ideas and enduring understandings that anchor the unit and establish a rationale for it. These are the big ideas that make the topic worthy of study for understanding. For the PLC Cowboys the enduring understanding is the same here as in the first design tool, but it is represented less formally as a list. The big ideas include data-based decision making, identifying trends, and making predictions. The understanding is the complex interaction of population, affluence, technology, and environment. Enduring understandings are assessed using performance tasks and projects which are complex, open-ended, and authentic.

At this point the PLCs were able to complete most of the Stage 1 Design Template. They had an idea of established goals, desired understandings, and key knowledge and skills. The only thing they lacked was essential questions focused on the enduring understanding. Understanding by Design emphasizes staying focused on the enduring understanding by specifying the desired understandings, framing goals related to the understanding in terms of essential questions, and then specifying key performance tasks (Stage 2). Essential questions should be open-ended provocative questions which lead students to engage in inquiry, uncovering ideas, and developing understanding. They help avoid activity-oriented or coverage oriented teaching by engaging students in the problem solving process. If we provide only a statement of the enduring understanding, then it may appear to the student as a fact that has already been established, versus an open conjecture that needs to be explored. National science standards and mathematics standards make the mistake of framing core content as fact-like sentences, rather than revealing them to be summary insights derived from questions and inquiries. UbD identifies several important characteristics of essential questions:

- Cause genuine and relevant inquiry into big ideas and core content;
- Provoke deep thought, lively discussion, sustained inquiry, and new understanding; lead to new questions;
- Require students to consider alternatives, weigh evidence, support their ideas, and justify answers;
- Stimulate vital, ongoing rethinking of big ideas, assumptions, and prior lessons;
- Spark meaningful connections with prior learning and personal experiences;
- Naturally recur, creating opportunities for transfer to other situations and subjects.

UbD classifies essential questions as having two levels of specificity: topical and overarching (Figure 5). Topical essential questions elicit topic specific insights, generalizations derived from the specific content knowledge and skills of the unit. Overarching essential questions elicit more abstract or general understandings that are transferable beyond the unit. They are broader in scope so involve generalizations that transcend the unit, forming bridges to other units and courses. UbD also classifies questions as guiding (closed) or open. Closed questions, whether topical or overarching, are intended to lead students to a desired understanding. Open questions do not converge to a settled understanding, but lead the student to draw their own conclusions, promoting intellectual freedom and an opportunity to question authority. The QR STEM project promoted interdisciplinary approaches, so we encouraged teachers to write overarching questions that would bridge areas of science and mathematics.

	Scope	
Intent	Topical	Overarching
Guiding (closed)	Unit specific questions, converge toward settled understanding	General questions, cut across unit/subject but still converge to desired understanding
Open	Stimulate inquiry and deepen understanding of important ideas within a unit, do not converge to settled understanding	Broad and deep questions that remain open in the discipline, cut across unit/subject boundaries

Figure 5. Understanding by Design essential question classification.
Wiggins, G. & McTighe, J. (2005). Understanding by Design,
Association for Supervision and Curriculum Development.

To engage teachers in writing essential questions, we used several UbD approaches. First we had them focus on their enduring understanding, converting it from a declarative statement to a question. We referred to this as the Jeopardy Approach; you have the answer, now frame the question. We practiced by having them select a science or mathematics standard from the national or state standards, then had them write it as a question. Then they took their enduring understanding statement and turned it into a question. Recall that the PLC Cowboys enduring understanding was: There is a complex global interaction between increasing demands for energy supporting transportation and electricity for an increasing population with desires to be more affluent, and maintaining environmental quality. Technology plays a central role in addressing this conflict between energy and environment. They converted this into the following overarching essential questions:

- What is the impact of increasing world population on energy resources that support transportation? What energy resources are most important for travel? (NOTE: a parallel question could be asked for electricity)
- How does the push for a higher quality of living by emerging nations interact with this impact?
- It's the environment as well, so how are choices we make about energy impacting the environment?
- What role does technology play in addressing the impact of energy use on the environment?

We asked the PLCs to check their essential questions against the essential question characteristics provided above. The proposed essential questions meet the intent of most of the six characteristics, but may be lacking in elements of engagement, specifically the characteristic calling for meaningful connections with prior learning and personal experiences.

The personal engagement of students is one potential barrier to using global grand challenges to drive the unit. This barrier is why we introduced the teachers to place-based education. The tenets of place-based education include personal connection to place. We asked the teachers to think about viewing the essential questions from a place-based perspective. How could they include the students' community in the questions? If this can be done, it personalizes the questions, which increases engagement. We also asked them to make the questions more provocative. The PLC Cowboys came up the following essential questions from a place-based perspective:

- What energy source will my car be using in 10 years?
- Is economic growth in India impacting my future life style?
- What will the climate change be in my community in 50 years?
- Can technology save the planet?

We also worked with the teachers on creating essential questions from an unexpected source, basic skills. Important understandings are often implicit or embedded in skill development. Often all you need to do is ask why processes you have automated work?

For example a student has mastered the quadratic formula, at least how to substitute into to it to find an answer. But do they know that the quadratic formula is just a general case of completing the square to find solutions? Do they know when it is more efficient to use square roots to solve a quadratic then to use the quadratic formula? The point is that high level use of skill often involves innovation, judgment, and efficiency. Genuine performance requires making choices from a repertoire of skills to solve challenging problems. Think of skills as tools. Do students know what tool to take out of their toolkit to solve a given problem? To be skillful is to work purposefully and strategically. It requires understanding of key principles that are at work.

Finally, we had the teachers consider the role that the UbD six facets of understanding could play in creating essential questions. The six facets can be divided into categories:

- 3 Facets represent performances one with understanding can do
  - ❖ Explain – provide thorough, supported, and justifiable accounts of phenomena, facts, and data (theoretical, explain why)
  - ❖ Interpret – tell meaningful stories, offer apt translations, provide revealing historical or personal dimension to ideas and events (personal, what does it mean to me)
  - ❖ Apply – effectively use and adapt what one knows in diverse contexts (pragmatic, how can I use it)
- 3 Facets represent types of insights one has
  - ❖ Perspective – see points of view through critical eyes and ears, see the big picture (dispassionate, whose point of view)
  - ❖ Empathize – find value in what others might find odd, alien, or implausible, perceive sensitivity on the basis of prior direct experience (passionate, what are you feeling)
  - ❖ Self-knowledge – perceive personal style, prejudices, projections, and habits of mind that both shape and impede one's own understanding, be aware of what one does not understand (introspective, my prejudices)

These facets are actions one performs that demonstrate understanding, so we can identify action verbs for each facet. For example, the Interpret facet includes the actions of create analogies, critique, evaluate, illustrate, predict, and translate. Chapter 3 Appendix: Figure 19) presents a tool developed by a teacher in the program for using facets to generate essential questions. For example, let's take facet 3 Application and choose the verb design. PLC Cowboys could have the following essential question: Can you design an IPAT model for the state of Wyoming? What data would you need? What restrictions would the model have?

Our final essential questions and enduring understandings task for the teacher was to complete the UbD Identifying Essential Questions and Understandings design tool (Chapter 3 Appendix: Figure 20). The design tool provides stem questions that prompted teachers to reevaluate and reformulate their proposed enduring understandings and essential questions. The PLC Cowboys used the question stems to engage in a dialogue about their enduring understanding and essential questions which is summarized below. The question stems are in italics.

Why study the impact of population on energy and environment? So what?

The PLC Cowboys found in the introductions to energy and environmental science offered by the QR STEM scientists a compelling case for focusing on the energy and environment nexus. The struggle between providing diverse energy sources for an increasing demand and its impact on the environment is a grand challenge for the next generation. Fossil fuels are a non-renewable energy resource and multiple models indicate we are nearing or have passed peak oil production. The technology allowing access to fossil fuel sources that were previously not economically viable, such as oil shale and hydraulic fracturing of low production wells, carry potential implications for the environment. What fuel sources will fill the gap upon the decline of oil? Biofuels are one possible source, but viable agricultural land is a precious commodity. Do we grow fuel or food for an increasing population?

What makes the study of this impact universal?

Energy and environment are universal by nature. There is a complex system tying our decisions on future energy sources to environmental impacts. Increased affluence for the human race is dependent on energy; it is the universal driver for economic prosperity. But energy cannot come at the cost of excessive environmental destruction. In addition, energy and environmental science are interdisciplinary, offering an excellent opportunity for the integration of STEM. This includes quantitative reasoning which is essential to understanding the energy and environment nexus.

If the unit on the impact of population on energy and environment is a story, what's the moral of the story?

The moral of the energy and environment story is that every choice has a consequence. Students will have to make decisions about energy resources as future citizens, those choices will carry environmental impacts.

What's the Big Idea implied in the skill or process of studying the impact?

To understand the energy and environment nexus, it is essential that students are scientifically literate and quantitatively literate. While students may have knowledge of these literacies, they often do not have an understanding of them. For example, students possess basic quantitative literacy skills but cannot apply them in context. They have knowledge of arithmetic processes such as addition and proportions, but lack the understanding to apply them in an energy or environmental context. So the big idea implied in these literacies is to enable students to know what tools to select from their tool box of skills and processes to explore the energy and environment nexus within context.

What larger concept, issue, or problem underlies the impact?

The larger concept underlying the impact is the ability to make scientifically informed data-based decisions about complex global challenges.

What couldn't we do if we didn't understand the impact?

Not understanding the impact of energy resource choices restricts the student as a citizen from making informed decisions that will impact their future environmental, social, and political world. A lack of literacy skills and quantitative reasoning restricts their future opportunities to become STEM professionals.

How is the impact used and applied in the larger world?

An understanding of energy science and environmental science can be used to make environmentally conscious decisions about energy resources. The grand challenge of energy and environment is a global issue. Decisions made in the United States to increase biofuel production have potential impacts on food production, which could impact third-world peoples.

What is a real-world insight about the impact?

A real-world insight about the energy and environment nexus is that there are a number of alternative energy resources, but each carries an environmental impact. Meeting future energy needs will be a challenge, we need an educated citizenry as well as future scientists to meet that challenge.

What is the value of studying the impact?

The value of studying the energy and environment nexus is a future generation of citizens and scientists who make informed decisions about energy resources and the impact of energy choices on the environment. In addition, the energy and environment nexus is an excellent example of a complex adaptive system that requires interdisciplinary approaches. STEM education needs to engage students in complex adaptive systems thinking and interdisciplinary STEM learning through real-world problem-based learning and place-based education.

The goal of this last task was to have teachers consider to what extent their proposed unit outcomes were enduring and transferable big ideas which have value beyond the classroom. The UbD framework refers to these as intellectual linchpins. We also wanted them to consider if their unit outcomes were big ideas and core processes at the heart of the discipline. They should elicit authentic learning and active construction of understanding on the part of the student. We wanted teachers to consider if their unit outcomes were abstract, counterintuitive, or often misunderstood concepts that require uncovering by the student. We also wanted them to consider that the big ideas may be embedded in facts and skills the students have memorized, but do not understand. What are the connections among facts that allow them to organize them into a meaningful structure? Why does the algorithm work?

Understanding by Design Stage 2:

Assessing Understanding

The first symposium provided the PLC Cowboys the opportunity to determine enduring understandings and essential questions for their unit on population and its impact on energy and environment. The second symposium moved them into Understanding by Design Stage 2: Assessing Understanding. While both conventional instructional design and UbD design begin with a stage of identifying goals for instruction, it is in the second stage that the two design strategies truly diverge. The conventional design follows goals with determining activities associated with those goals, then moves to assessing outcomes. UbD reverses these two stages, asking teachers to consider assessment before instructional activities. So in the second QR STEM symposium we focused on assessing the understandings the teachers had determined for their units. In reality, the UbD design process was not linear for our QR STEM project teachers. As with all creative processes, the teachers bounced around the stages of development, making connections to their personnel teaching experience and sharing new ideas with other teachers in their professional learning community. So upon arrival at the second symposium, many of the teachers had already tied favorite activities to the unit understandings. This is to be expected, it is part of the creative process. Our goal for UbD Stage 2 was to delay finalizing the activities and have them first consider assessment. We did this by employing the UbD frame of having them think like assessors.

Assessors ask three basic questions about the project they are assessing:

- What kind of evidence do we need to support the attainment of goals?
- What specific characteristics in student responses, products, or performances should we examine to determine the extent to which the desired results were achieved?
- Does the proposed evidence enable us to infer a student's knowledge, skill, or understanding?

The first question is seeking tasks that reveal understanding, such as comparing and contrasting key concepts, or summarizing key concepts. The second question is focused on development of criteria, rubrics, and exemplars as needed. The third question concerns issues of validity and reliability.

The conventional instructional designer, who selects activities before answering these questions, is in danger of falling into the activity designer teaching trap. The teacher implements activities that may even engage students, but the activities fail to provide evidence that students have developed understanding of the proposed unit outcomes. A summary of the differences, as identified by UbD, between a teacher thinking like an assessor and acting like an activity designer are provided in Figure 6.

An assessor uses a variety of assessment methods to provide evidence of student understanding. UbD identified a continuum of assessment methods which vary in several characteristics (Figure 7), including informal checks, observation/dialogue, quiz/test, academic prompt, and performance task. As we move along this continuum from left to right the assessment methods shift scope, time frame, setting, and structure. The scope of the assessments increases from simple on the left to complex on the right. Informal checks, such as teacher questioning, observations, examining student work, and think alouds, are simple in scope. Often they are not even graded, but provide formative assessment of student progress. Academic prompts and performance tasks are complex in scope, requiring students to think critically about divergent issues with no single best answer. Informal checks have a short term time frame, often no more than a few minutes. Performance tasks can have a short term time frame, but often they are longer term in duration, taking place over days, weeks, or even an entire school year. Teacher observations of students and classroom dialogues with them can have varied settings from decontextualized to authentic. However, these assessment methods are often decontextualized, focusing on student mastery of an abstract skill or process. Performance tasks have authentic settings. An authentic setting is grounded in a real-world situation, requires students to make judgments including formulating the problem and developing a plan for solving the problem, replicates challenging situations that are complex and messy, assesses the student's ability to use a variety of skills and knowledge within a multistage task, and allows for a feedback and revision cycle. Finally, informal checks are often highly structured or directive. The teacher is seeking a specific response. Academic prompts and performance tasks are much less directive and even ill-structured. The objective is to have the student clarify the task, formulate the question, and even personalize the task.

Think like an assessor	Acting like an activity designer
What should be sufficient and revealing evidence of understanding?	What would be interesting and engaging activities on this topic?
What performance tasks must anchor the unit and focus the instructional work?	What resources and materials are available on this topic?
Against what criteria will I distinguish work?	How will I give students a grade and justify it to parents?
How will I be able to distinguish between those who really understand and those who don't (though they seem to)?	What will students be doing in and out of class? What assignments will be given?
What misunderstandings are likely? How will I check for those?	Did the activities work? Why or why not?

Figure 6. Think like an assessor not an activity designer. Wiggins, G. & McTighe, J.(2005). Understanding by Design, Association for Supervision and Curriculum Development.

Continuum of Assessment Methods
- Vary in several characteristics
  - Scope: from simple to complex
  - Time Frame: short-term to long term
  - Setting: decontextualized to authentic
  - Structure: highly structured to ill-structured

- Move from snapshot to scrapbook
- Self-assessment of sources of evidence (HO)

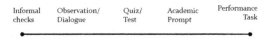

| Informal
checks | Observation/
Dialogue | Quiz/
Test | Academic
Prompt | Performance
Task |

Figure 7. Continuum of assessment methods. Wiggins, G. & McTighe, J. (2005). Understanding by Design, Association for Supervision and Curriculum Development.

We incorporated a more detailed discussion of assessment methods based on the work of Butler and McMunn (2012). Butler and McMunn classified assessments as selected response or constructed response Figure 8, further dividing constructed response into products and performances. Selected response assessment items are indicative of closed form quizzes and tests, useful for assessing the outer ring of the Clarifying Content Priorities design tool (Chapter 3 Appendix: Figure 18), but not the center ring representing enduring understandings.

Constructed response items are indicative of the left side of the assessment continuum. Performance tasks and academic prompts are the desired assessment type for the center ring of the Clarifying Content Priorities design tool. Teacher assessment items are often of the selected response or short answer constructed response variety. Our goal in the QR STEM project was to have teachers incorporate performance tasks such as those in the performances category listed in Figure 8.

While our goal was a performance task as a culminating activity, we also wanted teachers to use a variety of assessment types across the continuum of assessment methods. We shared with teachers ideas on incorporating assessment types. Informal checks and teacher observations can be informal or formal. Informal methods include taking anecdotal notes or writing narratives that address class wide behaviors and do not have predetermined criteria. Formal methods provide a tool such as the discussion matrix which has predetermined criteria. For example suppose a teacher is using student circles to engage small groups of students in critical thinking and reflection. The teacher can formalize the student circle assessment by using a discussion matrix to assess engagement (Figure 9). The discussion matrix provides predetermined criteria that will be assessed, such as contributions to discussion and substantiating ideas with reasoning. The teacher

Performance Tasks			
Debate between teams with two perspectives	Presentation to panel of experts	Engineering design to create a product	Research a real world problem in your community
Conducting a poster session	Create a YouTube video	Write a song	Present a play
Write a computer app or program	Create a diorama	Write a poem	Do a demonstration

Figure 8. Possible performance tasks.

Student Circle	Circle Members			
	Keith	Kris	Nick	Mitch
Participated in discussion				
Respected others input				
Provided math support for argument				
Interdisciplinary STEM viewpoints used				
Critical reasoning used				

Figure 9. Discussion matrix for assessing engagement in student circle.
Adapted from Butler & McMunn (2006). A Teacher's Guide to Classroom Assessment:
Understanding and Using Assessment to Improve Student Learning.

observes the student circle and simply places an X in the box under a student's name if they observe one of the criteria.

Another assessment method facilitating teacher observations are student self-assessments followed by goal-setting conferences (Figure 10). The teacher asks the student to rank their progress on a simple scale for predetermined criteria. The scale uses easy to comprehend language, such as not yet and getting there, with respect to the level students feel they understand. The predetermined criteria include comprehension, strategies, higher-order thinking skills, and motivation. Each criteria has a set of simple questions to prompt a response from students.

Moving from selected response to constructed response can be done at varying levels of sophistication. Simple product assessments are a good place to start. Teachers can ask students to provide diagrams and illustrations to convey understanding of concepts. Assessments can include graphic organizers which are mental maps that represent skills such as sequencing, comparing, contrasting, and classifying. Examples of graphic organizers include concept maps and webs, Venn diagrams to display overlap of concepts, flowcharts to sequence events or classify objects into categories. In fact, the UbD tools we have been using are examples of graphic organizers.

From a quantitative reasoning perspective, we asked teachers to incorporate multiple mathematical representations of concepts. Consider the rule of four with respect to representations: verbal, graphic, tabular, and analytic (equation or formula). When presenting a STEM concept, provide or ask the students to generate a story concerning the concept within a real-world context (verbal), data in a table (tabular), a graph of the data (graphic), and an equation modeling the data (analytic) such as a curve of best fit. Matrices are also a great tool for organizing characteristics or facts, allowing students to organize their thinking.

Self-Assessment: My progress in quantitative reasoning (QR).				
Progress level	Not yet	Getting there	Really improved	Mastered
Comprehension: • Do you understand using QR to support your arguments? • Can you solve problems using QR? • Can you provide a data-informed argument for your conclusion?				
Strategies: • Do you use estimation and measure? • Do you use multiple representations?				
Higher-order thinking skills: • Do you make connections across STEM disciplines? • Can you draw conclusions based on data?				
Motivation: • Do you enjoy using QR in STEM? • Do you feel confident in the QR you can do?				

Figure 10. Self-assessment of progress. Adapted from Butler & McMunn (2006). A Teacher's Guide to Classroom Assessment: Understanding and Using Assessment to Improve Student Learning.

Consider a portfolio as a means of assessing a product. A portfolio is a purposeful integrated collection of student work showing effort, progress, or degree of proficiency. There are a variety of types of portfolios. A best-worlds portfolio provides evidence of mastery of learning goals. A memorabilia portfolio can be used for dispositional learning targets such as student attitudes, interest, and self-esteem. A growth portfolio places the emphasis on change, assisting students to focus on their own learning. A skills portfolio provides evidence of employability skills. Finally, an assessment portfolio indicates student growth toward or proficiency in a standard of learning.

Performance assessments go beyond products. They require a performance by the student which is viewed by an audience. The performance is judged according to pre-established criteria presented in a scoring rubric. Examples of performance assessment include oral presentations; debates, which are structured arguments where teams attack or defend the informed opinions of others; panel discussions where predetermined criteria are addressed; senior projects that include research papers, portfolios, and presentations to a panel; logs that provide documentary evidence of events and concise summaries of information (i.e. scientific log of an experiment or a reading log); journals where students record thoughts, observations, and questions or have written dialogue with others (i. e. record of what you learned today or what anxiety was raised by the lesson); and notebooks, which are a collection of all information pertinent to a particular topic. Logs, journals, and notebooks can be used to teach organizational skills, as a source of verifying completion of assignments, and documentary evidence for a grade.

Understanding by Design presents two types of performance assessments: academic prompts and performance tasks. An academic prompt is an open-ended question or problem that requires students to prepare a specific academic response. Students are expected to think critically and construct a response under exam conditions – time limit and resources limited to what they are allowed to bring to the assessment. The academic prompt may be secure, meaning as in an exam they are not provided criteria to be assessed in advance. However an academic prompt may not be secure, such as providing students the rubric that will be used to score the assessment in advance. The academic prompt problem is often ill-structured, requiring the student to develop a strategy to solve it, and divergent in that there is no single best answer. The academic prompt engages the student in analysis, synthesis, and evaluation of the problem, so scoring is subjective. This requires subjective judgment based scoring using a rubric with set criteria. While this rubric must be developed in advance of grading of the academic prompt, it can be shared with students in advance (unsecure) or withheld until after students complete (secure) the academic prompt.

The performance task has many of the same characteristics as the academic prompt. A performance task is divergent, requires subjective judgment, is open-ended, and its goal is to engage students in critical thinking about a problem. However, a performance task differs from an academic prompt in a number of important ways. First, the performance task problem is a complex challenge that mirrors the issues and problems faced by adults. Therefore the performance task is an authentic assessment, meaning it is a real-world problem or at least a simulation of a real-world problem. Second, a performance task is never secure; the students are given the rubric with scoring criteria in advance of the task. Third, a performance task requires the student to address an audience through a performance, not in an exam setting. The performance task should also allow a greater opportunity to personalize the task. In the QR STEM project we incorporated place-based education for precisely this goal of personalizing the task by making it connect to the student's place.

At this point we asked the QR STEM teachers to complete an UbD self-assessment of their use of a variety of sources of assessment. They were asked in the self-assessment to rate their use of the above assessment tools in their classroom as:

0 No Evidence of Use, 1 Infrequent Use, 2 Sporadic Use, 3 General Use, 4 Frequent Use, 5 Extensive Use. The QR STEM teachers indicated most frequent use fell in the middle of the continuum of assessment (Figure 7) – tests, quizzes, and observations. Use of performance tasks was often rated as infrequent or no evidence of use. We then asked them to align the priorities for their proposed units with the assessment methods, using the handout in Figure 11. The evidence for worth being familiar with priorities was paired with selected response and more traditional quiz assessments. The evidence for important to know and do priorities was paired with constructed response product assessments. While the evidence for enduring understanding priorities was paired with performance tasks which allow for complex, open-ended, authentic assessments. This drove home our expectation that the unit they would develop would be anchored by a performance task.

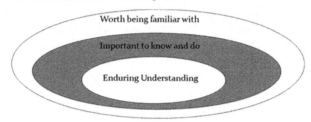

Collecting a Range of Evidence Activity

Determine a range of assessment evidence you may use related to the:
* Enduring understanding
* Topics important to know and do
* Worth being familiar with

Which assessment methods best fit the 3 categories?

Figure 11. Aligning assessment with level of content priority. Wiggins, G. & McTighe, J.(2005). Understanding by Design, Association for Supervision and Curriculum Development.

Quality assessment tasks encourage students to engage in higher-order thinking and require cognitive complexity. They target the upper levels of Bloom's Taxonomy which are analyzing, evaluating, and creating. They reflect the UbD six facets of understanding. These require students to engage in metacognitive activities such as self-regulation and self-awareness; literally they have to think about their thinking. Quality tasks have more than one right answer. Quality tasks move beyond promoting surface level learning about the big idea driving the unit; they promote a deep understanding of it. Quality assessment tasks also take into account four characteristics identified by Butler and McMunn:

• Appropriate: Is the task appropriate to the age level and preparedness of the students?

- Feasibility: Can the task actually be done in the time allotted or with the materials available?
- Authentic: Is the task motivating or engaging for students? Is it relevant to student's lives? Is it career-oriented?
- Inclusive: Does the task provide a learning entry point for diverse students? Does it address ideals such as equity, fairness, multicultural, learning style, multiple intelligences, and being culturally unbiased?

So how do teachers go about developing performance tasks that address all the issues above? UbD provides two approaches for developing performance tasks in which we engaged the QR STEM teachers: using the six facets of understanding to generate performance tasks assessing the enduring understandings of the unit and using the GRASPS technique to focus on engaging students through taking on roles. We will trace the PLC Cowboys first through using the six facets, then through implementing GRASPS, as they struggled with developing their performance task.

Performance Task – 6 Facets of Understanding

Recall the UbD six facets of understanding:

- ❖ Facet 1: Explanation – provide thorough, supported, and justifiable accounts of phenomena, facts, and data (theoretical, explain why)
- ❖ Facet 2: Interpretation – tell meaningful stories, offer apt translations, provide revealing historical or personal dimension to ideas and events, (personal, what does it mean to me)
- ❖ Facet 3: Application – effectively use and adapt what one knows in diverse contexts (pragmatic, how can I use it)
- ❖ Facet 4: Perspective – see points of view through critical eyes and ears, see the big picture (dispassionate, whose point of view)
- ❖ Facet 5: Empathy – find value in what others might find odd, alien, or implausible, perceive sensitivity on the basis of prior direct experience (passionate, what are you feeling)
- ❖ Facet 6: Self-knowledge – perceive personal style, prejudices, projections, and habits of mind that both shape and impede one's own understanding, be aware of what one does not understand (introspective, my prejudices)

We had already used the six facets to assist teachers in creating essential questions for the performance task. We now employed them to engage teachers in brainstorming assessment ideas for the performance task by asking them to complete another UbD design tool (Chapter 3 Appendix: Figure 21). The PLCs were to put their enduring understanding in the center of the array, then for each of the six facets brainstorm tasks through which students could demonstrate their understanding. The teachers' first question was if they had to provide a task for each of the six facets. We did not want them to feel that they had to artificially address a given facet if they did not see how it related to their desired understanding. So we did not require them to provide something for every facet. However, most of the PLCs did determine a task based on each of the facets.

To assist the teachers in brainstorming tasks, we provided two additional UbD handouts that supported the Brainstorming Assessment design tool. The first was a list of questioning for understanding stems for each facet (Chapter 3 Appendix: Figure 22) and the second was a list of performance verbs based on each facet (Chapter 3 Appendix: Figure 23). The PLC Cowboys began as all the PLCs did by placing their desired understanding in the center of the design tool: the complex interaction of population, affluence, technology, and environment. The PLC Cowboys selected explanation as the first facet they explored, running through the list of stem questions for explanation and using the action verbs for explanation to open up ideas about potential tasks. Teachers in the PLCs were at first vexed by believing they had to provide a response to every question stem on the handout. We assured them that this was just a brainstorming tool and they should use only those questions they felt fit their desired understanding. For the PLC Cowboys, the response to the question stems for explanation looked like this:

- *What is the key idea in the complex interaction of population, affluence, technology, and environment?* That increasing population growth requires increased resources, specifically energy resources. The push for affluence has a multiplying effect upon the desire for more energy. So we need alternative energy sources, but every energy resource comes with a cost, including an impact on the environment. Technology can improve energy production and provide renewable sources of energy, but can it offset the population and affluence factors?
- *What are examples of this complex interaction?* The current technological push for creating renewable resources that can supplement fossil fuel use, such as biofuels. But biofuels impact agricultural resources, creating a potential nexus between growing fuel stocks and food production. Having students play the Energy Wedge Game, where they select alternative energy resources to meet growing demand then consider the economic and environmental impacts, could be a task that would demonstrate understanding of the complex interaction.
- *What are the characteristics and parts of this complex interaction?* The complex interaction requires students to explore growth models for populations including linear, exponential, and logistic models; per capita consumption issues related to affluence; and environmental impacts such as climate change.
- *What caused the complex interaction? What are the effects of it?* The complex interaction is caused in part by increasing population and desire for increased affluence. The effects are a race to find technological solutions to provide increased energy resources, the limited resources available for those potential solutions, and the environmental impact of pursuing them.
- *How might we prove, confirm, justify the complex interaction?* Students could confirm the complex interaction by studying trends such as peak oil, population

growth, affluence change, and global environmental concerns such as climate change and sea water rise.

- *How is energy connected to environment?* Energy resources are natural resources, attaining them impacts the environment by exhausting those resources. Using them impacts the environment through pollution.
- *What might happen if we replace non-renewable resources with renewable energy resources?* Again having students consider the cost, both economically and environmentally, of switching from fossil fuels to a renewable energy resource. What renewable energy resources are sustainable for future energy needs?
- *What are common misconceptions about this complex interaction?* A common misconception is that we can meet future energy demands simply by increasing oil and coal production. Another misconception is that renewable energy comes without an environmental cost.
- *How did this come about? Why is this so?* An ever increasing population and a desire by third world countries to attain a higher standard of living are exceeding our capacity to provide energy. Technology has offset some of that demand, but can it continue to do so in the future?

The PLC Cowboys then examined the list of action verbs for the explanation facet. The performance task they were being asked to create requires the student to be actively engaged in constructing an enduring understanding of the complex interaction between energy and environment. This list of action verbs got them to think about what performances students could do that would demonstrate understanding. The PLC Cowboys proposed that students could do the following: model population growth and predict future energy needs; synthesize information on energy resources and environmental impact and show a connection between them; or they could build an exhibit that demonstrates the relationship. After considering the stem questions and action verbs for the explanation facet, the PLC Cowboys entered a task into the Explanation wedge of the Brainstorming Assessment Ideas design tool. They identified the potential task as: *Students will model the interaction of population growth with increased energy demand, then predict future energy resource use including issues of environmental costs and sustainability.*

So the PLC Cowboys now had a potential performance task that would address the explanation facet of understanding. They now repeated this process with each of the remaining five facets, considering the related question stems and action verbs to brainstorm potential tasks. Once the PLCs had completed one of the facets, they had already opened up ideas for some of the other facets. The result was a less formal discussion of individual questions and verbs, which was replaced with a more holistic discussion for each facet. A summary of the discussions for each facet is provided.

- Interpretation facet: The PLC Cowboys discussion of question stems for interpretation focused on what are the implications of this complex interaction and how does it relate to me or us? They wanted students to consider how the issue of energy resources and environmental impact would matter to them. Would they be driving electric cars in 10 years? Did they want wind turbines in their back yard? The action verbs led to actions such as: translate the global nature of the complex energy and environment relationship to your community; evaluate the energy resource question and critique current proposals for using a selected renewable energy source such as wind energy. Their entry in the Brainstorming Assessment design tool was: *Relate the proposed use of a renewable energy resource as part of the national energy strategy to how it impacts you and your place.*

- Application facet: The PLC Cowboys discussion of question stems for application focused on how we could use renewable energy resources to overcome future energy deficits due to reaching peak oil production? They wanted students to consider how renewable energy resources could fill the gap in energy needs and what the environmental impact of these choices would be. The action verbs led to actions such as: design a future energy policy that meets energy demands and accounts for environmental impact; test out different renewable resources as viable replacements for fossil fuels in transportation or generation of electricity. Their entry in the Brainstorming Assessment design tool was: *Play the energy wedge game with the goal of designing a future energy policy for the United States.*

- Perspective facet: The PLC Cowboys discussion of question stems for perspective focused on what are the different points of view about future energy resources and how might this look from the perspective of an environmentalist or petroleum engineer? They wanted students to consider the question of energy and environment from different perspectives. Wyoming is energy rich, with large coal deposits that drive the state's economy. But ranchers and outdoors enthusiasts have environmental concerns. So take the role of a rancher or coal miner and discuss the energy-environment nexus through their eyes. The action verbs led to actions such as: analyze the impact of renewable energy on the total energy picture from the perspective of an environmentalist; compare and contrast the views of an Exxon executive with an EPA Director on wind energy as a viable future energy resource. Their entry in the Brainstorming Assessment design tool was: *Student teams will debate the energy and environment nexus from different perspectives.*

- Empathy facet: The PLC Cowboys discussion of question stems for empathy focused on what would it be like to walk in the shoes of a third world citizen who desires to be more affluent and how might they feel about future energy resource allocations? They wanted students to consider the desire that we all have to improve our quality of living, the need for energy to increase economic opportunity, and the potential impact on third world countries of pursuing a given energy policy. The action verbs led to actions such as: assume the role of an educated third world or emerging economy (India or China) citizen, what are your concerns about energy availability? Imagine how they would respond to recommend future energy policies such as increasing biofuel production. Their entry in the Brainstorming Assessment design tool was: *Students will take on the role of a third world citizen and relate their view on the complex interaction of energy and environment as related to affluence.*

- Self-knowledge facet: The PLC Cowboys discussion of question stems for self-knowledge focused on what are my blind spots about the future of energy resources and their environmental impact and how are my views about this shaped by my prejudices? They wanted students to engage in self-reflection about how they have reached their current views on energy and environment. The action verbs led to actions such as: self-assess your current views on energy and environmental impact by reflecting on what is based in data and what is based on personal experience. Their entry in the Brainstorming Assessment design tool was: *Students will identify a misconception they held about the complex interaction between energy and environment and reflect on how they have developed a deeper understanding.*

Brainstorming assessment ideas through the six facets opened up the PLCs to the creation of engaging performance tasks. While separate potential tasks for each facet are presented, it does not mean that all of these tasks will be part of the unit. A unit for the QR STEM project could be anywhere from a week to a semester. Shorter duration units would have to select one of these tasks for the students to engage in or perhaps have a student select from one of the six, if the teacher is open to different performance tasks being conducted for the unit.

Performance Task – GRASPS

Some teachers in our project struggled with connecting the six facets to development of performance task. They found the GRASPS technique to be easier for them to use. We felt that having teachers go through both the six facets and GRASPS processes was important, so we delayed GRASPS until the teachers had brainstormed using the six facets. This ensured that the teachers were firmly focused on developing student's understanding.

GRASPS (Chapter 3 Appendix: Figure 24) is a design tool for developing a performance task with a focus on context and role playing. The acronym stands for the steps in the process which include creating: Goal, Role, Audience, Situation, Product-Performance-Purpose, and Standards-Criteria for Success.

The GRASPS design tool includes stem statements that a teacher can use to construct a scenario for a performance task. We had to tell teachers that they did not have to fill in all the blanks, but to use them as teasers for brainstorming. We encouraged them to select only one stem from each category or to make up their own stem. We also provided the teachers with two UbD handouts supporting the GRASPS design tool: Possible Student Roles and Audiences (Chapter 3 Appendix: Figure 25) and Possible Products and Performances (Chapter 3 Appendix: Figure 26).

With these design tools in hand, and having already gone through the process of brainstorming using the six facets, the teachers eagerly engaged in the GRASPS task. The PLC Cowboys had a lively discussion on constructing a task using GRASPS. Below is a summary of that discussion.

- Goal: The challenge is to understand the complex interaction between increasing global population, desire for increased affluence, the mitigating factor of technology, demand for energy resources, and the impact on the environment.
- Role: You are a scientist who has been assigned to one of the following research teams: population growth research, affluence and demand research, energy technology research, energy resource research, and environmental impact research.
- Audience: The target audience is an international panel of the United Nations Security Council (global scale body) and the Chamber of Commerce in your county (macro scale – place based). The UN bodies which will be represented on the international panel include the Commission on Population and Environment, the Commission on Science and Technology for Development, and the Commission on Sustainable Development.
- Situation: The challenge involves determining future energy resource use locally for your community as well as globally for the United Nations. You will be assigned to one of the five research teams and assume the role of either: local scientist focused on community impact, scientist focused on first world countries, scientist focused on emerging economy countries, or scientist focused on developing countries.
- Product, Performance, and Purpose: For your research team you will develop a study of current trends (i.e. population growth, affluence change, technology impact on energy production, energy resource development, or environmental impact), then develop future plans for energy resource development that account for environmental impact. The product will be a magazine article from each of the research teams reporting their findings and recommendations for the future of energy and its environmental impact. The article will be supported with visual displays such as graphs, maps, models, and photographs. The performance will be a debate between the research teams which is moderated by an expert panel of local energy and environment experts and chamber of commerce members.

- Standards and Criteria for Success: Your work will be judged through review of the expert panel and by the other research teams. The product and performance must meet the standards set within the Energy and Environment Rubic, which will be provided in advance of undertaking the project. Each research team must provide an analysis and predictions of trends in the areas of energy for transportation and production of electricity. The analysis must be data-based, providing quantitative (mathematical and statistical) arguments. Each team must also consider the environmental impact of meeting the future energy needs as related to their area of expertise.

The Standards and Criteria for Success component of GRASPS calls for the creation of a rubric. Most of our QR STEM teachers were very familiar with creating rubrics, so we did not focus extensively on rubric development in the project. However rubrics are essential to thinking like an assessor as is called for in Stage 2 of the Understanding by Design framework. So if teachers in your professional development program are not versed in creating rubrics then it is important to take the time to explore rubric development. We include here a brief discussion of rubrics.

UbD identifies the second question that assessors ask with respect to determining achievement as: What specific characteristics in student responses, products, or performances should we examine to determine the extent to which the desired results were achieved? This requires the creation of criteria, rubrics, and exemplars. A rubric is a criterion-based scoring guide for evaluating a product or performance along a continuum. A rubric consists of:

- Evaluative Criteria – qualities that must be met for work to measure up to a standard;
- Fixed Measurement Scale – often 4 or 5 levels;
- Indicators – descriptive terms for differentiating among degrees of understanding, proficiency, or quality.

Rubrics can be holistic or analytic. Holistic rubrics provide an overall impression of the elements of quality and performance levels in a student's work. Analytic rubrics divide a student's performance into two or more distinct dimensions, called criteria, and then judges each separately. For the QR STEM project we recommended development of an analytic rubric with criteria for understanding based on the six facets or Bloom's taxonomy, and criteria for performance. Rubrics can be generic or task-specific. Generic rubrics provide general criteria for a given performance area, such as a general problem solving rubric or a general rubric for understanding. Such rubrics can easily be found online, for example a search on Google for rubrics for understanding provided an extensive list of such rubrics, including one based on the six facets of understanding (Chapter 3 Appendix: Figure 27). Another example is the generic performance rubric created for the Delta Cooperative Model project (Chapter 3 Appendix: Figure 28).

The teachers were also encouraged to create task-specific rubrics that were designed for use with their unique performance task. Such rubrics are task dependent and so cannot be used to evaluate other performance tasks. A task-specific rubric for the PLC Cowboys would include specific criteria and descriptions related to the IPAT equation, stressing the interrelationships between the variables of population, affluence, technology, energy and environment.

We had the teachers peer review the generic and/or task-specific rubrics that they developed. An effective rubric has several key characteristics. First, it relates the specific task requirements to more general performance goals. Second, it discriminates among different degrees of understanding or proficiency according to significant features of the task. Third, it does not combine independent criteria in one column of the rubric. Fourth, all potential performances should fit somewhere within the rubric. Fifth, the rubric relies on descriptive language (what quality looks like) not comparative or value language to make distinctions. Sixth, the rubric avoids making the lowest score point sound bad, rather it describes novice or ineffective performance that needs to be addressed. Seventh, the rubric highlights judging impact of the performance as opposed to rewarding just process or effort.

We encouraged the PLCs to reflect back on the rubrics after they were used with their students. We urged them to use student anchors to improve the rubrics. This provided an opportunity to set standards that were based on student work, leading to improved consistency in judging student work. Student anchors also equip students to do more accurate and productive self-assessment.

The third question that UbD identified for assessors dealt with validity and reliability: Does the proposed evidence enable us to infer a student's knowledge, skill, or understanding? Inferring understanding from evidence requires the evidence be valid and reliable. Validity means did we measure what we meant to measure? Does the evidence indicate understanding of the expressed outcome? Are the performances appropriate to the understanding sought? UbD asks teachers to consider two key validity questions for an assessment task:

- Could a student do well on the performance task, but not demonstrate the understanding you are after?
- Could a student perform poorly on this task, but still have significant understanding of the ideas that they demonstrate in other ways?

Reliable assessments reveal a credible pattern, a clear trend. Reliability of the performance task is needed if it is to serve as more than just a snapshot of student performance. Reliability requires parallel assessments on the same concept using multiple assessment formats.

Understanding by Design Stage 3:

Plan Learning Experience and Instruction

The third QR STEM symposium moved the teachers into Stage 3 of Understanding by Design: Planning the Learning Experience and Instruction. This stage has two phases. Phase 1 is planning the learning experience. Phase 2 is exploring instructional techniques. The PLCs had determined what they wanted to accomplish (Stage 1) and how they would assess it (Stage 2), now we moved to thinking about who the learners are and what they will need to achieve the desired results (Stage 3). This is the first step in the design process where we leave what teachers want to address and move to what students will do. UbD Stage 3 asks three essential questions:

- Given the desired results and the performance tasks, what kinds of instructional approaches, resources, and experiences are required to achieve these goals?
- What do learners need, given the desired results?
- What is the best use of time in and out of class, given the performance goals?

We began the third symposium by having teachers share out their work on Stage 2, providing an opportunity for peer review of the performance task frameworks, continuum of assessments, and rubrics. We then engaged them in a variation of an UbD activity to explore the difference between engaging activities and effective activities. We assigned each of the PLCs to either discuss what it means for an activity to be engaging or what it means for an activity to be effective. They were provided the following focus questions, then given 10 minutes to come up with several characteristics of these two qualities of an activity.

Engaging Group: reach consensus within your PLC on what makes an activity engaging.

- When are students most fully engaged in/out of school?
- Under what conditions are learners most engaged?
- What makes them so engaged and what are the transferable elements from these exemplary cases?

Effective Group: reach consensus within your PLC on what makes an activity effective.

- When is student learning most effective?
- Under what conditions are learners most productive?
- What makes for the most effective learning and what are the transferable elements from these exemplary cases?

We drew a Venn Diagram on the board which had two overlapping circles, one representing engaging and one effective. We asked representatives from each of the PLCs to come to the board and enter an activity they use in teaching which elicited the characteristic they had been discussing. The effective circle included activities such as presentation of concept followed by student practice, work sheets for mastery, pop quizzes, and feedback with revision. The engaging circle included activities such as hands-on, real-world problem, personalizing problem for student, and group work. It was interesting to see which, if any, activities the teachers placed in the intersection of the Venn Diagram. What activities did they consider to be both engaging and effective? For surely the goal of the activities we choose to use with students should be both engaging and effective. We found that our teachers reflected what UbD found to be the characteristics of best designs, such as: clear goals based on a challenging task; hands-on approach; real-world applications; feedback systems that allow students to revise; personalized approach allowed to problem with multiple avenues to solution; focused reflection time; safe environment for taking risks; teacher as facilitator, student directed; and focused on big idea.

The UbD framework provides the WHERETO instructional planning tool (Chapter 3 Appendix: Figure 29) to reflect the key elements of designing tasks that are both engaging and effective WHERETO stands for:

- **W**here are we headed and Why?
- **H**ook the student and Hold their attention

- **E**quip the student with experiences, tools, knowledge
- **R**ethink big ideas, Reflect on progress, Revise work
- **E**valuate progress and self-assess
- **T**ailored to reflect individual talents, interest, style
- **O**rganized to optimize deep understanding

WHERETO can be used as a filter to determine curricular implementation. The task designer needs to ask: Where are we headed? The designer must make the goals of the activity clear to students, including what the overarching questions are. The designer must specify the desired performances and standards constituting achievement, including the final performance. Work must be purposeful from the students' perspective.

We began our teacher's work with the WHERETO tool by asking them to revisit their Stage 1 enduring understandings and essential questions and their Stage 2 assessment development with a focus on the performance task. UbD provides a design tool for each step of WHERETO. Let's walk through WHERETO with the PLC Cowboys.

The W in WHERETO

The W in WHERETO asks the question "Where are we headed and why?" Students should be aware of their performance obligations for the task. They should be able to answer the following questions with specificity and confidence as their work develops:

1. What will I have to understand by unit's end and what does understanding look like?
2. What are my final obligations? What knowledge, skill, tasks, and questions must I master to meet those obligations and demonstrate proficiency and understanding?
3. What resources are available to support my learning and performance?
4. What is my immediate task? How does it help me meet my overarching obligations?
5. How does today's work relate to what we did previously? What is most important about this work?
6. How should I allot my time? What has priority?
7. How will my final work be judged? What can I do to improve?

The W design tool was provided to the teachers to brainstorm on this aspect of WHERETO (Chapter 3 Appendix: Figure 30). The design tool asks the PLC Cowboys to clarify the goals, expectations, relevance and value, and diagnosis for their unit. A series of questions for each of these elements was provided to the PLC Cowboys, a summary of their responses is provided in the following exposition.

The goals for the PLC Cowboys unit will be presented on the first day of the unit. Where are we going in this unit? The goal is to develop an understanding of the complex interactions between population growth, desire for increased affluence, technology solutions, and impact on the environment. This will be explored through the topic of energy resources for the future. The PLC Cowboys had determined the NSTA (1996) and Common Core Mathematics Standards (2000) that the unit would address in Stage 1. The standards addressed will be shared with the students via a handout on connections of the unit to the overall course curriculum. What will students be learning? The students will be learning energy science, environmental science, and how to use quantitative reasoning to interpret and build models. They will also be learning to view STEM problems from an interdisciplinary perspective, where they bring biology, chemistry, earth science, physics, and mathematics to bear on a real-world problem.

What resources and learning experiences will help us get there? The STEM chapters of this text will provide significant resources for the students and teachers developing units with an energy and environment focus. The expectation, however, is that students will be involved in research related to the topic they are assigned, thus they are responsible for generating their own resources as well. The PLC Cowboys have developed a performance task which will serve as the primary learning experience.

The expectations for the PLC Cowboys unit is that they will complete the performance task, which includes researching their topic area, discovering trends, making predictions of future events, reporting out their findings through a magazine article, and completing a debate where they compare and contrast their area with the other areas. Students will be expected to demonstrate learning and understanding through the product of a magazine article and the performance of the debate, as well as a number of closed-form informal check and observation assessments. The informal checks will include the use of K-W-L charts, where students do quick responses to three questions: What do you know? What do you want to learn? What did you learn? The generic rubrics for understanding and performance will provide initial criteria and performance standards for the students. As student data are gathered, student anchors will be used to revise the generic rubrics into more task-specific rubrics.

What is the relevance and value of the unit? The unit will engage students in authentic real-world problem solving which requires them to take an interdisciplinary STEM approach. We need to move students out of the subject silos of science and mathematics, since in the real-world problems are addressed from interdisciplinary perspectives. The unit will also require students to use quantitative reasoning to provide data-based scientifically informed decisions, an important ability for citizens of a democracy. In addition, the topic of energy resources and its impact on environment is a grand challenge for the next generation; one they must be equipped to grapple with.

Diagnosis of students' prior knowledge and misconceptions will be conducted through a diagnostic quiz on energy, such as the National Geographic Great Energy Challenge quiz which students can take online (http:// http://environment. nationalgeographic.com/environment/energy/great-energy-challenge/energy-quiz/). Students will complete a short write on what they know about their assigned topic. For example for the population topic they would be asked to do a short write for

15 minutes on: What do you know about current trends in world population? What do you think are the consequences of the population trend on energy resources? On the environment? The short writes will be analyzed for student misconceptions and will provide data on which students can reflect concerning changes in their understanding upon completion of the unit. Students will also be surveyed on their learning styles and talents they bring to the performance task. For example, they would complete the online learning style quiz developed by Edutopia (http://www. edutopia.org/ multiple-intelligences-learning-styles-quiz).

The H in WHERETO

The H in WHERETO stands for techniques for hooking and holding students' attention. A hook can be an opening question that is provocative and engaging. The hook may or may not be the essential question, though we encouraged our teachers to make the essential questions into hooks when possible. The hook should instantly immerse students through prompting them to ask their own related questions. The hook is a problem, challenge, situation, or story that requires the student's wits, not just school knowledge. We asked our teachers to review their essential questions from Stage 1 and create engaging hooks from them. We then gave the teachers the UbD Hooking and Holding Students design tool (Chapter 3 Appendix: Figure 31), which provides a list of ideas that assist in brainstorming means of hooking and holding students attention.

The PLC Cowboys considered the list of ideas for hooking and holding attention. They began by developing provocative entry questions, such as: Will my next car be solar or wind powered? How much energy do I use each day? What is my carbon footprint? The PLC Cowboys also considered counterintuitive examples such as: About 1/3 of the energy that is sent from a power plant to your house actually arrives to light a bulb. What is going on here? These ideas are all phrased as personal experiences, which students often find more engaging. The PLC Cowboys considered a challenge to engage the students: What is the best source of renewable energy for the future – biofuels, wind, solar, other? They considered experiments where students had to predict an outcome: Determine how much energy is produced by a small solar panel, such as one that runs a solar toy car. Predict how big a solar panel would be required to provide energy for your school. The PLC Cowboys incorporated role-playing and simulation: You are a citizen of an emerging economy nation with dreams of a better standard of living. Argue your case for future energy resource allocation with a citizen of a leading industrialized country. They even considered using humor: Consider the following cartoons on climate change (Figure 12). What are the cartoons stating about climate change? What is your view on it? Create a cartoon of your own about climate change.

The goal of using hooks is to engage students. Hooks should be thought provocations using anomalies, weird facts, counterintuitive events, or mysteries. Hooks should provide experiential shocks that confront feelings and provide obstacles to overcome.

Hooks should allow for personal connections that engage students in pursuing a matter of interest to them. Hooks should allow students to bring different points of view to the problem, to look at a problem from multiple erspectives, and to shift perspectives.

Figure 12. Climate change humor. Mike Adams (2007). www.NaturalNews.com

The First E in WHERETO

The first E in WHERETO stand for equipping students to succeed through an integrated approach of experiential and inductive learning, direct instruction, and homework and out-of-class experiences. We provided teachers with the Equipping Students design tool (Chapter 3 Appendix: Figure 32) and asked them to brainstorm on how they would help students explore the big ideas, essential questions, and equip them to successfully engage in the performance task. The design tool provides three categories for equipping students:

- experiential and inductive learning which facilitates construction of meaning
- direct instruction which provides knowledge and skills that form a foundation for understanding
- homework and other out-of-class experiences that provide for mastery and connections

The PLC Cowboys began by discussing means of equipping students to engage in experiential and inductive learning. They selected some examples from the list of such activities provided by the design tool (Chapter 3 Appendix: Figure 33). The PLC Cowboys would equip students to achieve the desired understandings (Stage 1) through the research projects assigned in each topic. For example, the affluence research team would have to gather data on what nations are affluent, nations rising in affluence such as China and India, and third world nations. They would then have to relate increased affluence with increased resource demands, with a focus on energy resources. The students would engage in historic investigations of changing affluence so they could discuss trends. They would be involved in problem-based learning in determining the global impact of increased affluence; is there enough for everyone? They would also partake in place-based education by relating affluence to their place: How affluent is their community or county compared to nations seeking a better way of life or third world countries? Their expected performance includes engaging in creative expression and exploration of issues through writing a magazine article. Performance also includes the debate with teams from other topic areas which reflects elements of a Socratic seminar.

Direct instruction in the use of quantitative reasoning in the sciences will be provided for students to ensure data-based decision making. The PLC Cowboys will explicitly instruct students in the quantitative act, quantitative literacy, quantitative interpretation of models, and quantitative model building. This will be done by providing the students with QR vignettes that engage students in singular examples of using quantitative reasoning. Examples of vignettes are provided in Chapter 4. More extensive examples are also provided in Chapter 4.

The PLC Cowboys also discussed homework and other out-of class experiences that would equip students to succeed in the unit. They decided to scaffold the students' understanding by using graphic organizers such as the interdisciplinary graphic organizer in Figure 34 (Chapter 3 Appendix) . This graphic organizer would be used outside of class for students to organize information on interdisciplinary approaches to their enduring understanding and reflect on them. The vignettes for QR would provide possible homework problems. In addition, students would be asked to create a concept map that relates all the key components of their topic. They would provide students the opportunity to refine work by submitting drafts of their magazine articles and debate plans.

The R in WHERETO

The R in WHERETO represents the need to rethink, revise or refine, and reflect to build understanding. The likelihood of more sophisticated understanding depends on enticing and requiring the student to constantly rethink and reuse their concepts, points of view, and theories. The UbD design tool for this step of WHERETO asks teachers: How will you engage students in rethinking the big idea (Chapter 3 Appendix: Figure 35)? The PLC Cowboys had already built in an opportunity for students to revisit the big idea of the product, a magazine article, by engaging in a performance, the debate with other topic groups. For example, the debate will require the technology group to rethink their understanding in light of how it relates to the topics of population, affluence, energy, and environment.

The PLC Cowboys also built in an opportunity for the students to revise or refine their products and performances. Each of the topic teams will submit a draft of the magazine article to the editorial board, which consists of a representative from each of the topic teams and the lead editor, the teacher. The editorial board will review each topic teams' article, providing feedback and suggestions for improving the article. The topic teams will then resubmit the article, providing an explanation of how they addressed the editorial team's comments. To practice the performance, a mock debate will be held with the teacher as moderator. This will precede the actual debate, which will be performed in front of an expert panel consisting of teachers, community representatives, and scientists from local industries or colleges.

The reflect component of the R in WHERETO considers the cognitive science conception of metacognition. Developing understanding requires students to engage in self-assessment, self-awareness, and self-regulation. The PLC Cowboys incorporated a self-assessment task survey (Figure 13). This self-assessment would be completed once a week for the duration of the unit. If the self-assessment indicated a student was struggling, then a goal-setting conference would be held with student to get them back on track. In addition, the PLC Cowboys incorporated the K-W-L strategy as a means of self-assessment across the entire unit. Self-awareness of what students truly understand and where they have misconceptions will be challenged by the cooperative learning teams. The students will have to communicate their understanding to peers within their team. Self-regulation is the ability to step back from a problem and determine if the approach you are using is helping you get closer to your goal. The PLC Cowboys will facilitate self-regulation

Self-Assessment: My progress in the energy and environment unit (Put a check in the appropriate box)				
Progress level	Not yet	Getting there	Really improved	Mastered
Comprehension: •Do you understand the concept? •Can you solve problems using the concept? •Can you explain the concept to others?				
Strategies: •Do you use quantitative reasoning? •Do you use interdisciplinary approaches?				
Higher-order Thinking Skills: •Do you make connections? •Do you make judgments?				
Motivation: •Do you enjoy exploring energy and environment? •Do you feel confident in science and math you can do?				

Figure 13. Student self-assessment of progress. Adapted from Butler & McMunn (2006).
A Teacher's Guide to Classroom Assessment: Understanding and Using Assessment to
Improve Student Learning.

through teacher observation of groups as they work on their task. The teachers will reserve the right to ask three questions at any time:

- What are you doing?
- Why are you doing it?

- How is it helping you get closer to your goal?

These are question used by Schoenfeld (1992) to elicit appropriate problem solving behaviors in mathematics. Students will be told to expect these questions at any time and to be prepared to respond to them. We impressed upon the teachers the importance of having the enduring understanding recur within the task. Students should have the opportunity to rethink, revise or refine, and reflect through related but dissimilar experiences, shifts in perspective, or using contrasting theoretical approaches. The PLC Cowboy tasks incorporate these devices.

The Second E in WHERETO

The second E in WHERETO stands for encourage self-evaluation. This step is strongly connected to the R step we just discussed, and as such we have already discussed some self-evaluation methods that the PLC Cowboys are using. Developing self-understanding is one of the most important facets of understanding, which includes the ability to self-monitor progress and engage in self-adjustment to improve understanding. The UbD design tool for Encouraging Self-evaluation (Chapter 3 Appendix: Figure 36) is a series of question stems that can be used as prompts to guide student self-evaluation and reflection. The PLC Cowboys completed the question stems for their unit, providing the following list of questions for students:

- What do you really understand about the complex interactions in the IPAT model?
- What questions or uncertainties do you still have about the IPAT model?
- What was most effective and least effective in helping you develop on understanding of the topic in IPAT that you were assigned?
- How could you further improve your understanding of the IPAT model?
- What are your strengths and deficiencies in understanding the impact of energy choices on environment?
- How difficult was understanding the complex interactions in IPAT for you?
- How does your preferred learning style influence your engagement in the IPAT unit?
- What would you do differently next time with respect to making your energy resource choices?
- What are you most proud of and most disappointed in with respect to the IPAT unit? Why?
- What grade or score do you deserve on the magazine article and debate for the unit? Why?
- How does what you learned in the IPAT unit connect to other learnings in this class? In other classes you are taking?
- How has what you've learned about the interaction of energy and environment changed your thinking?
- How does what you've learned about IPAT relate to your present place and your future? The global place and future?

- What follow-up work is needed for you to develop a deeper understanding of energy and environment issues?

We finished our discussion of encouraging self-assessment by asking teachers to share ideas on how they did it. We then summarized the list of ideas and added others recommended by UbD and other resources. Here is our accumulated list of ideas:

- One-minute essay: So what have we concluded? What remains unresolved?
- Self-assessment as part of performance task
- Postscript where students confess to what they do not understand
- Peer review followed by self-assessment
- Pre-survey of burning questions, closure on how well they are addressed
- Explicitly indicate when beneficial learning strategies and relevant habits of mind are used
- Videotape vignettes of successful teaching episodes to share with students
- Case method or problem-based learning with open follow-up unit where students can frame and pursue inquiry
- Student self-profile of strength and weaknesses as learners

The T in WHERETO

The T in WHERETO stands for tailoring the design for diverse learners. This step involves differentiating instruction in terms of content, process, and product. Differentiating content addresses the question: How can content be differentiated to allow diverse learners to engage? Differentiating process asks: How can the process engage diverse learners with different learning styles? While differentiating product inquires: How can the product be varied to provide choices for students? UbD provides guidance for differentiating instruction across the three Understanding by Design stages. Tailoring instruction in Stage 1 does not affect the enduring understanding. The enduring understanding must remain constant for all students, as is reflected in national standards call for STEM for all students. However, the essential questions can be varied to accommodate diverse learners and knowledge and skills elements can be tailored to the needs of the students. Using diagnostic assessments like those proposed by the PLC Cowboys in Stage 2 can lead to adjustments in essential questions and foundational skills that address student deficiencies.

Tailoring instruction in Stage 2 entails selecting assessment options that provide students with appropriate choices of products and performances. The PLC Cowboys ensured a wide variety of assessments across the continuum of assessment options, which provides students with diverse abilities and learning styles multiple opportunities to show what they know and understand. The PLC Cowboys also included both a product and performance task, allowing for student diversity in learning style and preference. Another strategy for diversifying assessment would be to allow students to select the product or performance that they will complete to demonstrate understanding. In any case, while the performance task might change, the rubric for evaluating the task should not. It is important to maintain a common criteria for scoring student understanding.

In Stage 3 tailoring instruction can be done in a variety of ways. First, a variety of resources at different levels can be provided for students. For example, the PLC Cowboys could provide background science articles which are written at different reading levels. Second, the resources and directed instruction components of the unit should address multiple learning modalities. The PLC Cowboys discussed presenting material in three modalities: orally, visually, and in writing. Third, the instruction should address differences in learning styles and achievement levels. The PLC Cowboys are conducting a learning style and preference inventory which will then guide instructional methods and resource selection. Finally, students can be allowed options on how they work and how they communicate. While the PLC Cowboys will require cooperative groups, they will also include individual assessment items.

We provided teachers the UbD Tailoring Design for Diverse Learners design tool (Chapter 3 Appendix: Figure 37) and gave the PLCs time to brainstorm ideas for differentiating instruction. The design tool provides options for differentiating across content, process, and product. This led to a lively discussion by the teachers of both methods for differentiating instruction and the challenge of managing differentiation. The PLC Cowboys responses on content, process, and product differentiation are provided above in the discussion of tailoring by UbD stage.

The O in WHERETO

The O in WHERETO stands for organize for optimal assessment. The typical sequence of marching through content in a textbook is rarely the best choice for engagement or understanding. This results in a linear view of learning, where the student builds up component parts before seeing the big picture of how they go together. UbD proposes a constant movement back and forth between whole-part-whole and learning-doing-reflecting. An analogy for this is how students learn to use a cell phone or an I-pod. The coverage method used with textbooks would require them to carefully read the owner's manual, mastering each of the sub-skills needed to do specific operations, then making their first real call upon completion of the manual. In fact we know that students and adults begin by making the phone call, experimenting on how to save a phone number, sending a text message, or getting online. The point is they start with the whole, then move to parts when they have a task they wish to complete. So teachers should organize their instruction around enduring understandings and turn students loose on those understanding on day one. Problem-based learning, case methods, simulations to stimulate students, authentic learning, place-based education, and interdisciplinary STEM approaches are all means of moving towards whole-part-whole interactions. It is essential to immerse learners early on in intriguing issues, problems, situations, and experiences. Postpone teaching definitions, rules, and theories until they are needed to make sense of the experience. Teach for understanding by addressing the Why and What questions early and often.

The UbD Organizing the Learning design tool (Chapter 3 Appendix: Figure 38) focuses on the organization and sequence of design. Teachers are asked to consider two broad organizational patterns: Logic of Coverage versus Logic of Uncoverage. Coverage asks: What is most appropriately and effectively covered in a linear and didactic fashion? While uncoverage asks: What is most appropriately and effectively "uncovered" in an inductive, inquiry-oriented, experiential manner? This design tool elicited a lively discussion from the teachers as well. The issue of time to cover all the required content was clearly on the minds of the teachers. They asked, "I would love to incorporate more performance tasks in my classroom, but how do I find the time when the school district requires us to cover so much of the text?"

We understand the pressure that teachers are under to cover material for the standardized tests. At this point, it was not convincing teachers about the validity of uncoverage, but the practicality of it with respect to time. The teachers in QR STEM were excited about introducing a unit with a performance task as a focus. The UbD design tool was used to engage them in a discussion of when coverage was OK and when it was important to uncover. Since instructional time was the major concern we began by asking them how often they could squeeze in a performance task. Once a year? Once a semester? More? We wanted to get them to implement at least one performance task in the next year, so they would get a taste for it. We then reiterated that performance tasks should only be used for assessing enduring understandings, and they should identify no more than three enduring understandings for any given chapter in their text. So we are talking about creating only a few performance tasks per year. We found that our teachers in the QR STEM project who tested the water with one performance task were hooked. They would incorporate elements of UbD in their lessons and develop additional performance tasks.

The culminating effort for organizing for optimal effectiveness was to develop a learning sequence for the unit. The PLCs created a chronological list laying out the sequence of teaching and learning, with elements of WHERETO indicated. This sequence was then translated on to a calendar for the unit. Some units were done in a contiguous week to two week block. Other units were scheduled one day a week for multiple weeks, often on a laboratory or block scheduling day. We left the scheduling up to the teachers so they could fit the unit into their master plan for the semester. We only required that the unit be a multiple instructional day unit that was a minimum of three days.

Instructional Techniques

We finish this chapter with a discussion of our goals for introducing teachers to the Understanding by Design framework. We wanted the QR STEM project to move teachers beyond teaching for knowledge to teaching for understanding. We wanted this understanding to be from an interdisciplinary perspective, to be driven by authentic real-world place-based problems, and to incorporate quantitative reasoning supporting data-based and scientifically literate arguments. We also wanted to teach teachers to fish (create performance tasks), not give them a fish (hand them activities). The UbD framework was perfect for achieving these goals.

We wanted to change instructional techniques used by teachers in QR STEM from what UbD calls coverage to uncoverage. Coverage does not correlate with success in learning. There is simply too much material to teach in STEM and STEM knowledge is growing exponentially. Teachers have to make choices. We would like these choices to be based not on coverage of a textbook, but on enduring understandings. The irony of coverage lies within the egocentric fallacy: I taught it, so they learned it. This leads to the teacher lament: "I would like to go into greater depth, but I have to cover the content." UbD identifies a number of coverage concerns which are summarized in the list below:

- Learner's perspective: everything appears of equal value, facts to be memorized with no hierarchy, priority, or connected meaning;
- Textbooks cover up understanding: provide polished finished version of understanding leading students to see content as facts not concepts;
- Enduring understandings cannot be covered, they must be experienced and uncovered;
- Coverage leads students to believe there is only one official viewpoint to be memorized and recalled;
- Expert knowledge is the result of trail and error, inquiry, and argument – student's must struggle with enduring understandings, find issues, problems, gaps, perplexing questions, inconsistencies.

UbD also discusses issues of coverage versus breadth. Breadth implies extensions, variety, and connections are needed to relate disparate facts and ideas. Textbooks organize and summarize knowledge but mask depth. Without the fluid and flexible knowledge of how and why things work brought on by studying something in depth, one cannot accomplish real-world goals. Student misconceptions can be created by instruction that permits single representations for a concept to remain unchallenged. We must avoid overly simplistic and inquiry-ending coverage. Direct instruction has a place in the classroom for mastery of skills and knowledge, but we want teachers to move to a constructivist pedagogy when teaching for understanding.

Formative assessment is an essential aspect of uncoverage in teaching. We have discussed a variety of informal assessment techniques in our UbD Stage 2 presentation. We want to emphasize here that formative assessment should focus on providing feedback to students as they uncover knowledge, not on providing fodder for grading. The formative assessment cycle (Figure 14) proposed by Butler and McMunn (2006) clearly reflects the UbD stages of identifying enduring understandings, assessment, and planning learning.

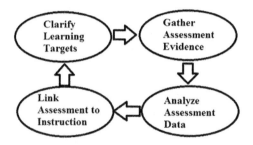

Figure 14. Formative assessment cycle. Adapted from Butler & McMunn (2006). A Teacher's Guide to Classroom Assessment: Understanding and Using Assessment to Improve Student Learning.

We have referred to the UbD six facets of understanding in Stages 1 and 2. We finish this chapter by summarizing the six facets relationship to instructional techniques (Figure 15). UbD recasts the facets as prompts for developing learning activities.

- What is the theory behind the statement of a big idea?
- What can you do with this knowledge?
- Are there other points of view besides the one expressed in the text? What are the critics or skeptics views?
- What would it feel like to think that way?
- Which of my beliefs or prejudices could be making it hard for me to believe or question this statement?

6 Facets	Facets Definition	Instructional Techniques
Explanation	Build, test, and verify theories	Problem-based learning
Interpretation	Build own interpretations, translations, and narratives	Oral history, literary analysis, case method, Socratic seminar
Application	Apply to real situations	Real or simulated tasks
Perspective	Take multiple points of view on same issue	Study even through different texts, challenge assumptions, role play
Empathy	Develop openness for other experiences and worldviews	Direct experience with ideas, recreate different characters simulating past events and attitudes
Self-knowledge	Ongoing self-assessment of what and how we know	Self-assessment and self-adjustment as key components

Figure 15. UbD six facets of understanding and instructional techniques. Adapted from Understanding by Design (Wiggins & McTighe) (2005).

REFERENCES

Ausubel, J. H. (1996). Can technology spare the earth. *American Scientist, 84*, 166–178.

Becker, J. (2004). Making sustainable development evaluation work. *Sustainable Development, 12*, 200–211.

Butler, S. M., & McMunn, N. D. (2006). *A teacher's guide to classroom assessment: Understanding and using assessment to improve student learning.* Indianapolis, IN: Jossey-Bass.

Chertow, M. R. (2001). The IPAT equation and its variants: Changing views of technology and environmental impact. *Journal of Industrial Ecology, 4*, 13–29.

DePaolo, D. J., & Orr, F. M. (2008). Geoscience research for our energy future. *Physics Today, 61*, 46–51.

Dewey, J. (1933). *How we think: A restatement of the relation of reflective thinking to the educative process.* Boston, MA: Heath.

Ehrlich, P., & Holdren, J. (1971). Impact of population growth. *Science, 171*, 1212–1217.

Harvard-Smithsonian Center for Astrophysics. (1997). *Minds of our own.* Annenberg Learner. http://learner.org/resources/series26.html

Hilbert, D. (1901). *Problemes mathematiques.*

National Research Council (NRC). (2001). *Grand challenges in environmental sciences.* Washington, DC: National Academy Press.

National Research Council. (2005). *Creating a disaster resilient America: Grand challenges in science and technology: Summary of a workshop.* Washington, DC: National Academy Press.

National Science Teachers Association. (1996). *Pathways to science education standards.* Arlington, VA: Author.

National Council of Teachers of Mathematics. (2000). *Principles and standards for school mathematics.* Reston, VA: NCTM.

Omenn, G. S. (2006). Grand challenges and great opportunities in science, technology, and public policy. *Science, 314*, 1696–1704.

Rios-Velazquez, C., Robles-Suarez, R., Gonzalez-Negron, A. J., & Baez-Santos, I. (2006). The delta cooperative model: a dynamic and innovative team-work activity to develop research skills in microbiology. *Journal of Microbiology & Biology Education, 7*, 20–27.

Schellnhuber, H.J., & Sahagian, D. (2002). The twenty-three GAIM questions. *Global Change Newsletter, 49*, 20–21.

Schoenfeld, A. H. (1992). Learning to think mathematically: Problem solving, metacognition, and sense making in mathematics. In D. Grouws (Ed.), *Handbook for research on Mathematics teaching and learning* (pp. 334–370). New York, NY: MacMillan.

Solomon, M. R. (1983). The role of products as social stimuli: A symbolic interactionism perspective. *Journal of Consumer Research, 10*, 319–329.

Steffen, W., Sanderson, A., Tyson, P. D., Jäger, J., Matson, P. A., Moore III, B., ... Wasson, RJ. (2004). *Global change and the earth system: A planet under pressure.* New York: Springer.

Varmus, H., Klausner, R., Zerhouni, E., Acharya, T., Daar, A. S., & Singer, P. A. (2003). Grand Challenges in Global Health. *Science, 302*(5644), 398–399.

Wiggins, G. P., & McTighe, J. (2005). *Understanding by design.* Ascd.

UNDERSTANDING BY DESIGN TEMPLATES

This appendix includes Understanding by Design (UbD) templates which the QR STEM project used with teachers in developing an energy and environment performance task.

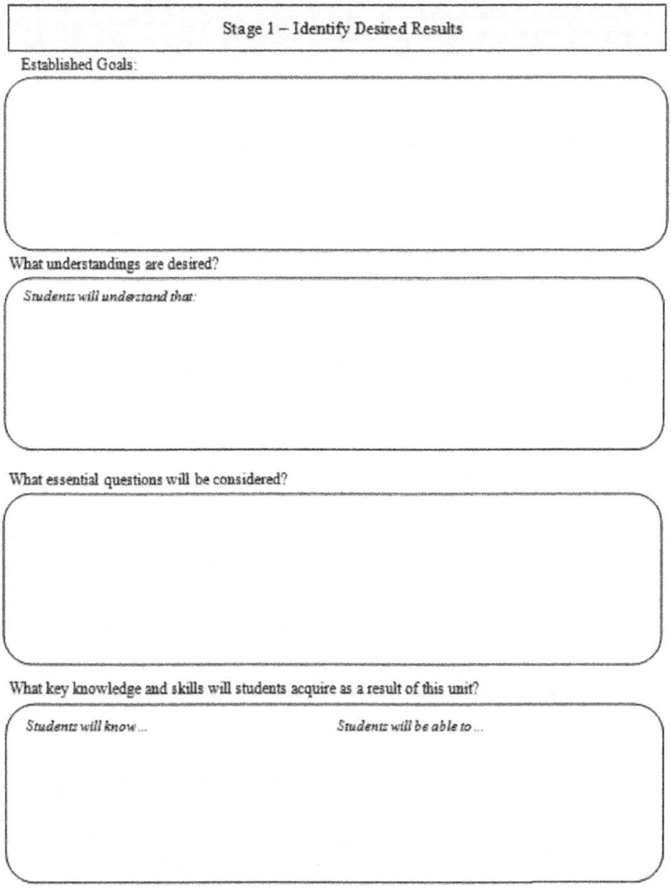

Stage 1 – Identify Desired Results

Established Goals:

What understandings are desired?

Students will understand that:

What essential questions will be considered?

What key knowledge and skills will students acquire as a result of this unit?

Students will know ...   *Students will be able to ...*

Figure 16. Identify Desired Results.

Structure of Knowledge

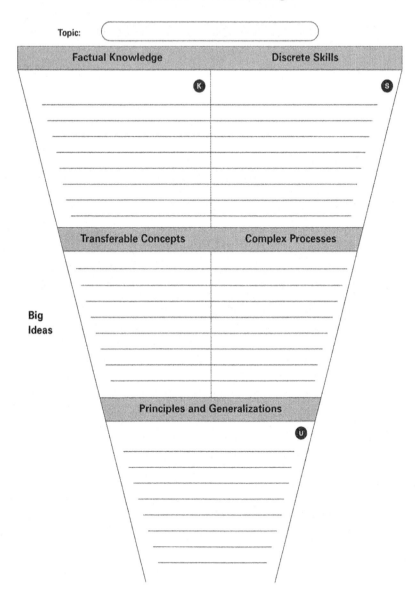

Figure 17. Structure of knowledge.

Clarifying Content Priorities

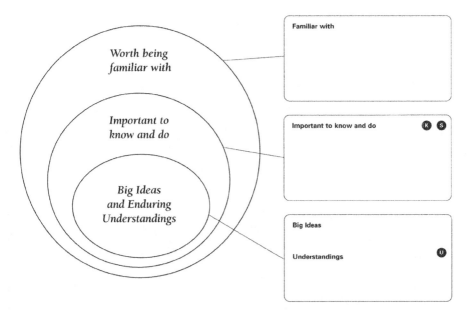

Figure 18. Clarifying content priorities.

Facet One: Explanation	Behavior or Action		Process or Product	
1. Demonstrate		by		.
2. Describe		by		.
3. Justify		by		.
4. Model		by		.
5. Prove		by		.
6. Show that		by		.

Facet Two: Interpretation	Behavior or Action		Process or Product	
1. Create analogies for		by		.
2. Critique		by		.
3. Evaluate		by		.
4. Illustrate		by		.
5. Predict		by		.
6. Translate		by		.

Facet Three: Application	Behavior or Action		Process or Product	
1. Adapt		by		.
2. Build		by		.
3. Design		by		.
4. Invent		by		.
5. Propose		by		.
6. Test		by		.

Facet Four: Perspective	Behavior or Action		Process or Product	
1. Argue for or against		by		.
2. Compare and contrast		by		.
3. Describe conflicting view point		by		.
4. Debate		by		.
5. Assess reasons for characters differing in their attitudes about		by		.

Facet Five: Empathy	Behavior or Action		Process or Product	
1. Assume the role of		by		.
2. Imagine you are		by		.
3. Recreate		by		.
4. Role-play		by		.
5. Simulate		by		.

Facet Six: Self-Knowledge	Behavior or Action		Process or Product	
1. Demonstrate your awareness of		by		.
2. Prove you realize		by		.
3. Confirm you recognize		by		.
4. Self-assess your ability to		by		.
5. Monitor your comprehension of		by		.

Figure 19. Six facets and essential questions.

Identifying Essential Questions and Understandings
Design Tool with Prompts

Use one or more of the following questions to filter topics or big ideas to identify possible essential questions and desired understandings.

Topics and Big Ideas:

What essential questions are raised by this idea or topic?
What, *specifically*, about the idea or topic do you
want students to come to understand?

Why study _____? So what?

What makes the study of _____ universal?

If the unit on _____ is a story, what's the moral of the story?

What's the Big Idea implied in the skill or process of _____?

What larger concept, issue, or problem underlies _____?

What couldn't we do if we didn't understand _____?

How is _____ used and applied in the larger world?

What is a real-world insight about _____?

What is the value of studying _____?

Essential Questions: Q

Understandings: U

Figure 20. Essential questions and understandings.

Brainstorming Assessment Ideas
Using the Six Facets of Understanding

Use the six facets of understanding to generate possible ways in which students might reveal understanding.

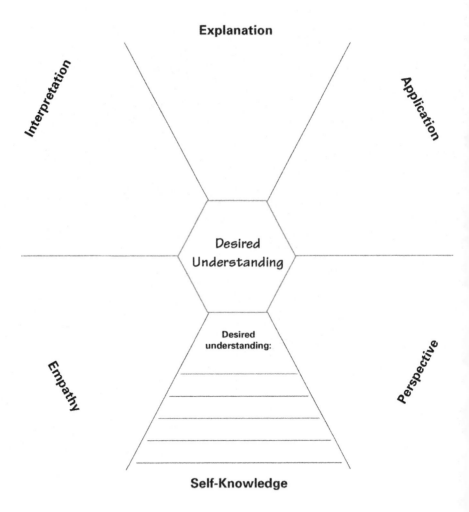

Figure 21. Six facets assessment ideas.

Questioning for Understanding

Explanation

What is the key idea in _____?
What are examples of_____?
What are the characteristics and parts of_____?
What caused _____? What are the effects of _____?
How might we prove, confirm, justify_____?
How is _____ connected to _____?
What might happen if _____?
What are common misconceptions about _____?
How did this come about? Why is this so?

Interpretation

What is the meaning of _____?
What are the implications of _____?
What does _____ reveal about_____?
How is _____ like_____ (analogy or metaphor)?
How does _____ relate to me or us?
So what? Why does it matter?

Application

How is _____ applied in the larger world?
How might _____ help us to _____?
How could we use _____ to overcome _____?
How and when can we use this (knowledge or process)?

Perspective

What are different points of view about _____?
How might this look from_____'s perspective?
How is _____ similar to or different from _____?
What are other possible reactions to _____?
What are the strengths and weaknesses of _____?
What are the limits of_____?
What is the evidence for _____?
Is the evidence reliable? sufficient?

Empathy

What would it be like to walk in _____'s shoes?
How might _____ feel about _____?
How might we reach an understanding about _____?
What was _____ trying to make us feel and see?

Self-Knowledge

How do I know _____?
What are the limits of my knowledge about _____?
What are my "blind spots" about _____?
How can I best show _____?
How are my views about _____ shaped by _____
(experiences, habits, prejudices, style)?
What are my strengths and weaknesses in _____?

Figure 22. Questioning for understanding.

Performance Verbs Based on the Six Facets of Understanding

Consider the following performance verbs when planning possible ways in which students may demonstrate their understanding. (See the design tool on the next page.)

explain
demonstrate
derive
describe
design
exhibit
express
induce
instruct
justify
model
predict
prove
show
synthesize
teach

interpret
analogies (create)
critique
document
evaluate
illustrate
judge
make meaning of
make sense of
metaphors (provide)
read between the lines
represent
tell a story of
translate

apply
adapt
build
create
de-bug
decide
design
exhibit
invent
perform
produce
propose
solve
test
use

perspective
analyze
argue
compare
contrast
criticize
infer

empathy
assume role of
believe
be like
be open to
consider
imagine
relate
role-play

self-knowledge
be aware of
realize
recognize
reflect
self-assess

Figure 23. Performance Verbs.

Constructing a Performance Task Scenario Using GRASPS

Consider the following set of stem statements as you construct a scenario for a performance task. Refer to the previous idea sheets to help you brainstorm possible scenarios. (Note: These are idea starters. Resist the urge to fill in all of the blanks.)

Goal:

- Your task is_____
- The goal is to _____
- The problem or challenge is _____
- The obstacles to overcome are _____

Role:

- You are _____
- You have been asked to _____
- Your job is _____

Audience:

- Your clients are _____
- The target audience is _____
- You need to convince _____

Situation:

- The context you find yourself in is _____
- The challenge involves dealing with _____

Product, Performance, and Purpose:

- You will create a _____
  in order to _____
- You need to develop _____
  so that _____

Standards and Criteria for Success:

- Your performance needs to _____
- Your work will be judged by _____
- Your product must meet the following standards: _____
- A successful result will _____

Figure 24. Grasps.

Possible Student Roles and Audiences

KEY ◯ = ROLES and ☐ = AUDIENCES

◯ ☐ actor
◯ ☐ advertiser
◯ ☐ artist/illustrator
◯ ☐ author
◯ ☐ biographer
◯ ☐ board member
◯ ☐ boss
◯ ☐ Boy/Girl Scout
◯ ☐ businessperson
◯ ☐ candidate
◯ ☐ carpenter
◯ ☐ cartoon character
◯ ☐ cartoonist
◯ ☐ caterer
◯ ☐ celebrity
◯ ☐ CEO
◯ ☐ chairperson
◯ ☐ chef
◯ ☐ choreographer
◯ ☐ coach
◯ ☐ community member
◯ ☐ composer
◯ ☐ client/customer
◯ ☐ construction worker
◯ ☐ dancer
◯ ☐ designer
◯ ☐ detective
◯ ☐ editor
◯ ☐ elected official
◯ ☐ embassy staff
◯ ☐ engineer
◯ ☐ eyewitness

◯ ☐ family member
◯ ☐ farmer
◯ ☐ filmmaker
◯ ☐ firefighter
◯ ☐ forest ranger
◯ ☐ friend
◯ ☐ geologist
◯ ☐ government official
◯ ☐ historian
◯ ☐ historical figure
◯ ☐ illustrator
◯ ☐ intern
◯ ☐ interviewer
◯ ☐ inventor
◯ ☐ judge
◯ ☐ jury
◯ ☐ lawyer
◯ ☐ library patron
◯ ☐ literary critic
◯ ☐ lobbyist
◯ ☐ meteorologist
◯ ☐ museum director/
　　 curator
◯ ☐ museum goer
◯ ☐ neighbor
◯ ☐ newscaster
◯ ☐ novelist
◯ ☐ nutritionist
◯ ☐ observer
◯ ☐ panelist
◯ ☐ parent
◯ ☐ park ranger
◯ ☐ pen pal

◯ ☐ photographer
◯ ☐ pilot
◯ ☐ playwright
◯ ☐ poet
◯ ☐ police officer
◯ ☐ pollster
◯ ☐ radio listener
◯ ☐ reader
◯ ☐ reporter
◯ ☐ researcher
◯ ☐ reviewer
◯ ☐ sailor
◯ ☐ school official
◯ ☐ scientist
◯ ☐ ship's captain
◯ ☐ social scientist
◯ ☐ social worker
◯ ☐ statistician
◯ ☐ storyteller
◯ ☐ student
◯ ☐ taxi driver
◯ ☐ teacher
◯ ☐ tour guide
◯ ☐ trainer
◯ ☐ travel agent
◯ ☐ traveler
◯ ☐ tutor
◯ ☐ t.v. viewer
◯ ☐ t.v. or movie
　　 character
◯ ☐ visitor
◯ ☐ Web site designer
◯ ☐ zookeeper

Figure 25. Roles and Audiences.

Possible Products and Performances

What student products and performances will provide appropriate evidence of understanding and proficiency? The following lists offer possibilities. (Remember that student products and performances should be framed by an explicit purpose or goal and an identified audience.)

Written	Oral	Visual
O advertisement	O audiotape	O advertisement
O biography	O conversation	O banner
O book report or review	O debate	O cartoon
O brochure	O discussion	O collage
O collection	O dramatic reading	O computer graphic
O crossword puzzle	O dramatization	O data display
O editorial	O interview	O design
O essay	O oral presentation	O diagram
O experiment record	O oral report	O diorama
O historical fiction	O poetry reading	O display
O journal	O puppet show	O drawing
O lab report	O radio script	O filmstrip
O letter	O rap	O flyer
O log	O skit	O game
O magazine article	O song	O graph
O memo	O speech	O map
O newscast	O teach a lesson	O model
O newspaper article		O painting
O play		O photograph
O poem		O poster
O position paper		O PowerPoint show
O proposal		O questionnaire
O research report		O scrapbook
O script		O sculpture
O story	Other:	O slide show
O test	O _____	O storyboard
O Web site	O _____	O videotape
		O Web site

Figure 26. Products and performances.

Explanation	Interpretation	Application	Perspective	Empathy	Self-Knowledge
Sophisticated: an unusually thorough, elegant, and inventive account (model, theory, or explanation); fully supported, verified, and justified; deep and broad; goes well beyond the information given.	Profound: a powerful and illuminating interpretation and analysis of the importance/meaning/significance; tells a rich and insightful story; provides a rich history or context; sees deeply and incisively any ironies in the different interpretations.	Masterful: fluent, flexible, and efficient; able to use knowledge and skill and adjust understandings well in novel, diverse, and difficult contexts.	Insightful: a penetrating and novel viewpoint; effectively critiques and encompasses other plausible perspectives; takes a long and dispassionate, critical view of the issues involved.	Mature: disposed and able to see and feel what others see and feel; unusually open to and willing to seek out the odd, alien, or different.	Wise: deeply aware of the boundaries of one's own and others' understanding; able to recognize his prejudices and projections; has integrity – able and willing to act on what one understands.
In-depth: an atypical and revealing account, going beyond what is obvious or what was explicitly taught; makes subtle connections; well supported by argument and evidence; novel thinking displayed.	Revealing: a nuanced interpretation and analysis of the importance/meaning/significance; tells an insightful story; provides a telling history or context; sees subtle differences, levels, and ironies in diverse interpretations.	Skilled: competent in using knowledge and skill and adapting understanding in a variety of appropriate and demanding contexts.	Thorough: a revealing and coordinated critical view; makes own view more plausible by considering the plausibility of other perspectives; makes apt criticisms, discriminations, and qualifications.	Sensitive: disposed to see and feel what others see and feel; open to the unfamiliar and different.	Circumspect: aware of one's ignorance and that of others; aware of one's prejudices; knows the strengths and limits of one's understanding.
Developed: an account that reflects some in-depth and personalized ideas; the student is making the work her own, going beyond the given – there is some "reading between the lines"; account has limited support/argument/data or sweeping generalizations. There is a theory here, but insufficient or inadequate argument or evidence.	Perspective: a helpful interpretation or analysis of the importance/meaning/significance; tells a clear and instructive story; provides a useful history or context; sees different levels of interpretation.	Able: able to perform well with knowledge and skill in a few key contexts, with a limited repertoire, flexibility, or adaptability to diverse contexts.	Considered: a reasonably critical and comprehensive look at all the points of view in the context of one's own; makes clear that there is plausibility to other points of view.	Aware: knows and feels what others see and feel differently; somewhat able to empathize with others; has difficulty making sense of odd or alien views.	Thoughtful: generally aware of what is and is not understood; aware of how prejudice and projection can occur without awareness and shape one's views.
Intuitive: an incomplete account but with apt and insightful ideas; extends and deepens some of what was learned; some "reading between the lines"; account has limited support/argument/data or sweeping generalizations.	Interpreted: a plausible interpretation or analysis of the importance/meaning/significance; makes sense of a story; provides history and context.	Apprentice: relies on a limited repertoire of routines; able to perform well in familiar or simple contexts, with perhaps some needed coaching; limited use of personal judgment and responsiveness to specifics of feedback/situation.	Aware: knows of different points of view and somewhat able to place own view in perspective; but weakness in considering worth of each perspective, especially one's own uncritical about tacit assumptions.	Developing: has some capacity and self-discipline to "walk in another's shoes" but is still primarily limited to one's own reactions and attitudes; puzzled or put out by different feelings or attitudes.	Unreflective: generally unaware of one's specific ignorance; generally unaware of how prejudices colour understandings.
Naive: a superficial account; more descriptive than analytical or creative; a fragmentary or sketchy account of facts/ideas or glib generalizations; a black-and-white account; less a theory than an unexamined hunch or borrowed idea.	Literal: a simplistic or superficial reading; mechanical translation; a decoding with little or no interpretation; no sense of wider importance or significance; a restatement of what was taught or read.	Novice: can perform only with coaching or relies on highly scripted, singular "plug-in" (algorithmic and mechanical) skills, procedures, or approaches.	Uncritical: unaware of differing points of view; prone to overlook or ignore other perspectives; has difficulty imagining other ways of seeing things; prone to egocentric argument and personal criticisms.	Egocentric: has little or no empathy beyond intellectual awareness of others; sees things through own ideas and feelings; ignores or is threatened or puzzled by different feelings, attitudes, or views.	Innocent: completely unaware of the bounds of one's understanding and of the role of projection and prejudice in opinions and attempts to understand.

Figure 27. Generic rubric for understanding based on the UbD six facets of understanding (Wiggins and McTighe, 1998) Available through http://ebookbrowsee.net/ubd-6-facets-rubric-pdf-d20426702.

CRITICAL THINKING RUBRIC for PBL

(for grades 6-12; CCSS ELA aligned)

Critical Thinking Opportunity at Phases of a Project	Below Standard	Approaching Standard	At Standard	Above Standard ✔
Launching the Project: **Analyze Driving Question and Begin Inquiry**	▸ sees only superficial aspects of, or one point of view on, the Driving Question	▸ identifies some central aspects of the Driving Question, but may not see complexities or consider various points of view ▸ asks some follow-up questions about the topic or the wants and needs of the audience or users of a product, but does not dig deep	▸ shows understanding of central aspects of the Driving Question by identifying in detail what needs to be known to answer it and considering various possible points of view on it ▸ asks follow-up questions that focus or broaden inquiry, as appropriate (CC 6-12.W.7) ▸ asks follow-up questions to gain understanding of the wants and needs of audience or product users	
Building Knowledge, Understanding, and Skills: **Gather and Evaluate Information**	▸ is unable to integrate information to address the Driving Question; gathers too little, too much, or irrelevant information, or from too few sources ▸ accepts information at face value (does not evaluate its quality)	▸ attempts to integrate information to address the Driving Question, but it may be too little, too much, or gathered from too few sources; some of it may not be relevant ▸ understands that the quality of information should be considered, but does not do so thoroughly	▸ integrates relevant and sufficient information to address the Driving Question, gathered from multiple and varied sources (CC 6,11-12.RI.7) ▸ thoroughly assesses the quality of information (considers usefulness, accuracy and credibility; distinguishes fact vs. opinion; recognizes bias) (CC 6-12.W.8)	
Developing and Revising Ideas and Products: **Use Evidence and Criteria**	▸ accepts arguments for possible answers to the Driving Question without questioning whether reasoning is valid ▸ uses evidence without considering how strong it is ▸ relies on "gut feeling" to evaluate and revise ideas, product prototypes or problem solutions (does not use criteria)	▸ recognizes the need for valid reasoning and strong evidence, but does not evaluate it carefully when developing answers to the Driving Question ▸ evaluates and revises ideas, product prototypes or problem solutions based on incomplete or invalid criteria	▸ evaluates arguments for possible answers to the Driving Question by assessing whether reasoning is valid and evidence is relevant and sufficient (CC 6-12.SL.3, RI.8) ▸ justifies choice of criteria used to evaluate ideas, product prototypes or problem solutions ▸ revises inadequate drafts, designs or solutions and explains why they will better meet evaluation criteria (CC 6-12.W.5)	
Presenting Products and Answers to Driving Question: **Justify Choices, Consider Alternatives & Implications**	▸ chooses one presentation medium without considering advantages and disadvantages of using other mediums to present a particular topic or idea ▸ cannot give valid reasons or supporting evidence to defend choices made when answering the Driving Question or creating products ▸ does not consider alternative answers to the Driving Question, designs for products, or points of view ▸ is not able to explain important new understanding gained in the project	▸ considers the advantages and disadvantages of using different mediums to present a particular topic or idea, but not thoroughly ▸ explains choices made when answering the Driving Question or creating products, but some reasons are not valid or lack supporting evidence ▸ understands that there may be alternative answers to the Driving Question or designs for products, but does not consider them carefully ▸ can explain some things learned in the project, but is not entirely clear about new understanding	▸ evaluates the advantages and disadvantages of using different mediums to present a particular topic or idea (CC 8.RI.7) ▸ justifies choices made when answering the Driving Question or creating products, by giving valid reasons with supporting evidence (CC 6-12.SL.4) ▸ recognizes the limitations of an answer to the Driving Question or a product design (how it might not be complete, certain, or perfect) and considers alternative perspectives (CC 11-12.SL.4) ▸ can clearly explain new understanding gained in the project and how it might transfer to other situations or contexts	

©2013 BUCK INSTITUTE FOR EDUCATION

For more FreeBIEs visit bie.org

Figure 28. Generic performance rubric for critical thinking in problem-based learning.
Source: Buck Institute for Education (2013).

WHERETO
Considerations for the Learning Plan

The acronym WHERETO summarizes the key elements that should be found in your learning plan, given the desired results and assessments drafted in Stages 1 and 2. Note that the elements need not appear in the same order as the letters of the acronym. Think of WHERETO as a checklist for building and evaluating the final learning plan, not a suggested sequence. For example, the learning might start with a Hook (H), followed by instruction on the final performance requirements (W), then perhaps some rethinking of earlier work (R).

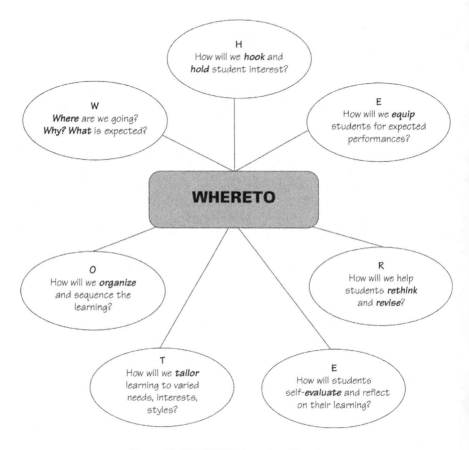

Figure 29. WHERETO Learning Plan design.

WHERETO
Questions to Consider for *W*

The W in WHERETO should be considered from the students' perspective. By working through backward design, designers should be clear about their goals and the evidence needed to show the extent that students have achieved them. Now, we seek to help the students become clear about the goals and expectations and the purpose and benefits of achieving them. Research and experience show that students are more likely to focus and put forth effort when they have clarity on the goals and expectations and see a purpose and value for the intended learning.

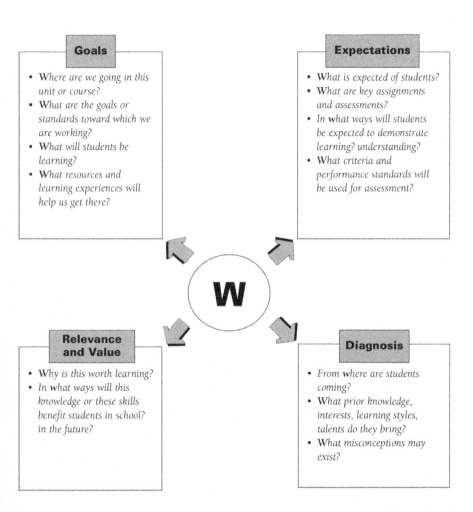

Goals
- *Where are we going in this unit or course?*
- *What are the goals or standards toward which we are working?*
- *What will students be learning?*
- *What resources and learning experiences will help us get there?*

Expectations
- *What is expected of students?*
- *What are key assignments and assessments?*
- *In what ways will students be expected to demonstrate learning? understanding?*
- *What criteria and performance standards will be used for assessment?*

Relevance and Value
- *Why is this worth learning?*
- *In what ways will this knowledge or these skills benefit students in school? in the future?*

Diagnosis
- *From where are students coming?*
- *What prior knowledge, interests, learning styles, talents do they bring?*
- *What misconceptions may exist?*

Figure 30. WHERETO questions for W.

175

wHERETO
Hooking and Holding Students

Effective teachers recognize the importance of *hooking* students at the beginning of a new learning experience and *holding* their interest throughout. The *H* in WHERETO directs designers to consider ways of engaging students in the topic and pointing toward Big Ideas, Essential Questions, and performance tasks—by design. Use the list below to brainstorm possible hooks for your unit design.

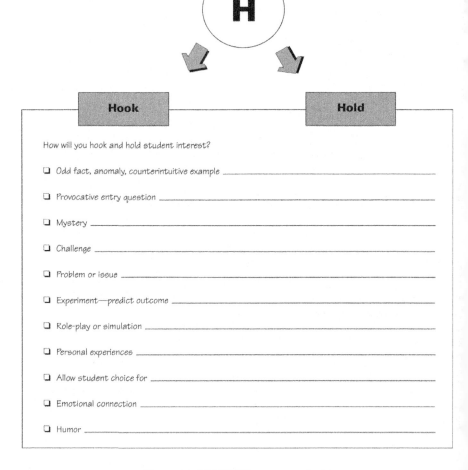

Figure 31. WHERETO questions for H.

WH**E**RETO, Page 1
Equipping Students

The first E in WHERETO prompts designers to think about (1) ways they will help students to *explore* the Big Ideas and Essential Questions, and (2) how they will *equip* students for their final performances. In order for students to come to an understanding of important ideas, they must engage in some inductive learning experiences that facilitate the "construction of meaning." In addition, direct instruction and out-of-class activities can play a role in equipping students with the knowledge and skills needed to perform. Consider using the six facets of understanding to generate effective and engaging learning activities.

Experiential and Inductive Learning	**Direct Instruction**
• What **experiential** or inductive learning will help students to **explore** the big ideas and questions —to achieve desired understandings (Stage 1)? —for their expected performances (Stage 2)?	• What information or skills need to be taught explicitly to **equip** students —to achieve the desired results (Stage 1)? —for their expected performances (Stage 2)?

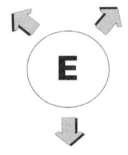

Homework and Other Out-of-Class Experiences
• What homework and other out-of-class **experiences** are needed to **equip** students —to achieve the desired results (Stage 1)? —for their expected performances (Stage 2)?

Figure 32. WHERE to questions for E – EQUIPPING part 1.

WH**E**RETO, Page 2
Equipping Students

Experiential and Inductive Learning	Direct Instruction
Examples:	To help students:
❏ Concept attainment	❏ Compare ideas and information
❏ Research/I-Search project	❏ Find information (e.g., research)
❏ Historical investigation	❏ Evaluate information and ideas
❏ Scientific experimentation	❏ Generate and test hypotheses
❏ Problem-based learning	❏ Communicate ideas
❏ Creative expression	❏ Manage their time
❏ Artistic or production	❏ Monitor their understanding
❏ Exploration of issues	❏ Organize information
❏ Construction project	❏ Persuade
❏ Socratic seminar	❏ Review each other's work
❏ Simulation	❏ Revise their own work
	❏ Use problem-solving strategies
	❏ Self-evaluate
	❏ Summarize key ideas

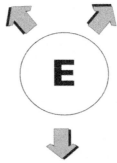

Homework and Other Out-of-Class Experiences

Examples:
- ❏ Practicing skills
- ❏ Reading with a purpose
- ❏ Working on project or performance task
- ❏ Studying and synthesizing information (e.g., create a concept map)
- ❏ Reflecting on ideas, process, or product (e.g., journal entry)
- ❏ Revising work

Figure 33. WHERE to questions for E – EQUIPPING part 2.

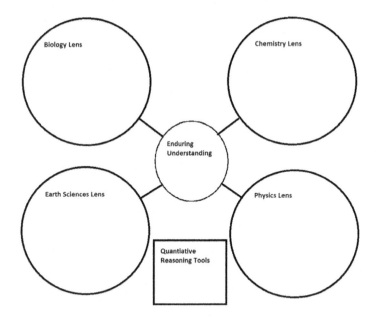

Figure 34. Interdisciplinary STEM.

WHE**R**ETO
Questions to Consider for *R*

The R in WHERETO reminds us that understanding develops and deepens as a result of *rethinking* and *reflection.* Thus, we should build in such opportunities by design. Consider the following questions as you plan learning experiences and instruction to cause students to *rethink* and *reflect* (i.e., to dig deeper into the Big Ideas), and to *refine* and *revise* their work based on feedback. Consider using the six facets of understanding to generate learning activities that require rethinking.

Rethink

- *What Big Ideas do we want students to* **rethink***?*
- *How will your design challenge students to revisit important ideas?*

Revise or Refine

- *What skills need to be practiced and rehearsed?*
- *How might student products and performances be improved?*

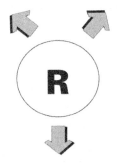

Reflect

- *How will you encourage students to* **reflect** *upon*
  —their learning and thinking?
  —the evolution of their understanding?
  —their use of strategies?
- *How will your design help students to become more metacognitive?*

Figure 35. Whereto questions for R.

WHERETO
Encouraging Self-Evaluation—*E*

Stage 2 of backward design specifies the assessment evidence needed for the desired results identified in Stage 1. The second *E* in WHERETO asks the designer to build in opportunities for ongoing evaluation, including opportunities for students to *self-evaluate*. The following questions may be used as prompts to guide student self-evaluation and reflection. (Note: This step connects with the *R* in WHERETO.)

E

- What do you really understand about _____?
- What questions and uncertainties do you still have about _____?
- What was most effective in _____?
- What was least effective in _____?
- How could you improve _____?
- What are your strengths in _____?
- What are your deficiencies in _____?
- How difficult was _____ for you?
- How does your preferred learning style influence _____?
- What would you do differently next time _____?
- What are you most proud of? Why? _____
- What are you most disappointed in? Why? _____
- What grade or score do you deserve? Why? _____
- How does what you've learned connect to other learnings? _____
- How has what you've learned changed your thinking? _____
- How does what you've learned relate to the present and future? _____
- What follow-up work is needed? _____
- Other: _____

_____

_____

Figure 36. Whereto questions for E – Encourage.

WHERETO
Tailoring the Design for Diverse Learners

The T in WHERETO refers to ways of *tailoring* the design to address student differences in background knowledge and experiences, skill levels, interests, talents, and learning styles. Designers consider ways in which lessons, activities, resources, and assessments might be personalized without sacrificing unit goals or standards. Appropriate differentiation of *content, process,* and *product* can accommodate diverse learners.

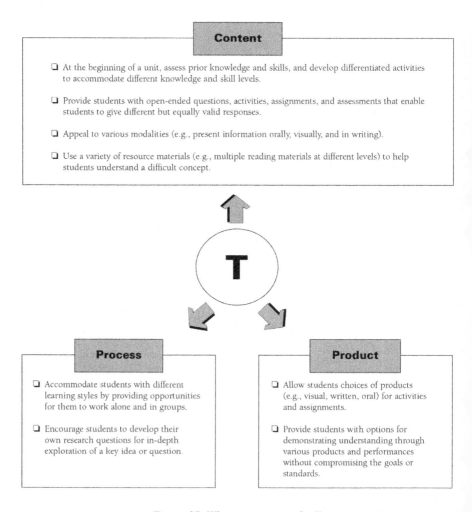

Content

❏ At the beginning of a unit, assess prior knowledge and skills, and develop differentiated activities to accommodate different knowledge and skill levels.

❏ Provide students with open-ended questions, activities, assignments, and assessments that enable students to give different but equally valid responses.

❏ Appeal to various modalities (e.g., present information orally, visually, and in writing).

❏ Use a variety of resource materials (e.g., multiple reading materials at different levels) to help students understand a difficult concept.

Process

❏ Accommodate students with different learning styles by providing opportunities for them to work alone and in groups.

❏ Encourage students to develop their own research questions for in-depth exploration of a key idea or question.

Product

❏ Allow students choices of products (e.g., visual, written, oral) for activities and assignments.

❏ Provide students with options for demonstrating understanding through various products and performances without compromising the goals or standards.

Figure 37. Whereto questions for T.

WHERETO
Organizing the Learning

The O in WHERETO relates to the organization and sequence of design. As they develop the learning plan, designers are encouraged to consider the following questions: How will the learning activities be *organized* to enable students to achieve the desired results? Given the desired results, what sequence will offer the most engaging and effective learning? How will the work unfold in a natural progression so that new teaching and activities seem appropriate, not arbitrary or meaningless, to students? Two broad organizational patterns are depicted below.

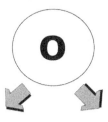

What is most appropriately and effectively covered in a linear and didactic fashion?	What is most appropriately and effectively "uncovered" in an inductive, inquiry-oriented, experiential manner?

The Logic of "Coverage"	**The Logic of "Uncoverage"**
❏ Present information in a logical, step-by-step fashion. (Teacher as tour guide.)	❏ Think of the unit as an *unfolding story or problem* rather than as a guided tour or an encyclopedia article.
❏ Follow the sequence of the textbook.	❏ Begin with a hook and *teach on an as-needed basis.* Don't front load all of the information before application.
❏ Move from the facts and basic skills to the more advanced concepts and processes.	❏ Make the sequence more surprising and less predictable.
❏ Expose students to a breadth of material dictated by established goals.	❏ Ensure that there are ongoing cycles of *model, practice, feedback,* and *adjustment* built into the unit.
❏ Use hands-on and other experiential activities selectively because these can take considerable time.	❏ Focus on transferable, Big Ideas.
❏ Teach and test the discrete pieces before having students apply what they are learning.	❏ Move back and forth between the whole and the parts rather than teaching all the little bits first, out of context. (Think of sports, the arts, and vocational technical projects.)

Figure 38. Whereto questions for O.

QUANTITATIVE REASONING IN STEM

What Does Quantitative Reasoning Look Like in Context?

INTRODUCTION

In Chapter 1 we introduced our framework for quantitative reasoning, which includes the components of the act of quantification, quantitative literacy, quantitative interpretation, and quantitative modelling. Here we want to provide specific examples within science contexts of elements of QR within each of these components. The examples will be short vignettes focused on a given element, so this section can be used much as you might use a dictionary. It provides an example that clarifies what we mean by the QR element and what it looks like in practice.

QUANTITATIVE REASONING LEARNING PROGRESSION

Trajectory of Learning for QR in Energy and Environment

We have been developing a learning progression for quantitative reasoning within the context of environmental science. This progression is built upon the QR Framework in Table 1. The framework provides four quantitative reasoning components and identifies some major elements within those components. We used the framework to construct QR assessments, which we then gave to students in several states across the United States. The assessment results and an in-depth literature review on quantitative reasoning were used to build a learning progression. The learning progression is provided in Table 2. The QR learning progression provides a trajectory of key levels that students achieve to engage in sophisticated quantitative reasoning in the sciences. Building up expertise along this progression requires students to engage in QR in varied contexts and to develop an array of quantitative tools.

We present QR vignettes as examples of using quantitative tools within a science context. The vignettes will be exemplars of the quantitative act, quantitative literacy, quantitative interpretation, and quantitative modeling. We integrate the discussion of quantitative act across the other three QR variables. So you can relate the exemplars to the Quantitative Reasoning Framework (Table 1). We will incorporate the elements within the Quantitative Reasoning Learning Progression (Table 2) throughout the exemplars as well.

Table 1. Quantitative Reasoning Framework

Quantification Act	Quantitative Literacy	Quantitative Interpretation	Quantitative Modeling
Variable	*Numeracy*	*Representations*	*Logic*
Identification	Number Sense	Tables	*Problem Solving*
Object	Small/large Numbers	Graphs/diagrams	Problem Formulation
Attribute	Scientific Notation	Equations	
Measure	Logic	Linear	*Modeling*
		Quadratic	Normal Distribution
Communication	*Measurement*	Power	Regression Model
Force-	Accuracy	Exponential	linear
dynamic	Precision	Statistical displays	polynomial
Scientific	Estimation	Translation	power
discourse	Units		exponential
Quantitative		*Science diagrams*	logarithmic
discourse	*Proportional Reasoning*	Complex systems	Logistic Growth
	Fraction		Model
Context	Ratio	*Statistics & Probability*	Multivariate Model
Avoids QR	Percent	Randomness	Simulation Model
Computation	Rates/Change	Evaluating Risks	Scientific Diagram
Driven	Proportions	Normal Distribution	Table & Graph
Situative	Dimensional	Statistical Plots	Models
view	Analysis	Correlation	
		Causality	*Inference*
Variation	*Basic Prob/Stats*	Z-scores	Inference
Causation	Empirical Prob.	Confidence Intervals	Hypothesis Testing
Correlation	Counting		Practical Significance
Covariation	Central tendency	*Logarithmic Scales*	

QUANTITATIVE REASONING EXEMPLARS

Quantitative Literacy Exemplars

Quantitative literacy (QL) is the use of numbers and arithmetic to quantify a context with the goal of understanding a phenomena so one can make informed decisions. Quantitative literacy has four major elements for which we will provide exemplars: numeracy, measurement, proportional reasoning, and descriptive statistics and basic probability. Numeracy is the ability to reason with numbers. This is the logic and problem solving aspect of QR on the arithmetic level. It includes having number sense, mastery of arithmetic processes such as the four basic operations, logic and reasoning with numbers, an understanding of orders of magnitude, and working with weights and measures. Number sense is defined as an awareness and

Table 2. *Quantitative Reasoning Learning Progression*

QR Progress Variable		
Quantification Act	*Quantitative Interpretation*	*Quantitative Modeling*
Level 4 (Upper Anchor) **4a** Variation: reasons about covariation of 2 or more variables; comparing, contrasting, relating variables in the context of problem **4b** Quantitative Literacy: reasons with quantities to explain relationships between variables; proportional reasoning, numerical reasoning; extend to algebraic and higher math reasoning (MAA) **4c** Context: situative view of QR within a community of practice (Shavelson); solves ill-defined problems in socio-political contexts using ad-hoc methods; informal reasoning within science context (Steen & Madison; Sadler & Zeidler) **4d** Variable: mental construct for object within context including both attributes and measure (Thompson); capacity to communicate quantitative account of solution, decision, course of action within context	**4a** Trends: determine multiple types of trends including linear, power, and exponential trends; recognize and provide quantitative explanations of trends in model representation within context of problem **4b** Predictions: makes predictions using covariation and provides a quantitative account which is applied within context of problem **4c** Translation: translates between models; challenges quantitative variation between models as estimates or due to measurement error; identifies best model representing a context **4d** Revision: revise models theoretically without data, evaluate competing models for possible combination (Schwarz)	**4a** Create Model: ability to create a model representing a context and apply it within context; use variety of quantitative methods to construct model including least squares, linearization, normal distribution, logarithmic, logistic growth, multivariate, simulation models **4b** Refine Model: extend model to new situation; test and refine a model for internal consistency and coherence to evaluate scientific evidence, explanations, and results; (Duschl) **4c** Model Reasoning: construct and use models spontaneously to assist own thinking, predict behavior in real-world, generate new questions about phenomena (Schwarz) **4d** Statistical: conduct statistical inference to test hypothesis (Duschl)

(*Continued*)

Table 2. Continued

QR Progress Variable		
Quantification Act	*Quantitative Interpretation*	*Quantitative Modeling*

| Level 3 | **3a** Variation: recognizes correlation between two variables without assuming causation, but provides a qualitative or isolated case account; lacks covariation
3b Quantitative Literacy: manipulates quantities to discover relationships; applies measure, numeracy, proportions, descriptive statistics
3c Context: display confidence with and cultural appreciation of mathematics within context; practical computation skills within context (Steen); lacks situative view
3d Variable: object within context is conceptualized so that the object has attributes, but weak measure (Thompson); capacity to communicate qualitative account of solution, decision, course of action within context, but weak quantitative account | **3a** Trends: recognize difference between linear vs. curvilinear growth; discuss both variables, providing a quantitative account
3b Predictions: makes predictions based on two variables, but relies on qualitative account; uses correlation but not covariation.
3c Translation: attempts to translate between models but struggles with comparison of quantitative elements; questions quantitative differences between models but provides erroneous qualitative accounts for differences
3d Revision: revise model to better fit evidence and improve explanatory power (Schwarz) | **3a** Create Model: create models for covariation situations that lack quantitative accounts; struggle to apply model within context or provide quantitative account
3b Refine Model: extend model based on supposition about data; do not fully verify fit to new situation
3c Model Reasoning: construct and use multiple models to explain phenomena, view models as tools supporting thinking, consider alternatives in constructing models (Schwarz)
3d Statistical: use descriptive statistics for central tendency and variation; make informal comparisons to address hypothesis |

(Continued)

Table 2. Continued

QR Progress Variable		
Quantification Act	*Quantitative Interpretation*	*Quantitative Modeling*
Level 2 **2a** Variation: sees dependence in relationship between two variables, provides only a qualitative account; lacks correlation, erroneously assumes causation **2b** Quantitative Literacy: poor arithmetic ability interferes with manipulation of variables; struggle to compare or operate with variables **2c** Context: lack confidence with or cultural appreciation of math within context; practical computation skills are not related to context **2d** Variable: object within context is identified, but not fully conceptualized with attributes that are measurable; fails to communicate solution, decision, course of action within context; qualitative account without quantitative elements (Thompson)	**2a** Trends: identify and explain single case in model; recognize increasing/ decreasing trends but rely on qualitative account or change in only one variable **2b** Predictions: makes predictions for models based on only one variable, provides only qualitative arguments supporting prediction **2c** Translation: indicate preference for one model over another but do not translate between models; acknowledge quantitative differences in models but do not compare **2d** Revision: revise model based on authority rather than evidence, modify to improve clarity not explanatory power (Schwarz)	**2a** Create Model: constructs a table or data plot to organize two dimensional data; create visual models to represent single variable data, such as statistical displays (pie charts, histograms) **2b** Refine Model: extends a given model to account for dynamic change in model parameters; provides only a qualitative account **2c** Model Reasoning: construct and use model to explain phenomena, means of communication rather than support for own thinking (Schwarz) **2d** Statistical: calculates descriptive statistics for central tendency and variation but does not use to make informal comparisons to address hypothesis

(Continued)

189

Table 2. Continued

QR Progress Variable		
Quantification Act	*Quantitative Interpretation*	*Quantitative Modeling*
Level 1 (Lower Anchor)		

	Quantification Act	*Quantitative Interpretation*	*Quantitative Modeling*
Level 1 (Lower Anchor)	**1a** Variation: does not compare variables; works with only one variable when discussing trends, **1b** Quantitative Literacy: fails to manipulate and calculate with variables to answer questions of change, discover patterns, and draw conclusions; **1c** Context: does not relate quantities to context or exhibit computational skills **1d** Variable: fail to relate model to context by identifying objects no attempt to conceptualize attributes that are measurable; discourse is force-dynamic; avoids quantitative account, provides weak qualitative account	**1a** Trends: do not identify trends in models **1b** Predictions: avoids making predictions from models **1c** Translation: fail to acknowledge two models can represent the same context **1d** Revision: view models as fixed, test to see if good or bad replicas of phenomena (Schwarz)	**1a** Create Model: does not view science as model building and refining so does not attempt to construct models **1b** Refine Model: accepts authority of model, does not see as needing refinement **1c** Model Reasoning: construct and use models that are literal illustrations, model demonstrates for others not tool to generate new knowledge (Schwarz) **1d** Statistical: does not use statistics; no calculation of even descriptive statistics

understanding about what numbers are, their relationships, their magnitude, the relative effect of operating on numbers, including the use of mental mathematics and estimation (Fennel & Landis, 1994). So number sense includes the concepts of magnitude, ranking, comparison, measurement, rounding, degree of accuracy, and estimation.

Below are examples of numeracy in a science context. Exemplar 1 provides examples from numeracy of small and large numbers, scientific notation, and order of magnitude. Order of magnitude arises in issues of scale in science. We view the world from a macroscopic perspective (what we can see with our naked eye), microscopic/subatomic perspective (what we can see with a microscope or smaller), and landscape/global perspective (what we can see with the aid of a telescope). We want students to enrich their macroscopic view by understanding the hidden mechanisms at the microscopic/atomic level that drive the world, as well as to see the global impacts at the landscape/global scale of what we do locally.

Science examples of a small and large numbers:

Diameter of a hydrogen nucleus is approximately 0.000000000000001 meters while the total energy consumption in the United States is 100,000,000,000,000,000,000 joules.

Scientific Notation: An alternative representation for these small and large numbers

     Hydrogen nucleus: 1×10^{-15} meters

     U.S. energy consumption: 1×10^{20} joules

Order of magnitude: How many orders of magnitude larger is the U.S. energy consumption than a hydrogen nucleus?   35

United States Consumption of Energy by Source

1.7×10^{-5} A

1.1 A

Exemplar 1. Numeracy – small and large numbers, magnitude.

Part of numeracy is bringing numbers into perspective. There are three techniques for doing this: estimation, comparisons, and scaling. Exemplar 2 is on estimation. Exemplar 3 focuses on making a comparison between an unfamiliar unit and one that has meaning for the student. Exemplar 4 is about scaling.

Provide an order of magnitude estimate of how much water U.S. citizens drink in a year.

Solution: Estimate that an average person drink 3-10 ounce (oz) glasses of water a day. There are 365 days in a year, and the U.S. population is on the order of 300 million or 3×10^8. So an estimate of water drunk is:

$$\frac{30\ oz}{1\ day} \times \frac{365\ days}{1\ year} \times (3 \times 10^8) = 3.285 \times 10^{12}\ \frac{oz}{year}$$

There is approximately 0.3381 oz in a milliliter, so an average person drinks 9.716×10^{12} mL/year.

The metric prefaces are another numeracy skill that students must master for science, for example there are 1000 mL in a liter, so our estimate, in liters, is 9.716×10^9 L/year.

Exemplar 2. Numeracy - estimation.

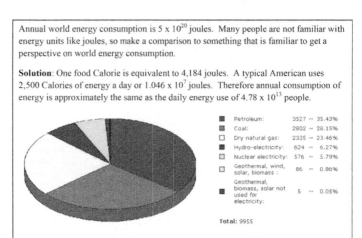

Annual world energy consumption is 5×10^{20} joules. Many people are not familiar with energy units like joules, so make a comparison to something that is familiar to get a perspective on world energy consumption.

Solution: One food Calorie is equivalent to 4,184 joules. A typical American uses 2,500 Calories of energy a day or 1.046×10^7 joules. Therefore annual consumption of energy is approximately the same as the daily energy use of 4.78×10^{13} people.

■	Petroleum:	3527 ~ 35.43%
■	Coal:	2802 ~ 28.15%
☐	Dry natural gas:	2335 ~ 23.46%
■	Hydro-electricity:	624 ~ 6.27%
☐	Nuclear electricity:	576 ~ 5.79%
☐	Geothermal, wind, solar, biomass :	86 ~ 0.86%
■	Geothermal, biomass, solar not used for electricity:	5 ~ 0.05%

Total: 9955

World energy consumption by type.

Exemplar 3. Numeracy - comparison.

An atom has a diameter of about 10^{-10} meters. Provide a scale that puts this into perspective.

Solution: If we multiply the diameter by 10^{10} then we get 1 meter. So there are 10×10^9 or 10 billion atoms in a line along a meter stick. A centimeter is $1/100$ of a meter, so there are 10^8 atoms along a centimeter line - that is 100 million atoms.

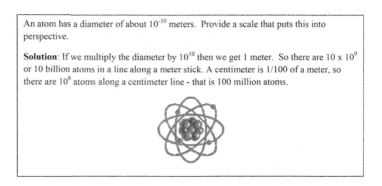

Exemplar 4. Numeracy – scaling.

A second element of QL is measurement. Science requires careful comprehensive measurement of quantities such as distance, area, volume, discharge (1 acre-foot of water per day), mass, density, force, pressure, work, moment, energy, power, heat, and many others. Measurement requires the student to select appropriate units of measure and to choose an appropriate instrument for measuring, such as a ruler for short distances, scales for weight, inclinometers for measuring angles of elevation or depression, spectrometers for measuring properties of light, or fluorometers to measure parameters of fluorescence which allow one to identify the presence of a specific molecule in a medium. Some of these instruments allow for direct measurement, such as the ruler, others are calculated from direct measures, for example volume, while still others are measured indirectly, for example using the fluorometer to determine amount of a specific molecule by measuring florescence. Measurement is an essential process in science and is not always a simple one. The fundamental characteristics of measure are:

- Accuracy: how close the measurement is to the actual value;
- Precision: how refined the measure is;
- Error: how far off the measure is which can be expressed as absolute error (true measure – value of measurement) or relative error (absolute error/actual height).

Exemplar 5 provides a science example of accuracy and precision. Exemplar 6 focuses on error, both absolute and relative. Exemplar 7 focuses on estimation, an essential skill for measurement. Finally exemplar 8 explicates dimensional analysis; the ability to track computations through units of measure.

The groundwater beneath a gasoline station was contaminated with methyl tert-butyl ether (MTBE), a gasoline additive used to increase gas mileage by increasing combustion. MTBE is also a cancer-causing agent. A groundwater sample was analyzed and MTBE measured 455 parts of MTBE per billion parts of water. The threshold measurement below which MTBE cannot be detected is 1 part per billion. What can we say about the accuracy and precision of these measures?

Solution: Precision is high since measure can determine 1 part per billion. Accuracy is unknown since we do not know the actual amount of MTBE in the water. Better to have accuracy first, then precision.

Exemplar 5. Measurement – accuracy and precision.

The General Sherman sequoia tree in Sequoia National Park has an actual height of 83.82 meters. Using an inclinometer and trigonometry a park ranger gets a measure of 84.71. What is the error in the measure?

Solution: The absolute error is 84.71 m – 83.81 m = 0.89 meters.
The relative error is 0.89 m / 83.82 m = 0.0106 or, as a percentage, 1.06% error. Note there is no unit attached to the ratio of relative error since meters cancel.

Exemplar 6. Measurement – absolute and relative error.

193

What is the volume of water an average household uses each year to wash dishes?

Solution: In this case an estimate is about the best for which we can hope. Assume the household does dishes once a day and uses 6-10 gallons of water per wash. Average these values to get 8 gallons of water per wash. There are 365 days in a year; to make the calculation easier round this to 400 days. Then calculate an estimated amount by paying attention to units:

$$\frac{8\ gal}{1\ wash} \times \frac{1\ wash}{1\ day} \times 400\ days = 3,200\ gallons$$

Exemplar 7. Measurement – estimation.

A small well in a rural village produces 3.5 gallons per minute. What is this discharge in m³/hour?

Solution: *Dimensional Analysis* is the tracking of units when performing calculations. It requires students to understand ratios. Students can track the calculations they need to perform by tracking the units. Students must also have knowledge of units in measurement systems and conversions between units.

$$\frac{3.5\ gal}{1\ min} \times \frac{60\ min}{1\ hr} \times \frac{1\ m^3}{264.172\ gal} = \frac{0.795\ m^3}{1\ hr}$$

Exemplar 8. Measurement – dimensional analysis.

A third element of QL is proportional reasoning. Proportional reasoning is a "form of mathematical reasoning that involves a sense of co-variation and of multiple comparisons, and the ability to mentally store and process several pieces of information" (Lest, Post, & Northern, 1988). Proportional reasoning is the most common form of structural similarity, a critical aspect in science for recognizing similar patterns in two different contexts. This type of reasoning underpins many concepts in numeracy and measurement. The essential characteristic of proportional reasoning involves reasoning about the holistic relationship between two rational expressions, such as fractions, quotients, rates, or ratios. Proportional reasoning is much more than the ability to employ the cross multiplication algorithm a/b = c/d implies that ad = bc. Students often do not understand this algorithm, they just know that "ours is not to reason why, ours is but to cross multiply". Early phases in proportional reasoning involve additive reasoning, where students add or subtract the values rather than setting up a proportion, or multiplicative reasoning, where they multiply the values. Traditional proportional reasoning tasks involve relationships of the type a/b = c/d where one of the values is unknown. But proportional reasoning is also the basis for linear relationships between two variables such as y = mx. To understand proportional reasoning, students first need to understand the concept of fraction, which at the most basic level is interpreted by students as a/b compares the part a to the whole b for like quantities. We need to move students beyond such basic understandings to understand ratio as change (Exemplar 9), ratio as parts per (Exemplar 10), normalizing data (Exemplar 11), percentage (Exemplar 12), percentage difference (Exemplar 13), and rate of change (Exemplar 14).

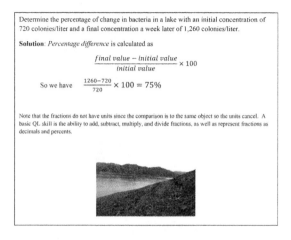

Exemplar 9. Proportional Reasoning – change.

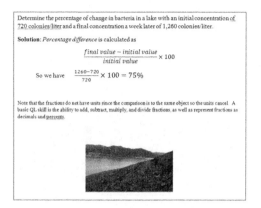

Exemplar 10. Proportional Reasoning – ratio as parts per.

The Little Snake prairie dog colony in Colorado has 36,875 prairie dogs on 31,624 hectares, while the Wolf Creek colony had 20,009 prairie dogs on 3,174 hectares. Which colony is more robust?

Solution: Normalize the data to find the number per hectare so you can make a comparison on a common scale. The density of prairie dogs per hectare in the Wolf Creek colony is $\frac{20,009\ pd}{3,174\ ha} = \frac{6.3\ pd}{1\ ha}$ while the Little Snake colony has only 1.17 pd/ha.

Exemplar 11. Proportional Reasoning – ratio normalize.

The total area of tropical forest in the Congo is 278,797 km^2 and in Zaire it is 1,439,178 km^2. The protected tropical forest in the Congo is 12,935 and in Zaire 93,160. What is the percentage of protected forest in the Congo? What is the percentage of total forest in the Congo to total forest in Zaire?

Solution: The percentage of protected forest in the Congo is an example of percentage as a fraction since we are comparing part-to-whole for like quantities:

$$\frac{12,935\ km^2}{278,797\ km^2} \approx 0.046\ or\ 4.6\%$$

The percentage of total forest is a part-to-part comparison, so it is an example of percentage as a ratio. Note we are still comparing like quantities.

$$\frac{278,797 km^2}{1,439,178 km^2} \approx 0.194\ or\ 19.4\%$$

Exemplar 12. Proportional Reasoning – ratio percentage.

Carbon is stored in various reservoirs on Earth. The amount of carbon in these reservoirs is measured in petagrams (Pg), where 1 petagram is 10^{15} grams. The amount of carbon stored in fossil fuels is 3,700 Pg while that stored in vegetation is 2,300 Pg. Using fossil fuels as a referent, what is the percentage difference between carbon stored in fossil fuels and in vegetation? (Langkamp and Hull, 2007)

Solution: $\frac{2300\,Pg - 3700\,Pg}{3700\,Pg} \approx -0.378 \; or -37.8\%$

So the carbon stored in vegetation is 37.8% less than that stored in fossil fuels.

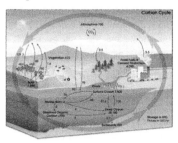

Exemplar 13. Proportional Reasoning – ratio percentage difference.

In 1990 the forests of the world covered 3,510 million hectares. By 1995 world forests had decreased to 3,454 million hectares. How much forest will be lost by the year 2010?

Solution: A pre-proportional reasoner might use additive reasoning, calculating change by taking the difference in forest area without accounting for the years over which it occurs: $3,454 - 3,510 = -56$ million hectares. If they disregard the years and consider this a yearly change they would grossly overestimate the amount of change. Calculating the rate of change per year requires finding the slope:

$$\frac{3,454 - 3,510 \; million \; hectares}{1995 - 1990 \; years} = -11.2 \; \frac{Mha}{yr}$$

So over the 20 years from 1990 to 2010 there will be a loss of

$$20 \; yrs \times -11.2\frac{Mha}{yr} = -224 \; Mha$$

Exemplar 14. Proportional Reasoning – rate of change.

True proportional reasoning requires a perception of structural similarity; a conception of n times as many. If a student reduces a/b = c/d to a = bc/d when solving, then they are not using possible structural relationships. As with cross multiplication, they are solving using algebra without regard to structure. Exemplar 15 provides an example of using the structural relationship underlying proportional reasoning.

A capture-recapture method is used to determine the size of the rat population on an island. A sample of 250 rats is captured and tagged. They are released and allowed to mix back into the population. Sometime later a random sample of 500 rats is taken and 21 are tagged. Estimate the total rat population.

Solution: A student may simply set up a proportion of tagged to total in the sample and tagged to total in the population

$$\frac{21\ tag}{500\ total\ sample} = \frac{250\ tag}{x\ total\ population}$$

which using the cross multiplication algorithm gives a population of about 5,952 rats. However such rote use of the cross multiplication algorithm may not indicate they are using proportional reasoning. To understand why the capture-recapture method works requires the student to use proportional reasoning. They understand that the population is about 24 times as much as the tagged rats and that this holds no matter how many rats are tagged in the original capture.

Exemplar 15. Proportional Reasoning – proportion.

We want students to build on the conception of proportional reasoning as equivalent ratios to understand linear direct variation, y = m x. where the slope m represents a ratio relating two variables x and y. Linear direct variation and the extension to indirect variation y = k/x are common in science. Variation requires an understanding not only of proportional reasoning, but the algebraic concepts of equivalence, variable, and transformations using structural similarity (Exemplar 16).

Ozone in the stratosphere is measured in Dobson units, where 300 Dobson units is a midrange value that corresponds to an ozone layer 3 millimeters thick. In 1991 the reported minimum in the Antarctic ozone hole was approximately 110 Dobson units. A 0 Dobson measure would correspond to 0 thickness of the ozone layer. What is the direct variation coefficient for a model of the relationship between Dobson units and ozone layer thickness?

Solution: To show the relationship between proportional reasoning and direct variation, consider solving the problem by setting up ratios of thickness to Dobson units: 3 mm/300 Du and y mm/110 Du. Now we have been told there is a direct linear variation between the models, so the ratio or slope is constant, so we can set these ratios equal and solve for y, so y = 1.1mm when the Dobson unit is 110. Take any ratio of thickness to units, call it y/x. Since the variation is linear we know that this general ratio is equal to the constant ration of 3 mm/300 Du. Setting them equal gives the proportion: y/x = 3/300 then solving for y gives the direct variation of y = (1/100)x where 1/100 or 0.01 is the constant of variation.

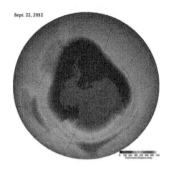

Exemplar 16. Proportional Reasoning – linear direct variation.

A fourth element of QL is basic probability and statistics. Probability is the chance of an event occurring, with theoretical probability defined as the ratio of the number of successful outcomes of an event to the total number of possible outcomes. Earth systems cannot be manipulated like dice to determine a theoretical probability. Often scientists can only estimate the probability through observations of the system, which is called empirical or experimental probability (Exemplar 17).

Descriptive statistics allow us to summarize and describe data. The fundamental descriptive statistics are measures of center of a distribution and measures of spread in a distribution. Measures of central tendency include the mean, median, and mode. Measures of spread include range, quartiles, five number summary, variation, and standard deviation. Exemplar 18 provides data for discussion of central tendency. The solution for Exemplar 18 is provided in the box below it.

From 1900 to 1998, there were 26 years in which a major flood occurred on the Mississippi River. What is the probability of a major flood on the Mississippi River in any given year?

Solution: The event is a major flood in a given year, which occurred 26 times. The total outcomes are the number of years in which a major flood could have occurred which is 99 (must count the year 1900). So the empirical probability of a flood is 26/99 or approximately 26%.

Odds for an event are the ratio between the event occurring and the event not occurring. For example the odds of having a major flood in a given year are $0.26/(1-0.26) = 0.26/0.74$ or about 1 in 3.

Exemplar 17. Probability.

E-waste is caused by the disposal of electronic products. Cathode ray tubes (CRT) from computer monitors and televisions contain lead that can leach into ground water. The table below provides data on leachable lead for 36 models of CRTs. Explore measure of central tendency for the data.

Year Made	CRT Maker	Lead (mg/L)	Year Made	CRT Maker	Lead (mg/L)	Year Made	CRT Maker	Lead (mg/L)
90	Clinton	1.0	93	Toshiba	3.2	94	Zenith	21.5
84	Matsushita	1.0	84	Matsushita	3.5	77	Zenith	21.9
85	Matsushita	1.0	84	Sharp	4.4	87	NEC	26.6
87	Matsushita	1.0	98	Samsung	6.1	96	Orion	33.1
89	Samsung	1.0	95	Samsung	6.9	85	Sharp	35.2
86	Phillips	1.0	98	Chunghwa	9.1	92	Phillips	41.5
84	Goldstar	1.5	89	Panasonic	9.4	84	Quasar	43.5
94	Sharp	1.5	97	Toshiba	10.6	92	Toshiba	54.1
94	Zenith	1.6	87	NEC	10.7	85	Toshiba	54.5
97	Toshiba	2.2	98	Samsung	15.4	93	Panasonic	57.2
97	KCH	2.3	92	Chunghwa	19.3	89	Samsung	60.8
91	Chunghwa	2.8	97	Chunghwa	21.3	89	Hitachi	85.6

Solution: The *median* is the middle number when the data are arranged in ascending order. If there is an even number of data values then the median is the average of the two middle numbers. There are 36 data values so we average the 18th and 19th values:

$$\frac{9.1 + 9.4}{2} = 9.25$$

The *mean* is the sum of all the values divided by the number of values:

$$\frac{\sum values}{36} = \frac{673.3}{36} = 18.7$$

The *mode* is the most frequently occurring value, which is 1.0. The mode is not often used in analyzing scientific data.

Notice that the mean and median values differ significantly, so it does make a difference what measure of central tendency is reported. The CRT makers may report the median to argue that the amount of lead is not as high, while an environmental group may report the mean.

Exemplar 18. Measure of central tendency with cathode ray tubes data.

Why have multiple measures of central tendency? When should we use mode? Median? Mean? Different data types require different measures of central tendency. Nominal or categorical data requires mode, ordinal data requires median, while interval and ratio data require median if skewed and mean if symmetric. A set of data is termed categorical if the values can be sorted into categories, for example gender has categories of male and female. These categories do not overlap and their choice can impact the outcome of an investigation. Thus categorical data cannot be averaged or placed in order, thus mode is the only possible measure of central tendency. A set of data is termed nominal if the values z`can be assigned a code in the form of a number which is simply a label. You can count but not order or measure nominal data. For example we could label females 1 and males 2 for gender. Since nominal data cannot be ordered then we cannot find a median. Since the numbers are only labels taking an average does not make sense. This leaves the mode as the only measure of central tendency. Ordinal data is a data set whose values can be ranked or put in order. You can count and order, but not measure ordinal data. For example, a rating scale from 1 to 5 of how much you dislike or like ice cream is an ordinal scale. You can rank observations on the scale, a 4 means you like ice cream more than a 3 does, but differences on the scale may not represent the same amount of like or dislike. Since you can rank the values you can find a median, but a non-uniform scale does not allow for calculation of a mean. An interval scale can be measured since the scale is uniform, such as measurement of longitude, but the zero point is arbitrary. If the scale can be measured then it can be ranked and counted, so we can use either the median or mean as a measure of central tendency. Finally ratio data is continuous, so it can be counted, ordered, and measured, such as height. For either interval or ratio data you can use either median or mean.

For interval or ratio data we must make a decision about using either median or mean. This decision is based on the type of distribution (Exemplar 19). Important characteristics of distributions are skewness, kurtosis, and modality. Skewness plays a key role in selecting either median or mode as a measure of central tendency. Exemplar 20 provides a figure of a normally distributed data set, skewed data sets, and a bimodal data set. For a normally distributed data set we would use the mean, which would be the same as the median. For a skewed data set we see that the mode, median, and mean can provide quite different values. The mean is pulled towards the tail of a skewed distribution, while the median is less affected by the skew. So we use the median as the measure of central tendency for a skewed data set. Notice for a bimodal data set the mean and median may be the same, but the mode provides important information about where data is clustered. Another characteristic of distributions which can impact the use of median or mean are outliers. Outliers are data points that are significantly larger or smaller than the majority of the data points. An outlier impacts the mean more than the median, since all values are used in the calculation of mean, but median just ranks the values. Outliers don't change rank. We have two choices when considering outliers. We use the median rather than the mean since it is less influenced by outliers or we drop the outliers from the data set and use the mean.

What does the shape of the distribution have to do with choice of mean or median?

Parameters of a distribution: *central tendency, variability, skew, kurtosis,* and *modality*

Example: scores from 6 sections of a statistics course
-A skewed distribution is therefore one that is askew, lopsided. Negatively (left) –
Positively (right). (Top figure)
-*Kurtosis* refers to whether the shape of a distribution is relatively short and flat, or tall
and slender. Types include *platykurtic* (flat-curved), *leptokurtic* (slender-curved), or
mesokurtic (medium-curved).
-*Modality* refers simply to the number of distinct peaks, or areas of cluster, that appear
within a distribution. Types include *unimodial* and *bimodal*. (Bottom figure)

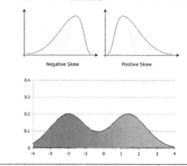

Exemplar 19. Distribution Types.

What does the shape of the distribution have to do with the choice of mean or median?

Solution: Often in biological data, the distribution is skewed to one side (most often to
the right hand side). In skewed data the mean is pulled towards the tail of the distribution
the most, but the median is also pulled in that direction. The mode is the least affected by
skewness, so you may want to consider using mode if the data set is skewed and mode
makes sense in the context. Also consider using median over mean in skewed data sets
since it is less impacted.

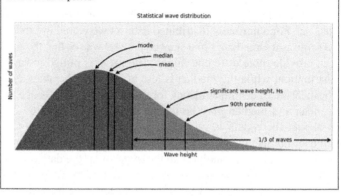

Exemplar 20. Distribution type impact on central tendencey.

The simplest measure of spread or variation in a data set is the range, which is the difference between the largest and smallest values in the data set. For the CRT problem the range is $85.6 - 1.0 = 84.6$. While range is easy to calculate it can be misleading. One outlier can make it appear the data set is much more spread than it is. To avoid this we use quartiles, values that divide the data set into quarters, and the 5 number summary: lowest value, lower quartile, median, upper quartile, and highest value. For the CRT problem the 5 number summary is (1, 1.9, 9.25, 29.85, 85.6). This indicates that the lower quarter only varies by 0.9 while the upper quarter varies much more at 55.75.

The most common measure of variation for normally distributed data is standard deviation. Standard deviation measures the average distance of all data values from their mean (Exemplar 20).

Chebychev's Rule provides a nice rule of thumb for data set distribution (Exemplar 21). The greatest proportion of data points lie within 3 standard deviations of the mean. So we call any point that lies outside of 3 standard deviations an outlier.

We have restricted quantitative literacy mostly to the realm of number and arithmetic. Standard deviation requires taking a square root, so it extends into algebraic operations, but primarily all of what we have explored under quantitative literacy is the sophisticated use of relatively simple mathematics. This is indicative

Standard deviation measures the average distance of all data values from their mean. Consider the CRT data given in Exemplar 18. Find the standard deviation.

Solutions: First find the *deviation* which is the distance of a value from the mean.

Second square the deviation so that positive and negative deviations don't cancel out when adding them, which could conceal spread.

Third, take the average of all deviations by summing them and dividing by one less than the total number of data values (this is an adjustment for working with a sample rather than a population). This result is called *variance*.

Finally, since variance is in squared units and our original data is not squared, square root the variance to get standard deviations, which is in the same units as the original data. So the standard deviation for the CRT data is:

$$s_x = \sqrt{\frac{\Sigma(x - \bar{x})^2}{n - 1}} \approx \sqrt{\frac{16818}{35}} \approx 21.92$$

Exemplar 21. Chebychev's Rule.

of the fact that being a quantitatively literate citizen does not require sophisticated mathematics. It is well within the reach of all citizens and focuses on mathematics learned at the elementary or middle school level. Commonly used statistics that border on moving from arithmetic to algebra are standard deviation, z-scores (number of standards deviations a data point lies above or below the mean), and confidence intervals. These require a basic understanding of algebra which is introduced at the eighth grade or ninth grade level. While there are more sophisticated mathematical and statistical concepts and processes commonly used in science, a student can go a long way with the basic mathematics included here.

Quantitative Interpretation Exemplars

Quantitative Interpretation (QI) is the ability to interpret a model of a given phenomena with the goal of understanding and making informed decisions. It is an essential ability for a scientifically literate citizen. QI is underpinned by the ability to quantify a problem, what we refer to as the quantification act (QA), as well as quantitative literacy (QL). QI may require students to go beyond the arithmetic that was the focus of QL, to engage in algebraic, geometric, and statistical modes of reasoning. Table 1 provides four elements of QI that arise in energy and environmental science: multiple representations, science models, statistics, and logarithmic scales. This list is not exhaustive, but includes common elements we came across in our work with teachers in creating an energy and environment performance task. Finally, in QI the model is provided for the student, they are not creating the model. We reserve the process of creating models for the quantitative reasoning component of quantitative modeling (QM). Table 3 provides the rule of four used in mathematics for representation types and clarifies the difference between QI and QM. The rule of four states that there are four categories of mathematical representations: verbal, tabular, graphic, and algebraic.

Table 3. Quantitative Reasoning Learning

	Verbal	Tabular	Graphic	Algebraic
QI	Mathematize	Interpret numeric data	Interpret visual representation	Interpret equation or formula
QM	Create written explanation	Create table through data collection	Create graph or visual representation	Create equation or formula

Working with multiple respresentations includes the ability to interpret a variety of representation types and to translate between different representations of the same phenomena. The most basic representation is a table of data. We consider a data table which is organized to display trends a model in and of itself. Students can use the table model to answer a variety of problems:

- Interpret a value in the table in the context of a problem;
- Determine trends;
- Interpolate and extrapolate values;
- Discover relationships when given bivariate data (2 quantities);
- Differentiate between cause and effect.

Exemplar 22 provides an example of a tabular representation for data collected on water temperature in a small closed-canopy stream. This data has been organized from lowest temperature reading to highest reading to make it easier to analyze. One way of organizing a data table is to consider frequencies of data within categories. A frequency table list categories or bins of data and frequency within each category. Relative frequency tables express frequency as a fraction or percentage of the total, while cumulative frequency tables express frequency as a total of frequencies for a given category and all previous categories (Exemplar 23).

Note that we have provided the frequency tables without discussing what the numbers mean. Too often students do the same thing, engaging in computation without understanding what is being represented. It is important to have students begin by engaging in the quantitative act, that is explicitly identifying the object, its attributes, and measure. The object is the variable temperature of water. It's attributes include that temperature varies by measure. This immediately raises the question of what is a normal temperature for a stream or are these temperatures a problem for fish in the stream? Both are questions about attributes of the variable that will help

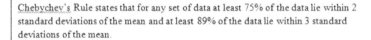

Chebychev's Rule states that for any set of data at least 75% of the data lie within 2 standard deviations of the mean and at least 89% of the data lie within 3 standard deviations of the mean.

Any data value that lies 3 or more standard deviations from the mean is called an *outlier* and it is common practice to discard them from the data set.

Example: In Exemplar 18, the CRT Hitachi (1989) model with lead at a level of 85.6 mg/L is an outlier since the mean is about 19 and 3 times the standard deviation is 66: 19 + 66 = 85 < 85.6. The graph below indicates what an outlier looks like when viewing data.

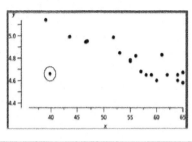

Exemplar 22. Chebychev's Rule.

205

Measurements of the temperature of small closed-canopy streams were taken in June 2013. Canopied streams have an umbrella of vegetation shading the water from the sun, keeping the water cool enough to be suitable for fish such as salmon. Provide a relative frequency and cumulative frequency for the data.

	Temperature		Temperature		Temperature		Temperature
1	11.0	9	13.0	17	15.0	25	15.9
2	11.5	10	13.0	18	15.0	26	16.0
3	11.7	11	14.0	19	15.0	27	16.0
4	13.0	12	14.0	20	15.0	28	16.0
5	13.0	13	14.4	21	15.0	29	16.0
6	13.0	14	14.4	22	15.5	30	16.5
7	13.0	15	14.4	23	15.6	31	16.5
8	13.0	16	14.7	24	15.6	32	17.0

Solution:

Temperature Categories	Relative Frequency	Cumulative Frequency
(11.0, 11.9)	3/32 or 9%	9%
(12.0, 12.9)	0%	9%
(13.0, 13.9)	7/32 or 22%	31%
(14.0, 14.9)	6/32 or 19%	50%
(15.0, 15.9)	9/32 or 28%	78%
(16.0, 16.9)	6/32 or 19%	97%
(17.0, 17.9)	1/32 or 3%	100%

Exemplar 23. Relative and cumulative frequency tables.

students relate it to potential other variables. Finally, the temperature appears to be measured on the Celsius scale. It is often instructive to have students select a specific point on the table and interpret what the point means, before they begin calculating, trying to determine trends, or making predictions.

Graphical representations are the most reported representation in articles for the general public. Consider the graphical representation on the front page of the U.S.A Today paper for every issue. Tables provide the data for graphs, but the table is often not presented to the reader. It is important that students make the connection between tables and graphs. Graphical representations have great variety including statistical representations such as pie graphs or bar charts, two or three dimensional coordinate graphs typical in mathematics, and science box models. Students often prefer graphical representations over equations and even over tables, due to the ability to visually interpret for trends and make predictions. However they may struggle to relate the variables in a graphic representation of bivariate data. Some will even struggle to interpret a specific point or instance in a graphical representation. Different representations for the stream data are provided in Exemplars 24 and 25.

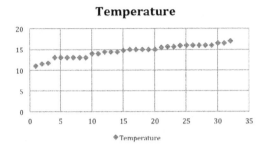

Exemplar 24. Scatter plot of stream data. Represents data as bivariate with observation by temperature.

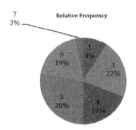

Exemplar 25. Pie chart for stream data. Represents data as categorical by percent frequency.

Science often presents graphical representations of models that are very different from what students see in mathematics, for example representations of systems through diagrams or box models and graphs with embedded variables. Box models represent complex adaptive systems with reservoirs and flows, such as the carbon cycle box model in Exemplar 26. Students may avoid the quantitative information in such models, focusing only on the flow and not the quantitative amount of the flow.

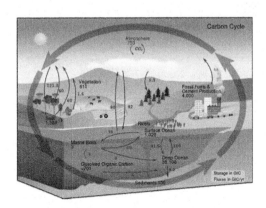

Exemplar 26. Science box model.

Models of flow have elements of box models, but are not representing closed systems, but rather how something passes through a system such as energy flow (Exemplar 27 and 28) or electricity efficiency (Exemplar 29).

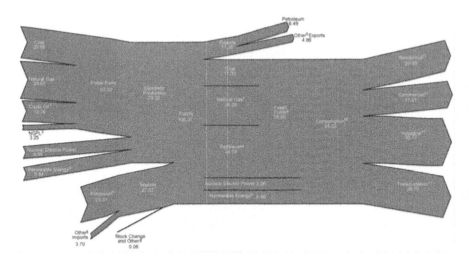

Exemplar 27. Energy flow model I.

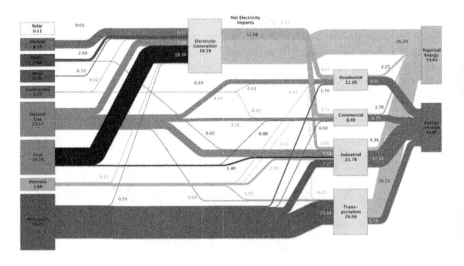

Exemplar 28. Energy flow model II.

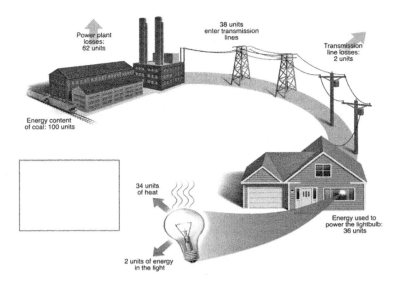

Exemplar 29. Electricity efficiency flow model.

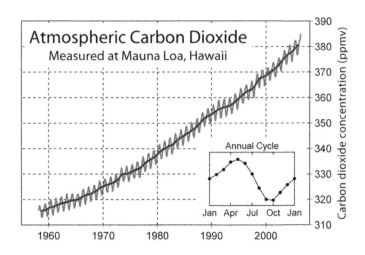

Exemplar 30. Atmospheric carbon graph.

Science graphs often embed multiple graphs on one set of axis (Exemplar 30) or have embedded information in the plot (Exemplar 31), such as location of country represented by color of the point plotted.

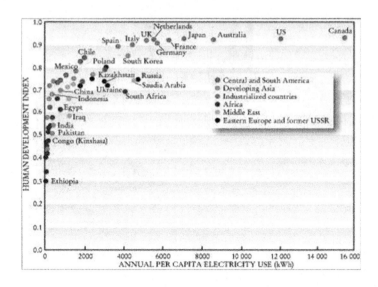

Exemplar 31. Electricity demand by affluence.

Maps are increasing in popularity as a means of representing information geographically. Interpreting maps such as the coal reserves map in Exemplar 32 combines map reading skills with data representation.

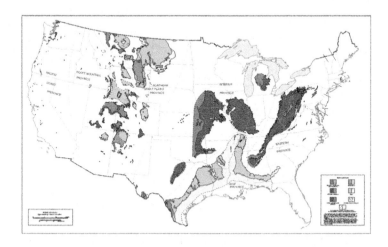

Exemplar 32. Coal reserves map. (U.S. Geological Survey, 1996).

Exemplar 33 presents a diagram that matches resources with uses. Such diagrams are examples of connected graphs from the mathematical area of graph theory.

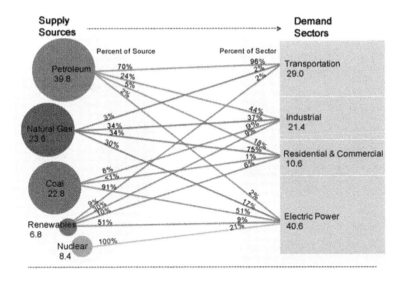

Exemplar 33. Connected graph of energy sources versus uses.

Even graphs on a familiar mathematical coordinator plane may be problematic for students, when combined with graphical representations of area under a curve (Exemplar 34) or the use of plotted points of varying size that indicate variation in the number of barrels of oil per day (Exemplar 35).

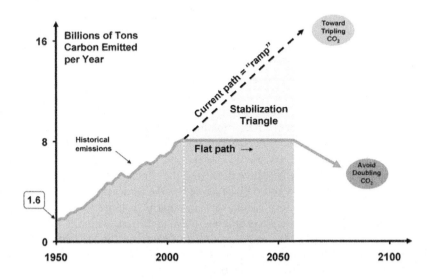

Exemplar 34. Stabilization of carbon emitted.

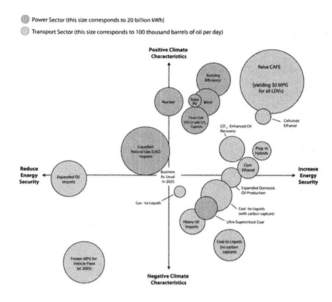

Exemplar 35. Power sector and transport sector.

Algebraic or analytic representations include formulas and equations, often representing bivariate data. A primary source of algebraic models are best fit curves for tables and scatter plots of data. The most used algebraic models in science are linear models of the form $y = ax + b$, power models of the form $y = ax^n$ where the base x of the power expression is unknown, and exponential models of the form $y = ab^x$ where the exponent x of the power expression is unknown. Some higher order (powers of 2 or more) polynomial models also appear, especially quadratic and cubic polynomial models. For example, alternative fueled vehicles have been increasing from 1995 through 2004 (Exemplar 36). If students want to make a prediction about the number of such vehicles on the road in 2010, then they need to determine a trend. Certainly the table indicates an increasing trend, but a scatter plot makes it easier to see if the trend is linear or curvilinear (nonlinear trend).

Exemplar 37 provides a scatter plot of the alternative fueled vehicle data plotted with a line of best fit. Students should estimate the line of best fit by sight before being provided the best fit line. Have them find the center of the data by averaging the x-values and then the y-values. Place a ruler on the center point of the data, then vary the slope of the ruler until you have a line that is as close to all the points in the data set as possible. They are estimating the line of best, which is the line with the smallest summed error for each actual data value and the estimated value on the line of best fit. This provides the student a concept of where the best fit curves come from. For more sophisticated mathematical students the formula for the line of best fit can be derived. The line of best fit provided by Excel for the AFV data is

Alternative fueled vehicles (ethanol, electricity, natural gas powered) are increasing on U.S. roads due to concern over environmental impacts and dependence on foreign oil. Can you predict the number of alternative fueled vehicles that will be on the road in 2010 using the data provided?

Year	Number of AFV
1995	246,855
1996	265,066
1997	280,205
1998	295,030
1999	322,302
2000	394,664
2001	425,457
2002	471,098
2003	510,805
2004	547,904

Exemplar 36. Alternative fueled vehicles.

$y = 35{,}443 \, x - 7 \times 10^7$. This is a great time to talk with students about scaling the years so that 1995 is year 1. This makes the line of best fit much easier to read and work with. Excel also gives a coefficient of variation of $R^2 = 0.967$. The closer this value is to one the better the fit of the line to the data. But is a line or a curve a better model for this data? A more sophisticated method to determine if one should use a line or curve to fit the data is to examine a plot of the residuals (errors) between the line of best fit and the actual data. Consider exploring this with higher level students.

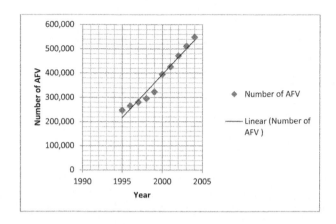

Exemplar 37. Scatter plot and line of best fit for alternative fueled vehicle data.

213

Consider the data on photovoltaic cells (Exemplar 38). The scatter plot for the cell data and the line of best fit are provided in Exemplar 39. Note how the data begins above the line of best fit, dips below in the middle, and then goes back above the line to the right of the graph. This pattern indicates that a nonlinear model may be a better fit. Depending on the sophistication of your students you may have them use a statistical package to find a power function and exponential model of best fit, then explore which appears to be the better fit.

Another approach uses logarithms to straighten out the data (make it linear) so you can fit a line to it. If the data is modeled by a power function the log-log plot of the data will be linear. The log-log plot is simply the plot of the log of both the x and y, (log x, log y) for all points in the data set. If the data is exponential then a semi-log plot will be linear. This is where you only log the y value and plot the points (x, log y). Fitting curves is a rich quantitative reasoning topic that can be addressed at all grade levels across middle school and high school.

Photovoltaic cells convert sunlight to electricity. The total capacity of U.S. shipments of photovoltaic cells has been increasing rapidly since 1985 (Year 0). Given the data here what can you determine about growth in capacity of these cells in the U.S.?

Year	Capacity MW
0	6.0
1	6.6
2	6.9
3	10.0
4	13.0
5	13.8
6	14.9
7	15.6
8	21.0
9	26.1
10	31.1
11	35.5
12	46.4
13	50.6
14	76.9

Exemplar 38. Photovoltaic cells. National Renewable Energy Laboratory (NREL), U.S. Department of Energy.

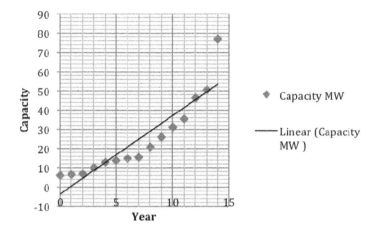

Exemplar 39. Photovoltaic cell scatter plot and line of best fit.

Statistical line plots or connected data plots provide graphical models that indicate trends without using best fit or other more complicated methods. Exemplar 40 is a line plot modeling historic use of different energy sources. Such plots are easy to create directly from data tables and are useful for making comparisons, finding differences, and trend analysis.

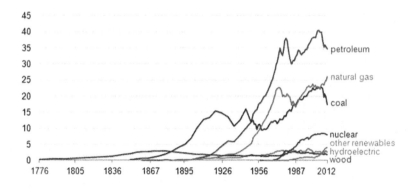

Exemplar 40. Historic energy sources.

Another model that is of importance in science is the normal distribution model. If we determine that a distribution is normal, then we already know a lot about the data set. Exemplar 41 shows a normal distribution. We can see that for a normal distribution approximately 68% of the data lies within one standard deviation of the mean; 95% within two standard deviations; and 99.7% within three standard deviations. This is called the Empirical Rule for normal distributions. Statistical packages can calculate skewness, which indicates if a data set is normal or not. If a distribution is skewed there are techniques for transforming them into a normal distribution so we can use the Empirical Rule. Techniques for transforming data depend on the type of skew (positive or negative) and the magnitude of the skew. Transforming positive-skewed data can be done using logarithms. If a distribution is determined to be normal, we can make predictions using the Empirical rule. For example if we have normally distributed data with a mean of 50 and a standard deviation of 10, then we know that a value of 85 is very unusual. This value is over 3 standard deviations from the mean, so it occurs only 0.3% of the time.

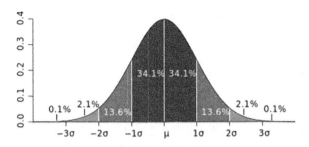

Exemplar 41. Normal distribution model.

Logarithmic functions are important in science. As we have discussed above, logarithms can be used to linearize data sets and transform skewed distributions into normal distributions. Logarithmic scales are another important use of this function in science. Scales that are very large can be difficult to work with, so we condense the scale using logarithms. Two common examples of this are the pH scale and Richter scale for earthquakes (Exemplar 42).

Logarithmic scales

pH (Power of Hydrogen) scale: concentration of hydrogen ions in a liquid.

$$pH = -\log(\text{concentration of } H^+)$$

Earthquake Moment Magnitude scale: size of an earthquake compared to a base quake with moment of $10^{10.7}$ dyne-centimeters

$$moment\ magnitude = \log\left(\frac{moment^{2/3}}{10^{10.7}}\right)$$

Exemplar 42. Logarithmic scales.

There are an almost endless number of examples of graphical and analytic representations for data. No matter what the representation is, students should be able to perform four elements of quantitative interpretation: determine trends, make predictions, translate between representations, and revise models.

Statistical processes and analysis play a key role in quantitative interpretation. We included basic descriptive statistics such as central tendency and spread in quantitative literacy, since they involve mostly arithmetic processes. Statistical processes that require algebra and are used to test for correlation or causality we include under quantitative interpretation, such as: z-scores, confidence intervals, randomness, evaluating risks, correlation, and causality. Due to space we will not include a discussion of hypothesis testing here.

Two commonly used statistical processes are converting raw scores to z-scores and confidence intervals. A z-score uses standard deviation to describe the position of a single data point in a data set. First you compare the score to the mean by finding the distance from the mean $x - \bar{x}$, then you compare this difference to the standard deviation to determine equivalence of how many standard deviations. The z-score then is:

$$z = \frac{x - \bar{x}}{S}$$

For example, given a data set with mean 17.5 and standard deviation 3.7, the z-score for the 10th data value of 13 is -1.2. This standardizes the data value of 13, telling us it is just over one standard deviation below the mean. Confidence intervals use margin of error to determine an interval of values that contain the true population mean within a given level of confidence. The margin of error E is based on spread (standard deviation), size of sample (n), and a parameter t which is 1.960 for sample sizes of 30 or more where a 95% confidence interval is desired. The confidence interval is expressed as $(\bar{x} - E, \bar{x} + E)$, where

$$E = t \cdot \frac{S}{\sqrt{n}}$$

Quantitative Modeling Exemplars

Quantitative Interpretation (QI) is the ability to interpret a model of a given phenomena with the goal of discovering trends and making predictions. Quantitative Modeling (QM) is the act of creating models like those presented in our QI discussion. However, in QI, the model is provided for the student to interpret. We think of this as the difference between being a consumer of information (QI) and the creator of the information (QM); or as the difference between being a scientifically and mathematically literate citizen and a scientist or mathematician. Table 1 provides four elements of QM that arise in energy and environmental science: logic, problem solving, model building, and statistical inference. We will discuss each of these below. QM is a creative act that requires students to perform at the upper level of Bloom's taxonomy.

Scientists build models to reflect reality and provide a simplified version of it that can be used to make data informed decisions about complex issues. Building a model requires critical thinking and reasoning to make an informed argument. Logic is the study of the methods and principles of reasoning, so it provides a foundation for modeling. Of course logic is critical to QL and QI as well, but we place it under QM to emphasize the importance of logic in the creation of a model. Consider the model as an argument, using facts or assumptions to support a conclusion. The argument must avoid fallacies where conclusions are not supported by the facts or assumptions. There are a number of common fallacies that are used to provide deceptive arguments supporting predetermined positions. Bennett and Briggs (2005) listed 10 types of fallacies:

- Appeal to Popularity or Majority: many believe that p is true, therefore p is true. Example: The majority of U.S. citizens do not believe that climate change is a reality, therefore there is no need to address it.
- False Cause: p came before q, therefore p caused q. Example: They used fracking on the oil well in June, and in December, I had problems with pollution of my water well. So fracking caused the pollution.
- Appeal to Ignorance: there is no proof that p is true, therefore p is false. Example: There is no concrete evidence that humans are causing global warming, so humans are not causing it.
- Hasty Generalization: p and q are linked a few times, therefore p causes q. Example: Several people living under high voltage power lines have gotten sick. The power lines must be causing the illness.
- Limited Choice (False Delemma): p is false, therefore only q can be true. Example: You are wrong about new oil fields being found in the U.S., so I am right about the U.S. being able to provide all its own oil.
- Appeal to Emotion: p is associated with a positive emotional response, therefore p is true. Example: Wind energy is clean energy, so we should invest only in wind energy.
- Personal Attack: a person or group claiming p is negatively perceived, so p is not true. Example: Energy companies claim that natural gas can provide for future U.S. energy needs. Since energy companies are driven by profits this is not true.
- Circular Reasoning: p is true implies restated version of p is true. Example: Nonrenewable energy resources are declining because we cannot produce more oil.
- Diversion (Red Herring): p is related to q and an argument for q is provided, therefore p is true. Example: Funding for renewable energy should be increased

for environmental ethics reasons. Environmental ethics is essential to preserving our future quality of life and we cannot afford to ignore it.

- Straw Man: a distorted argument for another person's version of p is provided, therefore you should believe my argument for what is claimed to be a real version of p. Example: An environmentalist provides an argument for the impact of constructing an oil pipeline across a nature preserve. The energy company lobby makes the distorted claim that the environmentalist is against any oil production in Alaska, then argues why this complete restriction of oil production would harm the U.S. economy.

When building models students must avoid basing them on such fallacies.

Students should also understand propositional logic. Propositions are statements that make a claim that may be either true or false. Such propositions underlie the research questions which models are built to answer. Basic propositional logic includes the following:

- Negation: the opposite of a proposition must be false if the original proposition is true, and vice versa. Example: Proposition - Oil is the primary energy resource. This is a true proposition so the negation is false: Oil is not the primary energy resource. Double negations are equivalent to the original proposition. Example: Oil is not the non-primary energy source.
- Conjunctions (And Statements): given two propositions p, q, the conjunction p and q is true only if p and q are both true. Example: Oil is the primary energy resource. Wind energy is the primary renewable energy resource. The first proposition is true, the second is false. So the conjunction of the two propositions is also false.
- Disjunctions (Or Statements): given two propositions p, q, the disjunction p or q is true if either proposition is true. Example: The disjunction of the oil and wind energy propositions is true.
- Conditionals (If .. then Statements): given two propositions p, q, the conditional if p, then q is true if both p and q are true or if p is false. The proposition p is called the hypothesis and q is called the conclusion. The condition proposes that the conclusion q is true on the condition that the hypothesis p is true. Example: If the U.S. maximizes oil production, then the U.S. can eliminate the need for foreign oil. If the U.S. does not maximize oil production (p is false) then no promise about oil independence is broken, so the conditional statement is true no matter if oil independence is reached (q is true) or not reached (q is false). If the U.S. does maximize oil production (p is true), then the promise is kept if the U.S. reaches oil independence (q is true), but is not kept if the U.S. does not reach oil independence (q is false).

Understanding the logic of conditional statements is essential to phrasing the research questions that should drive the creation of models. Changing the order of the propositions in the conditional statement "If p, then q" to "If q, then p" completely changes the meaning of the statement. This is called the converse of the conditional statement. For example the converse of our oil independence conditional statement is: If the U.S. eliminates the need for foreign oil, then the U.S. maximizes oil production. It is clear this statement carries a different meaning that would require a variation on the original model. Other common variations on the conditional are the inverse "If not p, then not q" and the contrapositive "If not q, then not p". Students should understand that the contrapositive is logically equivalent to the original conditional statement "If p, then q".

A second element of QM is problem solving. As with logic, problem solving is a component of QL and QI as well. We place it under modeling to emphasize the need for creative problem solving and critical thinking in creating models. Modeling requires students to engage in formulating the problem, a step in the problem solving process we often omit from the classroom. Students should develop their own research questions, ponder what data is needed to address the question, determine how that data should be gathered, analyzed, and presented. This requires determining what data to use and what data is extraneous. This process often places the student in the position of having a problem that they do not know how to attack. A heuristic is a general strategy for attacking such problems. The heuristic does not guarantee a solution, its purpose is to stimulate reasoning and guide problem solving efforts. There are a number of heuristics, such as Polya's four-step problem-solving heuristic (Polya, 1957). The scientific method could even be considered a heuristic. DECAL (Table 3) is a heuristic Mayes developed for an algebra book focused on modeling called ACT in Algebra: Applications, Concepts, and Technology in Learning Algebra (1998). While DECAL is focused on developing function models, it can easily be extended to include creation of tabular, graphic, and science models.

A third element of QM is the ability to create a wide variety of models like those presented in our discussion of QI. Models may be tables of data collected by the students and organized into frequency tables, tables of data represented in an appropriate statistical display, scatter plots of the data, regression models of the data using best fit linear, polynomial, power, exponential, and logarithmic equations, box models of a complex system, scientific diagram models, normal distribution models, logistic growth models, multivariate models comparing more than two variables, and even simulation models. The learning progression for QM identifies four elements of modeling: ability to create a model, ability to reason with the model, ability to use a variety of methods to construct models, and the ability to conduct statistical tests for significance. We provide some exemplars for creating models first, then finish with a discussion of statistical inference.

Displaying data is an essential aspect of communicating trends in data sets. There are a number of statistical displays available including frequency tables, pie charts, bar charts, dot plots, histograms, stem and leaf plots, box and whisker plots, and scatter plots. Creating a display from data is a basic step in developing models. Interpreting displays is essential to being a scientifically and mathematically literate citizen. How do we determine the appropriate display for a given data set? Exemplars 43 through 50 provide examples of when to use particular data displays as models.

Table 3. DECAL Problem Solving Heuristic

---

1. Describe the Problem: identify the parts or anatomy of the problem.
Setting: identify any known relationship or law which relates to modeling the problem situation.
Question: identify the unknown(s), label them as variable quantities.
Facts: list and identify all key facts.
Distractors: list all extraneous information (information which is not needed in solving the problem).

2. Explore: This is the critical thinking phase of solving the problem. You must determine how to formulate the modeling function in Step 3 from the anatomy of the problem in Step 1. You will have to apply problem solving **strategies**, which are specific methods of simplifying and understanding a certain class of problems. A variety of strategies may be employed, such as: deductive reasoning, inductive reasoning, analytic reasoning, recursive reasoning, and visualizing.

3. Create Model: write a mathematical sentence modeling the problem. In some cases the problem will be modeled by a system of equations or inequalities rather than a single function. It should be noted that for some problems such a function may not exist.

4. Apply the Model: use the modeling function to answer the question identified in Step 1. This part of the heuristic often requires a significant amount of computation, variable manipulation or function plotting. A Computer Algebra System (CAS) can be used to perform these operations so that we can focus on the more critical aspects of modeling the problem.

5. Link to New Situations: Review the problem and verify the solution. Does the solution make sense in the real world? For example are the size and units of the solution reasonable. Extend the problem by modifying the modeling equation to answer new questions related to the original problem.

Exemplar 43. Frequency Table.

Pie Chart

A pie chart is a way of summarizing a set of categorical data. It is a circle which is divided into segments. Each segment represents a particular category. The area of each segment is proportional to the number of cases in that category.

Example: Contribution to global wind generation by country in 2009.

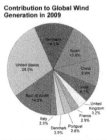

Contribution to Global Wind Generation in 2009

Source: U.S. Energy Information Administration, International Energy Statistics

http://www.eia.gov/cfapps/energy_in_brief/wind_power.cfm

Exemplar 44. Pie graph.

Bar Chart

A bar chart is a way of summarizing a set of categorical data. It is often used in exploratory data analysis to illustrate the major features of the distribution of the data in a convenient form. It displays the data using a number of rectangles, of the same width, each of which represents a particular category. The length (and hence area) of each rectangle is proportional to the number of cases in the category it represents.

Bar charts are used to summarize nominal or ordinal data.

Bar charts can be displayed horizontally or vertically and they are usually drawn with a gap between the bars (rectangles), whereas the bars of a histogram are drawn immediately next to each other.

Example: Energy prices by energy type across multiple years.

Figure 1. Average energy prices for manufacturers (1998-2010)
price (real 2005 dollars per million Btu)

http://www.eia.gov/consumption/manufacturing/reports/2010/ng_cost/

Exemplar 45. Bar Chart.

Dot Plot

A dot plot is a wary of summarizing data, often used in exploratory data analysis to illustrate the major features of the distribution of the data in a convenient form.

For nominal or ordinal data, a dot plot is similar to a bar chart, with the bars replaced by a series of dots. Each dot represents a fixed number of individuals. For continuous data, the dot plot is similar to a histogram, with the rectangles replaced by dots.

A dot plot can also help detect any unusual observations (outliers), or any gaps in the data set.

Example: Distribution of heights from a random sample of 500 students drawn from the U.S. Census at School database.

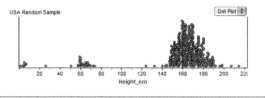

Exemplar 46. Dot Plot.

Histogram

A histogram is a way of summarizing data that are measured on an interval scale (either discrete or continuous). It is often used in exploratory data analysis to illustrate the major features of the distribution of the data in a convenient form. It divides up the range of possible values in a data set into classes or groups. For each group, a rectangle is constructed with a base length equal to the range of values in that specific group, and an area proportional to the number of observations falling into that group. This means that the rectangles might be drawn of non-uniform height.

The histogram is only appropriate for variables whose values are numerical and measured on an interval scale. It is generally used when dealing with large data sets (>100 observations), when stem and leaf plots become tedious to construct. A histogram can also help detect any unusual observations (outliers), or any gaps in the data set.

Example: Refer to the Frequency Table example, but now the focus is on examining the 71 cases where there is a non-zero difference in expenditures between the ESS and RECS-HS bill data. The bins for the histogram are centered at intervals of 40, for example the bin at 80 would have all differences in expenditures that fall between 60 and 100. The count is given as a percent on the vertical axis. Note that this is a negatively skewed distribution.

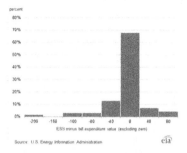

http://www.eia.gov/consumption/residential/data/2009/pdf/recs_ess_studypaper.pdf

Exemplar 47. Histogram.

223

Stem and Leaf Plot

A stem and leaf plot is a way of summarizing a set of data measured on an interval scale. It is often used in exploratory data analysis to illustrate the major features of the distribution of the data in a convenient and easily drawn form.

A stem and leaf plot is similar to a histogram but is usually a more informative display for relatively small data sets (<100 data points). It provides a table as well as a picture of the data and from it we can readily write down the data in order of magnitude, which is useful for many statistical procedures.

Example: Consider a random sample of 20 concentrations of calcium carbonate ($CaCO_3$) in milligrams per liter, measured to the nearest tenth. The stem is the whole number measure, the leaf is the decimal unit. The following is a possible stem and leaf plot for such data. In this plot 130 488 indicates there were three concentrations in the 130 bin – 130.4, 130.8 and 130.8.

```
127  5
128  69
129  35
130  488
131  25677
132  1389
133  26
134  5
```

Exemplar 48. Stem and Leaf.

Box and Whisker Plot (or Boxplot)

A box and whisker plot is a way of summarizing a set of data measured on an interval scale. It is often used in exploratory data analysis. It is a type of graph which is used to show the shape of the distribution, its central value, and variability. The picture produced consists of the most extreme values in the data set (maximum and minimum values), the lower and upper quartiles, and the median.

A box plot is especially helpful for indicating whether a distribution is skewed and whether there are any unusual observations (outliers) in the data set.

Box and whisker plots are also very useful when large numbers of observations are involved and when two or more data sets are being compared.

Example: Michelson was attempting to measure the speed of light while at the U.S. Naval Academy (1882). The experiment consisted of 5 trials each with 20 consecutive runs. For the first run of his experiment the median was around 950 km/s, the upper quartile around 980 km/s, and the extreme minimum value was around 740 km/s.

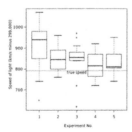

https://en.wikipedia.org/wiki/File:Michelsonmorley-boxplot.svg

Exemplar 49. Box and whisker.

Scatter Plot

A scatter plot is a useful summary of a set of bivariate data (two variables), usually drawn before working out a linear correlation coefficient or fitting a regression line. It gives a good visual picture of the relationship between the two variables, and aids the interpretation of the correlation coefficient or regression model.

Each unit contributes one point to the scatter plot, on which points are plotted but not joined. The resulting pattern indicates the type and strength of the relationship between the two variables.

Example: Waiting time between eruptions and the duration of the eruption for the Old Faithful geyser in Yellowstone National Park, Wyoming, USA.

Old Faithful Eruptions

http://commons.wikimedia.org/wiki/File:Oldfaithful3.png

Exemplar 50. Scatter plot.

Students should create table models for data they collect, organizing the data to highlight trends and make it easier to make predictions. We will use data collected on a glacier in the state of Washington as an example for developing a variety of models (Exemplar 51). The table is already organized by year and the data is continually decreasing so reorganizing the table is not necessary. Students can clearly see a trend in the table, the glacier is retreating. Many students struggle to make predictions from tables. So they may create a graphical model for the data. We used Fathom, a statistics packaged designed for teaching and learning, to produce a scatter plot of the data (Exemplar 52).

Glaciers store water that is used in irrigation. The table below provides data on recent changes in length of the Rainbow Glacier on Mt. Baker in Washington State. Position refers to the location of the glacier's leading edge, as compared to its 1985 position. Predict the length of the glacier in 2010 if it was 3,750 meters long in 1950. Explain how you arrived at your model.

Year	Position	Year	Position	Year	Position	Year	Position
1985	0	1989	-44	1993	-96	1997	n/a
1986	-11	1990	-55	1994	-116	1998	-201
1987	-22	1991	-60	1995	-137	1999	-241
1988	-33	1992	-75	1996	-161	2000	-246

Exemplar 51. Rainbow glacier data.

First we want students to recognize that the scatter plot has a definite trend. It is not a random set of points with no direction. There may still be some question as to whether the data is linear or curvilinear. Students should take a ruler and eyeball a line of best fit, then discuss what criteria they are using to determine their line of best fit. Some will try to get a line that goes through as many points as possible, we want them to focus on constructing a line that is as close to all the points as possible. Since it is a line they are looking for, then lines are determined by a point and a slope. We can find a point: the center of the data set is a point the line of best fit will pass through. The center of the data set point is simply (average of x values, average of y values). For the glacial data, the center point is (8.2,-100). Plot this point, place a ruler on the point, then rotate the ruler to estimate the slope that gives a line of best fit. The class can compare their different estimates and discuss which is the best fit. This leads naturally to a discussion of how to determine a line of best fit. The National Council of Teachers of Mathematics has a great applet for exploring visually the concept of a best fit line (Exemplar 53). The applet allows students to vary points or the line by dragging them, then seeing the impact on the calculated square error.

Fathom also allows for such an exploration. You can take the scatter plot, add a moveable line and eyeball a line of best fit by dragging it to fit the data. Then you can opt to see the squares representing square error, and refine your estimate by making the squares as small as possible. Now that students have a conception of what a best fit line means, have them use a technology tool to find the best fit line. There are many tools for fitting curves to data, including applets you can find online, programs like Fathom, or a graphing calculator. Using Fathom we get the line of best fit y = -16.8x + 38 with a coefficient of variation of $R^2 = 0.9647$ (Figure 54). An additional option in Fathom is the ability to drag data points and see directly the change in the line of best fit. This is a great opportunity to explore the impact of outliers on a line of best fit, simply select a point and drag it to make it an outlier. This raises the questions for students of cleaning the data. Should we remove outliers from a data set? Are the outliers due to natural variation or due to measurement error?

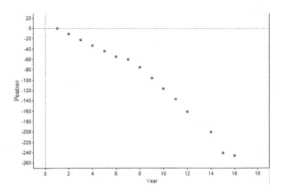

Exemplar 52. Rainbow glacier scatter plot.

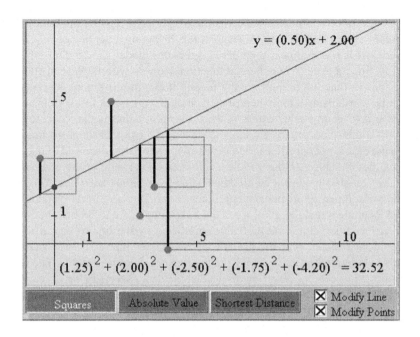

Exemplar 53. NCTM least-squares regression line applet.

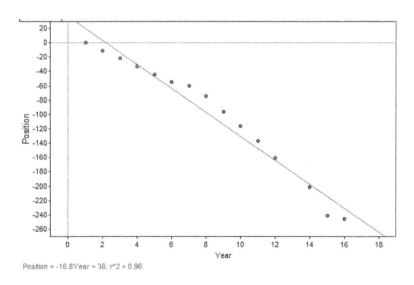

Exemplar 54. Fathom line of best fit for glacial data.

The next question for students concerns the trend of the data. Is the data linear or curvilinear (has a trend but is not linear)? If it is linear, then the line of best fit is the best model. If it is curvilinear then perhaps a better model is a quadratic function, power function, or even an exponential function. How do we tell? We can always use a higher power function to improve the fit. But if that improvement is very small it may not be worth using a more complicated model. One quick test for linear versus curvilinear is to examine the pattern of the scatter plot points with respect to the line of best fit. If there appears to be a random scatter of the points about the line of best fit, then the data is not curvilinear. However, if you see a definite trend of data points below on the left, above in the middle, and below on the right of the graph (or vice versa), then the data may well be modeled better by a curve then a line. The data for glaciers in Exemplar 54 displays a curvilinear trend. A more formal version of this test is to examine a residual plot. A residual plot graphs the difference between the actual vertical axis values and the values predicted by the line of best fit. Fathom can provide a residual plot for the glacial data (Exemplar 55). We examine the residuals to determine if they display the patterns we discussed above. The residual plot confirms our conclusions from above that the data appears to have a curvilinear trend. With this said, the coefficient of variation of the line of best fit indicates the line has a strong fit to the data. So we should be cautious about how much we will gain from fitting other models to the data.

We can use a graphing calculator or Excel to fit nonlinear curves to the data. Excel allows you to fit nonlinear curves including polynomial functions, power functions, logarithmic functions, or exponential functions. To fit a quadratic function to the glacier data using Excel, create a scatter plot of the data. Right click on one of the data points in the scatter plot, then select Add Trendline. If you want to see the equation of the curve select Display equation on chart. Select Display R-squared value on chart boxes to see the coefficient of variation. Have students begin with a familiar polynomial function, such as a quadratic or cubic. Exemplar 56 provides the quadratic best fit for the glacier data: $y = -0.71x^2 - 4.73x + 1.43$ with $R^2 = 0.9955$. Note that R^2 dropped from the value of 0.9647 for the linear model, but the increase in fit may not be worth using the more complicated quadratic model.

In real world applications the most common models fit to data are linear, power, and exponential functions. Let's explore another set of data and focus on the power and exponential models. Exemplar 57 presents data on fuel economy by engine size. A scatter plot of the data with the line of best fit is provided in Exemplar 58. Note the lower R^2 value indicates the fit is not as good as it was in the glacial data problem. This is due in part to increased spread in the data. So would a power function or exponential function fit the data better? We could do the analysis of residuals we discussed above, but we will do what many of the teachers and students do: generate all the models and compare them. Technology makes this easy to do and therefore a big temptation. Exemplar 59 provides a power function best fit model and Exemplar 60 an exponential function best fit model. We see that the lowest R^2 value of these three models is the power function $y = 44.7x^{-0.5}$, indicating this model has the best

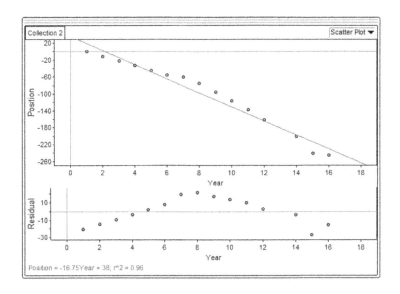

Exemplar 55. Residual plot for glacial data.

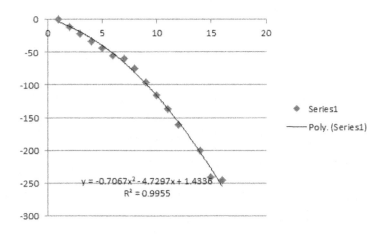

Exemplar 56. Quadratic of best fit for glacial data.

fit. The -0.5 power indicates this is near to a reciprocal of a square root model. This approach of generating multiple function models is function fishing for the correct model. Students will function fish. We should be considering other aspects of the data sets to determine what model makes the most sense, such as: does the data show characteristics represented by power functions or exponential functions; does the context of the problem indicate that exponential growth is likely. Let students fish, then explore the context of the problem to gain insight into what model to use.

Fuel Economy

The U.S. Department of Energy complied data on engine size and fuel economy for automobiles manufactured in 1999. Data for a random sample of 18 cars is given in the table. What can you say about the data?

Engine Size (Liters)	3.2	2.8	2.5	2.8	5.7	5.7	1.8	5.0	6.0	2.3	3.5	2.5	3.4	1.5	2.3	4.3	6.8	1.0
Fuel Economy (mpg)	26	26	27	26	28	13	29	23	19	30	23	26	25	41	31	25	16	47

Exemplar 57. Fuel economy.

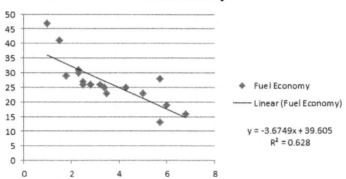

Exemplar 58. Fuel economy line of best fit.

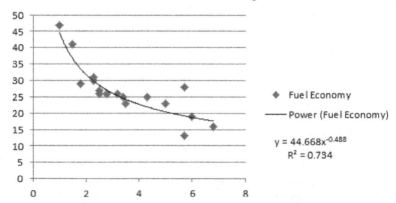

Exemplar 59. Fuel economy power function best fit model.

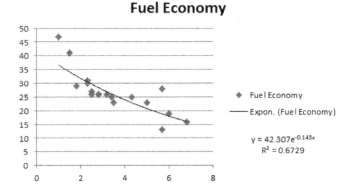

Exemplar 60. Fuel economy exponential function best fit model.

The above examples demonstrate that it is easiest to spot a linear trend, while determining which curve to use for curvilinear data is more difficult. So scientists will often take curvilinear data and straighten it out – transform it so the data appears linear – then determine what model to use. This is called linearization of data. Data that has a trend modeled by a power function of the form $y = ax^n$ can be linearized by plotting the log-log of the data points, that is instead of plotting (x,y) you plot $(\ln x, \ln y)$. Exponential data can be linearized by plotting the semilog $(x, \ln y)$. Exemplar 61 shows why this linearizes data.

Power Function	Exponential Function
Suppose data is modeled by $y = a \cdot x^n$	Suppose data is modeled by $y = a \cdot b^x$
Take the log of both sides and simplify: $$y = a \cdot x^n$$ $$\ln y = \ln a \cdot x^n$$ $$\ln y = \ln a + \ln x^n$$ $$\ln y = \ln a + n \cdot \ln x$$ Treat $\ln y$ as a single variable Y and $\ln x$ as a single variable X, then we have a linear equation: $Y = \ln a + n$ X. $\ln a$ is a real number, so call it A. We see that the log-log of the power equation is linear with respect to the logs: $$Y = A + n \cdot x$$	Take the log of both sides and simplify: $$y = a \cdot b^x$$ $$\ln y = \ln a \cdot b^x$$ $$\ln y = \ln a + \ln b^x$$ $$\ln y = \ln a + x \cdot \ln b$$ Treat $\ln y$ as a single variable Y, then we have a linear equation: $Y = \ln a + x \ln b$. $\ln a$ and $\ln b$ are real numbers, so call the first A and the second B. We see that the semilog of the exponential equation is linear with respect to the logs: $$Y = A + x \cdot B$$

Exemplar 61. Linearizing power and exponential data.

Exemplar 62 displays the log-log plot of the fuel economy data. The question is: Does the log-log data appear to be linear? If it does, the data can be modeled with a power function. Exemplar 63 displays the semilog plot of the fuel economy data. If this data appears linear then we can model the data with an exponential function.

231

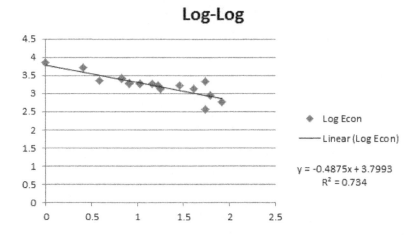

Exemplar 62. Log-log plot of fuel economy data.

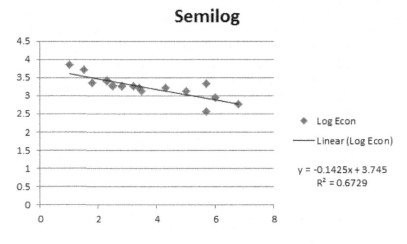

Exemplar 63. Semilog plot of fuel economy data.

Note that the log-log data has a line of best fit with a higher R^2 value, indicating a power function may be a better model then an exponential function for this data.

While equation models are the coin of the realm in mathematics, science uses a dazzling array of model types. The QI section provided a variety of creative models including box models, flow diagrams, and maps. These models often include engaging graphics, density of information, and embedded variables which can make them difficult for students to process. We do not have the space here to discuss creating all of the wide variety of models possible in science, so we will examine box models as an example of having students create science models. Consider the box model for the water cycle introduced in the QI section (Exemplar 26). This box model has beautiful graphics making it potentially very engaging for students. Students should be encouraged to create simpler versions of box models for complex cycles. First have the student research data on the water cycle. The primary components of any box model are reservoirs where something is stored and flows between those reservoirs. With some research we could determine the primary reservoirs for the global water cycle are: oceans, rivers, ground water, the atmosphere, and ice or snow. Represent each reservoir with a rectangle, even vary the size of the rectangles to indicate those with more and less volume. Now identify the flows between those reservoirs. How does water move between them? Flows include precipitation, evaporation, transpiration, and runoff. Students can now construct a box model that shows how reservoirs are connected by flows. Now increase the quantitative nature of the box model by embedding numeric data including measurement unit into the box model. For example the ocean stores $1,388,000 \times 10^3$ km^3 volume of water, with 436.5×10^3 km^3 per year flowing to the atmosphere through evaporation. Allow the students some freedom to be artistic and you have the box model in Exemplar 26.

We want to make a few quick comments on quantitative literacy and the act of quantifying with respect to the ocean water volume. First, the water volume unit is km^3. Take some time to be sure that students understand why volume is measured in cubic units, as well as to get a referent that helps them understand just how big a cubic kilometer of water is. Second, the magnitude of the volume is represented as $1,388,000 \times 10^3$ or a little over a million thousands. This is not a number students will be familiar with from a mathematics course. There the number would be represented as $1,388,000,000$ or a little over a billion. We need to be explicit about number representations and large numbers. The ability to understand large numbers is not innate; it is an acquired QL ability.

The final element we include in the modeling component of QR is statistical inference. We refer specifically to hypothesis testing, a foundational aspect of science research. We include inference under QM because it is essential to test constructed models against reality and refine them. Hypothesis testing provides a means for doing this. Here we provide a quick overview of the complicated conception of hypothesis testing. Suppose a student sees the model on carbon dioxide concentrations and global temperature change presented in Exemplar 64. They infer that carbon dioxide is impacting global average temperature. First, they run a statistical test of correlation to determine if there is a relationship between the two variables. There are a number of correlational tests to choose from, including: Pearson r correlation, Spearman rho correlation, point-biseral correlation, or Phi coefficient correlation. Since both variables are continuous, they choose the Pearson r correlation. The correlation indicates a positive correlation between 0.66 and 0.85, indicating that as one increases so does the other and allowing for good predictions for future temperatures based on CO_2 concentration. However, the student knows that correlation does not mean causation.

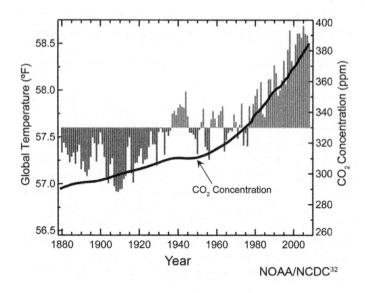

Exemplar 64. Climate change. Source: Global Climate Change Impacts in the United States, U.S. Global Change Research Program (NOAA/NCDC 2009).

The student cannot setup a control and experimental group for global CO_2 and global temperature change, making an inferential hypothesis test difficult. So the students conduct an experiment to see if through conservation they can significantly reduce the CO_2 they are releasing into the atmosphere over a month. Two classes of 30 students participate in the study. The control group does not alter their normal routine, estimating their normal personal carbon footprint for the month. The experimental group reduces their carbon footprint using a number of simple conservation practices. The research question is: Does the conservation group have a significantly different carbon footprint then the control group? The alpha level of significance is set at 0.05, meaning the maximum risk they are willing to take that any observed differences are due to chance is 5%. They decide to use a two-tailed test which means they will reject the null hypothesis if the alpha level is less than 0.25 in either tail (Exemplar 65).The students answered the following list of questions to determine what statistical test was best to use:

- Compare groups or correlate variables? Compare groups.
- Number of independent variables? One.
- Number of dependent variables? One.
- Number of covariates – control variables? None.
- Is independent variable categorical or continuous? Continuous – carbon footprint.
- Is dependent variable categorical or continuous? Categorical – treatment groups.
- Is dependent variable score normally distributed? Assume normality.

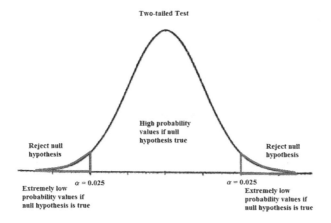

Exemplar 65. The normal curve of mean differences of all possible outcomes if the null hypothesis is true for a two-tailed test at alpha of 0.05. Reject the null hypothesis if it falls in the red outlier area.

This led them do conduct a t-test. The t-test produced a sample statistic p value of 0.03. The p-value is the probability that a result could have been produced by change if the treatment had no real effect. The p-value was less than the alpha value of 0.05 so they rejected the null hypothesis. There was a significant decrease in carbon footprint due to conservation measures. They understand that there are two types of possible errors in their outcome (Exemplar 66).

Researcher Decision	Population Reality	
	No Effect: null true	Effect Exists: null false
Reject null hypothesis	Type I Error: false positive Probability = Alpha	Correctly rejected: no error Probability = power
Do not reject null hypothesis	Correctly not rejected: no error	Type II Error: false negative Probability = Beta

Exemplar 66. Type I and Type II errors.

The students know that statistical significance does not always mean practical significance, so they ran a test of effect size. Effect size determines if the means are different in a practical sense by identifying the strength of the conclusions about group differences. Effect size tests vary by statistical test. For a t-test the effect size formula is:

$$ES = \frac{\mu_1 - \mu_2}{\left(\dfrac{n_1 \cdot sd_1 + n_2 \cdot sd_2}{n_1 + n_2} \right)}$$

where the numerator is the difference of means, n is the size of the control and experimental groups, and sd is the standard deviation of the groups. The effect size was 0.6 which indicates a medium effect size. An effect size of 0.6 indicates that about 70% of the control group would be below average persons in the experimental group.

CONCLUSION

We hope that the exemplars of QR in this chapter provide some clarification of what we mean by quantitative reasoning. QR includes a broad array of mathematical and statistical skills and concepts. While many of the skills and concepts are not complicated from a mathematical perspective, students struggle to implement them within a context. It is precisely the interdisciplinary nature of quantitative reasoning within real-world contexts that students need to experience if they are to improve in QR and become scientifically literate citizens.

REFERENCES/BIBLIOGRAPHY

Bennett, J. O., & Briggs, W. L. (2005). *Using and understanding mathematics: A quantitative reasoning approach* (3rd ed.). Reading, MA: Pearson Addison Wesley.

Fennell, F., & Landis, T. E. (1994). Number sense and operation sense. In C. A. Thornton & N. S. Bley (Eds.), *Windows of opportunity: Mathematics for students with special needs* (pp. 187–203). Reston, VA: National Council of Teachers of Mathematics.

Lesh, R., Post, T., & Behr, M. (1988). Proportional Reasoning. In J. Hiebert & M. Behr (Eds.), *Number concepts and operations in the middle grades* (pp. 93–118). Reston, VA: Lawrence Erlbaum & National Council of Teachers of Mathematics.

Mayes, R. L., & Lesser, L. M. (1998). *Algebra: Applications, concepts and technology in learning algebra*. Burr Ridge, IL: McGraw-Hill.

Polya, G. (1957). *How to solve it: A new mathematical method*. New York, NY: Doubleday.

PETROLEUM

Energizing the World's Transportation

OVERVIEW

The U.S. and world's transportation systems run on liquid fuels, which are almost exclusively produced from the refining of petroleum or crude oil. Since the 1970s, the U.S. domestic petroleum production has been unable to meet demand and the U.S. has imported a significant portion of its crude oil (Figure 1).

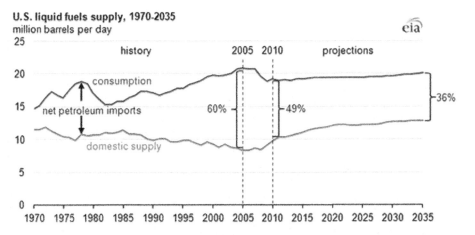

Figure 1. Comparison of the U.S. petroleum production and consumption curves over the time period 1965 to 2011. During this time, production has lagged demand and the difference has been made up by importing crude oil. Source: Energy Information Administration, Annual Energy Outlook 2012, Early Release.

The economy of the U.S. is heavily dependent upon oil (Figure 2). The fuels refined from petroleum, i.e. gasoline, diesel and jet fuel, power the cars, trucks and planes that move goods and people both long and short distances. Thus, crude oil is the major source of the energy responsible for the mobility of U.S. society.

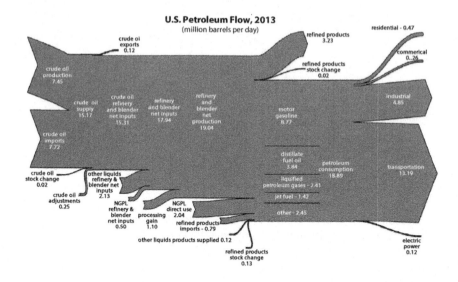

U.S. Petroleum Flow, 2013
(million barrels per day)

Figure 2. Sankey flow diagram showing how crude oil from domestic and foreign sources (left) moves through the oil and gas industry to the various sectors of the U.S. economy (right). Source: Energy Information Administration, Monthly Energy Review (May, 2014).

Other products from petroleum refining, e.g. heating fuel, asphalt, petroleum coke, etc., pave our roads, shingle our houses, heat our offices and homes, and power factories and industrial plants (Figure 3). At the same time, crude oil is a feedstock for petrochemical processes, which makes products (plastics, fertilizer, pharmaceuticals, etc.) critical to virtually all sectors of the world's economy.

Realistically, there are significant problems with importing a large percentage of the petroleum the U.S. uses. The nation must compete for oil on the open market with developing nations, e.g. China, India, whose demand for oil is sharply growing (Figure 4). At the same time, the global supply of oil is decreasing and its quality declining. In 2004, Indonesia's declining oil production curve fell below is growing consumption demand and the nation abruptly went from an oil exporter to an importer and consequently left OPEC. At the same time, most producing nations have declining production, e.g. Norway, and even the supergiant oil fields that have historically produced most of the world's crude oil are experiencing steady production declines (Sorrell et al., 2010). For example, Cantrell, Mexico's supergiant oil field, has been in a steady decline for decades. Another factor pressuring oil supply is the increasing domestic demand for petroleum within many of the exporting nations leading to less crude oil available for export, e.g. Saudi Arabia.

Politically, the world is also facing a rise of petro-nationalism where oil is not offered freely on the global oil market, but is distributed at discount prices to attain national political goals, e.g. Venezuela. Finally the character of oil readily available

Primary Energy Consumption by Source and Sector, 2013

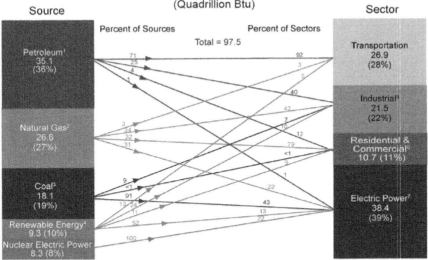

Figure 3. U.S. primary energy sources (left) and the economic sectors they supply (right). In addition to transportation, petroleum plays a large role in industry (44%) and commercial/ residential uses (10.6%). Only a small amount of petroleum is used to generate electricity. Nearly, 70 % of all petroleum used in the U.S. is used in the transportation sector, which is 93 % energized by petroleum. A quad is 10^{15} Btus. Source: Energy Information Administration, Monthly Energy Review (May, 2014).

on today's oil market is changing in physical and chemical character, e.g. light to heavy and sweet to sour. Because refineries are built to handle a particular range of crude oils, this causes problems in the downstream oil industry. All of these factors together produce more expensive oil and raise the risk of international conflict over the accessibility of oil.

The tightening of the global oil supply has not gone unnoticed in the United States. Repeatedly, there are calls for fixing the problem and making the nation 'energy secure' or 'energy independent'. Proposed solutions span the scientific, technological, and political spectrums. Some of the more widely publicized plans include: suing OPEC; reining in oil speculators; increasing domestic production by opening the Arctic National Wildlife Refuge (ANWR) to drilling; permitting oil exploration on the eastern U.S. continental shelf; encouraging energy efficiency, and conservation (low on the list); expanding domestic biofuels production; and replacing oil with domestic natural gas as a transportation fuel and powering electricity with wind (Pickens Plan). An answer or answers to the "US oil crisis" will result from a political discussion informed by a variety of perspectives, e.g. social, economic,

Top Consuming Countries, 1960-2006

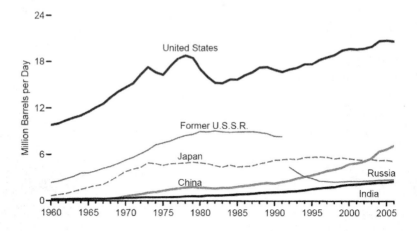

Figure 4. Oil consumption curves for the top oil consuming nations from 1960 to 2006. Although the U.S. is the top oil consumer, petroleum demand is growing significantly in developing countries like China and India. Source: Energy Information Administration, (http://www.eia.doe.gov/emeu/aer/pdf/pages/sec11_20.pdf).

etc. However, the discussion would benefit immensely from some basic science and rudimentary quantitative skills. Both may also be helpful in identifying potential solutions that are compatible with the limitations or constraints the physical world imposes on all human endeavors, e.g. the laws of thermodynamics.

This chapter will provide a background on petroleum that will place some of these issues in a more scientific context. Specifically, it will introduce liquid fuels, the reasons they are so valuable, and why it will be hard to replace them. The geologic processes that form petroleum will be reviewed. How petroleum is discovered, extracted, processed, and refined to create the products we use will also be discussed. In addition to this background material, this chapter will discuss three on-going petroleum debates: drilling in ANWR; replacing petroleum-based liquid fuels with alternatives; and Peak Oil and its ramifications. These social questions will demonstrate how science, technology, and engineering coupled with simple QR skills are critical for understanding the fundamental energy issues the nation faces.

LIQUID FUELS

Transportation is a major component of modern industrialized societies. It moves goods and people around the world at speeds unheard of during most of human history. This activity is extremely energy intensive. To maximize the material moved, transportation fuels must have a high energy density, be easy to handle, and remain stable over a wide temperature range. Thus, modern transportation is made possible by liquid fuels. Arguably, cheap, reliable access to modern liquid fuels is what makes much of our transportation system possible.

An Energy Carrier

Similar to electricity, fuel is an energy carrier (Figure 5). Thus, it must be created from a primary energy source. Unlike electricity, however, the energy in fuel must be transformed where it will be used, i.e. combusted in the vehicle or power plant. The energy released, i.e. mostly chemical, is converted to heat and transformed into useful mechanical work by a heat engine, e.g. internal combustion engine, jet engine, etc. The physical state of fuels can be gaseous, liquid, or solid. A fuel's physical state is important in determining the energy delivery system that is needed to harness the energy released when a particular fuel is combusted.

Properties

Perhaps the most successful transportation fuel in human history is liquid fuels. *Liquid fuels* are fuels that occur in the liquid state at most of the temperature and pressure conditions encountered on the Earth's surface. Liquid fuels have many

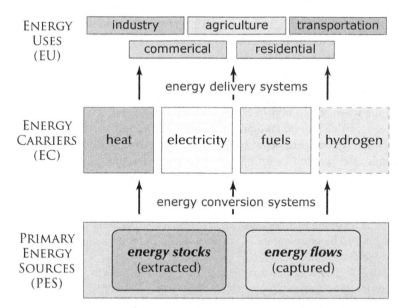

Figure 5. Fuels are an energy carrier. Many are produced from primary energy sources after extensive processing (secondary fuels), whereas others require little processing before use (primary fuels). Source: J. D. Myers. Used with permission.

practical engineering advantages over gaseous and solid fuels. They are easy to transport over long distances through pipelines, an option not available for solid fuels, but is possible with gaseous fuels. They can be pumped from storage to a vehicle easily. This makes refuelling a ship, car, train or airplane a relative easy task that can be done very quickly and by only a few or single individuals. In many instances, fuelling of the device itself, e.g. a furnace, becomes automatic. At the same time, the switch from solid to liquid fuel eliminates the need to deal with incombustible, solid waste. Liquid fuel combustion results in gas production (mostly CO_2 and H_2O with other minor pollutants) that is easily vented to the atmosphere. Compared to gaseous fuel, evaporative losses are also less with a liquid fuel.

The importance of the physical form of a fuel is clearly illustrated by a significant historical event. Winston Churchill's decision to switch the Royal Navy from coal to oil before World War I gave Britain a short strategic advantage than all naval powers ultimately had to follow even if they had no domestic source of liquid fuels. The move reduced the size of a warship's crew, cut refuelling time dramatically, extended a ship's range, and eliminated the need to acquire and crew coaling stations around the world. Today, activities such as refuelling at sea or in-flight would not be possible with solid fuels and would be even more dangerous with gaseous fuels.

Liquid fuels release their stored chemical energy by combustion. However, what actually combusts is vapors from the fuel, not the liquid itself. A good fuel must ignite easily, burn well but not explosively, yield a significant amount of heat, produce low smoke and ash, be inexpensive, and be easy to store and transport. How well a liquid fuel meets these criteria is determined by its physical and chemical characteristics. These include:

- *flash point*: The lowest temperature at which a liquid can vaporize to form an ignitable air-vapor mixture. It also marks the lowest amount of vapor necessary to ignite when an ignition source is applied. Flash point is useful in defining the degree to which individual liquid fuels are a fire hazard.
- *fire point*: The temperature at which a fuel will continue to burn for at least five seconds after ignition by an open flame. Below the fire point, evaporation of a liquid fuel is too slow to maintain combustive conditions.
- *cloud point*: The temperature at which dissolved solids are not completely soluble and precipitation of these solids gives the fuel a cloudy appearance. This behaviour results in clogging of filters and injectors thereby degrading performance.
- *pour point*: The temperature at which a liquid becomes semi-solid and loses its ability to flow readily.
- *viscosity*: A measure of the resistance of a fluid to deform under stress, i.e. its ability to flow. Low viscosity fluids flow easily whereas high viscosity fluids do not flow as freely. Molasses has a high viscosity and flows only sluggishly, whereas water has low viscosity and flows easily.

The combination of these variables determines a particular fuel's suitability for different applications. For example, a fuel with low cloud and pour points would be suitable for use in cold conditions. In contrast, a fuel with a high fire point is inherently safer to handle than one with a low fire point.

Energy Content

An ideal transportation liquid fuel, or any fuel for that matter, must have very high energy content. Higher energy contents means a vehicle can carry less fuel to go a given distance. At the same time, the lower amount of fuel carried allows the vehicle to move more people, goods and raw materials. Thus, the shift in transportation fuel has been historically from lower to higher energy content, i.e. wood to coal to oil.

Energy content can be measured using either energy density or specific energy (Figure 6). *Energy density* is the energy content of a fuel per volume, e.g. Btu/gal, J/l. It is sometimes referred to as volumetric energy density, which is actually a redundant term. In contrast, *specific energy* is energy per mass, e.g. Btu/lb, J/g. Specific energy is often called gravimetric energy density, but this term is inaccurate because density refers to a quantity per volume not mass. Since density refers to quantities per mass, the term is factually inaccurate in terms of energy content. The best transportation fuels have high energy densities and specific energies and will plot in the upper right corner of a plot of energy density versus specific energy (Figure 6a).

In terms of energy content, the best liquid fuels are those derived from petroleum or crude oil (Figure 6b). Fuels, such as diesel and gasoline, have high energy densities and specific energies. In contrast, biofuels, e.g. methanol, ethanol, have lower energy densities and specific energies. Vehicles burning these types of liquid fuels will have to consume more fuel to travel the same distance as a similar vehicle powered by

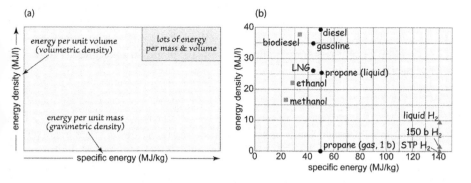

Figure 6. (a) Fuels can be gauged by their energy density (energy/volume) and specific energy (energy/mass). Both are high in a good transportation fuel. (b) Whereas the various physical forms of hydrogen, i.e. gas and liquid, have high specific energy, their energy density is low. For the most part, the best transportation fuels are liquid fuels derived from refining of petroleum. Source: J.D. Myers. Used with permission.

petroleum-derived liquid fuels. Although it is proposed as a transportation fuel of the future, hydrogen in all its physical states has energy densities much less than either bio- or petroleum fuels. Thus, a transportation system powered by hydrogen will require much larger quantities of fuel than our current system. The use of natural gas to power transportation suffers from a similar low energy density. Compressing the gas to a liquid state raises its energy density to near that of ethanol and methanol, but results in a much reduced energy return on investment (EROI).

The superior properties of gasoline and diesel can be illustrated by plotting energy content per unit weight (specific energy) versus energy content per volume (energy density). To make the plot more illustrative, gasoline is indexed to 1 on both axes and other fuels plotted relative to how they compare with gasoline (Figure 7). Plotted in this manner, the graph defines four quadrants or regions that quickly and visually show the value of different fuels relative to gasoline. Fuels plotting in the upper left quadrant are lighter than gasoline but will require a large fuel tank. This quadrant is occupied by the various phases of hydrogen fuels (Figure 7). Although fuel loads would be lighter, they would occupy a greater percentage of the vehicle's volume. Conversely, fuels in the lower right section are heavier than gasoline, thus they require less space. Currently, there are no reasonable fuel alternatives that occupy this quadrant. The lower left quadrant marks fuels inferior to gasoline with regards to both weight and volume (Figure 7). Biofuels, batteries, and compressed propane all fall into this quadrant. For the same distance travelled, vehicles utilizing these fuels would have to carry heavier fuel loads that occupy more space. Any fuel that plots in the upper right quadrant of the diagram would be a superior transportation fuel than gasoline. It would require less space and weigh less than an energy equivalent gasoline load. Thus, if a vehicle's fuel could be switched from gasoline to this fuel, it would carry a light fuel load and weigh less allowing for more goods and people to be moved further on an energy equivalent fuel load. Unfortunately, no fuels currently occupy this quadrant of the diagram (Figure 7). Clearly, the utility of gasoline will make it difficult to transform our transportation system to a new liquid fuel and still maintain the same services and energy performance.

Liquid Fuel Sources

To understand where our liquid fuels come from and the issues we face in powering transportation, it is useful to review current and future sources of liquid fuels. Liquid fuels can be divided into conventional oil and non-conventional liquids. *Conventional oil* includes those types of liquid hydrocarbons that flow freely to a production well. It consists of the better known crude oil as well as several other less known sources of liquid petroleum, including condensate and natural gas liquids. *Condensate* is the components of crude oil that at reservoir conditions, i.e. high temperature and pressure, is gaseous in form, but condenses to liquid when brought to the lower pressure and temperature of the Earth's surface. *Natural gas liquids*

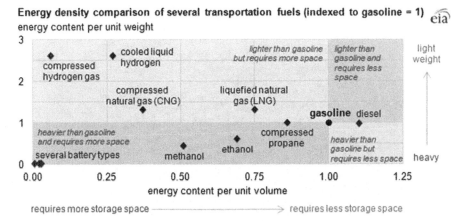

Figure 7. Comparison of gasoline versus other fuel sources on the basis of weight and volume. Fuels with better properties than gasoline will plot in the upper right quadrant. Source: Energy Information Administration, based on the National Defense University.

(NGL) are light hydrocarbon molecules in gas reservoirs that naturally liquefy at atmospheric conditions or can be easily liquefied by simple processing.

Non-conventional sources of liquid fuels consist of unconventional petroleum and non-petroleum sources that can be converted to liquid fuels. *Unconventional petroleum* is crude oil that needs some sort of stimulation to be produced and/or must be upgraded before it can be refined into a liquid fuel. Sources that fall solely into the stimulation category are heavy oil, shale oil, tight oil, and deep and ultra-deep oil. Conversely, oil shale and oil sands have hydrogen to carbon ratios (H/C) outside the range of typical petroleum based liquid fuels and must be chemically upgraded before they can be refined into secondary fuels. Theoretically, any high carbon and hydrogen feedstock can be converted to liquid hydrocarbons by altering their H/C ratio. Realistically, there are only three feedstocks that offer the potential for large-scale liquid fuel production in the future: gas-to-liquid (GTL); coal-to-liquid (CTL); or biomass-to-liquid (BTL), i.e. biofuels.

Not surprisingly, current production of liquid fuels is dominated by conventional oil. In 2007, production averaged 80.7 million barrels per day with the largest fraction coming from crude oil and a smaller fraction from natural gas liquids (NGL; Figure 9). Non-conventional liquid fuels comprised only a small fraction of total production (1.98 mb/d). The vast majority of this (1.2 mb/d) is from oil sands, i.e. a hydrocarbon source. Smaller fractions come from coal and gas to liquids, both sourced from hydrocarbons (Figure 9). Biofuels production, despite government mandates and rapid growth in recent years, is still only a small fraction of the liquid fuels needed to power global transportation.

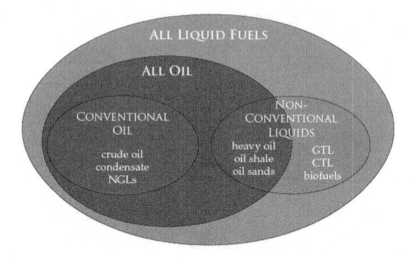

Figure 8. Potential sources of liquid fuels. Conventional oil supplies are declining whereas non-conventional are growing in importance. Source: after Sorrell et al. (2010).

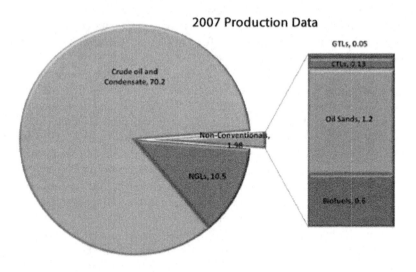

Figure 9. Relative percentage of liquid fuels derived from the different sources. Source: Sorrell et al. (2010).

THE NATURE OF CRUDE OIL

Petroleum is a naturally-occurring substance found in sold, liquid, or gaseous states and composed mainly of mixtures of chemical compounds of carbon and hydrogen, with or without other nonmetallic elements such as sulfur, oxygen, and nitrogen. It varies considerable in physical and chemical properties and is found on land, in the ocean basins, near the surface, deep underground, and in all types of physical environments.

Physical Characteristics

Petroleum or crude oil varies greatly in its physical properties. For example, heavy oils are opaque, black to dark brown and so viscous they barely flow at room temperature and pressure. In contrast, light oils are clear, green to yellow in color and highly fluid. This difference in physical nature determines, in large part, the economic value of a particular type of crude oil.

Three parameters are used to describe the physical nature of crude oil:

- *API gravity*: Specific gravity of oil measured at 60°F. Light oils have high API (35-45) and are highly valuable. In contrast, heavy oils have low API (10-25) and are correspondingly less valuable. API is the abbreviation for the American Petroleum Institute, an industry organization that sets many of the standards used in the oil and gas industry.
- *sulfur content*: Sulfur in crude oil causes problems during transport, refining, and combustion. Thus, oils with high sulfur must be treated to remove the sulfur and are less valuable than low-sulfur crude oils. Sweet refers to crude oils with less than 1 wt % sulfur. Crudes with higher sulfur content are classified sour.
- *pour point*: Whether or not a crude oil will pour at surface conditions is important in determining its value. The temperature at which a crude oil will pour is determined by its wax content. Waxes are hydrocarbon molecules with more than 18 carbons. Low pour point (low wax) means the oil remains liquid to very low temperatures. Because they are easier to handle over a range of surface conditions, low pour point oils are more valuable than those with higher pour points.

A common means of comparing and characterizing crude oil is by its density. The American Petroleum Institute has defined a density scale, the *°API gravity* that has become the global oil industry standard (Figure 10). The °API gravity scale was developed originally in the chemical industry and was only later applied to liquid hydrocarbons. The scale uses the specific gravity of the oil measured at 60°F. *Specific gravity* is the ratio of the weight of a given volume of liquid to the weight of an equal volume of a standard liquid under the same conditions. For liquids, the standard liquid is typically water. On the °API gravity scale, freshwater would have a value of 10. The API of a crude oil can be measured by placing a sample of it in a hydrometer and directly reading the value from a scale on the instrument.

One of the most common, undesirable contaminants in crude oil is *sulfur*. It causes problems both during refining and burning of crude oil or refined products. During refining, sulfur can damage some of the equipment in the refinery if it is not removed early during the process. When petroleum products containing sulfur

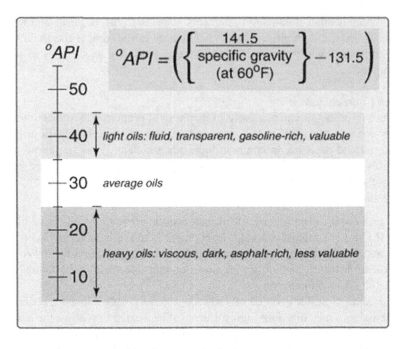

$$^{o}API = \left(\left\{ \frac{141.5}{\text{specific gravity} \atop (\text{at } 60^{o}F)} \right\} - 131.5 \right)$$

°API

50

40   light oils: fluid, transparent, gasoline-rich, valuable

30   average oils

20

  heavy oils: viscous, dark, asphalt-rich, less valuable

10

Figure 10. Definition of the API gravity scale for oil (top) and the numerical scale with some of t he corresponding oil characteristics. Source: J.D. Myers. Used with permission.

are burned, they release sulfur dioxide which when combined with moisture in the atmosphere produces acid precipitation, i.e. rain and snow. Because of these adverse effects, sulfur must be removed from crude oil during the refining process. Based on their sulfur content, crude oils are defined as sweet (less than 1 wt % sulfur) or sour (greater than 1 wt % sulfur). Sulfur in crude oil can occur in elemental form in solution or as hydrogen sulfide (H_2S), a deadly gas dissolved in the oil. The terms sweet and sour come from the historical practice of tasting a crude oil to determine its nature. Crudes with high sulphur had a sour taste, whereas those with low sulphur were sweet. This practice is rarely used today.

Hydrocarbon molecules with more than 18 carbons are waxes and have a significant influence on the physical characteristics of a crude oil. At the high temperatures of the oil reservoir, waxes are liquid. However, as the crude is lifted to the surface it cools and the waxes may solidify. Obviously, solidification of the waxes can have an adverse effect on crude oil handling. If waxes are a significant component of the crude oil, the oil can harden as it rises and clog production equipment forcing a shutdown of the well for workover. In contrast, crude oils with low wax content will not solidify as they are produced. Paraffins, a special type of waxes, are long straight hydrocarbon chains and important components of all crude oils.

Given their impact on physical nature, it is important to have a measure of the wax content of an oil. Wax content of crude oil is indicated by the *pour point*. This parameter is determined by heating the crude and pouring it as it is cooling. The lowest temperature at which the oil will still pour is the pour point. The range of observed crude oil pour points is 125°F to -75°F (52°C to -60°C). The higher the pour point, the greater the wax content. The color of the crude oil varies with wax content. Low or no wax crude oils, i.e. all paraffins have less than 18 carbons, are black whereas very waxy crudes are greenish. A yellow color marks crudes with only small amounts of waxes.

Chemical Characteristics

Crude oil is not a single chemical compound or molecule. Rather it is composed of hundreds perhaps thousands of different molecules. Each batch of crude oil has a different number of different molecules of varying amounts. All of these compounds are, however, *hydrocarbons*. They are molecules primarily composed of hydrogen and carbon in varying proportions. The number of hydrogens and carbons in each type of molecule differs as well as the physical arrangement of these atoms. A particular crude oil may contain hundreds of different types of hydrocarbon molecules and each crude oil is slightly different chemically from other crude oils.

Every crude oil is a mixture of molecules from three different hydrocarbon series, i.e. a general type of hydrocarbon molecule. In addition, the percentages of molecules within each series vary between oils. The types and percentages of hydrocarbon series molecules determine the chemical and physical properties of the crude oil.

Hydrocarbon molecules consist of different proportions of carbon and hydrogen chemically bonded together. In these molecules, carbon acts as a cation meaning that it carries a positive four electrical charge and can form four covalent bonds with other atoms. It can bond to either hydrogen or another carbon. The ability to bond to other carbons is what makes possible the large and complex variety of hydrocarbon molecules. The bond between carbons can be either single (one shared electron), double (two shared electrons) or even triple (three shared electrons). Hydrogen, in contrast, is an anion with a negative one charge. In hydrocarbon molecules, it can only bond to carbon atoms. Hydrocarbon molecules fall into five different series or classes:

- *alkanes*: Straight chains (*paraffins*) and branching chains (*isoparaffins*) hydrocarbon molecules, in which all carbon atoms are joined to other carbon atoms by single bonds (saturated). Their general formula is C_nH_{2n+2} where $n \geq 1$.
- *alkenes* (known historically as *olefins*): Straight hydrocarbon chains with double bonds between some carbon atoms (unsaturated). Their general formula is C_nH_{2n}.
- *cycloalkanes (known historically as naphthenes)*: Carbons arranged in cyclic rings with three or more carbons joined by single bonds (saturated hydrocarbons). The general molecular formula for the cycloalkanes is $C_nH_{2(n+1-g)}$ where g is the number of carbon rings in the molecule.

249

- *aromatics*: Six carbons arranged in a closed, hexagonal ring, but joined by alternating single and double bonds (unsaturated hydrocarbons). In very complex aromatic hydrocarbons, the rings may be joined or fused by sharing carbons to form a three-dimensional molecular structure.
- *asphaltics*: Very large hydrocarbon molecules with 40 to more than 100 carbons.

The *alkanes* are a group of hydrocarbon molecules with general formula C_nH_{2n+2}. In the general formula, the number of carbons, n, can vary indefinitely. The simplest alkanes are methane (n = 1), ethane (n = 2), and propane (n = 3). As n increases, the resultant alkane hydrocarbons change from gas (n ≤ 4) to liquid (n = 5-19) to solid or semi-solid (n ≥ 20). When n = 100, the alkane is hextane ($C_{100}H_{202}$). Although they share a common formula, there are, in fact, two alkane series with different structural forms. Paraffins form hydrocarbon molecules with the carbons arranged in straight chains and bonded through single C-C bonds (Figure 11). In contrast, isoparaffins are branched chains with some of the carbon atoms off the main chain and bonded to carbons atoms in the chain (Figure 11). As with the paraffins, all C-C bonds are single so the molecules are saturated. Despite their identical composition, paraffin and isoparaffin molecules have different boiling temperatures and chemical reactivity. Because of their different packing arrangements, they also have different densities. All of these physical differences are important in the refining of crude oil.

Another class of hydrocarbons, the *alkenes* have double bonds between some of their carbons. Because of the presence of the double bond, the number of hydrogen atoms in these molecules is reduced (Figure 11) and their general formula is C_nH_{2n}. The alkenes are unsaturated hydrocarbons. Somewhat surprisingly, the double C-C bond is weaker than the single C-C bond so alkenes are chemically reactive and react with other compounds to eliminate the double bond. Thus, they do not occur naturally in crude oil, but are produced in cracking processes during refining. They are particularly valuable because of their high chemical reactivity and are used to make a variety of other hydrocarbons during refining. They are also important in the formulation of gasoline and diesel.

The *cycloalkanes* are hydrocarbon molecules in which the carbon molecules are arranged in a cyclic ring structure with three or more carbons. The most important cycloalkanes with respect to crude oil have five and six member rings. The carbons are bonded to each other by single bonds so the molecules are saturated. Two hydrogen atoms are bonded to each carbon which is also bonded to two other carbons. Another class of closed cyclic hydrocarbons are the *aromatics*. In this class, the carbon atoms are centered at the apices of a regular hexagon and bonded to each other by alternating single and double bonds. Because the double bonds are weaker than single ones, these hydrocarbons are highly reactive. They do not occur naturally, but are important in refining processes because of their high reactivity. The largest hydrocarbons molecules make up the *asphaltics*. They contain more than 40 carbons and some have up to 100. They produce heavy, viscous oil, which alkanes (C_nH_{2n+2})   alkenes (C_nH_{2n})

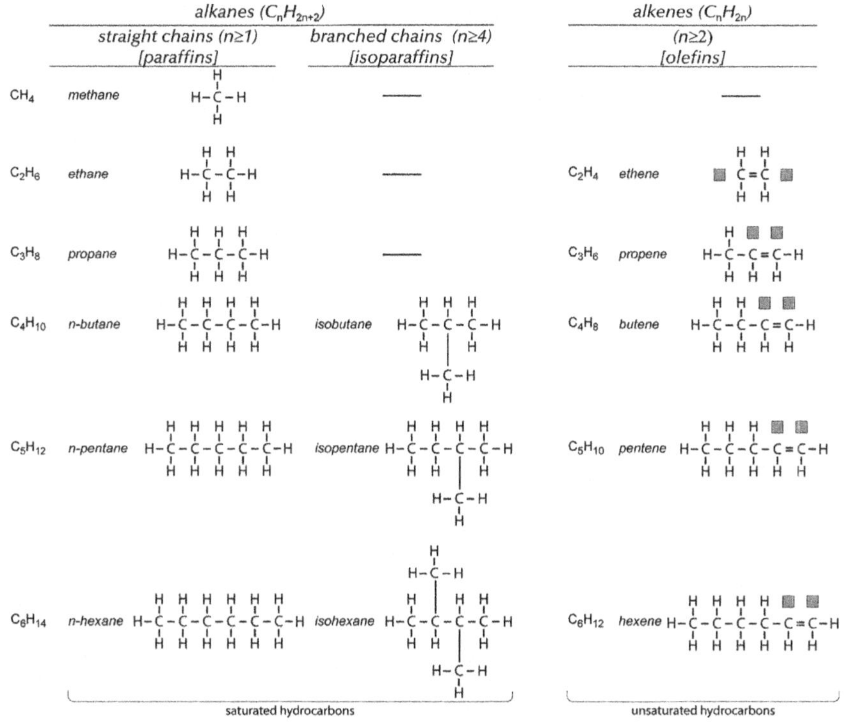

straight chains (n≥1) [paraffins]	branched chains (n≥4) [isoparaffins]	(n≥2) [olefins]

CH_4 methane

C_2H_6 ethane

C_3H_8 propane

C_4H_{10} n-butane   isobutane

C_5H_{12} n-pentane   isopentane

C_6H_{14} n-hexane   isohexane

C_2H_4 ethene

C_3H_6 propene

C_4H_8 butene

C_5H_{10} pentene

C_6H_{12} hexene

saturated hydrocarbons   unsaturated hydrocarbons

Figure 11. The structural formulas for the alkanes (paraffins) and alkenes (olefins). The alkanes (left) form straight and branched chains with all single bonds making them saturated. The alkenes (right) contain at least one double C-C bond thus they are unsaturated. The red squares near the alkene formulas mark positions of hydrogens replaced by the double C-C bond in the molecule. Source: J.D. Myers. Used with permission.

suggests their organic precursors did not reached very high temperatures during the oil formation process.

Of the thousands of hydrocarbon molecules in crude oil, the most important are the smaller molecules in the alkane series. The alkenes are also important because of their reactivity and ability to reduce engine knock. Since they do not occur naturally in crude oils because of their reactivity, they are produced during various refining processes.

Crude Oil's Value

Basic crude oils are identified by a two term combination that refers to viscosity (light vs heavy) and sulfur content (sweet - low and sour - high). Light, sweet crudes (e.g. West Texas intermediate) are low sulfur crude oils that are easy to process. They produce more transportation fuels per barrel and are easier to refine into cleaner-burning fuels. These oils fetch the highest prices on the spot market. Heavy, sour crudes are higher in viscosity, have greater sulfur contents, and require special equipment to refine. They produce less of the more desirable refined products, e.g. gasoline, diesel, jet fuel, etc., per barrel that light oils. Currently, they run $18-20 cheaper per barrel than light crudes. Petroleum from Mexico, Canada, Venezuela, and Saudi Arabia are dominantly heavy, sour crudes.

A *crude stream* is a characteristic crude oil that is produced by an oil-producing nation. It may be for export or internal consumption. Crude streams may represent petroleum from a single oil field or a blend produced by mixing one or more crude oils from different oil fields. The characteristics of important crude streams vary considerably (Table 1).

Another type of crude oil descriptor commonly encountered in media reports is the *benchmark crude*. A benchmark crude is a crude oil used by an oil-producing country or region as a standard for comparing oils and setting prices (Table 2). Each nation will have one or more different benchmark crude oils.

Crude oils from around the world have very different physical characteristics (Figure 12). Historically, most petroleum production produced was of light, sweet crudes. These crudes are easier to refine and produce a great proportion of the most valuable refined petroleum products. After decades of production, output from oil fields tapping these crude oils is falling steadily. In contrast, production of heavy, sour crude oils is steadily rising as more and more unconventional sources of petroleum are produced. Because of their physical and chemical nature, heavy crudes produce less of the most valuable refined products. Thus, they require more complex refiners for processing. Their higher abundances of sulfur and metals also

Table 1. Important crude oil streams, their country of origin and their physical characteristics. Data sources:EIA (2010), Hyne (2001)

crude stream	country	API gravity	S (%)	pour point (°F)
Brass River	Nigeria	40.9	0.1	-5
Bonny light	Nigeria	36.7	0.1	36
Arabian light	Saudi Arabia	33.4	1.8	-30
Iranian light	Iran	33.8	1.4	-20
Dubai	Dubai	31.1	2	-5
Kuwait export	Kuwait	31.4	2.5	0
Ekofisk	Norway	43.4	0.2	15
Brent Blend	Great Britain	38	0.4	-
North Slope	USA	38	0.3	-5
Bachequero	Venezuela	16.8	2.4	-10

Table 2. Important benchmark crude oils and their physical characteristics. Data sources: EIA (2010), Hyne (2001)

crude stream	country	API gravity	S (%)	pour point (°F)
Bonny light	Nigeria	36.7	0.1	36
Dubai	Dubai	31.1	2	-5
West Texas Intermediate	USA	40	0.3	-
West Texas Sour	USA	31.7	1.28	-
Brent Blend	United Kingdom	38	0.4	-

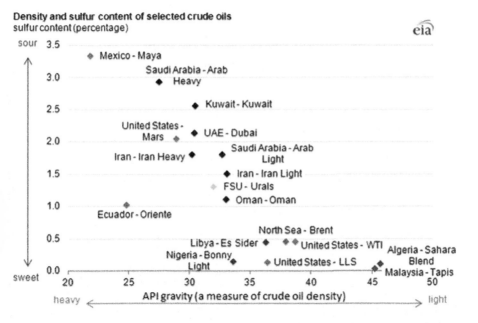

Figure 12. Sulfur content versus API gravity for a variety of different crude oils. The most valuable oils are the light, sweet crudes plotting in the lower right corner of the graph. The least valuable are the heavy, sours in the upper left corner. Source: Energy Information Administration, based on Energy Intelligence Group – International Crude Oil Market Handbook.

have a greater environmental burden and require specific refining processes to remove these pollutants. The continuing shift in production from light, sweet crudes to heavy, sour varieties has profound ramifications for the oil industry of the future (Figure 12).

PETROLEUM GEOLOGY

Formation

Petroleum is produced by alteration of organic matter by heat as it is buried in the Earth. Four factors that determine the type of petroleum formed are the: nature of organic matter accumulated; abundance of organic matter; maximum temperature the organic matter was exposed to during burial; and duration of maximum temperature.

The different geologic environments where fossil fuels can be formed are marked by the presence of three types of organic matter: algae from warm, freshwater lakes; single-celled organisms such as plankton, algae and bacteria living in parts of oceans; and plants including spores and pollen characteristic of land environments (Figure 13). Petroleum is mostly derived from marine organisms. Once buried, these organisms are subjected to organic decay that if it proceeded to completion would completely break down the organic matter and recycle its constituent elements back into the biosphere, hydrosphere, and atmosphere. To prevent complete decay during subsequent burial, organic matter must accumulate in oxygen-poor or deficient geologic environments or in sufficient quantity that when the oxygen is depleted by decay there is still organic matter remaining. Thus, the organic material that might eventually become petroleum accumulates in anoxic, marine environments. To a much lesser degree, organic matter that accumulates in poorly mixed freshwater lakes may produce petroleum upon burial.

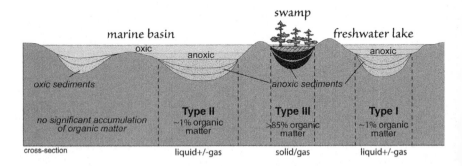

Figure 13. Different types of organic matter accumulate in different geologic environments. The accumulation of marine organisms in anoxic, restricted circulation marine basins is the most likely environment for oil formation. Only a small amount of organic material need accumulate in the sediment for oil to be formed. Source: J.D. Myers. Used with permission.

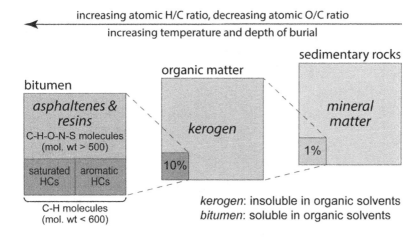

increasing atomic H/C ratio, decreasing atomic O/C ratio

increasing temperature and depth of burial

kerogen: insoluble in organic solvents
bitumen: soluble in organic solvents

Figure 14. The organic matter that must accumulate in sediments and be preserved in sedimentary rocks is very small. Source: J.D. Myers. Used with permission.

To produce petroleum, only a small amount of organic matter need to accumulate in the sediments (< 1%). Some estimates place the amount as low as 0.5 % organic matter (Figure 14).

To convert the organic molecules of organic matter to the hydrocarbon molecules characteristic of petroleum, the material must be buried to great depths under a thick blanket of accumulating sediment. Burial raises the temperature and pressure and produces chemical changes in the carbohydrate molecules of the organic matter. In particular, oxygen and water are driven off and the molecules are thermally cracked (broken) into smaller molecules, thereby increasing the H/C ratio. To start this process, the organic matter must attain depths where the temperature is around 75°C, i.e. the top of the oil window (Figure 15). If the rocks reach depths where temperatures are in access of 175°C, the oil is broken down to form the simplest hydrocarbon molecules and forms natural gas. Thus, the type of oil produced, e.g. heavy or light, depends upon the maximum temperature attained and how long the organic matter remained in the oil window (Figure 15).

Migration

The petroleum in a source rock is widely dispersed and low in abundance. If one were to drill into a source rock, the oil would not flow to the well in exploitable quantities. In addition, the low permeability of source rocks means the rate at which the oil reached the well would be uneconomic. However, petroleum is commercially extractable, sometimes at astonishing rates. Thus, petroleum must move from its source formations to reservoir rocks where it accumulates in greater volume. The important question is: How does this process occur?

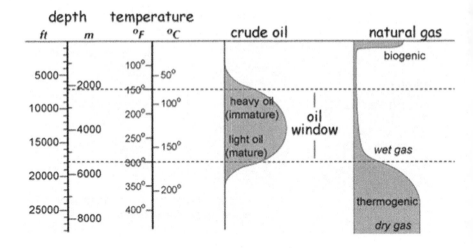

Figure 15. The oil window defines the depths and temperatures organic matter must reach before the process of oil formation begins. The type of oil produced depends on the maximum temperature attained in the oil window and the time spent at that temperature. Source: J.D. Myers. Used with permission.

The movement of petroleum out of its source rocks to reservoir rocks is a two-stage process involving primary and secondary migration (Figure 16). *Primary migration* is the movement of petroleum through and out of its source rock. Source rocks are typically fine-grained, organic-rich sedimentary rocks, e.g. shales. Shales commonly have low porosity and permeability, so migration of petroleum out of them is difficult. As the sediment is buried, they are compacted and squeezed, thereby forcing trapped water out and building up pressure. Oil may migrate from the source rock with the water and as a result of the pressurizing of the formation.

After exiting its source rock, petroleum begins *secondary migration* (Figure 16). This movement is generally through high permeability rock (a carrier formation). It moves petroleum from its source rock to it final accumulation point.

Accumulation

Once oil has left the source rock and begun secondary migration, it faces three possible fates. If it encounters no barriers to its upward migration, it could migrate to the Earth's surface where contact with air results in chemical changes that alters the petroleum forming tar pits or oil seeps. Conversely, the oil could simply dissipate or disperse throughout the carrier formations as it migrates. Finally, the oil may encounter an impermeable layer (cap rock) with a porous layer (reservoir) beneath and accumulate below the cap rock or seal (Figure 16). In this case, the reservoir

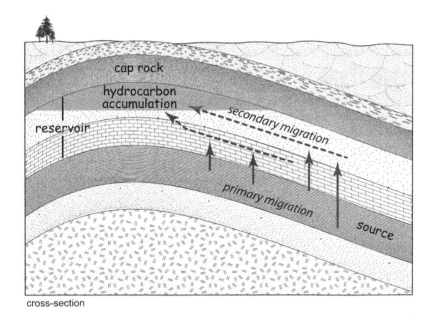

cross-section

Figure 16. After formation in the oil window, oil migrates out of the source rock into carrier formations through which it migrates to a site of accumulation. Source: J.D. Myers. Used with permission.

fills from the top down as the denser water is displaced by lighter petroleum and possibly natural gas. Of the three possible scenarios, only the last one might result in an economically recoverable hydrocarbon resource. It is estimated that only 10 % or less of all oil formed in the subsurface actually accumulates in a petroleum or oil trap.

Petroleum Traps

Petroleum is less dense than the water that it occurs with. Consequently, with time, it rises upward. If it does not encounter an impermeable layer, it will rise all the way to the Earth's surface where the lighter fractions will evaporate. This produces the oil seeps and tar pits that were important sources of early petroleum products. To prevent its loss and to form an oil field, petroleum must be trapped before it reaches the surface and allowed to accumulate. The combinations of natural geologic conditions that favour accumulation of oil define a *petroleum trap*. Oil companies spend considerable time, effort, and money looking for the right combination of geologic conditions that may have produced an oil trap.

The formation of an oil trap requires a number of different components and the arrangement of these components in a specific vertical sequence. The components of an oil trap include; a cap formation; a reservoir formation and a source rock. A *cap rock* is an impermeable geologic unit that slows the movement of the petroleum toward the surface. They are typically shales, i.e. fine-grained, clastic sedimentary rocks formed by the accumulation of solid particles. A *reservoir rock* is a unit that has high permeability and porosity which permits large volumes of petroleum to accumulate. This is the unit that an oil company will drill a well into to recover oil. Sandstones (coarse-grained, clastic sedimentary rocks) and limestones (chemical sedimentary rocks formed by precipitation of minerals from seawater) make the best reservoirs. The *source rock* is a geologic unit with the organic material that was exposed to elevated temperature and converted to oil and/or gas. As mentioned earlier, the most likely candidates are organic-rich shales.

The spatial arrangement of geologic units that produce traps are quite varied but fall into three broad categories. Structural traps are the products of folding and faulting produced by tectonic forces acting in the Earth's crust (Figure 17). Stratigraphic traps are produced by the processes of sedimentation that were active when the sedimentary rocks formed. In this situation, a combination of permeable and impermeable layers were originally deposited close to each other in a sedimentary environment.

Another very different but important type of oil trap is formed by *salt formations* (Figure 18). Salt is an evaporative mineral produced when seawater evaporates and produces a brine. When the concentration of dissolved solids reach about 3 %, the brine begins to precipitate salt. Further basin subsidence results in the salt layers being buried under a thick layer of overlying sediment. Under the weight of overlying units, the less dense and plastic salt begins to flow forming diapirs (blobs) that rise upward. This motion causes the overlying layers to be pierced and bent upward producing domes (Figure 18). It may also induce normal faulting above the rising diapir. Petroleum commonly accumulates along faults above the dome as well as immediately adjacent to the dome itself since salt is impermeable to fluid flow.

Oil is not the only fluid typically present in a petroleum trap. Water is also always present. In many petroleum traps, natural gas is often present as well. Because of their different densities, these fluid phases are commonly vertically stratified in a trap (Figure 19). Since it is the least dense fluid, gas, if present, will occupy the highest portion of the trap. Below the gas is the crude oil. At the bottom of the trap and below the oil zone is water. It may be freshwater, although more often it is highly salty, i.e. a brine.

Because the fluids in a trap are immiscible, they will be separated by liquid interfaces, referred to as contacts, between the different fluids (Figure 19). These contacts are mostly horizontal, because they represent the interface between two fluids under gravitational force. In some reservoirs, dynamic forces, e.g. groundwater flow, acting of the fluids may produce sloping contacts. Traps containing both gas and oil have two fluid contacts: GOC (gas-oil contact) and

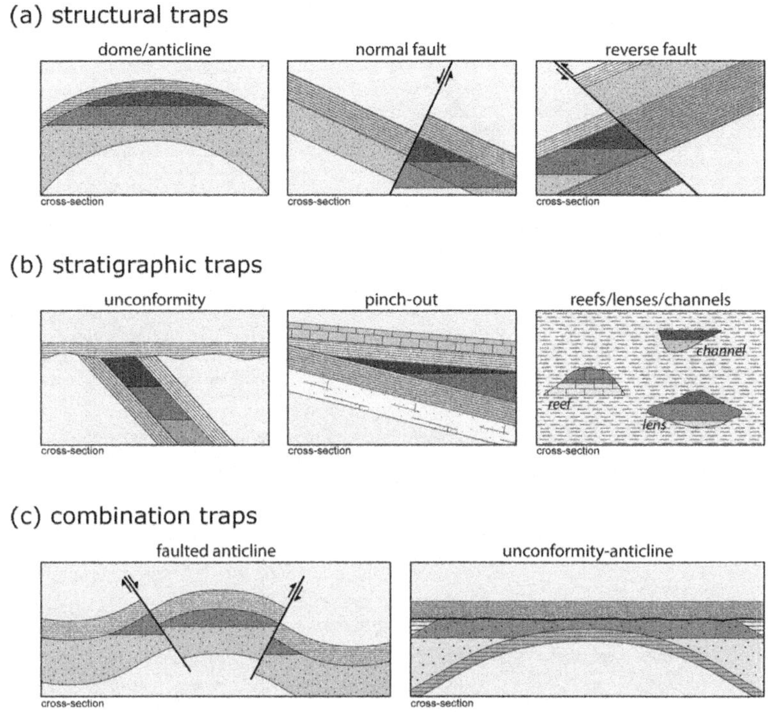

(a) structural traps

dome/anticline   normal fault   reverse fault

(b) stratigraphic traps

unconformity   pinch-out   reefs/lenses/channels

(c) combination traps

faulted anticline   unconformity-anticline

Figure 17. The three primary classes of petroleum traps. Source: J.D. Myers. Used with permission.

OWC (oil-water contact). In these situations, the gas is termed associated gas, i.e. it is associated with oil. When there is only one hydrocarbon in the trap, there is a single contact. For gas-only reservoirs, the fluid contact is GWC (gas-water contact) and the gas is non-associated gas. If it cannot be economically moved to a market, it is also referred to as stranded gas. When no gas is present only oil, the single fluid contact in the reservoir is an OWC (Figure 19). These contacts play a vital role in petroleum exploration and particularly in estimating the amount of hydrocarbons in a trap.

The oil industry uses a wide range of terminology to describe the practical aspects of a hydrocarbon trap. These terms are important because their dimensions and positions within a trap are useful in calculating the amounts of oil and gas in a trap. The highest point of the trap is the *crest* (Figure 19). Traps typically have a point at depth where the hydrocarbon fluids in the trap can leak out of the structure and migrate toward the surface or into other structures. This point is the *spill point* and it determines how much hydrocarbon fluids could be stored in the trap. The distance

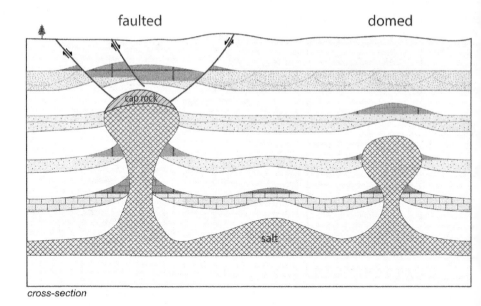

Figure 18. The various types of petroleum traps formed by the rising of salt formations to form salt domes and other types of traps. Source: J.D. Myers. Used with permission.

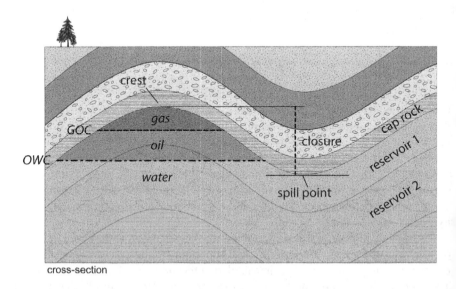

Figure 19. A structural petroleum trap is a geological structure that traps oil and possibly natural gas in a reservoir formation beneath a cap rock. Somewhere below these two units is the source rock where the petroleum was formed. Source: J.D. Myers. Used with permission.

between the crest and the spill point is the trap's **closure** (Figure 19). Depending upon the amount of hydrocarbon fluids held in the trap, the combined gas and oil columns may not equal the trap closure. The closure need not be vertically oriented, but depends on the orientation of the trap itself.

PETROLEUM PRODUCTION

Oil and natural gas are extracted using highly complex and engineered production wells. Offshore wells are now drilled in 5,000 feet of water and to depths of 40,000 feet below the seafloor. They can cost upwards of a $100 million and onshore wells are in the $5-10 million dollar range, with deeper, more complex wells much more costly. Drilling, completing, operating, and abandoning these structures require a wide range of geologic, engineering, and technological skills. Although understanding how an oil well is constructed and operated may seem like an arcane knowledge only useful to professionals, recent events prove otherwise. The cause of the Deepwater Horizon accident as well as the safety of hydraulic fracturing all turn on the details of oil and gas operations. Making decisions about these highly relevant social issues that are based on sound knowledge, not celebrity or politicians' sound bites or opinions, requires, at the minimum, a rudimentary understanding of how oil and gas wells are built and operated. This knowledge also provides a broader perspective for the factors that go into the cost of gasoline that you buy at the pump.

Drilling

Nearly all modern oil and gas wells are drilled using rotary drilling. *Rotary drilling* uses a rotating motion and weight to grind and fracture rock at the bottom of the hole thereby advancing the depth of the well. It is accomplished by a drill string with a bit on the end. Sections of hollow drill pipe of varying diameter and 30 feet long are screwed together to form a drill string. A derrick on the drill rig raises and lowers the drill string into and out of the hole (Figure 20). It also controls the amount of weight the drill string places on the drill bit, an important parameter in drilling. The drill string is rotated at the surface by either a kelly table or top drive and transmits this rotation down the hole, sometimes over 45,000 feet, to the drill bit. Drilling fluid, called mud, is circulated down the center of the drill string and up the annulus between the rock and drill string to the surface. The drilling fluid cools the bit, flushes cuttings from the bottom of the hole, and prevents formation fluids from entering the well. It also serves to stabilize the borehole against collapse.

The *drill bit* at the end of the drill string is the rig component that actually makes the hole. It grinds, cuts, scrapes, and crushes rock at the bottom of the well through its rotary motion. During drilling of a well, formations of different hardnesses and abrasiveness are encountered. To accommodate these variations, a variety of drill bit classes have been developed (Kennedy, 1983). Perhaps the most common is the two

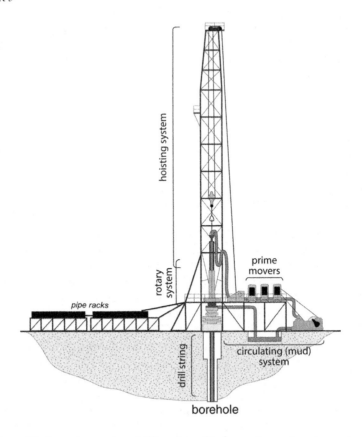

Figure 20. An onshore rotary drilling rig and is five major engineering systems.
Source: J.D. Myers. Used with permission.

or three cone rotary bit. This bit consists of the cones mounted on the drill bit pointing inward so that they intermesh. Each cone rests on a shaft that is anchored to the drill bit. Bearings around the shafts allow the cones to rotate as the drill string is rotated. The cones either have milled teeth or tungsten carbide insert teeth that actually do the drilling. For the hardest rocks, some tri-cones use natural or synthetic diamond inserts. To drill soft rock, the teeth on the bit are longer than on those bits for drilling hard rock. An alternative to the cone roller bit is the polycrystalline compact (PDC) bit, which uses synthetic diamond disks to shear the rock. Regardless of the type of bit, they all have openings through which drilling mud flows through to flush the cuttings being produced.

To provide information about particular formations intersect, core is often taken during drilling of a well, especially exploratory wells. A *core* is a solid cylinder of rock drilled out to preserve the spatial relations of the geologic formations. It may be hundreds of feet long and are usually taken in reservoir formations, but occasionally in the cap rock. When core is taken, a core bit consisting of a cylindrical, hollow tube is used. The bit cuts an annulus of rock leaving the center, i.e. the core, intact. For particularly hard formations, diamonds may be embedded in the bit face. As drilling proceeds, bits become worn, penetration rate decreases, and the bit must be replaced. To change a bit, the entire drill string must be pulled from the well and broken down into sections, a timely and costly procedure. A drill bit may also have to be changed when the hardness or abrasiveness of the formation being drilled changes. Excessive time changing bits results in longer drilling times and increases drilling costs.

As described above, a rotary drill rig, regardless of size or drilling environment, must perform three fundamental tasks: handle drill pipe and drill string; rotate drill string to turn bit at the bottom of the hole; and pump drilling mud to the bottom of the drill hole and back to the surface. These tasks are performed by five major systems on a rig (Figure 20). The *prime movers*, mostly diesel engines and electrical motors, provide the energy to power the other four systems. The *drill string* transmits the power produced by the rotary drives from the surface to the drill bit at the bottom of the hole. The *hoisting system*, the iconic representation of a drill rig, raises and lowers the drill string, supports the weight of the string and any casing run in the hole, and determines how much of the weight of the drill string is transmitted to the drill bit. The *rotating equipment*, either a kelly table or top-drive, generates rotation and transfers that rotation to the drill string. Finally, the *circulating system* pumps the drilling fluid down and up the hole, thereby permitting it to lubricate the bit, remove cuttings from the bottom of the hole, and control external pressures acting on the hole itself.

Well Configurations

Historically, oil and gas wells were drilled vertically or as near vertical as conditions permitted (Figure 21). Although this simplified drilling operations, *vertical wells* produced short production zones and development of a given oil field required drilling from multiple surface sites. These factors increase costs as well as environmental impacts. Such operations were adequate when recovery rates of individual wells were high and environmental regulations and concerns were lax.

As wells moved offshore, it became desirable to drill multiple wells from a single production platform to reach some target located outside the footprint of the platform. Directional drilling provided this capability. It involves drilling a borehole at a predetermined angle from the vertical (deviation) out away from the drill pad or platform (Figure 21). *Directional drilling* is slower and more expensive that vertical drilling, but can reduce environmental impacts and deployment costs. In recent years, directional drilling has progressed into horizontal drilling. In this type of drilling, a vertical well is drilled to a depth near the target horizon and deviated to the horizontal (Figure 21). This latter well section is drilled within and parallel to the dip of the reservoir unit thereby greatly increasing the length of a well's producing

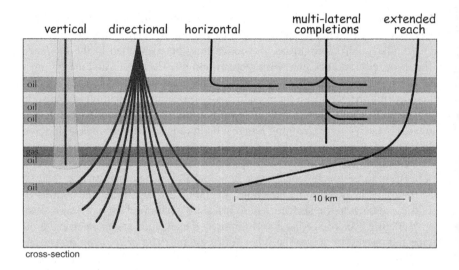

vertical   directional   horizontal   multi-lateral completions   extended reach

cross-section

Figure 21. Schematic cross-section showing the different types of wells drilled and constructed to extract oil and gas. Source: J.D. Myers. Used with permission.

zone. This can increase ultimate production 5-20 times that of a vertical well while increasing production rates. *Horizontal wells* are classified as short, medium or long-radius depending upon how sharply the well is deviated from vertical to horizontal (Figure 22).

Another new type of well, the *extended reach well*, is created using extended reach drilling (ERD). These are wells with horizontal or near horizontal segments (departures) that extend out long distances from the vertical segment of the well (Figure 21). Although not precisely defined in the oil and gas industry, an extended reach well typically has a horizontal distance to true vertical depth ratios of two or greater. ERD minimizes environmental impacts, reduces capital costs, allows access to offshore reservoirs from onshore; increases productivity and recovery; enhances production from shallow reservoirs; and increases flow of heavy oils by replacing flow through cold seafloor pipelines with movement along the wellbore at higher underground temperatures. ER and horizontal drilling allow production from oil zones only 42–72 feet (13-22 meters) thick. ER wells drilled from onshore in England reach 34,967 feet (10,658 m) into the North Sea to tap thin, shallow reservoirs (Allen et al., 1997). *Multilateral wells* consist of multiple production legs drilled from the same vertical wellbore (Figure 21). They are used to access oil zones that are thin and would not justify the cost of traditional drilling. The use of multilaterals in the Troll field in the North Sea has allowed the development of oil zones as thin as 42 feet (13 m) and added another 90 MMbbl of reserves (Oberkircher et al., 2004).

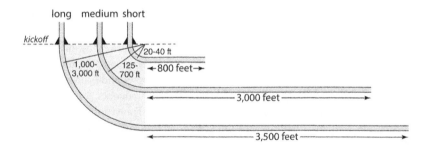

Figure 22. Horizontal wells are classified as long, medium and short radius depending upon how quickly they are deviated from vertical to horizontal. Source: J.D. Myers. Used with permission.

Casing and Cementing

Oil wells are commonly drilled to depths of 15,000 to 20,000 feet and increasingly to greater than 40,000 feet. These wells are subjected to a variety of large forces. For a variety of reasons, drilling wells in one single operation would be impractical (Hyne, 2012; Jahn et al., 2008). Near the bottom of the hole, pressures from the surrounding rocks would collapse the hole and entomb the bit (Figure 23). At shallow depths, the pressure of the drilling fluid column could damage shallow aquifers by forcing drilling fluids into the formations. At intermediate depths, drilling fluids might invade and damage oil-bearing formations (Figure 23). Alternatively, formation fluids from highly pressurized zones could enter the borehole and trigger surface blow-outs. These problems are overcome by drilling an oil well in stages and casing and cementing each stage before drilling to deeper depths (Hyne, 2012; Jahn et al., 2008).

Casing is steel pipe of varying diameter, wall thickness, and steel grade that is used to stabilize the hole, prevent formation fluids from entering the borehole, and protect shallow aquifers from contamination (Hyne, 2012; Jahn et al., 2008; Kennedy, 1983). A well will have multiple sets of casing strings, i.e. multiple sections (joints) of casing of the same diameter screwed together (Figure 23). Each string serves a different purpose. Casing consists of joints 16 to 42 feet long, but most commonly 30 feet long, which are screwed together as the string is lowered into the hole. A typical well will have: 1) a conductor casing; 2) a surface casing; and 3) a production casing. Depending upon the depth of the well and subsurface conditions, it may also have one or more intermediate casing strings. Sometimes the production casing is replaced with a production liner casing string at the very bottom of the well. Each successive string of casing extends deeper into the well and has a smaller diameter (Figure 23). Blow-out preventers will be attached to the top of the casing to prevent uncontrolled release of hydrocarbons in the case of an accident. Ultimately, when the well goes into production, the blow-out preventer will be removed and replaced by a wellhead or artificial lift device to control the flow of hydrocarbons from the well. These will be attached to the casing.

Before a drill rig is positioned, a conductor casing is either pile-driven into soft ground or set into a hole bored by a large diameter auger in hard ground. Conductor casing typically varies from 20 to over 40 inches in diameter and is driven to different depths depending upon the planned depth of the well. The deeper the well, the bigger the conductor casing diameter, and the deeper it is set. The conductor casing serves to stabilize the hole for drilling, confines drilling mud to the well pad, moves it to the mud tanks, and protects freshwater near the surface. All subsequent drilling operations are performed through the conductor casing (Figure 23).

After the conductor casing is set, a drill rig is brought in to start drilling. The rig drills through the conductor casing to below the deepest, shallow aquifer. The drill string is removed and surface casing set to protect groundwater aquifers. The casing is run (lowered) intro the hole using the drill rig's derrick for hoisting. The surface casing is run from the bottom of the hole to the surface. It has a guide shoe or round pipe with a hole in it at the bottom of the string. To clean the hole of drilling mud caked on the walls of the borehole, reamers are attached to the outside of the casing string. Arms extending from the reamers scrape the walls of the borehole as the

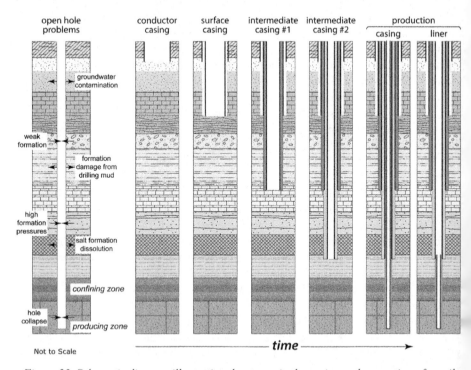

Figure 23. Schematic diagram illustrating the stages in the casing and cementing of an oil well. Source: J.D. Myers. Used with permission.

casing is lowered into the well and/or rotated. Centralizers with extended arms will be placed at intervals on the casing string to center the casing in the borehole.

When the entire casing string is set, it is cemented in place by a cement job. Cement slurry is pumped down the casing string, out its base and up the annulus between the casing and the borehole. When the cement sets or hardens (usually 8-10 hours), the casing is bonded to the formations. This bonding prevents fluid flow in the annulus and possible groundwater contamination or dilution of hydrocarbons by formation fluids (Figure 23).

With the surface casing set and cemented, drilling resumes by drilling through the cementing tools left from the cement job and the cement itself at the base of the surface casing. Depending upon the depth of the well and subsurface conditions encountered, one or more intermediate casing strings may also be set and cemented. These are used to control zones of weak rock or high formation fluid pressures as well as isolate salt formations that might dissolve if contacted by water-based drilling muds. Each of these casing strings is cemented using the same procedure as used for the surface casing.

Finally, production casing is run from the surface to the producing hydrocarbon zone. Normally, it is the smallest diameter casing used in the hole and is run the entire depth of the well. Depending on geology, a production liner may be run in place of or in addition to the production casing. Unlike production casing, a production liner is attached to the bottom of the production or intermediate casing and is not run all the way to the surface (Figure 23). This saves the expense of casing pipe in very deep wells. The production casing or liner may stop at the top of the producing formation or it may continue through to the bottom of the production zone. With the setting and cementing of the production casing or liner, the construction of the well is finished. However, it is engineered such that it cannot yet produce hydrocarbon fluids. The final stage in a well's development is well completion.

Well Completion

After the final casing string has been set and cemented, a well must be completed to enable it to produce hydrocarbons. Completing a production well entails: completing the bottom of the hole in the production zone; stimulating or treating production zones; running production tubing in the casing; placing packers to isolate different zones of the well; and attaching a wellhead or installing artificial lift. Since these activities occur both at the bottom of the well near the producing reservoir and in the upper section of the well above the reservoir, they are called lower and upper or reservoir or tubing completions (Jahn et al., 2008).

The lower completion is dependent upon where the production casing/tubing stops and the geological nature of the reservoir. The simplest is the barefoot completion used when the producing zone has been left open. An alternative is to run a production casing or liner with pre-existing holes into the producing zone, but not cement it.

There are three main completion options for a cased bottom hole. One of the most common is for a well cased and cemented through the producing zone. To allow fluid flow between the formations and well, the casing and cement are perforated using a special tool, the perforation gun that is lowered into the well on the drill string. At production depth, a series of shape charges are detonated sending high-velocity jets of gas through the casing and cement and into the reservoir formation. The charges are arranged so that they face in different directions and located at different heights. Perforating guns are expendable or retrievable and the charges can be adjusted to provide for maximum hole diameter or formation penetration length (Hyne, 2012).

The last two types of reservoir completions are used for production zones that consist of weak sands. In these formations, the main problem is keeping solids out of the well and ensuring they do not block fluid flow. In these situations, the zone around the well is packed with gravel. A screen is then run across the producing zone to keep solids from entering the well or the casing and the cement is perforated using a perforation, or perf, gun.

The upper completion determines how the produced fluids are conveyed from the producing zone to the surface as well as the components at the top of the well. Crude oil can be extracted to the surface through the production casing/liner or in production tubing. In a tubeless completion, crude oil is run to the surface in the casing itself. This provides for larger flow rates, but may lead to casing corrosion and does not provide adequate barriers to stop flow in the event of a loss of well control accident. An alternative approach is to run tubing down the well, and produce oil through both the tubing and casing. This is used for pumped wells producing at low rates and with significant gas. The gas is funnelled up the annulus between the tubing and the casing whereas the crude oil is pumped up the tubing. This arrangement produces better pump performance.

Tubing is small diameter (1.25-4.4 inch diameter), hollow steel pipe that is run down the casing to produce water, oil and/or gas. It comes in lengths of 30 feet and in different grades and types of steel. Tubing sections are screwed together like casing to produce tubing strings. Most tubing is centered in the casing using annulus packers that also seal off different portions of the casing from hydrocarbon fluids.

A single completion is used for wells with one producing zone (Figure 24a). A packer, which is made of a hollow rubber ring that can be expanded to press against the casing and tubing, is positioned above the producing zone. Once in the well, the fluid is confined to flowing up the tubing to the surface. In multiple completion wells, two tubing strings and multiple packers are used to separate two producing zones (Figure 24b). Thus, fluids from the different zones are not co-mingled, which could cause flow problems if the fluids were under different pressures and chemically and physically different (Jahn et al., 2008). The annulus between the tubing and casing can be filled with completion fluid to protect against corrosion. Tubing, since it is only hung in the well, is easier to remove and replace or repair if a problem occurs in the future than casing.

(a)   (b)

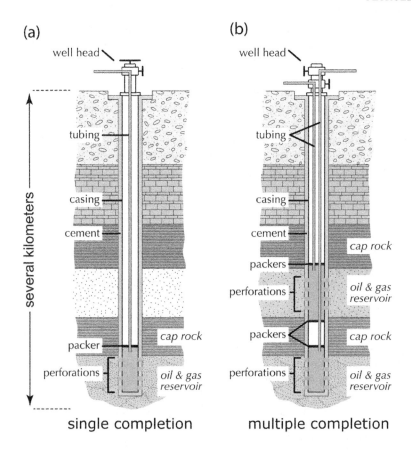

Figure 24. Diagrams illustrating a single completion (a) and multiple completion (b) of a free flowing oil well. Source: J.D. Myers. Used with permission.

The configuration for the topmost portion of a well depends upon the flow of produced fluids. For both free-flowing wells, i.e. wells in which hydrocarbons are forced all the way to the surface by reservoir drive, and non-flow, the top of the well is finished by installing a wellhead. A *wellhead* consists of a permanent forged or cast steel fitting that is welded to the conductor or surface casing. The wellhead from bottom to top consists of: the casing head, tubing head and Christmas tree (Figure 25). A *casing head* contains hangers for a casing string and a gas outlet for pressure release. Each casing string has a separate casing head and the lowermost and largest is for the surface casing. Above the casing head is the tubing head with the hanger for the tubing string. It also seals the casing-tubing annulus. The casing head allows opening and closing of the casing and in the case of pressure build-up bleeding of the gas in the casing. Monitoring casing pressure allows the operator to detect leaks in the tubing. Above the tubing housing is the *Christmas* or *production tree*. This device contains a series of values used to control the flow of oil and gas from the well. At the Christmas tree base is a master value to cut off flow from the well in an emergency (Figure 25). A pipe, the wing, extends horizontally out from the tree and is connected to a tubing string. It carries the flow of oil from the well. Whereas single completions will have one wing, multiple completions will have a wing for each tubing string. On each wing, there are chokes which are used to regulate the flow of hydrocarbons. Oil is rarely allowed to flow at the maximum rate possible. This would lead to a rapid depletion in reservoir pressure and decrease ultimate recovery. The large pressure difference between the well and reservoir created by high flow rates would also allow gas to exsolve from the oil and form bubbles. This could potentially block flow to the well. Above the wings are values that can be opened to lower wireline tools into the well for maintenance and testing. Finally, at the top of the wellhead is a pressure gauge that measures the pressure in the tubing (Figure 25). Because of their important safety role in controlling a well and its fluid production, Christmas trees are often machined from a solid block of steel (Hyne, 2012).

The majority of wells in the U.S. (~96 %) are not free-flowing, but require energy (artificial lift) to move the oil to the surface. In these cases, an artificial lift is deployed at the top of the casing. As reservoir pressure declines over time, free-flowing wells may reach a point where oil no longer makes it to the surface and they must be retrofit with artificial lift and the wellhead permanently removed. Artificial lift supplies energy to the oil in the well not the reservoir like EOR operations do. Artificial lifts can be divided into pumps and gas lift systems.

Pumps transmit mechanical energy to the oil by squeezing, pushing, or pulling it (Hyne, 2012; Jahn et al., 2008). There are five types of pumps used to produce oil:

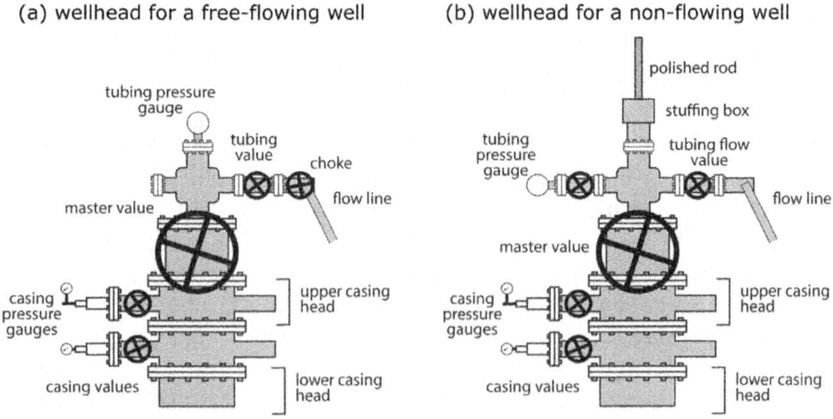

Figure 25. Schematic representation of a wellhead including the casing heads, tubing head and Christmas tree for a free flowing (a) and no-flowing well (b). Source: J.D. Myers. Used with permission.

beam pump; progressive cavity pump; electric submersible pump (ESP); hydraulic submersible pump (HSP); and jet pump. All require a source of energy to operate, so they increase production costs. A beam or rocker pump uses the up-and-down motion of a plunger to move oil up the well. Cavity pumps consist of a rotating corkscrew at the bottom of the well. The rotation of the screw moves oil upwards where it is lifted the rest of the way by a beam pump. This type of pump works well with heavy oils and low production volumes. ESPs consist of multistage centrifugal pumps that operate by lifting fluid a given vertical distance at each stage. Power is supplied by a downhole electrical motor. An HSP is a similar to an ESP, but powered by a turbine that is turned by a high-pressure fluid pumped down the hole from the surface. Because it turns faster, fewer stages are needed with a HSP, but there are problems with handling the power fluid. The jet pump is hydraulically powered but it creates a low-pressure region in the oil by passing the power fluid through a restriction. The low pressure region literally sucks oil up the well. Most of the world's oil wells using pumps employ beam pumps; however, they are stripper wells producing less than 10 b/d.

Gas lift systems do not involve transmitting mechanical energy to the fluid column. Rather, they add a low density fluid, i.e. gas, to the oil column thereby decreasing its density and reducing its resistance to upward flow. The gas is pressurized at the surface and passed down the casing outside the annulus. The different gas lift systems vary where the gas is added in the well column and whether it is added continuously or intermittently. Gas lift systems can use gas from the well itself after it is conditioned and do not consume the gas used in the process. It is, however, necessary to power the surface pump for pressurization.

PETROLEUM RECOVERY

After a well is drilled and completed, the task becomes one of getting the oil and/ or natural gas out of the ground. This process involves two steps: getting the oil/gas out of the reservoir rock and into the well; and lifting the oil/gas in the well from the producing zone to the surface (see previous section). A wide variety of equipment and processes are used to accomplish this task. In today's petroleum industry, great effort is expended to find the right combination of equipment and procedures that will maximize production from a well and an entire oil field.

Getting the oil or gas into the well cannot be accomplished by pumping. Rather it depends upon the energy stored in the reservoir to force hydrocarbons toward and into the well. Once these energy sources are depleted, oil will no longer flow and (economic) production ceases. This is the reason that initial recovery of petroleum from a reservoir is only 10-20 % with most of the original oil in place stranded in the reservoir. Recovering more of this residual oil requires adding energy to the reservoir through a variety of means. Improper management of hydrocarbon flow rates, spacing of wells too close together, producing too rapidly as well as a variety of other factors can result in rapid depletion of reservoir energy and reduced recovery.

CHAPTER 5

Thus, production and field management is critical in maximizing oil recovery and utilization of reservoir energy.

Production Curves

An oil well or, on a larger scale, an oil field goes through a series of different stages in which the oil is recovered by different means (Figure 26). Each stage results from different physical and geological conditions in the reservoir and dictates, in large part, how the well is managed. The three recovery stages are: primary recovery; secondary recovery; and tertiary recovery. Each stage involves more active intervention in oil extraction and consequently is increasingly expensive (Figure 26). In addition, each stage typically recovers a decreasing amount of hydrocarbons. Proper management of each stage is necessary to ensure maximum oil recovery from an individual well or oil field.

As production continues and the well matures, the height of the oil column adjacent to the well shrinks (Figure 27a). Because the well produces from a continually shrinking vertical distance, oil production falls over time. Ultimately, the cone of water formed below the crude oil due to extraction rises to the point where is increasingly produced by the well. Thus, as an oil well matures, oil production falls and the water cut grows (Figure 27b). Ultimately, the water to oil ratio of a well grows so large that it is no longer economically to operate the well and it is abandoned.

Primary Recovery

Primary recovery is the initial recovery stage for any oil and/or gas well and uses energy naturally present in the reservoir to drive oil/gas from the reservoir to the well. These energy sources are derived from the presence of fluids of different density in the reservoir and the lithologic and hydrostatic pressure the reservoir is subjected to. Thus, primary recovery involves four sources of energy or drives: gas drive; water drive; solution drive; combined drive (Figure 28).

As oil is extracted from the reservoir, the oil layer thins and water rises in the trap thereby maintaining pressure on the oil. This pressure forces oil into the well (Figure 28a). This *water drive* is the most efficient of the primary recovery drives. When there is a layer of natural gas above the oil, it expands as oil is removed thereby exerting pressure on the remaining oil below (Figure 28b). This *gas drive* helps to maintain natural drive in the reservoir. *Combined drive* occurs when oil is driven to the well by an expanding gas cap and a rising oil-water contact (Figure 28c). The final primary drive is *solution drive*. Petroleum commonly has gases dissolved in it. Two of the common gases are carbon dioxide (CO_2) and natural gas (Figure 28d). As the pressure in the reservoir decreases, these gases exsolve from the oil thereby expanding. The expansion of the solution gas helps maintain reservoir pressure and drives oil to the well.

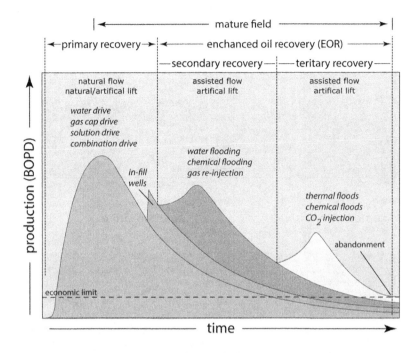

Figure 26. Cumulative oil well or field production curve showing the three principal types of oil recovery and the energy sources that drive the oil to the well. Source: J.D. Myers. Used with permission.

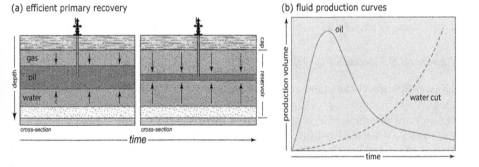

Figure 27. (a) As oil is extracted the height of the oil column shrinks and cones of gas above the well and water below the well develop. (b) With time, these changes in fluid heights cause the oil production curve to fall and the water cut to increase. Ultimately, when the cost of producing the water exceeds the value of the oil recovered, the well is abandoned. Source: J.D. Myers. Used with permission.

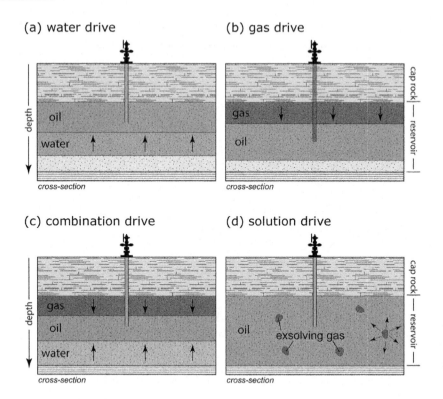

Figure 28. The four main types of primary oil recovery drives: (a) water drive; (b) gas drive; (c) combined drive and (d) solution drive. These are the natural reservoir energy sources for primary oil recovery. Source: J.D. Myers. Used with permission.

Enhanced Oil Recovery (EOR)

Even when good management procedures are used to pump an oil well or oil field, there is commonly 70-80 % of the original oil still in the reservoir when the natural drives are no longer capable of driving economic volumes of oil to the well. To recover additional oil, enhanced oil recovery (EOR) techniques are employed. There are two general classes of EOR: secondary recovery; and tertiary recovery. Although these processes increase the yield from a field, they also increase the production costs. Thus, EOR is only used when crude oil prices are high.

EOR processes are intended to restore some of the energy the reservoir has lost during primary production. In this manner, they enhance the movement of oil to the well. Although each additional EOR stage recovers more oil, the amount of oil in the reservoir that is recovered steadily declines from primary to secondary to tertiary recovery.

Secondary Recovery

The cheapest methods of EOR are *secondary recovery* methods that use the injection of water, chemical, or gas to increase the flow of oil. They produce increased cost but this is offset by the larger volume of oil produced. Even with the best secondary recovery techniques, the reservoir may still contain as much as 50% of its original petroleum when secondary methods become ineffective.

There are three primary mechanisms for secondary recovery of petroleum. These include: water flooding; chemical flooding; and gas re-injection. During *water flooding*, water is pumped through injection into the oil zone to displace the oil toward the production wells. Water used for injection is often separated from the oil extracted by production wells. This recycling lowers cost while disposing of a waste product that must otherwise be disposed of safely. Water flooding is the most common and economical of the secondary recovery methods. In many fields, water flooding is introduced early during well or field development. Saudi Arabia uses extensive water flooding with seawater to maintain production in most of their aging oil fields. *Chemical floods* inject chemicals that are soluble in oil into oil zone. As these chemicals dissolve into the petroleum, they alter its physical, e.g. viscosity, and/or chemical properties, e.g. surface tension, thereby allowing the oil to flow more freely. Generally, this technique is more expensive than water flooding because of the added cost of the chemicals. *Gas flooding* injects gas into a trap's gas cap to maintain gas pressure. For reservoirs with associated gas and highly dissolved gas contents, gas must be separated from the petroleum. Where the gas has a local market, it can be transported by pipeline and sold. However, when the gas is far from a potential market, i.e. stranded gas, it has no or limited economic value. Some of it may be used to power surface facilities, but a much larger volume must be disposed of. Historically, companies burned or flared the gas, but countries have increasingly banned this activity for environmental reasons. In these situations, the produced gas can be re-injected into the gas cap. Injection maintains, and in some instances, increases the gas cap pressure leading to an enhanced "natural gas drive". If the value of natural gas rises in the future, or cheaper means of transport are developed, the re-injected gas can be re-extracted with minimal costs.

All secondary and tertiary oil recovery methods require injecting fluid into the subsurface. Thus, a mature oil field undergoing EOR operations consists of a combination of injection and production wells. These wells must be arranged to facilitate production and maximize the benefit of the injected fluid. Well patterns are determined by the geologic nature of the reservoir and the character of the injected fluid. A large number of injection-production well patterns have been developed (Figure 29). Five and seven spot patterns systematically space injection and production wells. An alternative production-injection pattern arranges wells in straight lines. One variation (direct) has production and injection wells in line with each other whereas staggered line patterns do not align both types of wells in two dimensions.

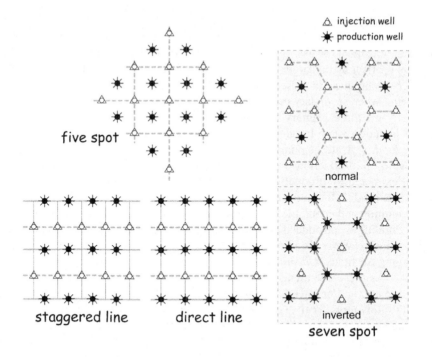

Figure 29. Common injection and production well patterns used for both secondary and tertiary enhanced oil recovery. These types of patterns are also used in in-situ mining operations for uranium, sodium, sulphur and copper. Source: J.D. Myers. Used with permission.

Tertiary Recovery

Tertiary recovery techniques have even higher costs than secondary ones. They also recover a relatively small amount of additional petroleum. At this time, they are used only sparingly. As oil prices climb, it is likely these techniques will become more common and may be used on fields that are now abandoned. Even with the best enhanced recovery techniques, as much as 30 % or more of the original oil in place may be left in the oil field when it is declared "depleted" and abandoned. As with secondary recovery, there are three principal types of tertiary recovery: steam flooding; CO_2 injection, and reservoir burning.

During *steam flooding*, superheated steam is injected into the reservoir to heat the oil and lower its viscosity. This makes the oil flow more readily. As the steam cools, it condenses so it also produces oil movement via secondary water flooding. Because large amounts of energy are required to produce the superheated steam, this procedure is quite energy intensive and hence expensive. Reservoirs can also be injected with carbon dioxide, i.e. *CO_2-EOR*, to improve oil recovery. There are two basics types of this type of tertiary recover. In one procedure a field is flooded with CO_2. Carbon dioxide is pumped down injection wells. At sufficient reservoir pressure, the CO_2 contacts the residual oil and the light hydrocarbon molecules dissolve into oil forming an enriched bank of gas of carbon dioxide and lighter hydrocarbon molecules. This bank sweeps the oil forward. Because carbon dioxide is highly mobile, the gas injection is followed by water injection (water after gas or WAG) to improve sweep efficiency and ensure all parts of the reservoir are sweep by the CO_2 flood. When the bank is produced, the dissolved gas exsolves providing extra gas-lift for production. The other type of CO_2-EOR involves a single well that serves as both a production and injection well. In a huff-and-puff operation, CO_2 is injected, the well shut-in for a period of time (soak period) and then opened for production. This process is repeated until its effectiveness decreases. Finally, gas and/or oil on the margin of the field can be ignited and burned by injecting air into the reservoir, i.e. *fire flooding* or *in-situ combustion*. Gases and heat produced force the oil toward production wells in the center of the field. Of course, this procedure results in oil or gas combusted and this fraction of oil cannot, therefore, be recovered. This tertiary recovery method is rarely used.

Examples

With sustained high oil prices in recent years, EOR has become a common method of extracting additional amounts of oil from aging oil fields worldwide. Because of its aging oil fields, the North American oil industry has been at the forefront of EOR for at least three decades. In the U.S., the large scale transport of carbon dioxide for EOR has been ongoing for over 50 years. More than 3,600 miles of pipeline in the mid-continent moves 50 $MtCO_2$ a year for EOR operations in Texas, Colorado, New Mexico, and Wyoming.

The Weyburn Oilfield located in the Williston Basin in Saskatchewan, Canada is an excellent example of the beneficial impact EOR can have on an oil fields ultimate recovery. Weyburn was discovered in 1954. Exploration work suggested the field contained 1.4 billion barrels of original oil in place (OOIP) and that this oil was a medium gravity crude. Production from the field began in 1955 with vertical wells (Figure 30). Primary production from Weyburn peaked in 1963 at 31,500 b/d. Secondary water flooding began in 1963 bumping production up to 47,200 b/d in 1966. However, as reservoir pressures declined, production fell to 9,400 b/d by 1986. Additional vertical and horizontal in-fill wells brought production to 22,000 b/d. With primary and secondary recovery, total production was 330 million barrels (23 % of OOIP) and was projected to only reach 25 % of OOIP (350 million barrels) before field abandonment.

In the late 1990s, Weyburn began receiving CO_2 for EOR operations from a gasification power plant in North Dakota. The carbon dioxide is moved to the oil field in a high-pressure, 205 mile (330 km) pipeline where it is injected using a 9-spot injection pattern of vertical wells with the injection well in the center of the

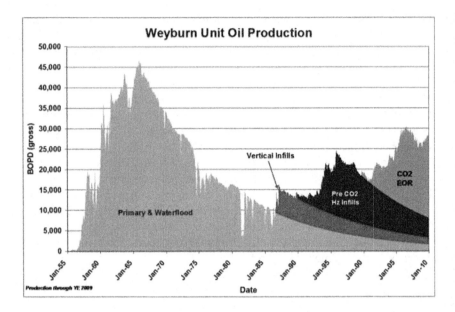

Figure 30. Cumulative production for the Weyburn Oilfield in Saskatchewan, Canada. Secondary and tertiary oil recovery has greatly increased the ultimately recoverable resource in this field. Source: Cenovus Energy Inc.

square and eight producer wells at the corners and mid-points (Figure 29). The wells are spaced 500 ft. (150 m) apart. Although the entire field has 720 wells, only 182 are involved in enhanced recovery (37 injection wells; 145 producer wells). It is projected that the CO_2-EOR phase will produce an additional 130 million barrels and extend the field lifetime 25 years (Figure 30). Over the course of the project, 20 million tons of CO_2 will be injected underground.

PETROLEUM PROCESSING AND REFINING

Petroleum, or crude oil, is a combination of hydrocarbon molecules. As it comes out of the ground, it is not very useful. To create high-value products, it must be refined by a variety of processes. The process of refining is complex and has evolved considerably over time. In the early stages of the petroleum industry, kerosene, a replacement for whale oil in lamps, was the product most in demand. Gasoline was considered a waste product that was hard to sell, because of its explosiveness and was often dumped into streams as a means of disposal. Today gasoline is the most desired product and jet fuel, a product that did not exist before World War II, commonly makes up about 10 % of refinery production.

Refining

Crude oil is not a chemical compound, but rather a combination of hundreds to thousands of different hydrocarbon molecules of varying size and shape. Each crude oil has a unique mixture of these hydrocarbons that determine its chemical and physical characteristics. Of these only a small fraction, e.g. gasoline and jet fuel, are desired by the market. *Petroleum refining* is a set of chemical and physical processes that change crude oil into a large range of more valuable refined products. Refining starts with distillation, the separation of hydrocarbon molecules based on boiling temperature. To improve yield, distillation products are often subject to a number of different secondary conversion processes including: cracking; reforming; alkalyation; blending; and hydrotreating. These processes squeeze more high-value refined products from crude. In addition to hydrogen and carbon, petroleum contains impurities such as sulfur, nitrogen, and oxygen as well as a range of metals. If released during combustion, these elements cause a variety of environmental and health problems. Thus, governmental regulations often place strict limits on how much of these elements may be in fuels. Refining must not only modify hydrocarbon yields, but also remove these unwanted contaminants.

Distillation

A liquid consisting of a single molecule, e.g. water or carbon dioxide, has a single boiling temperature. If the liquid's temperature is raised to the boiling point and held there, the liquid will ultimate evaporate away completely. In contrast, petroleum behaves very differently. When heated to a specific temperature, crude oil does not all evaporate. Only a fraction will boil away, regardless of how long the temperature is maintained. Increase the temperature a bit more, however, and another fraction of the liquid will boil away. Thus, through a series of temperature increases, crude oil can be evaporated completely. Chemically, this is the process of *distillation*, i.e. separation of molecules based on their boiling temperature. By plotting, the fraction evaporated versus temperature, a crude oil distillation curve can be constructed (Figure 31). Because they are comprised of different combinations of hydrocarbon molecules, each crude oil will have a different distillation curve.

Distillation occurs because the size or weight of a molecule determines, in part, its boiling point. The heavier the molecule, the more energy needed to convert it from the liquid to gaseous phases. Energy is added by heating and the higher the temperature, the more energy that is transferred to a molecule. Thus, distillation is a means of separating molecules based on their size. This fundamental principle, upon which atmospheric distillation of crude oil is based, is the first step in all refining processes.

The refining of a crude oil begins with distillation in an atmospheric distillation column (Figure 32). Crude oil is pumped from the storage tanks to a heater where its temperature is raised to approximately 750°F. At this temperature, the crude oil entering the distillation column is a mixture of liquid and gas. When this mixture enters the middle of the column, it is separated by gravity. Heavier liquids sink to

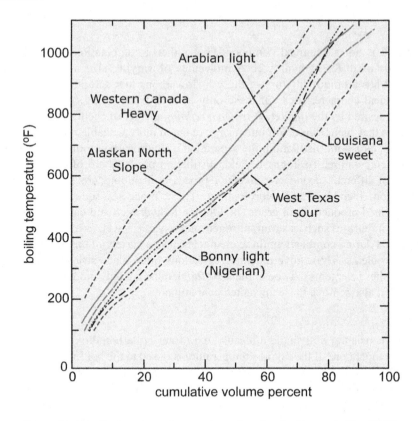

Figure 31. Distillation curves for a variety of crude oils. Source: Leffler (2000).

the bottom of the column and gas rises to the top. A series of trays with holes allow gas and liquid to move in different directions and maximizes separation. Different crude fractions, or cuts, are extracted at different heights, i.e. temperatures, from the column. Additional separation of the heavy hydrocarbon fraction that collects at the bottom of the column is achieved in a vacuum distillation unit.

The most valuable distillation products are those in the mid-range of the column, i.e. naphtha, gasoline, diesel and jet fuel (Figure 32). These are widely used as transportation fuels. Because distillation does not alter the hydrocarbon make-up of the original crude oil, the relative yields of the different cuts are determined by the nature of the feedstock (Figure 33). Heavier crude oils, i.e. lower API gravity, produce more of the heavy cuts and less of the valuable middle distillates. In contrast, the greatest percentage of valuable middle distillates is produced by the light crudes. All other factors being equal, heavy crude oils sell at a discount compared to light crudes. Because the majority of crude oils produced globally are heavy, simple distillation cannot meet the growing global demand for transportation fuels. Thus,

Crude oil distillation unit and products

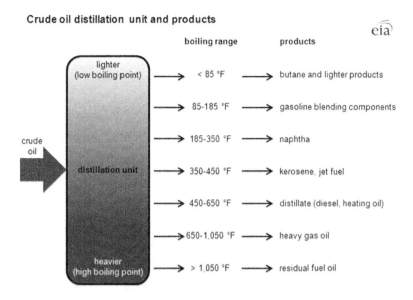

Figure 32. Schematic representation of a distillation column and the cuts or fractions extracted and their respective temperature ranges. Source: Energy Information Administration.

secondary conversion processes are used to change the light and heavy tails of the distillation column into the mid-range of products. This change can be achieved in one of three ways: lighter fraction molecules can be combined to increase their numbers of carbons; heavy fraction molecules can be split (cracked) to produce two molecules with fewer carbons; or molecules can be changed structurally while maintaining their original hydrogen to carbon (H/C) ratio (reformed).

Secondary Conversion Processes
Unlike distillation, *secondary conversion processes* change the very nature of the hydrocarbon molecules that originally made up the crude oil feedstock. By varying the number and types of processes used, even the heaviest crudes can be made to produce more of the middle distillates. The combination of processes required varies with crude API gravity and the desired product range. The major secondary conversion processes used in refining are: cracking, catalytic reforming, alkylation, and isomerization.

Cracking involves breaking large, heavy hydrocarbon molecules into two or more shorter, lighter molecules (Figure 34a). This is a chemical process that operates on fractions withdrawn from the lower part of a distillation column. Cracking can be accomplished using three different processes. Catalytic, or cat, cracking uses high temperatures and pressures along with a catalyst (typically a very fine powder) to

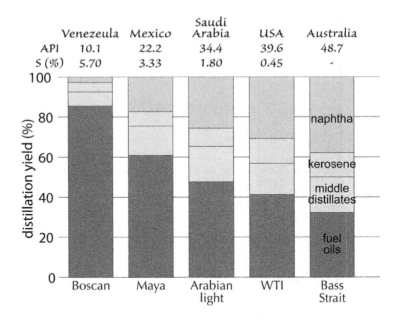

Figure 33. The relative yields of different benchmark crude oils. Heavier crudes produce less of the valuable mid-distillation range products. Thus, these oils need more extensive processing to produce large amounts of transportation fuel.

split the molecules. Thermal cracking relies solely on high temperature, like natural crude oil formation during catagenesis, to form smaller hydrocarbons. Coking is an extreme type of thermal cracking that is applied to the residual fraction (bottoms) from the base of the distillation column. In addition to producing middle distillates, coking also produces a coal-like, solid known as petroleum coke that is useful as a solid fuel in many industrial applications.

The fractions from the top of a distillation column have hydrocarbon molecules with two to four carbons. These smaller hydrocarbons are also the products of various secondary conversion processes, particularly cracking. Because they are highly chemically reactive, they are used in the petrochemical industry. However, they are too light to be used for fuel. These molecules can be combined by *alkaylation* to produce hydrocarbon molecules with six to eight carbons and octane numbers of around 100 (i.e. the gasoline cut) (Figure 34b). These motor fuel alkaylates are important in high-octane gasoline and aviation fuel. Another alkaylation process increases the octane number of straight run gasoline. This process treats gas with sulfuric acid, thus it is called sulfuric acid alkaylation and was responsible for producing most of the of the high-octane aviation fuel used by the Allies during World War II. Although not as important now, it was once one of the more important processes in the refining process

After distillation, some of the separated fractions have the right number of carbon-hydrogen atoms, but do not have the right properties. For example, straight-run gasoline from distillation has too low an octane number for modern internal combustion engines. To overcome this problem, the hydrocarbon molecules need to be structurally modified not built up or broken down. This is the process of *reforming*. There are two basic types of reforming used to rearrange molecular structure to increase octane number. *Catalytic reforming* uses special catalysts (different from those of cracking) to reform the molecules (Figure 34c). Using fine platinum powder supported by aluminium oxide, catalytic reforming changes straight run gasoline and naphtha to branched-chain isomers. Conversely, *isomerization* is a reforming process that converts linear, straight-chain paraffins to branched chain hydrocarbon molecules (e.g. isoparaffins) (Figure 34d).

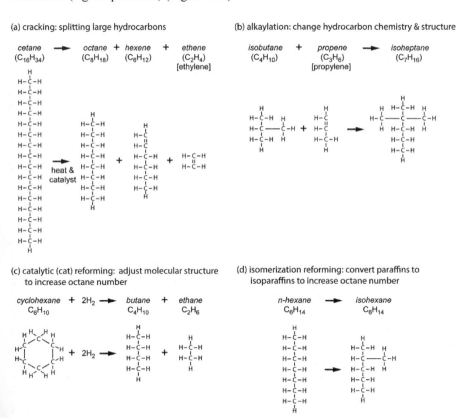

Figure 34. Four major secondary conversion processes used in oil refining. Source: J.D. Myers. Used with permission.

283

The engines of modern vehicles require fuels with very strict characteristics. These include the proper viscosity (to control flow), volatility (to prevent early volatilization leading to vapour lock) and octane number (to prevent engine knock – premature fuel ignition). For the latter, gasoline with octane numbers of 87, 89 and 93 are preferred. Unfortunately, many of the distillation fractions do not have sufficiently high octane numbers. To correct this problem, different distillation cuts can be mixed, a process called *blending*, with other refining products to produce gasoline of the proper octane number. Thus, streams from the cracking, reforming and aklyalation units are all mixed with appropriate distillation cuts, i.e. blended, to produce gasoline that satisfies market requirements.

In addition to hydrogen and carbon, crude oil has a range of contaminants, including nitrogen, sulfur and a variety of heavy metals. These elements adversely affect equipment in the refinery and have serious environmental impacts when refined petroleum products are combusted. Even sweet crude oils have some amount of sulfur in hydrocarbons with more than six carbons. Because they are chemically incorporated in the hydrocarbon molecules, these contaminants cannot be separated by physical processes, but must be chemically removed from the crude stream and its refined products. Contaminants such as sulfur are removed from crude oil using *hydrotreating*. It involves mixing the feed stream with hydrogen gas and heating the mixture to 800-900°F. The mixture is introduced into a reactor containing a catalyst in pellet form. Typically, this catalyst consists of cobalt and molybdenum oxides deposited on alumina (Al_2O_3) pellets. In the presence of the catalyst, several reactions occur: hydrogen reacts with sulfur to form hydrogen sulfide (H_2S); nitrogen compounds are changed to ammonia (NH_3); metals are deposited on the catalyst; unsaturated hydrocarbons become saturated, i.e. they acquire additional hydrogen; and associated cracking produces methane, ethane, propane and butane.

Oil Refineries

An oil refinery is an industrial complex designed to process crude oil into a range of higher value products, mostly fuels. Refineries vary markedly in capacity (throughput) and complexity, i.e. the number and type of secondary processing units they have (Figure 35). All refineries have an atmospheric distillation column, which is also the first unit the incoming crude is passed through. Refineries with just a distillation column are simple or topping refiners. They can handle only the very lightest and sweetest crude oils, but are relatively inexpensive and easy to operate. To process crude oils with a greater range of qualities, additional secondary conversion processing units are added to the refinery. These secondary units have a variety of purposes: increase separation; upgrade low-value distillation products; increase fuel octane number; and improve environmental fuel standards.

The complexity of a refinery is indicated by the *Nelson Complexity Index*. This index measures the variety and number of secondary conversion units a refinery has. Every refinery unit is assigned a number based on its complexity and cost relative

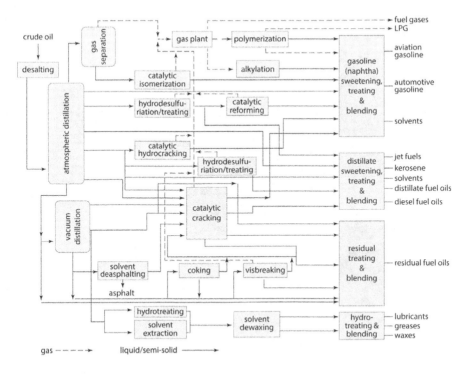

Figure 35. Schematic flow chart of a complex oil refinery capable of handling a wide variety of crude oil types because of the large number of secondary conversion process units present. Source: Modified from OSHA Technical Manual (OTM), Section IV: Chapter 2, Fig. IV-2-6. https://www.osha.gov/dts/osta/otm/oth_iv_2.html.

to a distillation unit, which is assigned a value of 1. For a given refinery, the factor for each type of unit present is multiplied by the number of that type of unit in the complex. The numbers from the various secondary conversion units are summed to produce a Nelson Complexity Index. The larger the index, the more complex the refinery and wider the range of crude oils it can process.

At the beginning of 2012, the U.S. had a daily refining capacity of 17.3 million barrels per day (b/d).These facilities were located near production centers, crude oil import ports or population centers (Figure 36). The largest concentration of refineries (44 % or 7.7 million b/d) is located along the Gulf coast close to that region's onshore and offshore oil fields. (The U.S. is divided into Petroleum Administration for Defense Districts (PADD). These districts were originally established during World War II to ration fuel across the country. They were abolished in 1946, but brought back during the Korean War. They are now used simply as a means of collecting data on petroleum products and analysing petroleum flows between the various regions of the country.)

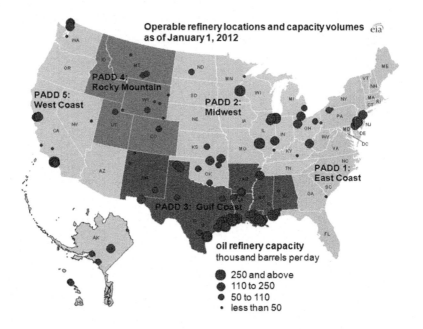

Figure 36. Oil refinery capacity in the U.S. Most refineries are located near oil production centers, import destinations or population centers. Fully 44 % of the U.S. crude refining capacity is located along the Gulf coast. Source: Energy Information Administration, Refinery Capacity Report, 2012.

The types of crudes that U.S. refineries can handle vary by region (Figure 37). Gulf coast refineries have many secondary conversion units so they are capable of handling the heavy, sour crudes from Mexico (Maya) and Venezuela (Bachequero). Because of their inferior qualities, these crude streams command a lower price than lighter, sweeter crude oils, e.g. Brent or Louisiana Light Sweet. In contrast, East Coast refineries have much less secondary conversion capacity and must buy light, sweet crude oils at a premium price. Shifts in North American crude oil production to heavy, sour Canadian and high-quality light, sweet U.S. crude have many refineries developing strategies to replace the more expensive high-quality crude oil.

PETROLEUM, STEM, QUANTITATIVE SKILLS AND PERFORMANCE TASKS

To this point, this chapter on petroleum has provided a comprehensive, but necessarily abbreviated overview of the entire petroleum exploration, production, and use value chain. Accordingly, it has provided the content knowledge necessary to create innovative, meaningful, accurate and, hopefully, engaging performance tasks to improve a student's science, technology and engineering understanding about an energy resource that impacts nearly every aspect of their daily life. At the

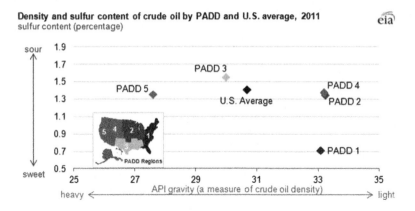

Figure 37. *The different crude oil handled by refineries in different parts of the U.S. These differences reflect, in large part, the types of crude oils available to the refineries. Source: Energy Information Administration, Petroleum Navigator.*

same time, it touches on many of the scientific concepts important in disciplines such as biology, chemistry, earth science, and physics. It also provides a means of connecting STEM and quantitative reasoning through these same tasks.

Petroleum is a subject that encompasses big numbers, simple mathematical skills and 'back of the envelope' calculations. Most importantly, serious debate about petroleum on a global or national basis must be grounded in fundamental quantitative data. The debate about U.S. biofuels mandates would benefit greatly if more discussion was focused on how the magnitude of mandated biofuels production compares to daily or yearly U.S. petroleum consumption and production. Similarly, figures on the amount of water necessary to produce these biofuels would place the discussion in a meaningful framework of sustainability and environmental impact.

The remaining portion of this chapter focuses on performance tasks developed around some key concepts of petroleum. These are: Peak Oil; the U.S. debate about oil production and the Arctic National Wildlife Refuge (ANWR); and strategies for replacing petroleum-derived liquid fuels with alternative hydrocarbon-based fuels. These debates all turn, in part, on quantitative information and require fundamental QR skills. At the same time, they focus on a topic that will impact all students' future mobility and their economic prospects.

Oil's Global Future: Peak Oil or Growing Supply

The modern world with its rapid transportation and economic globalization is dependent upon cheap, reliable transportation fuel. This availability makes it possible to jet around the world in a day, or to produce goods in China and transport them to anywhere in the world for sale. Our modern society is critically dependent upon enhanced mobility. Global travel, for vacations or business trips, are all possible because of the benefits of liquid fuels. Even less obvious is the impact transportation has on our everyday lives. It permits people to work in urban centers, but live in the suburbs. The food we eat, whether processed or grown locally and organically, all rely on inexpensive transportation to get to market. It is not difficult to image what will happen to the conveniences and comforts modern society provides if access to cheap inexpensive liquid fuels was permanently interrupted. If you live in the U.S. and are old enough to remember the 1973 Arab oil embargo, you know the economic, physical, social, and political stresses that are placed on an industrialized society by the shortage of liquid fuels. Perhaps surprisingly for some, petroleum is critical for modern, high yield agriculture. It powers the mechanized equipment that is so prevalent in the western agricultural sector and is important for the generation of ammonia, a key ingredient of fertilizer. Thus, the lack of cheap, reliable petroleum could drastically impact agricultural output negatively and hence the ability to feed an expanding global population.

The majority of liquid fuels used in the world today are derived from refining of petroleum or crude oil. It is the only energy source with high enough energy density and specific energy to fuel many forms of transportation (Figure 7). The internal combustion and diesel engines are dependent upon fuels refined from petroleum or crude oil. Despite the hype about solar and wind for producing electricity, an all-electric airplane is not likely any time soon, if ever. Consequently, the entire airline industry, the millions of passengers moved globally each day, and the goods shipped are critically tied to the availability of cheap and reliable petroleum supplies. In the U.S., 73 % of petroleum is used in the transportation section, nearly three times the amount used in the second most oil dependent economic sector (Figure 3). Similarly, 93 % of U.S. transportation is powered by petroleum.

Since the beginning of the 1900s, petroleum has been the fastest growing of all energy sources (Figure 38). Mid-way through the 20th century, petroleum passed coal as the United States' most important primary energy source. A similar evolution in energy is also true for the rest of the industrialized world. In the foreseeable future, there is no reason to believe that petroleum will be dethroned from its dominant role in the world's energy picture. In fact, both the EIA and IEA predict that the demand for petroleum will steadily increase in the next 30 years.

Petroleum is a non-renewable fossil fuel. It represents an energy stock; therefore, there is a finite amount of it in the ground. In addition, it is increasingly difficult to find and extract. The world's oil supply is increasing sourced from more extreme climates, e.g. the North Sea, and physically demanding environments, e.g. deepwater Gulf of Mexico and offshore Brazil. In addition, many producing nations are now on the downward side of their national production curves. Given these factors, it is clear that at some point the world will run out of usable crude oil. The questions are, therefore, when and what will replace petroleum?

History of energy consumption in the United States (1776-2012)
quadrillion Btu

Figure 38. U.S. energy growth by primary energy source. Petroleum is now the dominant primary energy source in the United States. Source: Energy Information Administration, AER Energy Perspectives and MER.

The History of Peak Oil

The concept of running out of petroleum to power the world's transportation system is captured in the concept of *Peak Oil*. Although many believe that Peak Oil refers to the physical exhaustion of petroleum sources, this is not, in fact, true. Instead, Peak Oil refers to the peaking of the production of petroleum. On a global, cumulative petroleum production curve, it represents a maximum. After Peak Oil, global oil production will always be less than what it was at maximum production.

Probably the first person to publish on Peak Oil was M. King Hubbert, at the time a geologist working for Shell Oil. In 1956, Hubbert presented a paper to a meeting of the American Petroleum Institute in which he predicted U.S. oil production would peak sometime in the late 1960s or early 1970s (Hubbert, 1956). Because it was a time of sustained 7%/year growth in oil production, his findings were ridiculed within the oil industry. Yet, U.S. oil production peaked in 1972, well within Hubbert's suggested time frame. Hubbert also drew peak curves for U.S. coal and natural gas production as well. In addition, he estimated global peak oil. Because of his success in predicting the peak of U.S. oil production, the characteristic shape of a peaking oil production curve is called *Hubbert's curve* and the procedure for quantitatively modelling the production curve the *Hubbert model*.

The concept of peak oil was revisited in 1998 by two former oil geologists, but on a global scale (Campbell and Laherrere, 1998). These authors provided a somewhat more detailed explanation of their mathematical procedures for predicting the timing of peak oil and discussed in detail the sources of their data. Despite apparent problems with the available data, Campbell and Laherrere (1998), using nearly five more decades of oil industry data than available to Hubbert, projected that global production of conventional oil would peak in the first decade of the 21st century. In their discussion, they also listed the three primary reasons many critics of the concept of a near-term peak in oil production cited to dispute Hubbert peak predictions. These include future discovery of large, remote oil fields, technological advances in recovery, and a switch to unconventional sources of petroleum.

The Mathematics of the Oil Production Curve
Conceptually, the peak oil production curve is a relatively straightforward concept and should provide a convenient means of calculating when production of any non-renewable resource will peak. Initially, production starts at zero and increases rapidly and exponentially according to numerous historical data sets, as the easiest to find and biggest resources are developed first. Ultimately, production will flatten and peak as reserves become harder to find and produce. With time, production continues to fall and the resource is exhausted or becomes uneconomical to extract. Although this concept is intellectually simple, the details in how to model it mathematically and where to find the historic data necessary for modelling are exceedingly complex.

In his 1956 paper, Hubbert provided few details about the mathematical procedures he used to calculate his curves. In his figure describing the curve, he showed a symmetrical bell curve and noted that the area under the curve was the ultimate cumulative production (Figure 39). Because it is simply the area under a curve, the cumulative production is the integral of the production rate (P) through time (dt). By plotting historic production and estimating what the ultimate recovery would be, Hubbert was able to make his predictions for U.S. and global oil, coal, and natural gas production.

In his figure for global oil production, Hubbert identified the key variables necessary to predict the timing of peak production (Figure 40). These include the cumulative production, the proven reserves and future discoveries.

Subsequent articles have pointed out that a symmetrical production curve does not match historic data for non-renewable resource production. Rather, an exponential growth and tailing decline are more prevalent. This has led many authors to use a logistics curve to approximate production (Brecha, 2012). A logistics curve is often used for growth in a system constrained by a finite capacity. For this type of curve, production initially grows exponentially. As extraction becomes more difficult, the rate of production decreases and hits a maximum. After peaking, the curve ultimately falls to zero. Unfortunately, fitting historical production data to a logistic curve does not provide a very accurate estimate of when peak production will occur. This only happens once the amount produced becomes a significantly fraction of the ultimately recoverable resource (Brecha, 2012). Thus, these types of curves are good at identifying peak production after it happens, but not in predicting when beforehand. Obviously, for policy planning purposes an early, reliable prediction of when peaking will happen is necessary.

Regardless of the exact mathematical form used for the production curve, there are several variables that are important for all mathematical forms (Figure 41). These include the cumulative production and proven reserves. Proven reserves are those oil resources that have been discovered and can be extracted given current technological

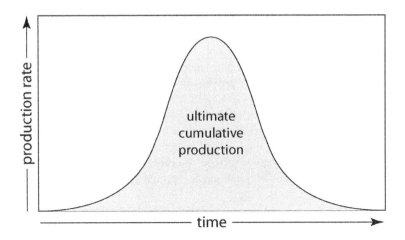

Figure 39. Hubbert's schematic representation of the production curve for a non-renewable resource. Source: Modified from Hubbert (1956).

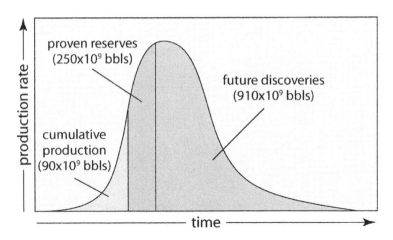

Figure 40. Hubbert's curve for global oil production identifying his 1956 estimates for cumulative production, proven reserves and future discoveries. Source: Modified from Hubbert (1956).

and economic conditions. Obviously, production results come from historical data and is the best constrained of the variables, because oil companies meter the amount of oil they produce. There are, however, still gaps in this knowledge set. For example, the amount of oil produced during the first Iraq War when the retreating Iraqis sabotaged Kuwaiti oil wells is unknown. Both of these variables represent quantities that can be determined from published data.

291

There is, however, considerable variability in the quality of reported reserves. In the U.S., the Securities and Exchange Commission (SEC) places strict rules on what U.S.-based oil companies can report as proven reserves. The same is not true in other countries where such data may be influenced by political or economic pressures. To illustrate, consider the case of proven oil reserves in several important OPEC nations. In the early 1980s. there was a significant increase in proven reserves for six OPEC members (Figure 42). Yet, observers have noted that none of these countries reported major exploration projects or advances in oil extraction technologies during this time. In addition, under OPEC rules, the amount of oil a member can produce and export is determined by their proven reserves. Thus, many industry observers view these reserve increases as 'phantom barrels' and question what this means for Peak Oil predictions.

The other two factors important for estimating the timing of peak production is the reserve growth and the yet-to-find oil (Figure 41). Reserve growth is "..the commonly observed increase in recoverable resources in previously discovered fields through time" (Klett and Schmoker, 2003). Reserves grow for a variety of reasons including improvements/application of new production technologies, evolving geologic knowledge of a field or region, economic factors prolonging a

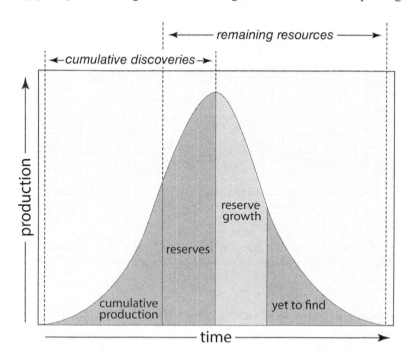

Figure 41. The four factors that are important for defining the timing of the peaking in the oil production curve. Source: J.D. Myers. Used with permission.

field's production, revision of reserve reporting definitions, and new or revised data estimates (McGlade, 2012). Although this number could be negative or positive, historical evidence shows that it is usually almost always positive. The yet-to-find oil is the oil that exists in oil fields that have not yet been found, that is they are unknown fields. Both reserve growth and yet-to-fine oil are unknown quantities.

Since the publication of Hubbert's paper and especially that of Campbell and Laherrere (1998), a virtual cottage industry has sprung up in the academic world regarding the issue of Peak Oil, its timing and the consequences of a near-term peak.

(a) top OPEC producing countries

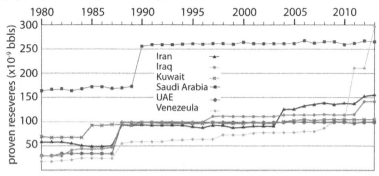

(b) non-OPEC producing countries

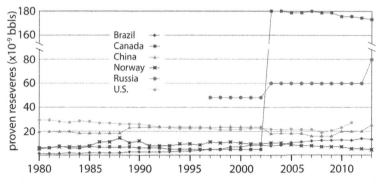

Figure 42. (a) Stated reserves for six major OPEC producers jumped dramatically in the early 1980s without any obvious exploration work or technology breakthroughs. These large increases have lead many observers to question the validity of reserve numbers from some of the most important oil-producing nations. (b) During the same period, the stated reserves for six non-OPEC oil producing nations show few large changes. The major reserve change for Canada in 2002 represents reclassification of oil sands reserves as conventional petroleum.

These papers extended and refined the original mathematics and have the benefit of a much longer and richer dataset. Yet, these papers have still failed to provide a conclusive answer to the fierce debate about the likelihood of a near-term peak in conventional oil production. At the same time, there is a continuing debate on the blog-o-sphere about the timing of Peak Oil and its consequences for modern society and humankind. The number of popular books on the topic is also staggering with viewpoints all over the political, economic, and social spectrum.

A Simple Peak Oil Exercise
Clearly, the topic of Peak Oil provides a multitude of potential QR exercises that tie directly to an important social and political topic. In many cases, investigating the details of the curve-fitting techniques used may be beyond the skills of many grade levels. However, in high school math and science course such activities might be useful and would demonstrate real world use of QR skills that are often taught without relevant social context.

In lower grade classes, an important exercise could be the plotting of production data by region or country. This would introduce large numbers, the use of datasets, and could be used as a meaningful introduction to the use of spreadsheets and their sorting, plotting, and curve fitting functions. Production datasets can be obtained from a number of sources on-line including EIA, BP Statistical Review of Energy, and IEA. Most of these datasets are available in spreadsheet or pdf format. A meaningful part of any such exercise could be to have students actually use the Web to find the data that they will manipulate. This type of activity offers the possibility of discussing data error, data accumulation, and the uncertainty in measuring a quantity such as global oil production. This concept could later be transferred to other STEM principles such as how one measures fluxes to different water and carbon sinks and sources in the hydrologic and carbon cycles, respectively.

At lower grade levels, some simple calculations about R/P calculations can convey the fundamental concept of Peak Oil in simple quantitative form. R/P calculations are a quick means of estimating how long a company, nation, or region's known oil supplies will last. R is reserves, i.e. identified and recoverable amounts of a resource, expressed in mass or volume units. Production is the rate at which a reserve is produced. It is expressed as volume or mass per time. Obviously, dividing R by P will yield a quantity with units of time. This time is the time to resource exhaustion. R/P is a crude estimate, because production fluctuates and reserves grow with exploration and decrease with production. Activities can be developed looking at R/P at an instant in time or using data sets from different years to show how R/P changes temporally. The latter allows a discussion of what factors influence R/P estimates.

Appendix A provides reserve (R) and production (P) data for 48 nations. It also has aggregated data for some political entities, e.g. Organization for Economic Cooperation and Development (OECD), Organization for Petroleum Exporting

294

Countries (OPEC), European Unit and the states of the former Soviet Union. The data also use a multiplier that may be unfamiliar to students, but is commonly encountered in scientific and technical publications, i.e. reserve data is reported as x10^{-3}. Thus, the reserves for Algeria are, in fact, 12,270,000,000 barrels not 12,279,000 barrels as reported in the table body or 12,270 barrels (12,270,000 barrels multiplied by 10^{-3}). (This notation is a source of confusion even for first year graduate students.) Although these data can be used in a number of different ways, the worksheet in Appendix A illustrates one approach used in multiple teacher professional development programs to demonstrate how such performance tasks are used. Working through this example will illustrate some of the principles used to design this task.

Before beginning the task, familiarize yourself with the data by asking yourself some simple questions. How many nations are included in the data set? To your knowledge, are any major oil producers left out? What is the range of magnitudes of reserves and production? Are the units for the two terms consistent? With a better understanding of the data set, answer the first two questions in the worksheet about R and P. Do not forget to consider a number of different perspectives when formulating your answers. Calculate R/P for each nation in the first table and for different political organizations in the second table. Plot your calculated results as histogram with the countries arranged from largest R/P on the left to shortest on the right. Using this new quantitative information, answer the second set of questions in the worksheet. Having worked through this example, it should be apparent that despite its simplicity it covers a large number of important QR skills covered at different grade levels. Plotting, data sorting, large numbers, and simple quantitative calculations are some of those important skills.

There are multiple ways in which this exercise can be extended or enhanced to address other perspectives of Peak Oil. For example, students could use the Web to locate the different countries in the table. They could be asked to identify which countries belong to which of the political organizations identified in the second table. After entering it in a spreadsheet, they could sort the data according to different criteria. After sorting, they could see where the U.S. stands in relation to oil production and reserves. These answers might surprise them and hopefully help them think about the issue of petroleum usage in a different and more realistic light.

Some Signs of Peak Oil's Arrival?

Because of the inconclusive nature of the mathematical forms appropriate to modelling the cumulative production curve in predicting the time of peak production and the inherent uncertainty in compiled data, it is appropriate to ask if there are other indicators of a pending, near-term peak in global conventional oil production. Several authors have attempted to address this question in a number of ways.

According to a study by Sorrell et al. (2010), conventional oil production is influenced by three factors. First, production for individual regions typically rises to a peak or plateau and then decline. The majority of fields begin their decline when

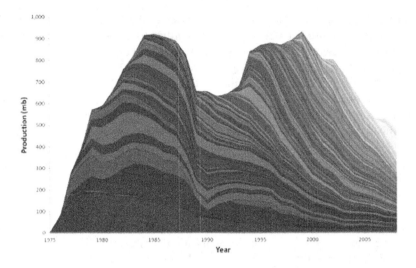

Figure 43. Oil production from individual fields from UK's continental slope in the North Sea. Early on production is dominated by a smaller number of larger fields (left side of diagram). Later production is mostly from a larger number of smaller fields (right side). This later production is, however, not able to reverse the decline in large field production. Source: (Sorrell et al., 2010).

less than half of the field has been produced. Second, the majority of a region's oil is located in a small number of large fields with a large number of smaller fields producing the rest. Large fields are discovered first and the smaller ones later. This type of behaviour is clearly illustrated by production from the continental shelf of the United Kingdom (Figure 43). Initial production is from a small number of large fields followed later by development of a larger number of smaller fields. The production from these fields is, however, not capable of offsetting the terminal decline in large field production late in the development cycle. The early peak in the U.K. cumulative production is not related to the physical constraints, but to production delays resulting from the disastrous explosion and fire of the Piper Alpha oil platform and the time it took to institute new and improved safety procedures.

Sorrell et al. (2010) also found that 60 nations have already passed peak production. This list includes some large producing nations. Using a simple bell-shaped curve with a symmetric production cycle and a peak at 50% production, these authors estimated the timing of peak production for ultimately recoverable resources (URR) ranging from 2,000 to 4,000 Gb (Figure 44). With the low estimate, the peak occurs in 2009 and for the high in 2032. Maximum production in the first case is 92 mb/d and 115 mb/d in the second. Most importantly, these results show that an 80 % increase in URR delays the production peak only 23 years. Delaying

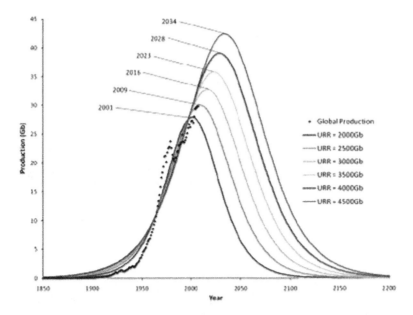

Figure 44. Bell-shaped production curves for different estimates of ultimately recoverable resource. Increasing URR by 80% (2,000 to 4,000 Gb) delays peak production by only 23 years. Source: (Sorrell et al., 2010).

the peak one year requires increasing URR by ~80 Gb, an amount that exceeds the current discovery rate (Robelius, 2007).

As discussed above, one of the physical factors determining the nature of future conventional oil supply is the occurrence of most of the oil in a region in a small number of larger (Sorrell et al., 2010). Of the 70,000 oil fields in production globally, half of that production comes from just 110 fields. Clearly, large fields play an oversized role in global conventional oil production. Giant oilfields, or elephants as they are called in the oil industry, are defined in a couple of different ways (Robelius, 2007). One definition focuses on the field's URR and sets the minimum at 0.5 Gb (1 Gb = 10^9 barrels). In contrast, Simmons (2002) defines a giant field as one capable of maintaining a production rate of 1 mbd or more. Robelius (2007) has shown that the vast majority of giant fields defined by URR are also giant fields by production as well. These giant fields have played a very significant role in global oil production (Figure 45).

Regardless of how they are defined, giant oil fields are very rare (Figure 46). They comprise only about 1 % of all the known oil fields, but 100 of the largest have produced nearly half of the world's conventional oil production. They also contain over 50 % of the URR oil left in the world.

297

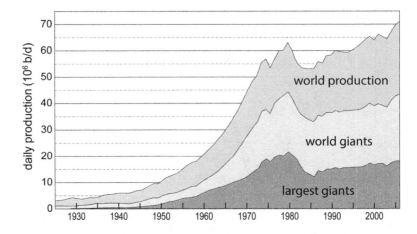

Figure 45. The role of giant field production in total global conventional oil production is substantial. Source: Robelius (2007).

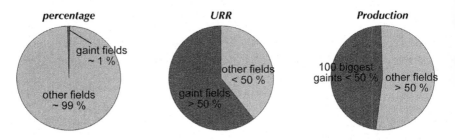

Figure 46. (Left) Giant fields comprise only 1 % of the total number of producing oil fields. However, their URR and production greatly exceed that for all smaller fields. Source: (Robelius, 2007).

Yet, giant fields are mostly old and rapidly maturing. For example, the largest oil field in the world is Saudi Arabia's Ghawar field with an URR estimated conservatively at 100 Gb (Robelius, 2007). The field was discovered in 1948 and production started in 1951 and has continued ever since. Peak production was in 1980 at 5 Mbpd and is still around this figure today. It is estimated to have produced a staggering 60 Gb of oil and still is in plateau production stage. Thus, Ghawar plays a crucial role in global oil production. There is debate about when Ghawar will go into decline. Saudi Aramco maintains the field is not nearing decline, but an extensive study of Ghawar production by Simmons (2005) lead him to predict that decline is imminent. Mexico's offshore Cantrell field is another giant in decline with average decline of 14%/y. With many giant fields aging and starting their decline phases, discovery of new giants is imperative to keep global production high to meet current and growing oil demand. Yet, the discovery of giant fields has fallen

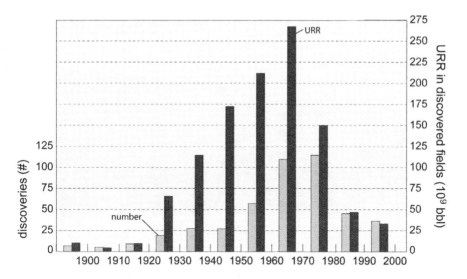

Figure 47. Giant oil field discovery by number (top) and size (bottom). Clearly, the discovery of giant fields has fallen off sharply. With few geologically unexplored parts of the world left, this trend is unlikely to be reversed by future exploration efforts. Source: (Robelius, 2007).

steeply in recent years. The most prolific discovery period for giant fields, in terms of number and size, was in the 1960s-1970s (Figure 47). Historic data suggests that the production from these large giant fields cannot be made up by the discovery of a large number of smaller fields. This trend has major relevance to the timing of global peak production and is cited by some of evidence of a near-term production peak in conventional oil production.

U.S. Oil Production, ANWR and Energy Policy

As discussed previously, the United States is heavily dependent upon crude oil to power its transportation system. In 2010, 37 % of the primary energy used in the U.S. was derived from oil and other liquid fuels. Despite growing interest in renewables in powering our transportation sector, the EIA projects that consumption of oil will remain largely unchanged for approximately the next 20 years (Figure 48). Because the nation is so critically dependent upon crude oil, changes in the price of oil ripple throughout the entire economy. Thus, it is not surprising that the cost of gasoline, a refined product of petroleum, and the supply of oil are topics that resonate with the U.S. public.

In the 2008 U.S. presidential election with gasoline prices topping $4/gal, domestic oil production was an important campaign issue. Republican vice-presidential candidate Sarah Palin, governor of Alaska, advocated expanding

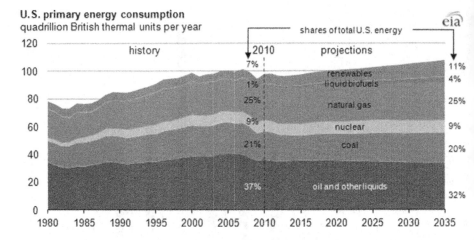

Figure 48. Crude oil comprised a significant percentage of U.S. energy sources from 1980 through 2010. Projections to 2035 by EIA indicate this reliance on petroleum will change little in the next 20 years. Source: Energy Information Administration, Annual Energy Outlook 2012, Early Release.

drilling with her famous sound bite "drill, baby, drill". Although the issue had many perspectives, one important issue focused on drilling for oil in Alaska's Arctic National Wildlife Refuge (ANWR). ANWR was portrayed as a means of immediately lowering gasoline prices, providing the U.S. the means to become independent of oil imports, and a potential economic boon to Alaska and the nation. Unfortunately, as with most political debates, the discussion often lacked creditable quantitative information. How much oil was estimated to lie beneath ANWR? How much could be recovered? How did the amount of recoverable oil compared to the U.S. daily and yearly consumption? Similarly, there was very little discussion of the uncertainty in the quantitative data that was available. Such information could have provided a means of moving past the rhetoric and on to more meaningful discussion.

Although drilling in ANWR has receded from the national debate, an examination of the ANWR drilling controversy provides a convenient and engaging means of illustrating the size of oil fields, and the quantitative and statistical methods used to estimate the amount of recoverable oil (or other resources as well). It also demonstrates how simple quantitative analysis can provide some easily understandable objective data on which to ground political discussions.

The History of U.S. Oil
The U.S. oil industry began in 1859, when the first well drilled specifically to retrieve oil was completed in Pennsylvania. The nation was one of the early pioneers globally in producing oil. Demand at the time was for kerosene as an alternative

source of illumination to whale oil, which was becoming increasing expensive due to over-hunting of whales (Kolb and Kolb, 1979; Yergin, 1992). Therefore, crude oil was distilled mostly to produce kerosene. The heavy distillation ends increasingly displaced animal and vegetable fats as lubricants and the heaviest were used to pave roads with asphalt. Because of their volatile nature, there was little market for the middle distillations, e.g. naphtha and gasoline. To dispose of these unwanted by-products, oil refiners poured them into nearby streams.

With the invention of the internal combustion engine and the advent of the automobile, gasoline became a useful product and demand increased. At the same time, electricity was displacing kerosene as a lighting source, especially in the cities. Thus, the middle distillates became more important and methods of refining other than distillation were developed.

To feed this demand, oil companies scoured the country for oil reservoirs. Major finds in California and Texas supplied the nation with all the oil it needed. During World War II, the U.S. supplied its allies with most of the oil they required. Oil production continued to grow until about 1972, when production peaked in the U.S. (Figure 49). Since that time, oil production has steadily fallen until recently when the development of shale oil reversed the historic decline.

U.S. Field Production of Crude Oil

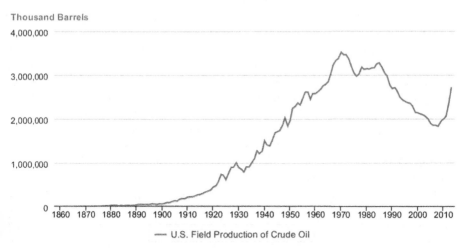

Figure 49. U.S. oil production peaked in 1972 and steadily declined through the decade of the 2010s. The development of shale oil has slowed and even reversed this decline in recent years. Source: EIA, 2014, http://www.eia.gov/dnav/pet/hist/LeafHandler. ashx?n=pet&s=mcrfpus1&f=a.

Despite the peaking of domestic production, U.S. demand for oil continued to grow (Figure 1). The shortfall in production compared to consumption led to ever increasing imports. In 2005, nearly 60 % of all oil used in the United States was imported. The lower demand for oil due to the economic downturn of 2008 and the increase in shale oil production shrank this figure to 49 % in 2005. Regardless of the increased domestic production, EIA projections show imported oil still making up 36 % of total U.S. consumption in 2035 (Figure 1).

Alaska's North Slope
The North Slope of Alaska is a vast region sandwiched between the Brooks Range to the south the Arctic Ocean to the north (Figure 50). It stretches from the Canadian-U.S. border west to the Chukchi Sea, a marginal sea of the Arctic Ocean. The area is largely uninhabited except for small villages along the coast. Ecologically, it consists of tundra, the layer that thaws with the seasons, and the permanently frozen permafrost below. The relatively flat terrain means water flows north to the Arctic Ocean in shallow, braided streams or collects into pools and ponds that dot the land. Within the North Slope is a mixture of federal, state, and native lands with the latter mostly along the coast. The National Petroleum Reserve in Alaska (NPRA) and the Arctic National Wildlife Refuge (ANWR) comprise a large portion of this remote region. It is cut approximately down the center by the Trans-Alaska Pipeline System (Figure 50)

After World War I, the U.S. Navy was converting its ships from coal to oil. To secure a possible future source of oil for the navy, President Harding established the Naval Petroleum Reserve Number 4 in 1923 along Alaska's North Slope. Except for some naval and U.S.G.S. surveys, the area was mostly untouched wilderness until the 1990s. In 1976, the area was renamed the National Petroleum Reserve in Alaska (NPRA) and transferred from navy to Bureau of Land Management control, an agency within the Department of Interior. In the late 1990s and early 2000s, oil and gas leasing occurred within the area. Currently, there are proposals from conservation groups to designate the refuge as the National Pleistocene Refuge.

To the east of NPRA is the Arctic National Wildlife Refuge (ANWR). The refuge was established in 1960 and expanded in 1980 by Congress with the passage of the Alaska National Interest Lands Conservation Act. At 19 million acres, ANWR is the largest refuge in the nation. Eight million acres in the refuge are designated wilderness (Figure 50) and another 10.1 million acres are designated 'minimal management', which means they are managed to preserve natural conditions and resources. The remaining 1.5 million acres of the refuge are part of the 1002 area (Figure 51). This area is assumed to have significant petroleum reserves, and unique flora and fauna as well.

Congress left the decision about how to manage the resources in this part of the refuge to future politicians. Drilling in ANWR requires authorization from Congress. Because it has potentially large oil and gas reserves as well as significant wildlife habitat, a decision on how this area was to be managed for resources was deferred to the future. ANWR is managed by the U.S. Fish and Wildlife Service.

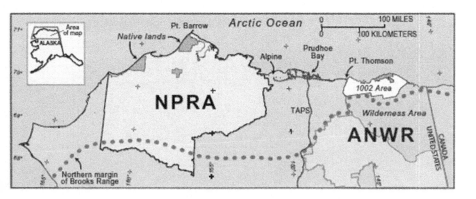

Figure 50. The North Slope of Alaska is bounded on the north by the Arctic Ocean and to the south by the Brooks Range. It contains the National Petroleum Reserve in Alaska (NPRA) and the Arctic National Wildlife Refuge (ANWR). Source: USGS (2002).

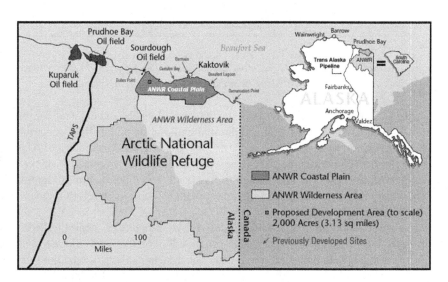

Figure 51. 1002 area is a coastal region along Alaska's Arctic coast that was set aside when the Arctic National Wildlife Refuge was established in 1980. How its resources would be managed were left to the future to decide. The coastal plain, shown in green, is the 1002 area in ANWR. Source: Alaska Department of Natural Resources.

The North Slope Oil Province

Despite its role as an importer of oil, the U.S. is the third or fourth largest oil producer depending upon production year. Although most of the oil fields are concentrated in the continental U.S., the largest oil field is, in fact, on Alaska's North Slope

303

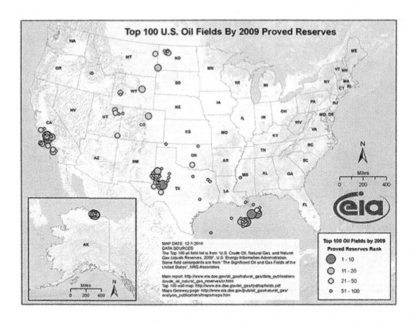

Figure 52. Top 100 hundred oil fields in the United States. The biggest field is Prudhoe Bay located on Alaska's North Slope. Source: Energy Information Administration.

(Figure 52). The Prudhoe Bay oil field, the largest in the U.S. and eighteen largest in the world, was discovered in 1968. Additional exploration and drilling confirmed a large number of oil fields in the region (BP, 2006). Along the Arctic coast of Alaska, there have been 36 petroleum discoveries with another 48 in Canada's Mackenzie River delta to the east. The Alaskan coast has commercial petroleum production at Prudhoe Bay. This region of Alaska has an estimated 15 billion barrels of recoverable oil and 45 trillion cubic feet of recoverable gas.

To move this oil to market, the Trans-Alaska Pipeline System (TAPS) was constructed between 1974 and 1977 from Prudhoe Bay on the North Slope to Valdez on Prince William Sound in southern Alaska. The system consists of feed lines on the North Slope that bring oil to the pipeline near Prudhoe Bay, the 12 pumping stations located along the pipeline, and the Valdez Marine Terminal. It is 800 miles long with a diameter of 48 inches (122 cm) and privately owned. Oil from the pipeline comes from a number of fields including: Prudhoe Bay, Kuparuk, Alpine, Endicott and Liberty. Out of the ground, the oil has a temperature of 129°F (49°C), but cools to 111°F (44°C) as it transits the feeder system to the pipeline itself. The oil travels at 3.7 mph and makes the trip from Prudhoe Bay to Valdez in 11 days. Although the pipeline can move 2.14 million barrels per day and peaked in 1988 at 2.03 mbpd, its flow in 2012 was only 600,000 bpd. If the flow decreases below 200,000 bpd, major operational problems ensue and the pipeline would probably not be economic to operate (NETL, 2012).

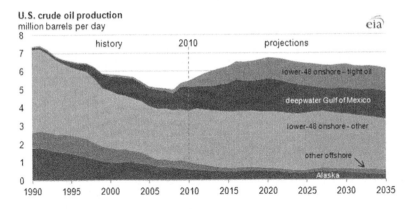

Figure 53. U.S. oil production by region since 1990 and forecast to 2035. Alaska oil has played a major role in production, but has been steadily declining for several decades. In the future, it will be eclipsed by production from tight formations and deepwaters of the Gulf of Mexico.

Oil from the North Slope has played a significant role in U.S. oil production since it came on line in 1977 (Figure 53). Production peaked in 1988 at about 2 million barrels per day and is in a steady decline ever since.

1002 Area Oil Assessment

In 1987, the U.S. Geological Survey submitted a report to Congress describing the resources, including oil, in ANWR's 1002 area. Since that time, additional wells outside of, but adjacent to ANWR were drilled (Figure 54). Using new data from these wells as well as pre-existing well data and seismic results, 40 U.S. Geological Survey (USGS) scientists conducted a three year study to re-evaluation the resource potential of the area (USGS, 2001). The new study also re-analyzed 1,400 miles of seismic data collected in 1984 and 1985 by an oil and gas consortium. Because conducting seismic surveys in the area requires an act of Congress, this survey is the only one that has been performed in the 1002 area.

Methodology

As discussed earlier, the amount of oil a reservoir holds depends upon the thickness of the reservoir and its permeability and porosity among other factors. Rather than simply assigning a value to these factors, the U.S.G.S. used a probabilistic method to assign likely values and evaluate multiple scenarios (a procedure commonly used by oil companies). They also concentrated on accumulations that were bigger than 50 million barrels of oil and 250 billion cubic feet for gas, since these are oil fields large enough to be developed economically on the North Slope. Summed together, these accumulations defined the oil in-place, that is, the oil in the pores of the reservoir formations (Figure 55). Modern oil extraction techniques can extract

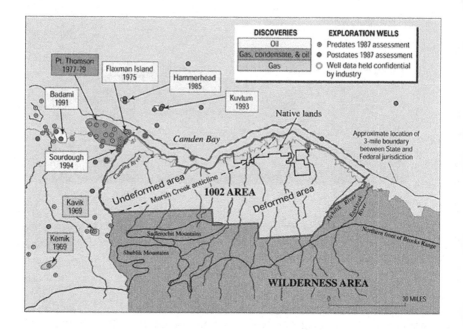

Figure 54. Map showing wells drilled after the 1987 assessment of 1002 that were used in the 2001 assessment. Also shown are the deformed and undeformed areas of 1002. Source: USGS (2001).

only a portion of this resource depending upon the recovery factor, i.e. the ratio of producible oil reserves to total oil in-place for a given field. By multiplying the oil in-place by the recovery factor, estimates of the technologically recoverable oil are obtained (Figure 55). For the assessment, the U.S.G.S. used recovery factors of 30-50 % for oil and 60-70 % for gas. Finally, economic factors further limit the amount of technically recoverable oil that can actually be extracted and cover costs and generate a profit (Figure 55). Higher oil prices move this curve to greater recoverable volumes whereas lower price lowers the recoverable amount. It is this last curve that determines how much oil can be recovered from ANWR.

To account for the uncertainty in the estimates, the recoverable volumes are expressed as probabilities. For example, an F_{90} estimate means that there is a 95% chance that the stated amount of oil will be found (Figure 55). This is a conservative estimate so its value with be small, i.e. it is the minimum estimate. At the other end of the probability range is F_5. This means the stated volume has only a 5 % chance of being found. Thus, it is a maximum estimate.

Assessment Results

Based on the new seismic and drilling results, the U.S.G.S. reassessment of ANWR's oil potential identified a resource of 7.7 billion barrels of oil with the range between

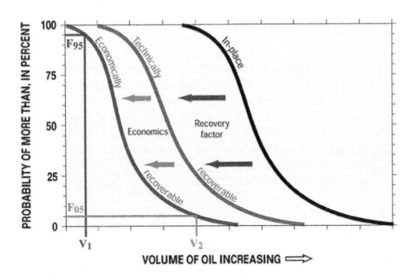

Figure 55. Schematic representation of oil in-place, technically recoverable and economically recoverable amounts of oil. F95 and F50 probabilities correspond to min and max estimates, respectively. Source: (USGS, 2001).

Table 3. U.S.G.S. 2001 assessment of recoverable oil in ANWR's 1002 area

Part of study area	Volume of oil, in millions of barrels		
	F95	Mean	F5
Entire Assessment area	5,714	10,360	15,955
ANWR 1002 area (Federal) TOTAL	4,254	7,668	11,799
undeformed part	3,403	6,420	10,224
deformed part	0	1,248	3,185

4.3 and 11.8 billion (Table 3). They suggested that the oil will not be found in a single, large supergiant field, but in numerous accumulations in the 100 million barrel range. In addition, the oil is probably not uniformly distributed throughout the 1002 area. Most of the oil would be found in the undeformed part of the area in the west. This location has advantages because it is closet to pre-existing oil infrastructure.

How Big an Oil Province is ANWR?
Seven billion barrels of oil certainly sounds like a lot, but how much is it really. To grasp, the significance of such an oil field on a national or global basis it is

important to have a quantitative understanding of how this compares to U.S. daily consumption. This activity helps you to place the amount of oil likely recovered from ANWR in its proper context, a key issue in the ANWR drilling controversy. Scan the graphs and tables on page 1 and 2 of the ANWR assessment in Appendix B of this chapter. Using the information provided in the appendix, answer the questions on pages 3-4. As you are doing the exercise and from the viewpoint of a citizen engaged in the ANWR debate: 1) review the geology and setting of ANWR; and 2) consider how opening ANWR will impact U.S. oil imports and the price of oil on the U.S. and perhaps the global market. At the same time from the perspective of an educator think: 1) of the quantitative skills you are using; and 2) how this type of activity might be adapted to your class, state or region.

The Future of U.S. Oil

For some, the prospect of opening ANWR to oil exploration and eventual production is a game changer in the U.S. energy forum. Others argue that the amount of oil is trivial and the environmental impact not worth the cost. Hopefully, the simple calculations you performed help you put this issue in a broader quantitative context. Regardless, two studies help provide a more detailed background picture.

In 2002, the U.S.G.S. published a oil and gas assessment for NPRA using methodologies similar to those of the ANWR study (USGS, 2002). In this study, they estimated recoverable oil at 9.3 billion barrels (mean) with a range of 5.9 to 13.2 billion barrels and non-associated gas at 59.7 trillions of cubic feet and a range of 39.1 to 83.2 Bcf (USGS, 2002). This was based on extrapolating the geologic features of the large, recently found Alpine field on the NPRA border into the reserve. Based on this discovery, oil and gas companies leased land within the reserved and drilled 30 exploration wells on federal and native lands. Most of the wells were within 50 miles of the Alpine field. Surprisingly, only five oil discoveries were made. Based on this information as well as the lapsing of leases in the NPRA, the U.S.G.S. believed a new reassessment was warranted. Using methodology similar to that for ANWR, the estimates for NPRA were reduced to 896 million barrels, a nearly 90 % reduction. In contrast, non-associated gas was estimated at 52, 839 Bcf, only a 10% decrease (USGS, 2010). The reasons for the change were entirely geological. They found an abrupt transition from oil to gas 5-20 miles west of the Alpine field and a significant decrease in reservoir quality. Since much of the data for the ANWR assessment is also extrapolated from locations outside the refuge, NPRA is a sober reminder that assessments may be incorrect.

In its *Annual Energy Outlook 2008*, the EIA conducted an analysis of crude oil production from ANWR (EIA, 2008). They evaluated three resource cases for ANWR: a high, mean and low. In all cases, ANWR production begins in 2018 (a decade after the study) and grows but ultimately declines before 2030, the end of the projection period. Production peaks at 780,000 barrels per day in 2027 for the mean case. The low and high cases both peak in 2028 with the high at 1,450,000 bpd and the low 510,000 bpd. Total oil production for the mean case is 2.6 billion barrels

(1.9-4.3). This production would represent 0.4-1.2 % of global oil consumption and affect oil prices only marginally, e.g. $0.41/b (low resource case) to $1.44/b for the high. These price changes could easily be nullified by shifts in OPEC production.

ANWR production does replace imported oil on a 1 to 1 basis (EIA, 2008). The opening of ANWR would extend the life of TAPS out beyond 2030. The availability of transport could result in the prolonging existing fields' lifetimes and opening of new, small fields. Similarly, ANWR production would reduce expenditures on imported oil $135 to $327 billion (2006 dollars) with a corresponding reduction in the U.S. trade deficit.

Clearly, making a decision about ANWR drilling is difficult and multifaceted, but good, simple quantitative data can help the discussion and decision making.

Replacing Petroleum

Given its importance in powering our economy as well as our military, the potential peak in global crude oil production has significant national security implications. Thus, the Department of Energy's National Energy Technology Laboratory (NETL) sponsored a study of the potential replacements for petroleum-based liquid fuels (Hirsch et al., 2005). The study considered eight alternatives to our present liquid fuels system. These included improved energy conservation in the transportation sector; better conventional oil recovery; expansion of heavy oil and oil sands production; ramp up of gas-to-liquids (GTL); establishment of a large-scale coal-to-liquids (CTL) industry; expansion of liquids from U.S. domestic sources; fuel switching to electricity; other fuel switching; and using hydrogen as a transportation fuel.

The study focused on large-scale, physical mitigation. It considered systems to reduce consumption of liquid fuels and construction and operation of facilities designed to produce large quantities of liquid fuels. For the purposes of the study, mitigation involved an overnight go-ahead decision, i.e. a crash program. The possibility of project delay or blockage due to not-in-my-backyard (NIBMY) opposition was not considered.

Mitigation Wedges

To illustrate the impact of the different alternative liquids fuel strategy, the study used wedges to approximate the scale and pace of market penetration of mitigation efforts. A *mitigation wedge* has two parts (Figure 56). First, the time needed to penetrate the market and displace, replace, or reduce significant amounts of petroleum-derived liquid fuels. This part of a wedge addresses the need to redesign and/or retool existing facilities or to plan and construct entirely new production facilities. The second part addressed implementation of the mitigation option. That is, the ramp up in production as measured in barrels per day (bpd) of production or savings.

All the options originally identify as possible sources of liquid fuels were subsequently screened for feasibility. In particular, any potential wedge mitigation option must be able to substitute for current fuels on a large scale and in a short time

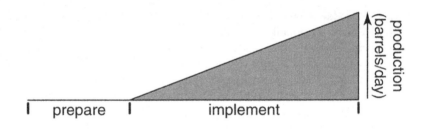

Figure 56. Illustration of the two components of a mitigation strategy's wedge. Source: Hirsch et al. (2005).

frame. Given the massive use of liquid fuels in U.S., viable petroleum alternatives had to be capable of producing fuel on a massive scale in a relatively short timeframe. The technology has to be commercial or near commercial now, energy efficient, and environmentally clean. Any electricity savings produced from the technology was deemed irrelevant given the difficulty of quickly changing the nation's current vehicle fleet to electricity. After screening, the possible wedge options identified were: increased fuel efficiency; expanded EOR; greater heavy oil and oil sands production; implementation of coal-to-liquids; and creation of a gas-to-liquids industry (Hirsch et al., 2005).

Heavy oils
Heavy oils are those crude oils with API gravity of 22° or less. They also have very high viscosities (100 centipoise) and consist of hydrocarbons that relative to lighter oils are carbon-rich and hydrogen-poor. Heavy oils often contain significant amounts of sulfur and metals. Given these physical and chemical characteristics, they require special processing and can be handled by only the most complex oil refineries. Because they are semi-solids at reservoir temperatures, heavy oil recovery requires special stimulation processes to get them to flow to the well. There are, however, very large global reserves of heavy oils. The Orinoco Heavy Oil belt of Venezuela alone contains an estimated 1.2 Gb of original oil in place, of which 367 Gb is believed to be recoverable.

Oil sands
Oil (tar) sands are a complex mixture of bitumen, sand, clay, and water. Bitumen is naturally occurring assortment of long hydrocarbons with an API gravity of 8-14°, which is heavier than water. It has a viscosity of 10,000 cP (similar to molasses). Bitumen must be upgraded before it can be refined into useful products. Upgrading of bitumen is both energy and water intensive. The basic formula for upgrading is two tons of oil sands, 0.5-0.7 mcf of natural gas, and 2-4 barrels of water for one barrel of syncrude (upgraded bitumen from oil sands production) produced. The syncrude must be refined like conventional petroleum to produce liquid fuels. As with heavy oils, there are large global reserves of oil sands. The oil sands of

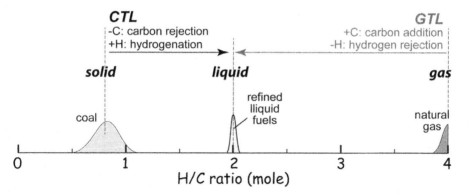

Figure 57. The H/C ratios of coal, refined petroleum products and natural gas. Refined products have an H/C ratio of around 2. Because its H/C is lower than refined products, carbon must be removed or hydrogen added to adjust its H/C to 2. In contrast, natural gas' hydrogen content must be decreased or carbon increased. Source: J.D. Myers. Used with permission.

Canada's Alberta province are estimated at 1.7-2.5 Tb. Of this amount, 15 % or 255 Gb are believed recoverable with current technology.

Coal to liquids/Gas to liquids

The final two mitigation options involve converting less valuable, but abundant forms of fossil fuels, i.e. coal and natural gas, into liquid fuels. These are known as *coal-to-liquid* (CTL) and *gas-to-liquid* (GTL). Both are proven technologies that have been deployed on commercial, albeit small, scales. Malaysia has a GTL plant that converts its stranded gas to liquids for export and South Africa has several CTL plants that produces most of the diesel fuel consumed domestically. Both technologies involve adjusting the H/C ratio of the starting feedstock (Figure 57).

Because coal has a low H/C relative to refined petroleum products, its H/C must be raised by some combination of carbon loss and/or hydrogen addition. For gas, the process is the opposite, i.e. carbon gain and/or hydrogen loss. This adjustment is accomplished using a Fischer-Troposch (F-T) process originally developed in Germany between the world wars, but refined in numerous countries since then. The process uses a gas feedstock and adjusts the H/C through a series of reactions of the form:

$$\underbrace{(2n+1)H_2}_{\text{hydrogen gas}} + \underbrace{nCO}_{\substack{\text{carbon} \\ \text{monoxide}}} \rightarrow \underbrace{C_nH_{(2n+2)}}_{\text{alkanes}} + \underbrace{nH_2O}_{\substack{\text{water} \\ \text{vapor}}}$$

311

The products, i.e. $C_nH_{(2n+2)}$, produced are in the alkane hydrocarbon series consisting of paraffin and isoparffin molecules (see petroleum chemistry section). . By adjusting the reaction so that n is between 3 and 8, propane through octane are created, which are liquid at standard temperature and pressure or can be readily liquefied. These are ideal for the production of diesel fuel as well as other refined products. Since the feedstock for the F-T process must be a gas, CTL includes an initial gasification step in which the coal is chemically converted to a syngas of carbon monoxide and hydrogen.

Estimated Production
When the NETL study was conducted, U.S. petroleum consumption was approximately 20 million barrels per day. Because of the economic downturn in 2008, consumption was greater then than in 2013. If crash programs in all identified mitigation options were started at approximately the same time, they could ramp up to slightly over 20 million barrels per day within fifteen years (Figure 58). The biggest contribution would be from expanded heavy oils and oil sands production (8 mbd) and the least from a new GTL industry (2 mbd; Table 4).

Transition Impact
The results from this study suggest a significant time interval is needed to deploy the technologies and build the infrastructures that can replace a significant amount of the conventional petroleum the United States uses. Given this lead time, Hirsch et al. (2005) investigated how the timing of the start of the crash program would impact the transition from petroleum to other fuels, that is, would it be a smooth or hard transition. They consider three different scenarios for the beginning of the crash programs relative to the peaking of conventional petroleum production: starting at the peak (Scenario 1); 10 years before peak (Scenario 2); and 20 years before peak (Scenario 3).

Waiting until conventional petroleum production has peaked to institute a mitigation strategy (Scenario 1) results in immediate and continuing shortfalls of liquid fuels (Figure 59a). These shortfalls continue and increase markedly over 20 years. Conversely, a crash program started 10 years before peaking delays shortages for a decade, but the increase in magnitude for the following decade (Figure 59b). Of the different choices, only Scenario 3 provides for a smooth, 'easy' transition from conventional petroleum to the five proposed alternatives (Figure 59c). Only with far-sighted, energy policies can the world's liquid fuels demand and supply sides be balanced. Failure to plan early for peaking in conventional petroleum production will lead to massive shortfalls and significant negative economic impact (Hirsch et al., 2005).

Because production peaks are recognized only after they pass, it will be hard to determine when mitigation strategies should be implemented. Wait too long and

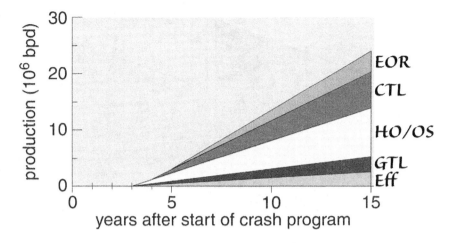

Figure 58. The petroleum mitigation triangle consists of five different replacement/reduction strategies. Within 15 years of the start of crash programs for all strategies, daily liquid fuel production would exceed 20 mbd. This would satisfy present U.S. demand for liquid fuels. Abbreviations: EOR – enhanced oil recovery; CTL – coal-to-liquid; HO/OS – heavy oil/oil sands production; GTL – gas-to-liquid; and Eff – energy efficiency. Source: Hirsch et al. (2005).

Table 4. Delay times and production maximums for the five petroleum replacement or reduction strategies

Wedge	Delay (y)	Production (10⁻⁶ bpd)
Gas-to-liquid (GTL)	3	2
Energy efficiency	3	3
Enhanced oil recovery (EOR)	5	3
Coal-to-liquid CTL	4	5
Heavy oils/oil sands	3	8
Total	-	21

there will be significant social and economic costs. Start too early and resources might be wasted on premature technology. Because signals of pending conventional peaking are likely to be weak at best, identifying when to start preparing for a global downturn in conventional petroleum production will be daunting, but a key factor in adequate dealing with the problem (Hirsch et al., 2005).

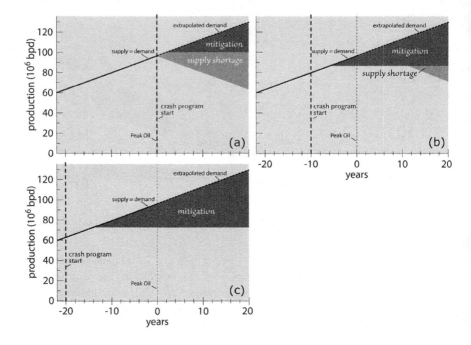

Figure 59. Relation between timing of Peak Oil and initiation of crash program of fuel replacement. Only an early, careful planned mitigation strategy will allow a smooth transition away from conventional petroleum-derived liquid fuels. Source: Modified from Hirsch et al. (2005).

Economic Cost

Although the NETL study suggests there are no significant engineering and technological barriers to crash programs to replace petroleum-derived liquid fuels, it did not examine other issues associated with such programs. In particular, it did not consider the economic costs of such a massive construction and engineering endeavour. An excellent quantitative task for students is to calculate how much such a project might cost.

Using the information in the handout in Appendix C, complete the following tasks. For the coal-to-liquids wedge, calculate: 1) the number of CTL plants built 10 years after the initiation of the crash program; 2) the cost of these plants (indicate if your estimate is a high or low estimate); and 3) the amount of coal needed to support annual production at the end of the 10 year period. To evaluate the feasibility of the gas-to-liquids wedge calculate: 1) the number of GTL plants built 10 years after the initiation of the crash program; 2) the cost of these plants (indicate if your estimate is a high or low estimate); and 3) the amount of gas needed to support annual production at the end of the 10 year period. Based on your results, identify those countries which you think might develop GTL capability.

SUMMARY

Petroleum-derived liquid fuels power the world's transportation because of their high energy per volume *and* mass. They are converted into refined liquid fuel products that are used in nearly all modes of transportation. It is a non-renewable fossil fuel formed by the chemical and physical transformation of organic remains from single cell, marine organisms. These transformations occur only when these remains have been buried to depths that place them in the oil window. Once formed, oil is mobile and migrates from source rocks to lower depths. If the oil encounters the proper geologic structures, i.e. a petroleum trap, it may accumulate in economically recoverable quantities. Petroleum traps are classified as structural, stratigraphic or salt dome.

Once found the extraction of hydrocarbon fluids is a complex and very expensive process. In fact, most exploration wells drilled in search of oil fail to find economic amounts of hydrocarbons, i.e. they are dry holes. Wells are drilled to great depths and in very deep water. The construction and engineering of an oil or gas well not only determines how successful it is in extracting hydrocarbons, but also how effective it is in protecting other underground resources, e.g. groundwater. Drilling has evolved considerably from the vertical wells first drilled at the beginning of the oil era. Now directional and extended reach drilling minimizes environmental impact while allowing oil reservoirs that were previously unrecoverable to be extracted successfully.

Crude oil directly out of the well has a range of physical and chemical characteristics, e.g. API gravity, sulfur content, pour point, that determines its ultimate economic value as well as how it is processed and refined. Crude oil refining consists of a preliminary separation step, distillation, and six secondary conversion processes. Unfortunately, crude oil distillation, i.e. the physical separation of hydrocarbon molecules based on boiling point, alone cannot meet market demands for the transportation liquid fuels a growing human population and expanding economy needs. Thus, there are a wide range of secondary conversion processes that modify the chemical structure of hydrocarbon molecules to enhance the production of gasoline, jet fuel, and naphtha. These include: cracking, reforming, alkalyation, blending, and hydrotreating. These processes change both the physical and chemical structure of hydrocarbon molecules. Oil refineries vary greatly in complexity and the types of crude oils they can or cannot process.

Because of its complex nature and the critical role it plays in powering modern societies great mobility, petroleum and the petroleum industry are a useful means of introducing STEM concepts to students. The topic is socially relevant, commonly in the media, and touches virtually all students in an industrialized society. Petroleum spans the scientific disciplines of chemistry, biology, earth science, and physics. At the same time, understanding petroleum and the impact it has on the modern world requires fundamental quantitative reasoning skills. Thus, the study of petroleum provides the ideal means to tie science and QR together in a meaningful and topical social context.

Given the breadth and diversity of the petroleum industry, there are countless subjects and concepts that can be presented at varying grade levels and across different subject areas. Armed with a basic, but meaningful, understanding of the global-spanning and immense petroleum industry, the reader should be able to identify a number of fundamental principles and big questions around which to develop a variety of meaningful performance tasks that introduce the various QR skills while providing authentic practice in their application. At the same time, these tasks have the ability to weave all the various strands of STEM into a meaningful context. This subject, because of its breadth, complexity, and global span, has the potential to break down the instructional silos between disciplines, and demonstrate to students how these subject areas are woven together in the natural and built worlds.

REFERENCES

Allen, F., Conran, G., & Lesso, B. (1997). Extended-reach drilling: breaking the 10-km barrier. *Oilfield Review (Winter)*, 32–47.

BP. (2006). Prudhoe Bay Factsheet. British Petroleum.

Brecha, R. J. (2012). Logistic curves, extraction costs and effective peak oil. *Energy Policy, 51*, 586–597.

Campbell, C. J., & Laherrere, J. H. (1998). The end of cheap oil. *Scientific American*, 78–83.

EIA. (2008). *Analysis of crude oil production in the Arctic National Wildlife Refuge*. Energy Information Administration.

EIA. (2010). *Monthly foreign crude oil acquistion report: Appendix A: Crude stream codes* (p. 18). Washington, DC: Energy Information Administration.

Hirsch, R. L., Bezdek, R., & Wendling, R. (2005). *Peaking of world oil production: Impacts, mitigation, and risk management*. Pittsburgh, PA: National Energy Technology Laboratory, Department of Energy.

Hubbert, M. K. (1956). *Nuclear energy and the fossil fuels* (Publication No. 95). Houston, TX: Exploration and Production Research Division, Shell Development Company.

Hyne, N. J. (2001). *Nontechnical guide to petroleum geology, exploration, drilling and production* (598 pp). Tulsa, OK: PennWell Corporation.

Hyne, N. J. (2012). *Nontechnical guide to petroleum geology, exploration, drilling & production* (724 pp). Tulsa, OK: PennWell Corporation.

Jahn, F., Cook, M., & Graham, M. (2008). *Hydrocarbon exploration and production. Developments in petroleum science* (444 pp). Amsterdam, the Netherlands: Elsevier.

Kennedy, J. L. (1983). *Fundamentals of drilling--technology and economics* (216 pp). Tulsa, OK: PennWell Publishing Company.

Klett, T., & Schmoker, J. (2003). *Reserve growth of the world's gaint oil fields*. American Association of Petroleum Geologists.

Kolb, D., & Kolb, K. E. (1979). Petroleum chemistry. *Journal of Chemical Education, 56*(7), 465–469.

Leffler, W. L. (2000). *Petroleum refining in nontechnical language* (3rd ed., p. 310). Tulsa, OK: PennWell Publishing Company.

McGlade, C. E. (2012). A review of the uncertainties in estimates of global oil resources. *Energy, 47*(1), 262–270.

NETL. (2012). *Fossil energy—Trans-Alaska pipeline system*, A.E. Office (Ed.). Pittsburgh, PA: National Energy Technology Laboratory, Department of Energy.

Oberkircher, J., Smith, R., & Thackwray, I. (2004, March/April). Boon or bane: 10 years of multilateral completions. *Drilling Contractor*, pp. 39–40.

Robelius, F. (2007). *Giant oil fields—The highway to oil Giant oil fields and their importance for future oil production*, Uppsla University, Uppsala, Sweden, 168 pp.

Simmons, M. (2002). *The world's giant oilfields*, Simmons & Company International.

Simmons, M. R. (2005). *Twilight in the desert—The coming Saudi oil shock and the world economy* (422 pp). New York, NY: John Wiley & Sons, Inc.

Sorrell, S., Miller, R., Bentley, R., & Speirs, J. (2010). Oil futures: A comparison of global supply forecasts. *Energy Policy, 18,* 4990–5003.

USGS. (2001). *Arctic National Wildlife Refuge, 1002 Area, petroleum assessment, 1998, including economic analysis* (6 pp). Washington, DC: U.S. Geological Survey.

USGS. (2002). *U.S. geological survey 2002 petroleum resource assessment of the National Petroleum Reserve in Alaska (NPRA)* (6 pp). Washington, DC: U.S. Geological Survey.

USGS. (2010). *2010 updated assessment of undiscovered oil and gas resources of the National Petroleum Reserve in Alaska (NPRA)* (4 pp). Washington, DC: U.S. Geological Survey.

Yergin, D. (1992). *The prize—The epic quest for oil, money & power* (885 pp). New York, NY: Simon & Shuster.

APPENDIX A: HOW LONG CAN WE PRODUCE OIL?

The R/P or reserves to production ratio is an important quantity for understanding the long-term viability of non-renewable resources such as oil, natural gas, copper, and gold to name just a few. R is the reserves a nation or region is thought to contain and expressed in some unit of mass, e.g. tons, ounces, or volume, e.g. barrels, Tcf, etc. P represents the production rate, which is volume or mass per unit of time. Thus, R/P has units of time and is a crude measure of how long a non-renewable resource can be produced.

Based on your new knowledge of how petroleum is formed, produced and refined, answer the following questions.

1. How do reserves (R) of a nation change over time?

2. List some factors that impact production (P).

Calculating the R/P for petroleum for a nation, provides a quick and effective way of evaluating sound bites like "Drill, baby, drill". In this activity, you will calculate the R/P values for the top petroleum producing nations in the world. From the data in the table below:

- Calculate the R/P values for each country in the first table and for the different political organizations in the second table.
- Using your results, create a histogram of national R/P arranged from longest (on left) to shortest (on right) R/P.

Using this information, answer the following questions:

- Which nations are likely to still be pumping oil toward the end of the petroleum era?

319

— In light of the R/P values you calculated, does it make much sense to press for expanded U.S. domestic drilling at the expense of the environment? Why or why not?

In light of difference in total reserves for different countries, are all of the R/P results equally meaningful for global Peak Oil discussions? Explain your answer.

Global Petroleum Statistics

Country	Reserves(b) *	2007 Production (bpd)
Algeria	12,270,000	2,000,133
Angola	9,035,000	1,723,000
Argentina	2,586,762	698,194
Australia	4,157,565	560,801
Azerbaijan	7,000,000	867,889
Brazil	12,623,830	1,832,658
Brunei	1,200,000	194,212
Canada	27,664,029	3,308,661
Chad	900,000	143,562
China	15,493,400	3,743,368
Colombia	1,510,000	560,846
Denmark	1,113,297	312,000
Ecuador	4,269,278	520,088
Egypt	4,070,000	709,962
Equatorial Guinea	1,755,000	363,309
Gabon	1,995,000	230,000
India	5,459,250	800,798
Indonesia	4,370,000	969,095
Iran	138,400,000	4,401,055

Country	Reserves(b)*	2007 Production (bpd)
Iraq	115,000,000	2,144,699
Italy	781,296	121,682
Kazakhstan	39,828,000	1,490,356
Kuwait	101,500,000	2,625,795
Libya	41,464,000	1,847,740
Malaysia	5,357,000	755,282
Mexico	12,186,500	3,477,192
Nigeria	36,220,000	2,355,859
Norway	8,171,588	2,556,093
Oman	5,572,000	717,834
Peru	1,097,288	113,869
Qatar	27,436,200	1,196,680
Rep. of Congo (Brazzaville)	1,940,000	222,126
Romania	477,700	105,450
Russian Federation	79,432,085	9,978,022
Saudi Arabia	264,209,000	10,412,699
Sudan	6,614,500	457,000
Syria	2,500,000	393,947
Thailand	461,000	309,183
Trinidad & Tobago	793,800	154,129
Tunisia	596,000	97,649
Turkmenistan	600,000	197,818
United Arab Emirates	97,800,000	2,914,880
United Kingdom	3,592,500	1,636,148
US	29,444,000	6,879,000
Uzbekistan	594,000	114,068
Venezuela	87,035,000	2,612,521
Vietnam	3,410,000	340,025
Yemen	2,780,000	336,000

*$x10^{-3}$

	2007	
Country	Reserves(b)*	Production (bpd)
TOTAL WORLD	1,237,875,465	81,532,910
European Union	6,797,440	2,394,438
OECD	88,344,547	19,170,373
OPEC	934,739,200	35,204,154
OPEC 10	810,704,200	31,336,456
Non-OPEC £	174,990,180	33,524,262
Former Soviet Union	128,146,085	12,804,494

*x10^{-3}

Source: BP Energy Summary, 2008

APPENDIX B: ASSESSING ANWR'S OIL IMPACT

The Arctic National Wildlife Refuge was established by Congress in 1980 with the passage of the Alaska National Interest Lands Conservation Act. Because it was recognized at the time that the coastal region was the potential source of hydrocarbons, Congress delayed deciding how this portion of the refuge would be managed in the future, e.g. preserved or utilized. The area in the refuge that might be open to hydrocarbon exploration and production is called 1002 Area. This is the area on which the current political battle is focused.

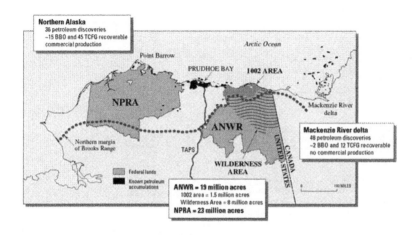

U.S. Oil Production and Consumption

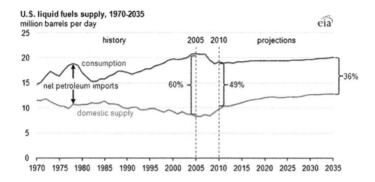

U.S. Oil Consumption and Production, 1965-2007

	1965	1966	1967	1968	1969	1970	1971	1972	1973	1974
production*	9,014	9,579	10,219	10,600	10,828	11,297	11,156	11,185	10,946	10,461
consumption*	11,522	12,100	12,567	13,405	14,153	14,710	15,223	16,381	17,318	16,631

	1975	1976	1977	1978	1979	1980	1981	1982	1983	1984
production*	10,008	9,736	9,863	10,274	10,136	10,170	10,181	10,199	10,247	10,509
consumption*	16,334	17,461	18,443	18,756	18,438	17,062	16,060	15,295	15,235	15,725

	1985	1986	1987	1988	1989	1990	1991	1992	1993	1994
production*	10,580	10,231	9,944	9,765	9,159	8,914	9,076	8,868	8,583	8,389
consumption*	15,726	16,281	16,665	17,283	17,325	16988	16,713	17,033	17,236	17,719

	1995	1996	1997	1998	1999	2000	2001	2002	2003	2004
production*	8,322	8,295	8,269	8,011	7,731	7,733	7,669	7,626	7,400	7,228
consumption*	17,725	18,309	18,621	18,917	19,519	19,701	19,649	19,761	20,033	20,731

	2005	2006	2007
production*	6,895	6,841	6,879
consumption*	20,802	20,687	20,698

* bbl/d (x10^{-3})

U.S.G.S. 1998 ANWR Assessment

Part of study area	Volume of oil, in millions of barrels		
	F_{95}	Mean	F_{05}
Entire assessment area[1]	5,724	10,360	15,955
ANWR 1002 area (Federal), TOTAL	4,254	7,668	11,799
Undeformed part	3,403	6,420	10,224
Deformed part	0	1,248	3,185

[1] Includes 1002 area shown on figure 2, Native lands, and adjacent State water areas within 3-mile boundary (see fig. 2).

Current U.S. Oil Production and Consumption

1. In 2007, how much oil did the U.S. consume daily?

2. How much domestic oil was produced each day in 2007?

3. What was the daily U.S. oil shortfall in 2007?

4. How much oil did the U.S. consume in 2007?

5. What was the total U.S. domestic oil production in 2007?

6. What was the difference in U.S. oil consume and produced in 2007?

7. Imports in 2007 represented what percentage of the total U.S. oil consumption?

Historic Trends in U.S. Oil Production and Consumption

8. From 1982 to 2007, by what percentage did U.S. oil consumption increase?

9. How much recoverable oil does the U.S. Geological Survey estimate ANWR contains that is under Federal jurisdiction?

10. At 2007 consumption rates, how many years of U.S. consumption does this represent?

11. Is this a high or low estimate?

12. Why?

13. From 1982 to 2007, by what percentage did U.S. oil consumption increase?

---

14.   What was the yearly average increase?

15.   Doing the same time period, by what percentage did U.S. domestic oil
           production decrease?

16.   What was the average yearly decline?

Even after discovery, oil fields take a long time to develop and bring into
production. It is estimated that if ANWR were to be opened for production
(assuming economic amounts of oil are found) its oil would not make it to market
for at least 10 years or so. Obviously, such a delay would have a profound impact
on the role ANWR might play in dealing with our dependence upon foreign oil.

17.   Assuming no major changes in U.S. oil production, estimate daily U.S. oil
           production in 2018.

18.   What will annual production be?

19.   What will U.S. oil consumption be in 2018?

20.   How much oil will the U.S. consume annually in 2007?

21.   What happens to ANWR's significant as an oil producing region in this future
           scenario?

APPENDIX C: REPLACING CONVENTIONAL PETROLEUM

In their study of petroleum peaking, Hirsch et al. (2005) looked at different ways of replacing petroleum-based liquid fuels. They identified five options with the potential to replace petroleum-based fossil fuels on a massive scale in the near term, i.e. decades. These were: enhanced oil recovery, coal-to-liquids, heavy oils/oil sands, gas to liquids, and improvements in vehicle fuel efficiency. Their wedges are shown below. In this activity, you will investigate the magnitude of the change from petroleum-based liquids for two of the five options: GTL and CTL.

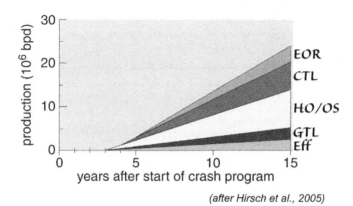

(after Hirsch et al., 2005)

Coal-to-liquid:
For the coal-to-liquids option, Hirsch et al. (2005) assumed typical plants would have a production capacity of 100,000 bpd and five could be built annually after the preparation period had passed.

For the coal-to-liquid wedge, calculate the:

1. number of CTL plants built 10 years after the initiation of the crash program

2. cost of these plants (indicate if you estimate is a high or low estimate)

3. amount of coal needed to support annual production at the end of the 10-year period

4. identify the countries which might have the capacity to develop CTL

Gas-to-liquid:

Hirsch et al. (2005) do not provide many details for their gas-to-liquid wedge except to say that it will provide 1 MM bpd in five years. Assuming an average plant size of 140,000 bpd, there would 2 constructed a year.

For the gas-to-liquid wedge, calculate the:

1. number of CTL plants built 10 years after the initiation of the crash program

2. cost of these plants (indicate if you estimate is a high or low estimate)

3. amount of gas needed to support annual production at the end of the 10-year period

4. identify the countries which might have the capacity to develop CTL

plant type	capital costs ($ per barrel of daily capacity)	feedstock requirements
CTL	$50,000-$70,000	6×10^7 tons/yr – 1.3×10^8 tons/yr
GTL	$25,000-$45,000	$500\text{-}600 \times 10^6$ scf/d
BTL	$140,000	

Source: Nonconvential Liquid Fuels, EIA Issues in Focus, AEO2006

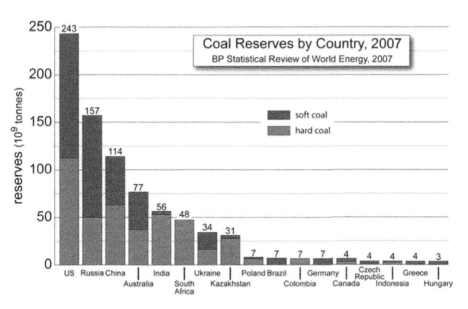

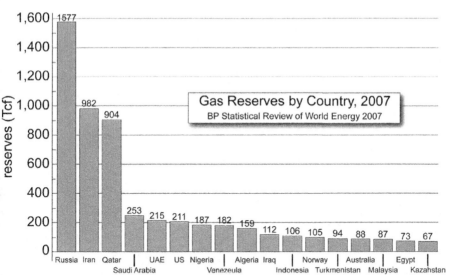

COAL

Can Humanity Afford to Use It? Can Humanity Afford Not to Use It?

INTRODUCTION

Coal is the fossil fuel that powered the Industrial Revolution and changed humanity's life on Earth in ways that are hard to imagine. Before tapping into this energy source, life was hard, work was never ending and back breaking, food supplies were uncertain, and one's world was defined pretty much by the places one could walk to (Baer, 1998). Access to coal and the energy it supplied changed industry, made long distance travel more accessible and easier, and opened new markets for a variety of goods. Because of increased travel, communication and exchange of ideas between cultures became more widespread. After waning in importance because of the rise of petroleum as a dominant primary energy source in the early 20th century, coal has made a comeback by becoming the primary energy source for much of the world's electricity. Yet, today many view coal as a menacing evil whose use threatens global climate and must be abandoned at all costs, even if it entails economic sacrifice and a drop in the standard of living for many. Others, particularly in the developing world, see coal as a way to grow wealth and lift millions out of economic and energy poverty. Thus, the use of coal in the developing world is growing rapidly in contrast to the developed world where there is virtually no growth in the demand for coal (Figure 1). Given the abundant coal resources in much of the developing world (e.g. China), and the proven technologies of coal-fired electricity generation, it is clear that coal will not be eliminated from the world's primary energy mix any time soon.

Globally, the role of coal as a primary energy source has changed dramatically in the last two centuries. These world-wide changes are mirrored by the evolving role of coal in the U.S. energy portfolio (Figure 2). The earliest known use of coal in the U.S. goes back about 2,000 years (Schweinfurth, 2009a). It was mined in Virginia between 1720 and 1750. With the expansion of railroads in the 1800s, the demand for coal grew. In addition to using coal, the railroads provided a convenient means of moving it from mine to market. At the same time, railroad construction stimulated the growth of the iron and steel industry. By this time, the iron industry had switched from charcoal to coke for reducing iron ore to pig iron. Coke was physically stronger than charcoal so it could better withstand the weight of a furnace charge while burning at a higher temperature. Because coke is a form of fuel produced by burning coal in an oxygen-poor environment, expansion of the iron and steel industry also further

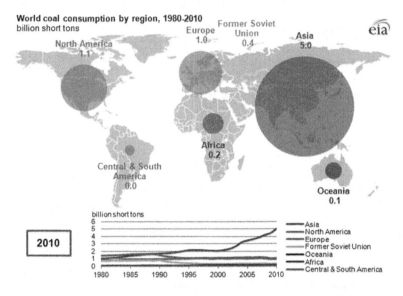

Note: With about 15 million short tons in total consumption, the Middle East was by far the smallest coal-consuming region and was too small to show on the map.

Figure 1. In recent decades, the consumption of coal has grown rapidly in Asia whereas it has decreased slightly or remained the same in much of the rest of the world. Asia has abundant coal resources and they are a cheap and accessible energy source. Source: U.S. Energy Information Administration, International Energy Statistics. (http://www.eia.gov/todayinenergy/detail.cfm?id=4390).

increased the demand for coal. The invention of the turbine-generator combination for the generation of electricity by electromagnetic induction in the 1880s led to an additional demand for coal. These generators were powered by new improved versions of the steam turbine that were all fuelled by coal.

Because of these technological changes, the demand for coal increased rapidly and it passed wood as the dominant primary energy source (PES) around 1885 (Figure 2). As global population grew, industry expanded, and the world's economy recovered from World War II, the use of coal continued to grow from the end of the 19th century through the 1950s. However during the same time period, petroleum was making inroads as a source of primary energy. Consequently, petroleum soon passed coal as the primary PES in the United States by the end of the 1950s. With the transition from coal to petroleum, the use of coal fell from just after World War II through the mid-1970s. With the Arab Oil Embargo dramatically increasing the cost of petroleum, coal progressively displaced petroleum as a fuel source for electricity generation. Since then coal has experienced a steady, upward trend in demand (Figure 2) until the falling price of natural gas from shale and worries about greenhouse gas (GHG) emissions reversed, or at least slowed, this growth pattern.

History of energy consumption in the United States (1776-2012)
quadrillion Btu

Figure 2. Change in primary energy sources (PES) from 1776 to 2012 for the United States. Coal was the dominant PES for much of the 19th century and early part of the 20th century. It is still an important PES, but its role in the U.S. economy has changed significantly. Source U.S. Energy Information Administration, AER Energy Perspectives and MER (http://www. eia.gov/todayinenergy/detail.cfm?id=11951&scr=email).

In 2011, coal supplied 19.7 quads[1] or 20% of the 97.3 quads of energy the U.S. consumed (Figure 3 – petroleum chapter). Energy from coal was used primarily in only three sectors of the U.S. economy. Industry used 8% of U.S. coal primarily in the iron and steel and cement industries. A small percentage (<1%) went to residential and commercial uses. However, the majority of coal (92%) was combusted to generate electricity. To supply this energy, the U.S. produced 1,094 million short tons[2] of coal, but consumed only 1,003 million short tons (Figure 3). The bulk of the consumption (929 million short tons) was burned in power plants to generate cheap, reliable electricity.

Despite its contribution to global economic growth over the last three centuries, coal has had a negative perception from the very beginning of its use. In Elizabethan England, the transition to coal, because of deforestation, was resisted by noble and commoner alike (Rhodes, 2007). People complained about the smell of coal smoke, the soot it released, and its dirtiness compared to wood. Only the growing expense of wood propelled the switch to coal. Later after World War II, coal was again identified as 'dirty' because of the haze and smog created by industrial use, and more importantly the thousands of coal-fired home furnaces that were poorly adjusted and operated. Fledgling environmental laws passed in the early 1970s resulted in the clean-up of coal particulate emissions through the installation of baghouses and electrostatic precipitators and visibility improved. With these changes, coal went off the radar again.

In the 1970s, concern about acid rain and the damage it was doing to forests, lakes, streams, and buildings downwind of coal-burning electric power plants became a growing concern. Coal was once again 'dirty', but now because of its sulfur (SO_2)

333

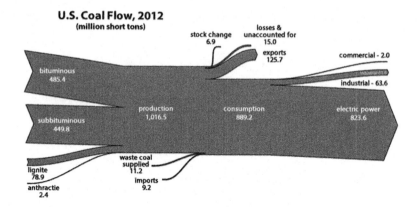

Figure 3. Sankey flow diagram depicting the flow of coal in the U.S. economy in 2012. Most of the coal produced was subbituminous or bituminous and went almost exclusively to electricity generation. Source: U.S. Energy Information Administration, Monthly Energy Review (January, 2014) (http://www.eia.gov/totalenergy/data/monthly/#coal).

and nitrogen (NOx) emissions. The industry once again sought ways to make coal clean. With passage of the Clean Air Act, power plants in the U.S. began installing scrubbers to reduce SO_2 emissions. Acid precipitation decreased and forests and lakes started to recover. Coal was 'clean' again. Today, coal has come full circle and is once again considered a dirty fuel source. It is viewed by many as highly polluting fuel that spews carbon dioxide, an important greenhouse gas, into the atmosphere at unprecedented rates. Once again, technological solutions are being actively pursued to produce 'clean coal' and preserve its role in the global and U.S. energy mixes. Carbon capture and storage (CCS) is viewed as one of the technologies capable of making coal a clean fuel once again.

As with all energy and mineral resources, coal moves through a materials flow cycle that begins with extraction and ends with the energy services consumers' demand. This cycle consists of a number of different stages (Figure 4). Extraction begins with mining either at the Earth's surface or deep underground. Once coal is produced, it must be prepared for transport by crushing, sizing, and cleaning to improve quality by removing contaminants and unwanted impurities. Coal is transported distances ranging from local to global. Depending upon distance moved, transport can be by conveyor (mine-mouth power plants), truck, rail, or water. Transport by water varies in size from small river barges to large, ocean-going bulk carriers. At a smaller scale, some coal is moved as slurry in pipelines. The final use for coal is determined by the type of coal (Figure 4). Thermal coal is low-quality coal valued for its ability to provide heat. It is used primarily in electricity generation and the manufacture of cement. In terms of volume or mass, trade in this type of coal dominates national and international coal markets. Metallurgical or coking coal has a specific set of physical and chemical properties that make it suitable for the production of iron and steel. It commands a higher price and comprises a significant portion of the global coal trade.

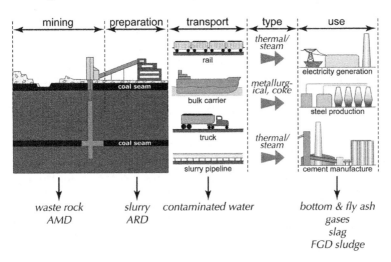

Figure 4. Schematic representation of the coal life cycle from production (left) to final end use (right). Intermediate stages in the cycle include preparation and transport. Potentially harmful waste streams are produced at every stage of coal's life cycle (bottom). Source: J.D. Myers, used with permission.

As in any material life-cycle, there are outputs at all stages of the coal life-cycle. Some of these are capable of creating environmental damage. Before the environmental awareness of today and stringent environmental laws, many of these waste streams damaged the environment and ecosystems. During mining, improper handling of mining waste and abandonment of mines generated acid mine drainage (AMD) and problems with waste rock disposal. Similar problems arose from the waste streams associated with coal preparation. Poorly constructed disposal sites for waste produced acid rock drainage (ARD), resulted in containment system failure, adversely impacted stream turbidity and sediment load, and altered water chemistry. Transport has the potential to impact hydrologic systems. At the point of combustion, coal produces a variety of solid, liquid, and gaseous wastes. Bottom and fly ash as well as flue gas desulfurization (FGD) sludge are all solids that must be disposed of safely. Atmospheric emissions include sulfur dioxide (SO_2), nitrogen oxides (NOx), mercury, heavy metals, and particulate matter (PM). Although not recognized legally as a pollutant under U.S. environmental law, there is also growing concern about the emission of the greenhouse gas (GHG) carbon dioxide (CO_2) during coal combustion. In this chapter, we will explore each step of the coal material life-cycle and its corresponding STEM and QR connections.

COAL RESERVES, CONSUMPTION, AND PRODUCTION

Coal is one of the most abundant of the conventional fossil fuels. In 2013, global coal reserves were estimated to be 860 billion tonnes (BP, 2013). Of this total, slightly more than half (456 billion tonnes) is soft coal, which consists of lignite and subbituminous coal (also known as brown coal). The remaining reserves consist of bituminous and anthracite or hard coal. These reserves are unequally distributed around the world. Nearly 90% of coal is found in North America (28.5%), Europe (35.4%), and Asia (30.9%). Combined, the Middle East and Africa have only 3.8% of the world's coal reserve with virtually none found in the Middle East. South America has even less coal than the Middle East and Africa (i.e. 1.5%) (BP, 2013). Slightly over 91% of the world's coal is held by nine nations (i.e. U.S., Russia, China, Australia, India, Germany, Ukraine, Kazakhstan, and South Africa) (Figure 5). Of these, the top three hold 59.1% of global coal reserves. In Africa, only South Africa has significant coal deposits and they are almost exclusively hard coal. Columbia, Brazil and Venezuela are the only nations in South America with significant coal reserves. Outside of these nine nations, coal reserves in all other nations are less than 7 million tonnes, but are widely distributed (Figure 5).

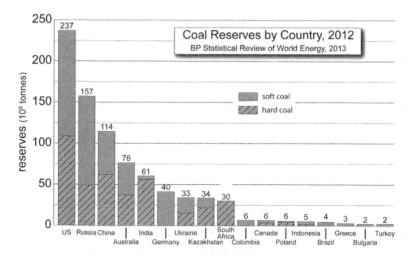

Figure 5. Coal reserves plotted by country with both soft and hard coal shown. Over 90% of the world's coal is concentrated in nine nations and nearly 60% in just three nations. Soft coal encompasses lignite and subbituminous coal whereas bituminous and anthracite coals comprise hard coal. Although most nations have a mix of hard and soft coal, Germany (soft) and South Africa (hard) have only one type of coal. Data source: BP Statistical Review of World Energy, 2013.

In 2012, the world consumed 3,730 Mtoe[3] of coal, nearly 2.6 times the consumption in 1965 (i.e. 1,429 Mtoe (BP, 2013). Almost 70% of total coal use was in Asia with Europe and Eurasia a distant second (13.9%) and North America third (12.6%). Together, the Middle East, Africa, and South and Central America consume less than 4% of global coal. The majority of coal use was in non-OECD countries (71.8%). As for coal reserves, global coal consumption is concentrated in a small number of nations (Figure 6). China, U.S., and India consumed over 100 Mtoe each, but most nations used much less coal. Between 2011 and 2012, twenty-eight nations had a decrease in coal use with declines range from 26% to a few percent (BP, 2013). Three nations experienced declines in coal use of greater than 20% whereas an additional three recorded a decrease of more than 10%. At the other end of the spectrum, twenty-five nations witnessed an increase in coal consumption with a significant number (9) showing gains of more than 10% (BP, 2013).

Although consumed on a commercial scale in over 70 countries, coal is produced in only 50. Together, these nations produced 7,864 million tonnes of coal in 2012, a 2% increase over 2011 and a doubling since 1981. Most of this coal was produced in the Asia Pacific region (67.8%) with nearly equal amounts in North America (14.5%) and Europe-Eurasia (12.2%). No coal was produced in the Middle East reflecting their near complete lack of reserves. Non-OECD production represents nearly three quarters of all coal produced globally. Of the fifty or so nations that produced commercial amounts of coal in 2012, China dominated production with 3.65 billion tons (Figure 7). The U.S. was a distant second.

In 2011, only 15% of coal produced was traded internationally (WCA, 2013a). Thus, most of the coal produced is consumed domestically in the country that produced it. Unlike for other globally traded fossil fuel commodities, a large share of the cost of internationally traded coal is transportation. Thus, the coal trade revolves around regional markets centered on the Pacific and Atlantic Oceans (Figure 8). Both steam or thermal coal and metallurgical or coking coal are traded. In 2012, the top exporters of coal were (in order of size of trade): Indonesia, Australia, Russia, U.S., Columbia, South Africa, and Canada (WCA, 2013b). There is a large variation in the amount of coal exported with Indonesia and Australia individually exporting over 300 million tonnes. Whereas Australia exported nearly equal amounts of thermal and metallurgical coal, Indonesia's output was almost exclusively (99%) thermal coal. The other major coal exporting nations all exported individually less than 150 Mt. Except for Germany and the United Kingdom, all top coal importing countries (China, Japan, India, South Korea, and Taiwan) in 2012 were located in Asia (WCA, 2013b). All these nations imported far more thermal coal than metallurgical coal.

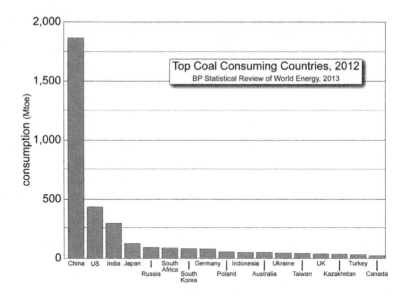

Figure 6. Coal consumption plotted, in millions of tonnes oil equivalent, by country. Only three nations, China, U.S., and India, consumed more than 100 Mtoe. China consumed more than four times the amount the U.S. used. Data source: BP Statistical Review of World Energy, 2013.

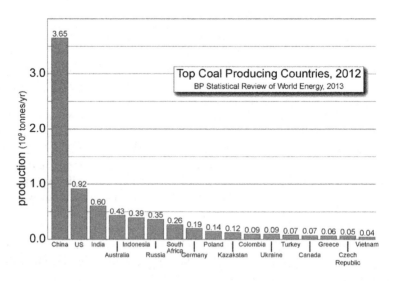

Figure 7. China produced a staggering 3.65 billion tonnes of coal in 2012. No other nation produced more than a billion tonnes, although the U.S. was close. Data source: BP Statistical Review of World Energy, 2013.

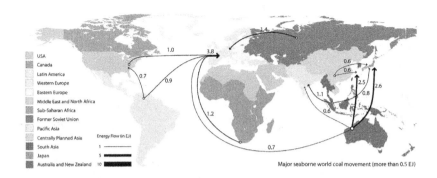

Figure 8. Although it is traded globally, coal is not moved on the same scale as oil. The top coal exporting nations in 2012 were Indonesia, Australia, Russia, U.S. Columbia, South Africa, and Canada. The top five importers of coal (China, Japan, India, South Korea, and Taiwan) were all located in Asia. Source: GEA (2012). Reproduced with permission from the International Institute for Applied Systems Analysis (IIASA).

Australia

Australia has an estimated 76 billion tonnes of coal ranking it fourth in the world in terms of reserves (Figure 5). This represents 8.9% of world coal reserves (BP, 2013). Coal fields in Australia are concentrated in the eastern part of the country (Figure 9), although small deposits are found along the west coast and in Tasmania (Mohr et al., 2011). Eastern coals are primarily exported whereas western coals are used mostly for domestic electricity generation (Thomas, 2002). Seams in Queensland are low ash and sulfur, high volatile subbituminous coal of Mesozoic age, which can attain thicknesses of 4 meters (13 feet). In New South Wales, coal is found in seams that may have thicknesses of 10 meters or less (<33 feet). Lignites found in Victoria are shallow, flat-lying, and can attain thicknesses of 300 meters (Thomas, 2002). Coal production in this state is primarily for electricity generation.

China

Given its large population and rapid economic growth, it is perhaps not surprising that China is the world's largest consumer of coal (Figure 6). Because its coal reserves are large (13.3% of global total, BP (2013)), China has historically been able to fulfil its coal demand by domestic production. This production makes China the world's largest producer of coal by a large margin (Figure 7). Although many are not surprised to learn the China is such a large producer and consumer of coal, this has not always been the case. China's coal use changed dramatically in the last half century (Figure 10). In 1965, China consumed only 114 Mtoe of

Figure 9. The majority of Australia's coal fields are located in the east. Coal produced from Queensland and New South Wales are primarily for export as thermal or coking coal. Coal from Western Australia and Victoria are used domestically to produce electricity. Modified from Jaireth and Huleatt (2012).

coal. Compared to its 2012 use of 1,873 Mtoe, this represents a 16-fold increase in the last 47 years. This increase in consumption has been steady since 1965, but it accelerated dramatically around the turn of the current century (Figure 10). During the period 1965-2012, China's share of global coal consumption has grown dramatically. In 2012, China consumed nearly as much as the rest of the world's nations combined.

With 114 billion tonnes of coal reserves, China holds the third largest reserves in the world (Figure 5). It also has 13.3% of world's coal (BP, 2013). The majority of China's coal is bituminous and anthracite. Coal is not uniformly distributed across China (Figure 11). Most proven and recoverable deposits are found in the north far from population centers where demand is greatest. The provinces of Inner Mongolia, Shanxi, Shaanxi, and Xinjiang each contain more than 100,000 Mt of coal. Coal fields along the Inner Mongolia-Shanxi border contain undisturbed coal seams up to 10 meters in thickness with low sulfur content (< 1%). These coals

340

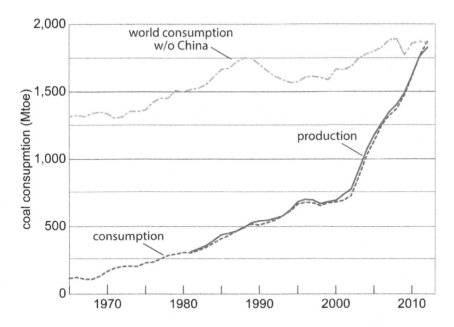

Figure 10. China's consumption of coal has grown dramatically since 1965. During much of this time, domestic production matched or slightly exceeded demand. In the last two years, China's coal production has lag behind consumption. When compared to the rest of the world's coal consumption, it is perhaps surprising to learn that China uses as much coal as the rest of the world combined. Data source: BP Statistical Review of World Energy, 2013.

are produced by underground mining and used primarily for electricity generation (Thomas, 2002). Coal seams in Lianoning province can attain thicknesses of 100 meters.

Coal mines in the China are typically owned by different levels of government (Tao and Li, 2007). Key state mines are run by provincial governments and are highly mechanized. In 2001, there were 100 of these mines. Local mines are administered by provincial, prefecture, and county governments. They are smaller and less mechanized and numbered about 2,000 in 2001. The largest number of mines (21,000-23,000) consists of township or village enterprises. These are run by small collectives or individuals. Unlike the other two classes of mines, these are small, use manual labor, and have low productivity. They also have, however, low production costs (Tao and Li, 2007). Many of these mines are run without official permission and attempts have been made recently to close them.

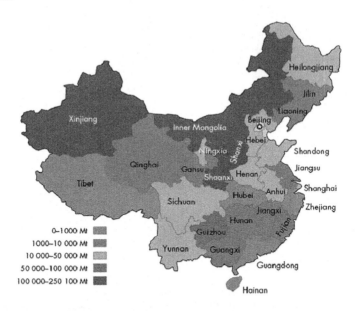

Figure 11. Most of China's coal is located in the north and northwest. The majority of coal reserves are found in Inner Mongolia, Shaanxi, Shanxi, and Xinjiang Provinces. The separation of the coal fields in the north from the population centers of the south creates logistical problems in moving coal from production to consumption sites. Source: (Tao and Li, 2007).

United States

With an estimated 237 million tons, the United States holds the world's largest reserves of coal (Figure 5). These reserves represent approximately 27.6% of the world's coal (BP, 2013). The U.S. Geological Survey has divided the nation into six coal provinces: Eastern, Interior, Northern Great Plains, Rocky Mountain, Pacific Coast, and Gulf Coastal Plain (Figure 12).

The Eastern province contains the Appalachian Basin, a 1,500 kilometer long (932 miles), NE-SW trending basin that is nearly 400 kilometers (248 miles) wide at the NE end but shrinks to 25 kilometers (15 miles) wide at the SW. It is divided into three compartments (Figure 13) each with 26 to 60 coal seams of economic value ranging in thickness from 0.5 to 3.6 meters (1.6-12 feet) (Thomas, 2002). The seams are mostly high and medium volatile bituminous coals of Carboniferous (Pennsylvanian) age. Small amounts of anthracite also occur in this province. Bituminous coals of Carboniferous age are widely distributed in the Interior Province and the province is divided into an Eastern and a Western section (Figure 13). Coals in the east have high sulfur (3-7%) and vary in thickness from 0.5 to 2.5 meters (1.6-8 feet). Most production in the Interior Province is from these coal seams. In the Western Interior,

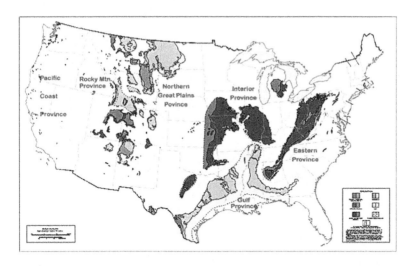

Figure 12. U.S. coal occurs in six major provinces (Eastern, Interior, Northern Great Plains, Rocky Mountain, Pacific Coast and Gulf Coastal Plain). Coals in the east are typically older and of higher rank than those in the west. Source: U.S.G.S.

seams are thinner (<1.5 meters (1.6 feet)), but laterally extensive, and are mined by surface methods (Thomas, 2002). The Northern Great Plains Province contains the extensive Tertiary coals of the Powder River Basin of Montana and Wyoming (Figure 13). These coals are extensive, low sulfur, and mostly subbituminous with thicknesses averaging 6-30 meters (5-250 feet) (McClurg, 1988). Mining in this region is primarily by surface methods conducted on a large scale. The Pacific Coast Province contains mostly small deposits of coal in isolated basins except for the subbituminous deposits of Alaska, which may be very large (Thomas, 2002). Extensive lignites of Tertiary age are found in seams 1 to 7.5 meters (3.2-25 feet) thick in the Gulf Coastal Plain Province (Figure 13).

There is a significant difference between eastern and western U.S. coals (Figure 14). Coals in the east are older, occur in thinner seams, and for the most part have higher sulfur contents. In contrast, western coals are lower in rank, have lower sulfur contents, and are much thicker.

Coal has been mined in the U.S. since colonial times (Schweinfurth, 2003; 2009b). Production has grown from just under 200 million short tons in 1950 to just under a billion tons in 2012 (Figure 15). In 2012, the U.S. was the world's second largest producer of coal with just under a billion tonnes (Figure 7). Since 1950, coal mining in the U.S. has changed dramatically (EIA, 2012). During this time, there has been a steady growth in the amount of subbituminous coal mined in the U.S. (Figure 15). Additionally, the amount of lignite mined has grown whereas anthracite production has declined and bituminous coal production levels have remained constant and even

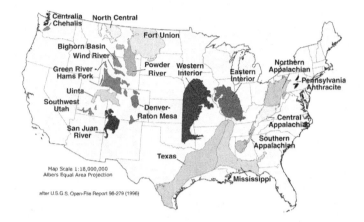

Figure 13. U.S. coals occur in six major provinces (Eastern, Interior, Northern Great Plains, Rocky Mountain, Pacific Coast and Gulf Coastal Plain. Coals in the east are typically older and of higher rank than those in the west. Source: U.S.G.S. Open-file Report 96-279.

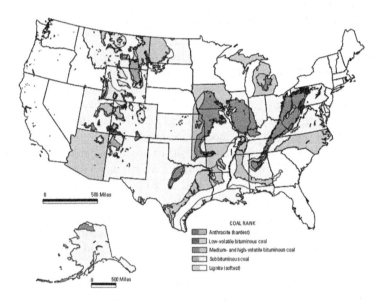

Figure 14. The rank of U.S. coal varies regionally as well as between fields. Anthracite is found in small eastern fields of Appalachia. Bituminous coal is primarily located in eastern and mid-western coal fields. The Northern Great Plains contain large deposits of subbituminous coal and lignite. Large deposits of lignite are found in the southeast and northern plains. Source: Modified from Schweinfurth (2003).

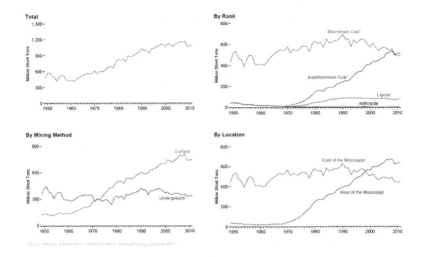

Figure 15. In addition to growing production (top left), the U.S. coal mining industry has undergone significant changes in the last half century. Whereas anthracite production has declined over this period, lignite and especially subbituminous production have increased markedly (upper right). Surface mining production has grown dramatically whereas output from underground mining has remained fairly constant (lower left). Coal mining activity has also shifted from the east to the west (lower right). Source: U.S. Energy Information Administration, Annual Energy Review 2011.

declined slightly. Thus, the rank of coal produced in the U.S. has steadily declined over the past fifty years. In addition to changes in the rank of coal mined, there has been a steady move toward more surface mining in large mines located west of the Mississippi River (Figure 15).

COAL'S NATURE, CLASSIFICATION, AND COMPOSITION

Nature

Coal is a brown to black, organic sedimentary rock that is combustible and composed predominantly of carbon with some hydrogen and lesser amounts of other elements. It represents an accumulation of both organic and inorganic sediments. Coal consists of two components. Macerals are organic components derived from the plant remains that accumulated to form coal. They are equivalent to minerals in inorganic rocks. Mineral matter consists of primary and secondary minerals formed at all stages of coalification. It is incombustible and when coal is burned forms the solid ash that remains.

When observed under the microscope, the identifiable organic units of coal are *macerals*. There are many types of macerals and their names all bear the suffix

"-inite". Despite their complexity, macerals are grouped into only three main classes. *Vitrinite* is a maceral group derived from lignin of humic (woody) material such as stems, roots, and vascular leaf tissue. Nearly 90% of North American coals are comprised of vitrinite macerals. They impart a shiny appearance to coal. *Liptinite* is derived from the resins and waxes of spores, cuticles, and pollen. They are richer in hydrogen compared to macerals of the vitrinite group. The last maceral group is *inertinite*. Their name reflects their inert behaviour during thermal alteration. They have high carbon contents and represent organic matter that was oxidized during coal formation. This oxidation may have been from burning of the peat or simply biological decay during low water periods. Within each maceral class, there are many different subtypes each derived from a different part of the original organic precursor. For example there are many types of woody plants in a swamp that contribute to the organic matter of coal. Each of these, in turn, consists of a variety of components (e.g. leaves, bark, etc.) that will become macerals. Thus, it is not surprising that there is a large variety to macerals.

Although nearly 130 minerals have been identified in coal, only thirty-three are commonly present (Schweinfurth, 2003). Of these, quartz, kaolinite, illite, montmorillonite, chlorite, pyrite, calcite and siderite are major components. These minerals may occur embedded in the coal matrix as single crystals or in clusters of crystals. Alternatively, they may occur within voids or spaces in coal. The presence or absence of this mineral matter has important implications for the economic value of coal. Arguably, the most important of these from an environmental view is pyrite, a sulfur-bearing mineral that has environmental implications at virtually every stage of the coal life-cycle. Mineral matter also has impacts on the operation of power plants. For example although they do not burn, mineral matter may melt at the high temperatures of boilers. Consequently, high concentrations of low-fusion minerals can result in scaling or slagging of boilers and combustion equipment. Alternatively, mineral matter with high fusion temperatures produce fly ash which must ultimately be removed from the flue gas before it is exhausted to the atmosphere.

Classification

Coal is classified in a number of ways including rank, grade, use, physical nature, and origin. *Rank* is a measure of the degree to which peat has undergone thermal alteration. The higher the rank of a coal, the higher its carbon content. A coal with high carbon content produces more heat when burned. Shiny, reflective macerals in a coal indicate higher rank. The different ranks of coal, in order of decreasing rank, are: *anthracite, bituminous* (divided into A, B and C classes based on heat content), and *subbituminous. Lignite* is not technically coal, because it has not undergone the necessary chemical and physical changes produced by thermal processes. It is, however, often portrayed as having a rank below subbituminous coal. Subbituminous coal and lignite are commonly referred to as *brown* or *soft coal* whereas bituminous and anthracite are termed *black* or *hard coal* (Figure 16).

Coal *grade* is defined on the basis of ash content with four different categories recognized: bone coal (15-50%); very high ash coal (8-15%); high ash coal (6-8%) and low ash coal (less than 3%). A 'coal' with greater than 50% ash is not combustible and is not technically coal. Low grade corresponds to high ash coal and high grade to low ash coal. Low grade coals release less energy when burned, because a greater portion of the coal is incombustible. For coal used in electricity generation, grade is important because it determines the amount of incombustible material (ash) that must be transported to a power plant as well as disposed of after combustion. Coals used for metallurgical purposes require low ash contents to prevent the introduction of impurities into the metal-making process.

In addition to rank and grade, coal can also be classified on how it will be used. There are two broad classes. *Steam coal* is used in electrical power plants to produce the steam used to generate electricity. It is also used in industrial applications to generate process heat (e.g. heating of clinker in cement production). Steam coal is the most widely used coal and is the most used by volume. *Metallurgical coal* consists of coal suitable for making coke for use in industrial applications. Coke is produced by burning coal in a reduced oxygen atmosphere (i.e. coking). Coking removes most of the gasses and leaves a solid (coke) that burns with a higher temperature than coal. There are two grades of coke. *Chemical grade coke* is of a lower grade with higher ash content as well as greater amounts of trace element impurities. It is used for reducing phosphate rock in electric furnaces and in the production of calcium carbide. *Metallurgical grade coke* burns at a much higher temperature and is used as the heat source in blast furnaces for making iron and steel. It also has low ash content and trace impurities.

In addition to being classified based on rank, grade, and use, coal is also described based on the nature of the organic matter that it is made from. *Humic coal* is derived

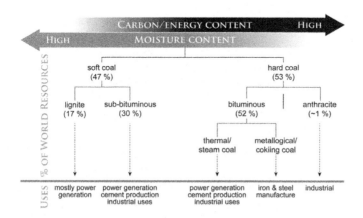

Figure 16. Representation of the relationship between coal type and use. Source: After World Coal Institute, 2005).

primarily from woody tissue (i.e. macroscopic plant remains) and has gone through a peat stage of development. Volumetrically, this is the most important type of coal. Coal derived primarily from spores and algae (i.e. microscopic plant debris) is *sapropelic coal*. There are two types of sapropelic coal. Coals that are made up of microspores that settled underwater are called *cannel coals*. In contrast, *boghead coal* is derived primarily from algae.

Characterizing Coal

Coal is a very complex substance that is used for a variety of very different purposes (Figure 16). The suitability of a particular coal for any given purpose is determined by its physical and chemical properties. Thus, it is important to establish a coal's nature by physical and chemical analyses. These analyses are performed at virtually all stages of the coal life-cycle (e.g. during mining, ship loading, receiving, etc.). Coal analyses fall into two classes, physical and chemical (Figure 17). Various physical properties are determined by petrographic analysis and proximate analysis. In addition, there are a variety of other specialized test to determine various physical characteristics of coal. In contrast, only the ultimate analysis is commonly used to determine the chemical composition of coal.

Physical Properties
The physical characteristics of coal are determined by four basic properties (i.e. moisture, volatile matter, ash, and fixed carbon). Coal when mined is always wet (i.e. it contains moisture). Coal moisture is derived from four main sources: 1) surface

COAL ANALYSIS OPTIONS

physical analyses			chemical analysis
petrographic	special	proximate	ultimate
- macerals	- abrasiveness &	- moisture	- carbon
- minerals	grindability	- volatile matter	- hydrogen
- reflectance	- coking & caking	- ash	- oxygen
- microlithotypes	properties	- fixed carbon	- nitrogen
	- slagging & fouling		- sulfur
	properties		- +/- phosphorus
	- ash analysis		- +/- trace elements
	- washability		
	- float/sink		

as-recieved (ar), air-dried (ad), dry-basis (db), dry, ash-free (daf)

Figure 17. Schematic chart illustrating the various types of chemical and physical analyses used to characterize the nature of coal. The coal properties routinely measured during each type of analysis are also shown. Source: J.D. Myers, used with permission.

348

moisture (water on the surfaces of coal macerals and minerals); 2) hydroscopic moisture (water held in pores and microfractures); 3) organic moisture (water held in the macerals); and 4) mineral moisture (water that is part of a mineral's crystalline structure). Moisture represents the water in coal at the location, time, and conditions when it was sampled. *Volatile matter* consists of those compounds or components liberated when coal is heated to high temperature in the absence of air. It generally consists of short and long chain hydrocarbon molecules as well as some sulfur. High volatile matter content increases the risk of spontaneous combustion of coal. *Ash* is the non-combustible residue left after coal is burned. Because minerals often undergo physical and chemical changes during coal combustion, ash does not equate exactly to mineral matter. Ash is measured by weighing a sample of coal, burning it completely, and weighing the residue. *Fixed carbon* is the carbon in coal that is left after all the volatile matter has been driven off. It represents the solid combustible component of coal. A *proximate analysis* measures a coal sample's moisture, volatile matter, ash, and fixed carbon (Table 1).

Because coal is primarily used at high temperatures, it is important to know coal properties at elevated temperature as well as at ambient conditions. Thus, proximate and ultimate analyses are frequently conducted in several different ways. *As-received* performs the analysis on a sample of coal as it is received without preparing the coal in any way. Thus, it measures all the relevant variables. It is perhaps the mostly widely used of analyses. *Air-dried* is conducted after the coal is dried in air and the surface moisture is driven off. If the coal is analysed after all the moisture is driven off, it is referred to as *dry-basis*. Finally, *dry, ash-free* includes only the volatile matter and fixed carbon. The impact of these different types of analyses are shown in Table 1 and Table 2.

Chemical Composition
An *ultimate analysis* of coal reports, in weight percent, its major element abundances. Elements measured during an ultimate analysis include carbon, hydrogen, nitrogen, oxygen, and total sulfur (Table 2). There are national and international standards

Table 1. An example of a proximate coal analysis for the four different ways of reporting coal characteristics

	unit	as-received	air-dried	dry-basis	dry, ash-free
moisture	wt. %	3.3	2.7	-	-
ash	wt. %	22.1	22.2	22.8	-
volatile matter	wt. %	27.3	27.5	28.3	36.6
fixed carbon	wt. %	47.3	47.6	48.9	63.4

Table 2. Results of an ultimate coal analysis for the four different ways of reporting coal characteristics

	unit	as-received	air-dried	dry-basis	dry, ash-free
carbon	wt. %	61.1	61.5	63.2	81.9
hydrogen	wt. %	3.00	3.02	3.10	4.02
nitrogen	wt. %	1.35	1.36	1.40	1.81
total sulfur	wt. %	0.4	0.39	0.39	-
oxygen	wt. %	8.8	8.8	9.1	-

describing how an ultimate analysis is to be performed. As with the proximate analysis, ultimate analyses can be reported on the basis of as-received, air-dried, dry-basis, or dry, ash free. Compared to hydrocarbons, coal is deficient in hydrogen with a H/C ratio of approximately 0.9 or less, half that of crude oil. It is also richer in oxygen with approximately one oxygen per five carbon atoms. Often times, an ultimate analysis is recast into a quasi-chemical formula expressing the relative atomic abundances of these five major elements. For example, a bituminous coal may have a formula of $C_{137}H_{97}O_9NS$ whereas a high-grade anthracite might have a formula of $C_{240}H_{90}O_4NS$. Expressing coal composition in this manner makes it easy to quickly assess how the carbon, hydrogen, and oxygen contents vary between coals as well as how their H/C ratios differ. It also provides a quick indication of the relative abundances of the potential air pollutants nitrogen and sulfur.

Chemical Structure of Macerals
Not surprisingly, the chemical structure of the organic matter (i.e. it's macerals) in coal is extremely complex, heterogeneous, and varies by rank. Unlike the minerals in coal, macerals are not crystalline and therefore do not have unique and specific chemical formulas or atomic structures. In contrast, they vary with the nature of their organic precursors, the degree of decay they have gone through, the maximum temperatures they have experienced, and the duration of those temperatures. Consequently, it is not surprising that the chemical structure of coal is only poorly understood. In terms of their chemical structure, macerals are polymers. That is, they are large molecules or macromolecules composed of many repeating subunits or *monomers*. For coal, the basic monomer is the planar, six member carbon hexagon (i.e. the *aromatic ring*) (Figure 18a). The six carbons of the ring each occupy an apex of the hexagon and are bonded to the other carbons by alternating single and double chemical bonds. Symbolically, the aromatic ring is depicted by omitting the carbons and drawing the ring as a simple hexagon. In one symbolic form, the positions of the double C-C bonds are indicated by short lines within the ring (Figure 18b). For

(a)　　　　　　　(b)　　　　　　　(c)

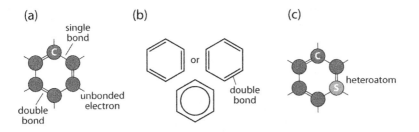

Figure 18. (a) The basic chemical building block of coal macerals is the aromatic ring, a six carbon molecular structure with the carbon centers defining a regular hexagon. The carbons are joined by alternating single and double C-C bonds. (b) An aromatic ring is represented symbolically by a hexagon with either three internal lines or an inscribed circle. The lines represent positions of the double C-C bonds and occupy different positions in the hexagon depending on coal structure. (c) Hetroatoms (i.e. non-carbon atoms) can freely substitute into the aromatic ring structure and in coal are mostly nitrogen, oxygen, and sulfur. Source: J.D. Myers, u sed with permission.

the other form, a circle is inscribed within the hexagon signifying the sharing of electrons between the carbons. Elements, *heteroatoms*, commonly substitute for carbon in the ring (Figure 18c). The most common heteroatoms in coal are nitrogen, oxygen, and sulfur.

Because the basic aromatic ring contains free electrons, the ring carbons bond to elements and/or molecules external to the ring. This external bonding is what produces the polymeric chemical structure of coal. In the simplest form, each carbon bonds to a single hydrogen producing the important ring - benzene (C_5H_6), which is not a major component of coal. More complex molecules are created when the rings share carbons or bond to bridging atoms or groups of atoms (i.e. functional groups) (Vasireddy et al., 2011). Common elements of the functional groups are carbon, hydrogen, and/or oxygen in various combinations (Figure 19). A wide range of functional groups are present in low rank coals and there is limited cross-linking of the aromatic rings. As rank increases, the functional groups decrease in number and the cross-linking of the aromatic rings increases markedly.

COAL FORMATION

Coal is produced by the accumulation and alteration of organic matter by biological decay and chemical changes due to increasing heat with burial. Four factors determine the type of coal formed: nature of organic material that accumulated; abundance of organic matter; maximum temperature the organic matter was exposed to; and the duration of the maximum temperature. Numerous lines of evidence suggest that coals are formed in wetlands and in a particular type of wetland (i.e. a swamp) (Figure 20).

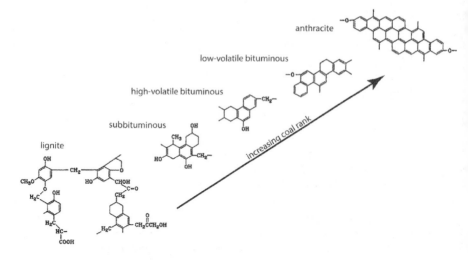

Figure 19. The structure of the organic components of coal varies significantly with coal rank. As rank increase, there are fewer functional groups present and the cross-linking of aromatic rings becomes much more extensive. Source: After Vasireddy et al. (2011).

Figure 20. Okefenokee Swamp in Georgia is a peat-forming swamp. This swamp illustrates the diversity of plants that contribute to peat formation and ultimately coal. Low topographic relief and consistent standing water are other characteristics that contribute to coal formation. Source: Photograph by W.H. Orem, U.S. Geological Survey photo (Schweinfurth, 2003).

Coalification is the suite of physical and chemical processes that convert dead organic matter into coal. There are two stages of coalification: 1) *peat formation*, which is dominated by biological activity; and 2) *bituminization* or the alteration of gytta by chemical reactions driven by rising temperature due to increased burial. At and just below the swamp floor, peat consists of a recognizable mass of leaves, roots and woody tissue. With increasing depth and as biological decay proceeds, the organic matter in peat becomes less and less recognizable as plant material and more of a "muck-like" layer. At 6-10 meters (19-32 feet), peat has been transformed into a dark brown to black hydrophyllic (water-loving), incompressible gel called *gytta* (Figure 21). This transition is the result of biological decay active in the top 10 meters (32 feet) of the swamp floor.

Wetlands: Coal-Forming Swamps

Wetlands are unique geological, physiographic, chemical, and biological environments that occur between land and water (Figure 22). They are characterized

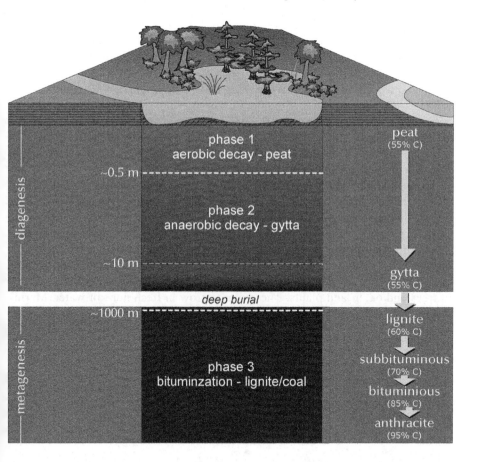

Figure 21. The first stage in the coalification process is biological decay. It consists of both aerobic and anaerobic decay, which occur at different depths. Biological decay produces gytta, which is converted to coal by the process of bituminization (the application of heat). Source: J.D. Myers, used with permission.

353

by water above, at, or near the surface, unique soils, vegetation adapted to wet conditions (hydrophytes), and the absence of flood-intolerant plants. Wetlands are variable in character with variations in water depth, dry/wet conditions, location, size, and dominant plant species.

There are three primary types of inland wetlands: bogs, marshes, and swamps (Figure 22). *Bogs* are characterized by the presence of mosses, shrubs, and possibly sedges. Freshwater bogs consist almost entirely of mosses, particularly sphagnum. Bogs are most common in the tundra regions of northern latitudes. Grasses, reeds, and rushes with or without cattails are the primary vegetation of *marshes*. Freshwater marshes have water depths of less than a meter and are characterized by rushes, reeds, and grasses. *Swamps* are characterized by the presence of trees. Freshwater swamps are forested regions that are flooded all or most of the year. Water depths range up to three meters. Fossils preserved in coal seams indicate swamps are the primary depositional environments in which coal forms.

Coastal wetlands are influenced by tides and storm surge flooding, therefore they exhibit a range of salinities. Commonly, salt marshes contain grasses and rushes adapted to high salinity, periodic flooding, and a wide temperature range. Coastal mangrove swamps have waters that range from freshwater to highly saline and emergent vegetation. Inland wetlands are removed from the influence of the ocean and, except for a few near saltwater lakes, are freshwater.

To form thick accumulations of coal, swamps must have a specific set of characteristics: freshwater; stagnant or slow moving water; standing water; long period of stable conditions; and accommodation space for peat accumulation (McClurg, 1988). Despite the widespread occurrence of coal, not all wetlands satisfy the conditions necessary to produce peat, the forerunner of coal. The presence of woody materials indicates the freshwater wetland that produced coal must have been a swamp not a marsh or bog. Coal is formed from the remains of trees and other land plants. These plants grow in fresh not salt water. Marine waters also have too low an acidity (high pH) and too high oxygen levels to preserve peat.

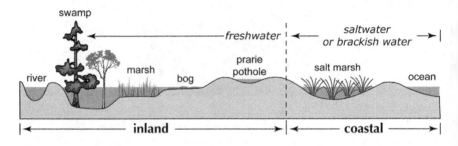

Figure 22. The various types of wetlands. Coals are formed mostly from organic remains of trees so they likely formed in swamps. Source: J.D. Myers, used with permission.

Currents in a swamp oxygenate water, which promotes organic decay and destroys the material that can become peat. They also dilute the acids produced by plant decay, thereby preventing a lowering of the pH. High acidity ultimately kills aerobic and anaerobic bacteria thereby slowing biological decay. Dynamic water also tends to bring in sediment while eroding some of the decaying plant material. For all these reasons, peat accumulation is favored by stagnant swamp water. If peat or decaying organic matter is exposed to air for any significant amount of time, it undergoes complete oxidation and decay. Thus, decaying organic matter must be covered by stagnant, acidic water most of the time to permit accumulation of large amounts of organic material. The generation of gytta, the precursor to coal, requires 10 meters (30 feet) of peat. Since peat accumulates at a rate of approximately 1-4 millimeters (0.03-0.15 inches) per year, the accumulation of such a thickness of peat requires time intervals on the order of 150,000 years.

Wetlands are, by their very nature, shallow with rarely more than 5 meters of water. With time as organic and inorganic material accumulate on the swamp floor, the elevation of the floor rises and the swamp evolves into dry land. Yet, coal seams are up to 100 meters thick. How is it possible for such thicknesses to be developed from shallow swamps? Unlike a normal swamp which dies quite rapidly, a coal-forming swamp must maintain a relatively constant water depth for thousands of years, thereby allowing the accumulation of enough organic matter to create the very thick coals seen around the world. There are two potential mechanisms for maintaining a long-lived swamp. One way is for the water surface of the swamp to rise in conjunction with the rising column of accumulating organic matter. The rising water level maintains the swamp and permits continued accumulation of organic matter on the bottom of the wetland. This process produces a domed swamp, but can be maintained for only a short period of time before the swamp floor becomes emergent. A second means of maintaining constant water depth is to allow the floor of the swamp to sink. To maintain a constant water depth, subsidence of the swamp floor must match the rate of organic and inorganic matter accumulation. If the floor sinks too rapidly, water levels in the swamp rise and the plants are drowned thereby producing a lake. If organic matter accumulates at a rate faster than the swamp floor sinks, the swamp eventually fills with sediment. The sinking of the swamp floor creates space for thick accumulations of organic matter. The space created by the sinking swamp floor is called the *accommodation space* and is critical for the formation of thick, uniform coals.

Peat Formation: Biological Activity

As organic matter accumulates on the swamp floor, bacteria and fungi begin to decompose it through aerobic decay. This decay produces carbon dioxide (CO_2), methane (CH_4), and a variety of carbon and nitrogen compounds. Initially, the aerobic organisms in the peat live on oxygen originally trapped in the accumulating debris. Because peat is impermeable, air and the oxygen it contains cannot circulate down through the swamp bottom litter. Thus as aerobic decay proceeds and organic matter is buried by more accumulating debris, the amount of oxygen in the lower parts of the peat column steadily decreases. At about 0.5 meters, biological decay has consumed all the oxygen, thereby killing the aerobic bacteria and causing aerobic decay to cease. This stage of biological decay reduces the initial organic matter by as much as 50%. At this time, the peat is approximately 55% carbon.

Below 0.5 meters (1.6 feet), anaerobic decay becomes the primary biological decay mechanism in the peat column. As decay proceeds, the organisms produce acids. One of these acids (i.e. tannic acid) produces the characteristic brownish tint of swamp water. The accumulation of acid raises the acidity of the water. When the pH of the swamp water drops below 4.5, the anaerobic bacteria die and anaerobic decay stops. At this depth (~10 meters (32 feet)), biogenic processes have ceased and further transformation of the organic material results from inorganic chemical reactions at much deeper depths and driven by high temperatures. Thus, the peat layer in a coal swamp never gets more than 10 meters (32 feet) thick as the swamp evolves.

At this stage of coalification (i.e. the end of biological activity), a black, hydrophilic, gel-like substance, *gytta*, forms a layer beneath the decaying peat. Although estimates vary, it appears that less than half of the original peat becomes gytta. Decomposed lignin makes up most of the gytta. It still only has about 50% carbon and lots of moisture. As the swamp evolves, a relatively constant 10 meter layer of decaying peat is maintained above the gytta (Figure 23). However, over thousands of years more and more peat is converted to gytta thereby increasing the

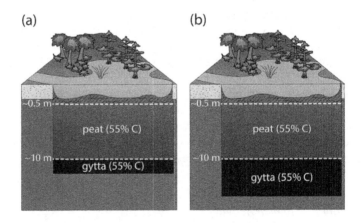

Figure 23. (a) At about 10 meters (32 feet) depth, organic decay has converted the peat into a black gel-like substance called gytta. (b) As long as the conditions remain constant, the base of the peat layer in the swamp remains at 10 meters (32 feet) (left). With time, the gytta layer thickens as a continual flow of organic matter passes through the peat section to become part of the gytta. Source: J.D. Myers, used with permission.

thickness of this gel-like layer. If the gytta layer is subjected to temperatures above 100°C, it will become coal and the resultant coal seam will be the same thickness as the original gytta layer.

Bituminization: The Role of Inorganic, Thermal Reactions

The final step in the formation of coal requires that the temperature of the gytta be raised to over 100°C. This is accomplished by burying it under a continually accumulating blanket of sediment. When 600 to 1,200 meters (2,000-4,000 feet) (the exact depth depends upon the geothermal gradient) of sediment accumulates over the gytta, it raises the temperature above the critical coalification temperature of 100°C. At this temperature, the organic molecules are thermally "cracked" or broken into smaller H-C-O compounds, thereby producing the various macerals that make up coal (bituminization).

To form coal, the amount of organic material must be extremely high. Combustible coal is only produced when organic matter makes up over 85% of the rock (Figure 24). Below this critical threshold, the rocks are not combustible. Lower amounts of organic matter produce a variety of sedimentary rocks rich in organic matter, but that will not combust.

Coalification vs. Hydrocarbon Generation

Clearly, there are major differences between the formation of coal and hydrocarbons (i.e. oil and natural gas) (Figure 25). Coal is formed by the accumulation of large amounts (> 85%) of Type III organic matter that is mostly derived from land

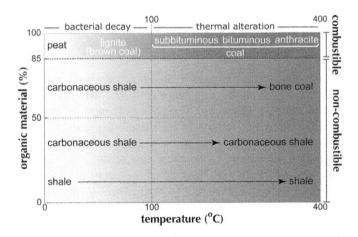

Figure 24. Very high accumulations of organic matter (>85%) are necessary to form coal. Source: J.D. Myers, used with permission.

357

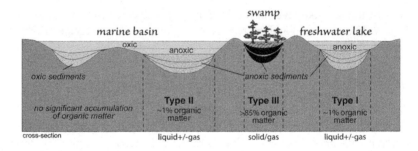

Figure 25. Although both are fossil fuels, there are significant differences in the formation of coal and the hydrocarbons oil and natural gas. Source: J.D. Myers, used with permission.

plants. In contrast, hydrocarbons result from the alteration of Type I and II marine organic matter. In addition, coal formation usually results predominantly in the formation of a solid with or without gas. Although chemically possible, there is generally very little liquid produced during coalification. Because it is solid, coal does not migrate in the subsurface like oil and gas do thus the need for larger organic accumulations to produce economically viable coal deposits. Another difference between the formations of these two fossil fuels is the much smaller degree of thermal cracking of organic molecules. The molecules that make up coal are not hydrocarbons rather they are complex carbon-hydrogen molecules with lower H/C ratios, abundant oxygen in several chemical forms, and trace amounts of nitrogen and sulfur chemically bound to the molecules. In contrast, crude oil and natural gas consist of hydrogen-carbon molecules with much higher H/C ratios, and smaller molecular sizes that produce gas and liquid at surface temperatures and pressures.

COAL SEAMS

In the strictest geological sense, coal is a sedimentary rock that happens to be combustible. Whereas for most sedimentary rocks the majority of sediments that comprise it are inorganic solids, coal is comprised of mostly organic sediment with a smaller amount of inorganic sediment. Yet, these organic sediments were subject to some of the same surficial geologic processes that normally act on sediments as they accumulate (i.e. deposition, compaction, dewatering, etc.). Thus, the physical nature of coal units will be, in part, determined by sedimentary processes. It is not unreasonable then to anticipate that coal on a macroscopic scale will vary in character from one coal unit to another, much as other sedimentary rocks (e.g. sandstones) do.

As with all sedimentary rocks, the primary initial physical form of a coal unit is a tabular unit oriented horizontally. A *tabular* body is one in which its width and length are of similar magnitude, but both are very much greater than the height or thickness (Figure 26). An example of an object with a tabular form is a pizza box.

Tabular bodies of coal that are recognizable at the map scale on the surface and in the subsurface are termed *coal seams*. Because of the many geologic processes they may be subject to after coalification, coal seams come in all shapes and sizes. They can vary in thickness from the centimetre scale to nearly 300 meters (984 feet) in thickness (Figure 26). Coal seams can also have areal extents of hundreds of square kilometers. Unless they have been tilted by subsequent tectonic forces acting in the crust, they are horizontal or have only shallow dips. The combination of tabular form and horizontal orientation has important implications for how coal seams are ultimately mined. In tectonically active areas, coal seams can be highly deformed with very contorted shapes and may even be faulted and displaced. If they have been deformed too much, coal seams may be uneconomic to mine.

If all geologic factors across the coal-forming swamp were spatially constant for the duration of a seam's accumulation, a coal seam would be a uniform, tabular body. However, examination of coal seams in a variety of geologic settings clearly shows that individual coal seams vary across their length and breadth. Omitting those changes that are the result of tectonic forces for the moment, many of the irregularities and features of coal seams can be traced back to sedimentary and biological processes operating during organic and inorganic sediment accumulation. On the map scale level, the most important of these are interrupted organic sedimentation by clastic sediment accumulation, and destruction of previously deposited organic sediment by oxidation.

These processes lead to a variety of physical forms that characterize coal seams. A *washout* is a lens of the roof rock that projects down into a coal seam (Figure 27). They produce steep dips and thin the seam. Washouts may extend through an entire seam, remove only part of the seam or alter the nature of the rock at the roof of the seam. The opposite of a washout is a *floor roll*, a ridge or dome of floor rock that juts up into the seam (Figure 27). These too produce a thinning of the seam and steep dips of contrasting rock types. Both features

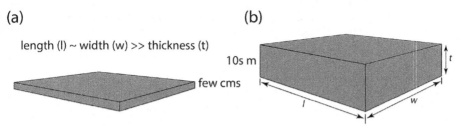

Figure 26. Coal units that are recognisable at map scales are coal seams and are characterized by tabular shapes that, unless tilted and deformed by tectonic forces, are horizontal or dip at only shallow angles. Coal seams vary in thickness from a few centimenters (a) to seams tens of meters thick (b). In rare instances, lignites 300 meters thick are known. Source: J.D. Myers, used with permission.

can also result from differential accumulation of organic sediment. In this case, the position at which the floor roll formed may have had a larger percentage of inorganic sediment resulting in less organic decay and compaction than in the surrounding sediment.

A commonly observed and important feature of coal seams is *splits* (Figure 27). Splits result when a coal seam traced laterally along an outcrop divides into two distinct coal beds separated from each other by a non-coal unit, the *parting*. Splits can have very simple geometric configurations or consist of a complex set of many different splits. A more complex type of split is the S split where a stem of coal from an upper seam extends down into a lower seam. Splits suggest an interruption of organic sedimentation by a pulse of clastic sedimentation. Simple splits probably result from variations in swamp water levels that caused some regions of the swamp to dry out producing a hiatus in peat formation whereas the central core of the swamp retained its standing water and peat formation continued uninterrupted (Jones, 2010; McClurg, 1988). The more complex S-split may

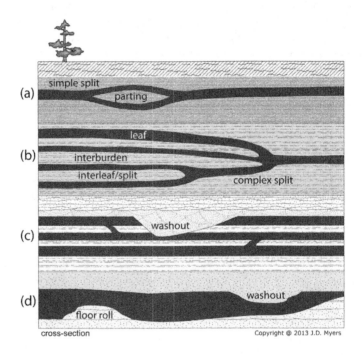

Figure 27. Illustration of the macroscopic features of coal seams. Washouts and floor rolls result in a thinning of a seam. Splits are where a seam separates into two or more individual seams. In contrast, partings are sections of a seam that encapsulate a lens of sedimentary rock. Source: J.D. Myers, used with permission.

result from a complex combination of variations in the rate of organic sediment accumulation and decay.

The geologic and geomechanical variations of a coal seam produced by these types of features can materially impact mining, particularly underground mining where there is less flexibility in dealing with unexpected conditions. Splits can so reduce the size of individual leafs that a seam that was thick enough economically to mine may no longer be so. Rolls and washouts can interfere with longwall mining (see next section) by damaging cutting heads and diluting the mined coal with incombustible material. Thus, coal exploration programs must carefully note the presence and locations of such features when conducting geologic mapping and drilling programs.

Coal is normally characterized by two sets of joints, *cleats*, that formed during coalification (Figure 28). The two sets are oriented at right angles to each other and marked by different degrees of development. The better developed and longer set of cleats is referred to as the *face cleats*. They are the more through going set of joints. At right angles to the face cleats are the *butt cleats*. This set terminates against the face cleats. The development of cleats varies with coal rank. Anthracite coal has poorly developed cleats, whereas they are strongly developed in bituminous coal. Cleats in brown coal (i.e. lignite and subbituminous coal) are only poorly defined presumably because of lesser degrees of coalification. Cleats are form by shrinkage of gytta due to dewatering and loss of volatile organic material during bituminization and cooling.

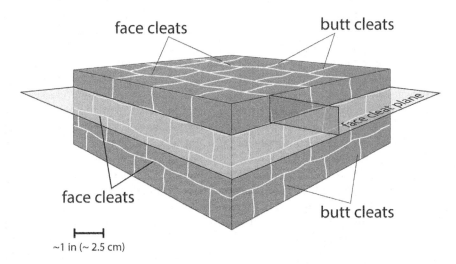

Figure 28. Coal is characterized by two sets of joints oriented approximately at right angles to each other. Face cleats are better developed and more through-going, whereas butt cleats terminate against the face cleats. Source: J.D. Myers, used with permission.

COAL PRODUCTION

Coal production consists of three distinct stages. *Mining* removes the coal from the ground using a variety of different mine types and mining methods. *Preparation* prepares the run-of-mine (ROM) coal for market. It often involves multiple operations and is designed to enhance heating value, remove environmental pollutants, and reduce shipping weight. Preparation plants are commonly located close to mines to reduce transportation costs. Finally, *transportation* moves cleaned coal from the preparation plant or mine to the point of end use. It may be moved only a short distance (to a mine mouth power plant) or shipped half way around the world.

Mining

The first step in the utilization of coal is extracting it from the Earth in a manner that yields a profit. The process of extracting any useful resource from the Earth is *mining*. Humans have been mining various Earth resources for thousands of years. Given the many different ways in which these resources occur geologically, a wide range of mining classes and methods for extracting metallic ores, non-metallic minerals, and fossil fuels have been developed. However, the unique geologic form of coal, i.e. horizontal to flat, thin tabular seams with only moderate mechanical strength, means that only a small number of these different types of mining methods are of importance in the coal mining industry.

Coal mining can be classified based on mine type, mine class, subclass, and mining method (Figure 29). Mine types fall into one of two broad categories. *Surface mines* extract a resource using an open excavation or one operated from the surface. In contrast, *underground mines* use openings that permit human entry into the subsurface where the majority of the mining activity occurs. Obviously, surface mines are used from coal seams that are shallow, whereas underground mines are appropriate for deep-lying coal seams. Although there are two mine classes for surface mines[4], only *mechanical mines* are used for coal extraction. This class of mine uses a variety of mechanical equipment to uncover a seam and excavate its coal. Mechanical surface mining has no subclasses. In contrast, underground mining has no mine classes, but it does have three sub-classes. Of these, only two (unsupported and caving) are used for coal mining (Figure 29). *Unsupported mining* does not use artificial pillars to support the roofs of mine openings. It may leave pillars of the deposit as support, but it relies primarily on the strength of the roof rock to keep mine openings from collapsing. Still, roof-bolting and other localized support methods are commonly used in this subclass of mines. Unsupported mining is especially effective for tabular, flat, thin deposits that are of moderate strength with mechanically strong overlying rock, all characteristics of many coal seams. In contrast, *caving* actively induces collapse (i.e. caving) of the ore or coal and the overlying rocks. It is a prime choice for coal seams with weak overlying rocks and appropriate for tabular seams that are flat and thin. Caving often produces land subsidence at the surface and typically has higher production and recovery rates than unsupported mining.

The last category in mine classification is mining method (Figure 29). A *mining method* encompasses the systems and procedures, physical layouts, and mining equipment used to exploit an ore body or coal seam. The type of mining method appropriate for a given deposit is determined by its internal attributes as well as external factors. The spatial, geologic, hydrologic, geomechanical, and mineralogical qualities of a deposit are some of the internal properties important in selecting a mining method. External factors that influence mining method selection include miner health and safety, environmental concerns, economic factors, legal limitations, technological controls, and engineering constraints. Given the variety of Earth resource deposits, a large variety of mining methods have been developed. However, coal is excavated using only four surface mining methods or two underground methods (Figure 29). The four primary surface mining methods used for coal recovery are: open-pit, open-cast (strip), contour, and mountain-top removal. The only underground mining methods of importance for coal extraction are room-and-pillar and longwall (with shortwall a variation of this more common mining method). Each mining method has distinct advantages and disadvantages and the selection of the proper method for a given deposit is perhaps the key decision in determining whether or not a particular mine is successful economically and environmentally. Details of each mining method are provided in the next sections.

In the U.S., the percentage of coal produced by surface mining has steadily grown from 25% in 1949 to 68% in 2011 (Figure 30). It surpassed underground

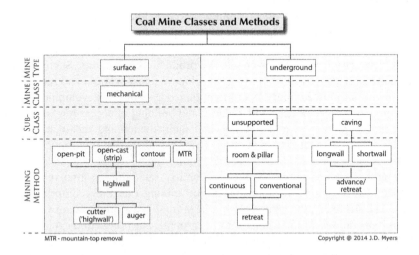

Figure 29. The different types of mining methods used to extract coal. Perhaps surprisingly, room-and-pillar mining is classified as unsupported because no artificial means are used to re-enforce the mine roof. Source: J.D. Myers, used with permission.

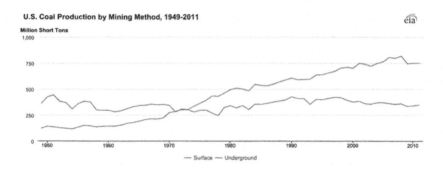

Figure 30. Surface mining has steadily grown in importance since 1949. It surpassed underground mining as the primary supplier of coal in 1971. In 2011, surface mining accounted for 68% of U.S. coal production. Source: U.S. Energy Information Administration, Annual Energy Review, Table 7.2.

mining in the production of coal in 1971. This change reflects the opening of large, surface coal mines in the western United States. Unlike some other mineral and energy resources extracted by mining, coal has a very low unit value, so the costs of extracting, processing, and transporting coal are critical in determining the economic viability of a particular coal seam. In this regard, surface mining, which is much less expensive, has a definite advantage over underground mining.

Mining, both surface and underground, involves a large number of *unit operations* to extract coal from the ground. These operations are divided into two broad classes. *Production operations* are those mining activities directly responsible for coal extraction (i.e. those that make money). These include operations such as drilling, blasting, loading, hauling, and hoisting coal. *Auxiliary operations* are those activities that are necessary to support or enable the production operations. Such operations occur during all stages of mining (e.g. development, excavation, and reclamation). Some of the various auxiliary operations that occur during development are site preparation, topsoil removal, shaft sinking, and building of access roads. Water and flood control, ventilation and lighting, and maintenance and repair are auxiliary operations that occur during extraction. During reclamation, auxiliary operations include revegetation, erosion control, and monitoring.

The unit operations of both surface and underground mining involve an ordered sequence that is continually repeated during mining (i.e. they comprise a cycle) (Figure 31). Arguably, the primary cycle in mining is the production cycle, that is, those unit operations that win coal from the ground. The production cycle obviously includes those processes that directly produce coal. It may also include auxiliary operations to ensure miner safety (e.g. roof bolting in underground mining). At its most fundamental, the production cycle consists of breakage and handling. Within each cycle stage, there are a number of operations that vary from one mine type and mining method to another. Grasping the difference between how coal is mined requires understanding the different coal mining production cycles.

Stripping Ratio and Cut-off Depth
Many factors go into the determination of whether a coal deposit will be mined from the surface or underground. These include surface topography, surface and groundwater hydrology, overburden thickness and hardness, seam thickness, number of seams present and, for multiple seams, the interburden thickness(es). Since it costs to remove and handle the overburden, the amount of coal exposed and extracted must cover its own extraction cost as well as that of the overburden. Stripping costs vary with the nature of the overburden (e.g. hardness, density, etc.).

The relationship between overburden and seam thickness is quantified by the *stripping ratio*. It is the unit amount of overburden that must be removed to access a similar unit of coal. Thus, a stripping ratio of 3 means three units of overburden must be removed for each unit of coal extracted (Figure 32). The types of physical

production cycle = breakage → handling

Figure 31. The general production cycle for both surface and underground mining. The different types of mines and mining methods implement this cycle in very different ways thereby impacting production volumes and environmental outcomes. Source: J.D. Myers, used with permission.

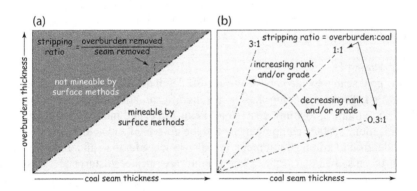

Figure 32. (a) Overburden depth versus coal seam thickness. Straight lines from the origin on this diagram define a fixed stripping ratio. If the stripping ratio for a coal seam plots above the line, the seam is too deep for surface mining. (b) The rank, grade and quality of a coal seam all influence the permissible stripping ratio for a given coal seam. Better quality coal can support a higher stripping ratio than poor quality coal. Source: J.D. Myers, used with permission.

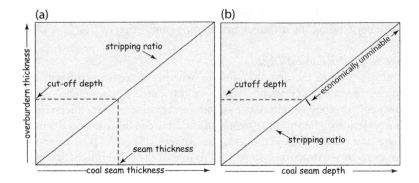

Figure 33. Overburden vs. seam thickness illustrating the cut-off depth for surface and underground mining. Any seam plotting to the right or above the dashed line is too deep to be successfully mined by surface methods. Source: J.D. Myers, used with permission.

properties that are used to calculate stripping ratio include: thickness, volume, and weight. Stripping ratio varies with coal quality and rank. For example, higher rank or grade coal increases the stripping ratio, whereas lower rank or grade lowers it (Figure 32a). High abundances of contaminants will lower the stripping ratio, but low contaminant concentrations will raise the stripping ratio (Figure 32b).

Obviously, the concept of the stripping ratio only works to a certain depth. Below this depth (i.e. the *cut-off depth*), surface mining is not economical (Figure 33). The cut-off depth depends on coal rank and quality. A lower stripping ratio has operational benefits because it means less material has to be moved to gain the same amount of coal.

Surface Mining
Shallow coal seams located above the cut-off depth are extracted by surface mining (Figure 34). Surface mining has some significant advantages including: large production volumes, low unit cost, small labor force, and increased opportunity for mechanization. Surface equipment can also be up-scaled and automated more easily than underground mining equipment. It is also much safer than underground mining. Among the disadvantages of surface mining are surface disturbance, destruction of soil horizons, habitat destruction, wildlife displacement, dust and noise disturbance during operation, significant effect on viewscapes, and major surface and groundwater hydrologic impacts. Mining operations can also be impacted by weather and climate.

For a surface mine, the typical mine development sequence is surface infrastructure construction, top soil removal and stockpiling, overburden removal (stripping), coal extraction, and reclamation. Each stage in the general mining production cycle (Figure 31) consists of two components (Figure 35). Breakage involves drilling and blasting both overburden and coal. For surface mining, handling is straightforward

Figure 34. A Wyoming surface coal mine after a winter storm. Coal and overburden are removed from the numerous benches (shelves or ledges). The active mining area is on the right. The two topmost benches are for removing overburden, whereas coal is extracted from the lowest bench face with shovels located on the mine floor in the center background. Overburden spoils piles are visible on the left. Photo by Linda Taylor.

PRODUCTION CYCLE: SURFACE MINING

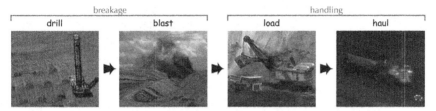

Figure 35. The production cycle for a surface coal mine consists of four basic stages (i.e. drill and blast, which comprise breakage, and load and haul for handling). Source: J.D. Myers, used with permission.

and encompasses only loading and hauling. This cycle is considerably simpler than that for underground mining and consists of only production operations. Thus, surface mining will tend to produce more coal in a given period of time than underground mining.

Surface Mining Methods
Once it has been determined that surface mining will be used to extract the coal, a host of factors are used to determine the type of surface mine to employ. Based on these factors, one of four main types of surface mining methods is selected for extraction: open pit, open cast (strip), contour, or mountain top removal (MTR) (Figure 29). Each type employs different machinery, workforces, and production cycles while producing different annual volumes of coal.

Open pit mining is used in areas where flatlands or gentle rolling topography overlie horizontal or shallow dipping coal seams. They have surface dimensions (i.e. width vs. length) that are roughly equi-dimensional thereby defining a large areal footprint. They are appropriate for thick (> 15 meters (50 feet)) or multiple

367

seams separated by thin interburdens underlying a large area. The best candidates for open pit mining are horizontal or shallow dipping coal seams. Because such seams are often too thick for the reach of most excavating equipment, these seams are often mined using a series of mining benches (11-12 meters (35-40 feet) high) connected by inclined roads (i.e. haul roads) (Figure 36). As the depth to coal increases, successive benches are developed at deeper and deeper levels. Depending upon its thickness, overburden is excavated from a single or multiple benches using shovels or hydraulic excavators. The overburden may be evacuated directly or, if hard, blasted before excavation. It is loaded into a fleet of trucks that move the overburden away from the active benches and dump it in a mined out portion of the pit for ultimate reclamation. Coal is extracted from the lowermost bench with a production cycle consisting of drilling, blasting, loading, and hauling. Shovels or hydraulic excavators reach the seam from the mine floor to load another fleet of haul trucks that transport the coal to a primary crusher. Depending upon the nature of the coal, it may be sent to a preparation plant for additional processing or stockpiled to await transport. After mining is complete, the backfilled pit is reclaimed by restoring as nearly as possible the original topography, re-establishing water courses and wetlands, and reseeding the area with native vegetation. Because coal is exposed on multiple faces throughout the mine, an open pit mine provides the operator flexibility in planning and carrying out mining operations. Accordingly, there is much greater ability for dealing with problems that arise during mining and avoiding significant down time. Coal can be stockpiled and blended to overcome any variations in run-of-mine (ROM) coal quality, grade, and/or rank to meet contractual obligations. Open-pit mines can produce in excess of 907,184 tonnes (1,000,000 short tons) of coal a year. In 2010, eight large surface mines in the Powder River Basin of

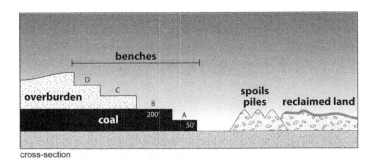

cross-section

Figure 36. Schematic cross-section of a typical open-pit coal mine. These mines are used to mine thick or multiple coal seams covering a large areal extent. Benches are designated with A being the deepest. As the mine deepens and additional benches are added, the lettering shifts downward and the next letter in the alphabet is added for the new topmost bench. This odd naming scheme ensures that the deepest bench (i.e. the coal producing bench) is always designated A. Source: J.D. Myers, used with permission.

Wyoming produced over 18 million tonnes (20 million short tons) each with the top two producing in excess of 90 million tonnes (100 million short tons) (EIA, 2011).

Open-cast or *strip* mining is used for horizontal or shallow dipping coal seams overlain by areas with limited topographic relief. These mines consist of a single excavation several tens of meters wide and thousands of meters long (Figure 37). The long dimension parallels the strike of the deposit and mining advances down dip. A dragline removes overburden from above the coal seam and casts (places) it in the excavated portion of the mine in one single operation. Mining generally begins near a coal outcrop where the overburden is thinnest and advances toward thicker parts of the overburden. Mining proceeds until the mine property boundary is reached, the overburden thickness becomes too great, the operating limit of the equipment is reached, or the stripping ratio becomes too high. The production cycle for a strip mine is the same as for an open-pit mine and is also carried out by truck and shovel. Reclamation begins early during mining. As soon as possible, the spoils area is contoured, topsoil replaced, and vegetation planted. Many of the physical and operational characteristics of an open-pit mine also hold true for an open-cast mine.

In the hilly and steep mountainous terrain of Appalachia, thin, horizontal coal seams are often buried by too much overburden to remove the entire seam

Figure 37. An open-cast or strip coal mine. Overburden is removed by the dragline (center background) to expose the coal seam (center and left middle ground). The dragline casts (places) the overburden in a spoils pile (triangular shape on horizon) with a single rotation of the unit. A truck and shovel operation is used to mine the exposed coal seam. Photo by James McClurg.

economically. Because the thickness of the overburden varies, some of the seam can, however, be removed by *contour mining*. Contour mining removes overburden in a pattern that follows the contours of a mountain or ridge (Figure 38). It produces a long, narrow, winding bench with a highwall on the mountain side. The trace of the highwall mimics a contour line on the hill side, hence the mine name. Originally, overburden was placed downslope from the cut, but this resulted in additional land disturbance and landslide and erosion problems. Now only the original cut disposes of overburden downslope. Material from subsequent cuts fill in previously mined areas. Mining progressively cuts into the mountain thereby increasing the height of the highwall and the amount of overburden that must be removed. The exposed coal is removed by truck and shovel using the typical surface mining production cycle. Mining ceases when the highwall becomes too unstable, the limit of the excavation equipment is reached, or the stripping ratio is no longer economical. A ridge of undisturbed material 5-6 meters (16-20 feet) wide is left on the outside of the cut to provide stability during mining. When mining is complete, the overburden is moved back against the highwall and graded such that the highwall is buried and the hill slope restored. Overburden is graded, topsoil replaced, and native vegetation replanted to stabilize the restored slope. Contour mines commonly have 5 to 10 workers and high, but limited productivity. They typically produce less than 100,000 tons of coal a year. Although contour mines are the most common type of surface coal mine in the U.S., they produce the least amount of coal. They are typically confined to the mountainous terrain of Appalachia.

When an open-pit, open-cast mine or contour mine has reached the end of its operational lifetime, a steep or near vertical mine face (i.e. the *highwall*) exposing a coal seam at its base still exists (Figure 39). In many instances if the conditions

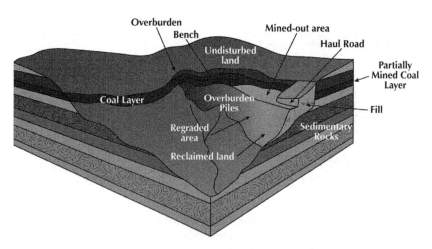

Figure 38. Schematic representation of a contour mine. Contour mines are used mostly in rugged, hilly topography. Source: J.D. Myers, used with permission.

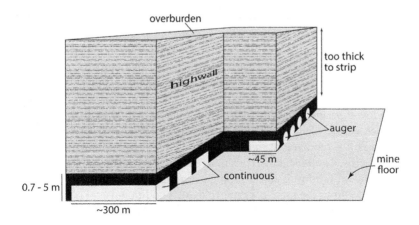

Figure 39. Highwall mining options. Auger mining produces circular openings that extend about 45 meters (150 feet) into the highwall. Conversely, continuous highwall mining reaches further 305 meters (1,000 feet)) under the highwall to extract coal and creates a rectangular opening. Source: J.D. Myers, used with permission.

are favourable, the mine may switch to underground mining to recover additional coal. However, this switch is expensive and requires considerable lead-time for mine planning and development. In addition, the switch can only be made for relatively thick coal seams. An alternative to underground mining is the initiation of *highwall mining* to extend the production life of the original mine (Figure 39). Highwall mining uses a variety of equipment to extract coal from the seam without removing the overburden above it. It is an unsupported type of mining that requires strong overburden. Two types of mining methods, auger and cutter, are used in highwall mining (Shen and Fama, 2001; Walker, 2001).

Auger mining extracts coal by boring beneath the final highwall of a surface mine. An auger is a large spiral screw (similar to a wood borer) that crushes the coal and moves it out of the hole by the rotatory motion of the auger. It produces circular entries that can extend up to 45 meters (150 feet) under the high wall. Augering can remove 25-30% of the coal in the buried portion of the seam. It has high productivity, but has difficulty dealing with rolls or dips in the seam. An alternative highwall mining method is *cutter mining*[5]. A cutter highwall miner consists of a cutter unit attached to a power unit backed by pushbeams. The cutter unit has evolved from the continuous miner used in underground mining (see underground mining section). Pushbeams are rigid rectangular boxes each six meters (20 feet) long and enclosing two counter-rotating screw conveyors that move the crushed coal toward the cut. The pushbeams push and pull the cutter and power units into and out of the seam allowing it to penetrate and bore out the coal. As the miner advances, additional pushbeams are attached. Cutter highwall miners can work in

371

seams 76 cm (30 inches) to 5 meters (16 feet) thick and penetrate up to 305 meters (1,000 feet) under the highwall. Unlike augers, they produce a rectangular entry. These miners are operated remotely using laser-guidance and camera-monitoring systems and require only a 3-4 person crew. Depending upon coal seam thickness, these types of mining systems can produced 40,000 to 110,000 tonnes (44,000-121,000 tons) of coal a month. In contrast to the auger, the highwall system can readily follow dips and rolls and can be used in seams with dips up to 8°. In addition, the enclosed nature of the pushbeams prevents mined coal from being diluted by rock debris as it is removed from the seam. When highwall mining is complete, the coal mine is closed and reclaimed in a manner similar to a contour or open-pit mine. Clearly, highwall mining is not a primary mining method. Rather, it is a salvage operation that allows the mine operator to extract additional coal before the mine is closed and reclaimed. It is primarily used in the mountainous eastern United States, although it has also been deployed in some Australian coal mines (Shen and Fama, 2001; Walker, 2001).

When covered by hilly, steep mountainous terrain, horizontal coal seams are often too thin, areally limited, or slopes and soils above them are too unstable to be mined by underground methods. Similarly, stripping ratios maybe too great or variable to justify open-pit, strip, or contour mining. Steepness may also limit the effectiveness of the common types of surface mining. If geologic, technical, and economic conditions are favorable, these coal seams can be extracted by *mountain top removal (MTR) mining* (Figure 40). Overburden, that is the top of the mountain, is removed in a series of parallel, horizontal cuts by truck and shovel or dragline. In some MTR operations, 300 meters (1,000 feet) of overburden is removed to expose the underlying coal seams. Because of the hardness of the overburden, it must be drilled and blasted before removal, a potential source of conflict with adjacent property owners. Overburden removal greatly expands the volume of spoils (i.e. rock and soil). Thus, they all cannot be accommodated by disposal in the mined out areas. In addition, the steep terrain creates stability issues with respect to spoils piles. Thus, spoils are deposited in adjacent valleys or hollows producing *valley fills* adjacent to the levelled mountain (Figure 40). A single valley fill can be 300 meters (1,000 feet) wide, extend up valley for two kilometres or more, and contain 191 million cubic meters (250 million yd^3) or more of material (Copeland, 2008). A similar production cycle of drill, blast, load, and haul is used to extract the exposed coal. If multiple coal seams are stacked on top of each other, the interburden exposed by the removal of the topmost seam is excavated and the next lower seam mined. This process is continued until all the seams are removed or the cost of overburden removal exceeds the value of the remaining coal. This type of mining significantly changes the original topography leaving in its place levelled mountain tops and buried valleys that form extensive flattened plateaus. These changes in topography are accompanied by drastic changes in surface hydrology, ecosystem modification, and wildlife displacement. MTR operations produce 300,000 to 1,000,000 tons of

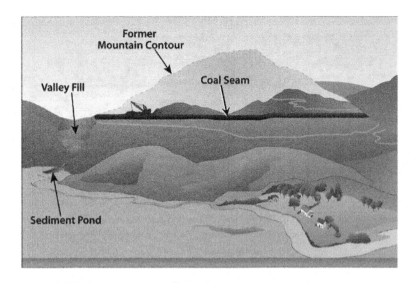

Figure 40. Mountain top removal (MTR) mining excavates the top of a mountain to expose the coal seams below. The overburden is disposed of in adjacent valleys forming what are known as valley fills. Source: (EPA, 2011).

coal per year. Very large mountain top removal mines can have a lifetime of up to 30 years.

Surface Mine Development Sequence
Regardless of the type of mining method, surface mines all have a similar development pattern. First, topsoil is stripped typically by scrapers similar to those seen on highway construction projects. The soil is stockpiled in topsoil banks for use later during reclamation. To ensure the viability of the organic matter in the topsoil, stockpiles cannot be stored indefinitely because soil organism necessary for successful reclamation will not survive indefinitely in the stockpiles.

Next the overburden is excavated and transferred to spoils piles. The piles are located mostly in mined out portions of the mine. Historically, overburden was removed by large electrical stripping shovels, but these have mostly been replaced by newer types of equipment. Overburden is generally stripped using one of three different methods: dragline, bucketwheel excavators (BWE), or truck and shovel. *Draglines* are among the largest and heaviest mobile equipment on the planet (Figure 41a). A dragline has a large bucket (typically 30-60 m³ (39-78 yd³)) suspended from a long (45-100 meters (147-328 feet)) boom by a hoist rope or, more accurately, chain. The bucket is dropped on the surface and dragged across it by a drag chain that runs from the bucket to the front of the dragline cabin. As

(a)   **(b)**

Figure 41. (a) Dragline showing boom and bucket and dumping overburden. Photo by
J.D. Myers. (b) Bucketwheel excavator with boom and bucket on right and conveyor system
on the left. Photo by © ThyssenKrupp AG, http://www.thyssenkrupp.com/en/presse/bilder.
html&photo_id=1259.

it drags across the surface, the bucket's teeth break up the overburden and scoop
up the loosened material. When filled, it is lifted by the hoist line. The boom and
loaded bucket are swung over the spoils pile and the drag rope released causing the
bucket to tip and dump. Draglines are usually operated in strip mines where they can
reach the digging and discharge points by simply swinging their booms. Draglines
'walk' on a set of feet that lift the dragline off the ground, push it backward and
lower it to the ground again. They run on electric power and because of their high
power demands are directly tied to the electrical grid. A dragline can cost $50-100
million and is so large that it is shipped to the mine in pieces where it is assembled.
It can take several years to assemble a dragline on-site. Although mostly used to strip
overburden for coal mining, they are also used in oil sands mines in Canada where
they strip the overburden.

A *bucket wheel excavator (BWE),* another large piece of mining machinery, is
a continuous digging machine used to remove soft overburden and coal (Figure
41b). It has a large wheel with buckets equipped with cutting edges mounted
around the circumference of the wheel. The wheel rotates against the digging face,
breaking the soft overburden and filling each bucket as the wheel rotates against
the mine face. As the bucket rotates downward, it dumps its load onto a discharge
boom, which moves material to a mine conveyor system for removal to the spoils
piles.

Overburden is also removed by truck and shovel operations. Depending upon the
hardness of the ground, the overburden may have to be drilled and blasted prior to
excavations (Figure 42). Otherwise it is excavated directly using scrappers. Blasted
overburden is excavated using either electric shovels or hydraulic excavators with
either a clam shell or front bucket configuration. These units load a fleet of haul
trucks that continually move between the overburden face and the spoils piles. The

trucks can move hundreds of tons of material in a single trip. They are mostly rear dump. Truck movement is timed with shovel operations so that an empty truck is arriving as a full one is leaving. Truck and shovel overburden removal is used where it is too difficult for large dragline equipment to operate. They also provide for greater flexibility in mine operation.

After exposure, the coal is extracted in a variety of mining methods determined by the nature of the coal. Soft or brown coal can be extracted continuously using a BWE. This approach is widely used in Germany for the mining of areally extensive, shallow lignite and brown coal seams. Hard coal is generally mined using the conventional surface production cycle of drill, blast, load, and haul. In the thick

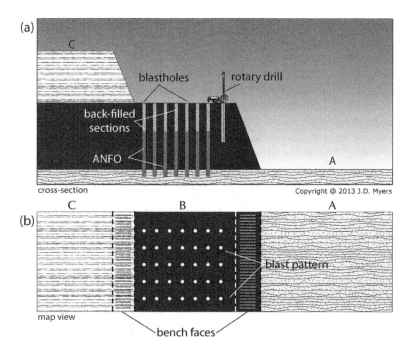

Figure 42. Schematic representation of procedure for loading blast holes. (a) Blastholes are drilled through the seam in a regular grid pattern. Each hole is fill with ANFO, an explosive comprised of a mixture of ammonium nitrate and fuel oil, and backfilled with coal cuttings from the drilling. It is generally pumped into the boreholes in the form of a slurry. (b) Individual blasholes are detonated electronically following a precise timing and spatial sequence. Holes near the coal bench face are fired first directing the coal outward and providing free space for successive holes to blast coal into. The goal of the blast is to break the coal into the proper size for the equipment while keeping the blast pile from scattering widely. Source: J.D. Myers, used with permission.

coal seams of the western U.S., rotary drills are used to drill 15 centimeter (6 inch) diameter holes extending up to 15 meters (50 feet) into the seam (Figure 42). The holes are dewatered, if necessary, partially filled with explosive and topped off with back-filled coal. A booster is placed in the explosive in each hole and wired in sequence to other holes. The explosives are fired electronically in a precisely timed pattern. The objective of the blast is to fracture a large amount of coal into pieces that can be easily handled by the mine's equipment. If properly planned, the blast will not move the coal far from its original location. With the coal blasted, a shovel moves in to start loading it into haul trucks. The shovels are either electric shovels or hydraulic excavators with either a front bucket or back-hoe configuration. They load the haul trucks in a highly choreographed sequence to minimize machine wait time. Haul trucks are specifically designed and built mining equipment that can carry upwards of 399 tonnes (440 short tons) of coal. They are mostly rear dump, but some bottom dump trucks are also used as are coal haulers. Shovels and trucks are carefully matched for their capabilities.

In India, a significant coal producer and consumer, coal mines are often situated close to populated areas and blasting cannot be used to loosen coal because of safety issues. Here, coal is stripped from seams using surface miners (Schimm, 2001). These are tracked vehicles with a cutting drum mounted horizontally underneath the unit. As the unit advances, the drum rotates and changeable cutting bits shatter and fracture the coal. The shattered coal is picked up and moved to a conveyor that either fills trucks positioned next to the surface miner or side casts it into rows for later loading and hauling. This system works well in areas where safety prohibits more traditional excavation techniques.

Machinery

The basic operations of a surface coal mine include: clearing land; overburden removal; bank preparation; excavating/loading; transport (hauling); and reclamation (grading and revegetation). The operation of a surface coal mine requires a wide variety of equipment (Figure 43). Generally, this equipment falls into two categories. The first consists of equipment typically used for highway construction and other earth-moving projects. This equipment includes the familiar bulldozers, front end loaders, trucks, scrappers, etc., seen on highway projects each summer. The other class consists of specialized equipment (e.g. power shovels, draglines, haul trucks (haulers)) specially designed and manufactured for surface mining.

The mobile mining equipment commonly found in surface coal mines can be divided into eight major classes: draglines; stripping shovels; scrapers; dozers; rotary drills; front-end loaders; hydraulic excavators; loading shovels; and haul trucks. In some instances, the equipment performs only one function in the operation of a surface mine (e.g. rotary drills) whereas in others the equipment performs a variety of functions (e.g. scrapers). Within any one class, there are a wide variety of different designs and models produced by a variety of manufacturers.

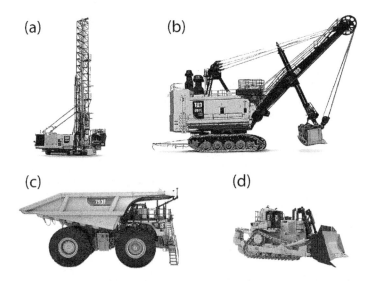

Figure 43. Surface mining uses a variety of specialized equipment including: (a) rotary drills for drilling blastholes; (b) electric rope shovels for loading coal; (c) haul trucks for moving coal and overburden; and (d) large dozers for road building and preparing platforms for draglines and shovels. Source: Caterpillar (http://www.cat.com/en_US/ products/new/equipment/off-highway-trucks/mining-trucks/13894258.html).

Underground Mining

When coal seams are too deeply buried for surface mining, they are extracted using underground mining. The typical development sequence of an underground mine is construction of the surface infrastructure, sinking of a shaft or slope, development of mine haulways either in the coal itself or through the surrounding rock, installation of support systems (e.g. ventilation, lighting, maintenance shops, etc.), development of working mine faces, and installation of conveyage and hoisting systems. Clearly, the development of an underground mine is much more complex and time consuming than for a surface mine. The advantages of an underground mine include: the ability to extract coal at depth; operations are unaffected by weather; minimal surface disturbance; the absence of dust problems at the surface; reduced impact on surface hydrology; and limited impact on viewscapes. The disadvantages include: higher unit production costs; greater capital outlay; longer development times; higher labor costs because of the need for a highly skilled workforce; greater safety and health issues; small production volumes; and limited opportunity for mechanization and automation.

The production cycle of an underground coal mine is much more complex than for a surface mine (Figure 44). As before, breakage consists of drill and blast. After breakage, there is an auxiliary bolting operation which provides roof support. Instead of two operations, handling now consists of loading, hauling and hoisting. Haulage production cycle = drill $\rightarrow$ blast $\rightarrow$ bolt $\rightarrow$ load $\rightarrow$ haul $\rightarrow$ hoist

$\underbrace{\qquad\qquad\qquad}_{\text{breakage}}$ $\underbrace{\qquad\qquad\qquad\qquad}_{\text{handling}}$

Figure 44. Typical production cycle for unsupported, underground coal mining. Compared to surface mining, two new processes or stages (i.e. bolting and hoisting) have been added. Source: J.D. Myers, used with permission.

entails transporting the mined coal from the active mine face to the shaft or slope. Here it is transferred to a hoisting system that lifts it out of the mine. Thus, the mined coal must be handled twice and transferred between different systems. The more involved production cycle is partly responsible for the lower production volumes of underground mines compared to surface mines. It also results in a higher production unit cost. Thus, underground coal seams must be of higher grade, quality, and/or rank to support the additional mining costs.

Types of Underground Coal Mines
There are three primary entries for an underground mine: audit, slope and shaft. The choice of which to use is dependent upon surface topography, seam depth, mine surface acreage, and cost. In areas where the coal seam is nearly horizontal and outcrops on the surface, the mine is developed directly from the surface using a horizontal entrance called a *drift* (Figure 45a). Entry to the seam is at the outcrop and mining progresses inward. For these mines, there is little preparatory work for the mine itself and coal production begins almost as soon as work underground commences. The mine simply follows the seam underground.

When a coal seam is not too deep, it can be reached using an inclined or sloping tunnel (i.e. a *slope mine*). The coal is removed by a conveyor belt or haul cars (Figure 45b). The slope of the access tunnel is determined by the angle at which coal will no longer stay on the conveyor belt or which is too steep for haul cars. Generally, this angle is 18°. The access tunnel or *decline* can be developed by drilling and blasting or using a tunnel boring machine. It is commonly lined with 2.5-5 centimeters (1-2 inches) of concrete. Where the rock is not very strong, the tunnel may be lined with steel arches for additional support.

As the depth to the coal seam increases, the length of the decline becomes greater and greater thereby producing an excessively long entry way and increasing transport times and mining cost. To reach deeper coal seams, a *shaft mine* that employs a vertical shaft is used to access the coal seam (Figure 45c). The shaft is generally circular in cross-section and lined with concrete. It may be compartmentalized with one compartment used for ultility connections and another for moving material and personnel in and out of the mine. The latter is accomplished using a cage (skip) that is lowered and raised via a cable connected to hoists in a headframe above the shaft (Figure 45c). Depending on the mine design, some mines have a separate shaft to move coal.

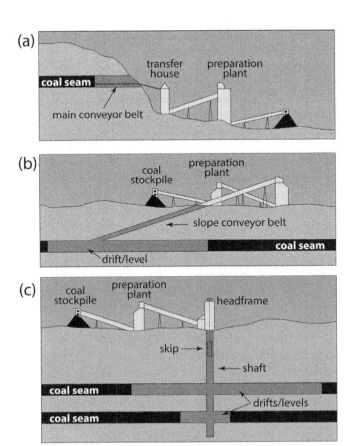

Figure 45. Three different types of access for an underground mine. (a) drift mine; (b) slope mine; and (c) shaft mine. Source: J.D. Myers, used with permission.

Underground Mining Methods

Because of diverse geology, geometric arrangements, and geomechanical characteristics of underground ore bodies and their host rocks, a wide range of underground mining methods have been developed. However, the relatively limited nature of underground coal seams (i.e. horizontal or shallow dipping tabular bodies) dictates that only a limited number of these numerous underground mining methods are appropriate for coal mining. In particular, room and pillar or longwall mining are the two choices for extracting coal underground (Figure 29). Each mine type employs different machinery, workforces, and production cycles. They also produce coal at very different rates.

Room-and-pillar mining is an older, well-established mining procedure that drives two sets of parallel openings at right angles to each other and at regular intervals (Figure 46). This procedure produces a rectangular grid of rooms where coal has been removed and pillars where coal has been left. The rooms are typically 6-9 meters (20-30 feet) on a side, whereas the pillars have sides of 6-27 meters (20-90 feet). This type of mining recovers 50-60% of the coal in a seam. Room-and-pillar mining is accomplished using one of two very different mining methods (i.e. conventional mining and continuous mining). Both mining methods are a form of unsupported mining. Nearly three-quarters of the coal removed in the United States is by continuous mining.

Conventional room-and-pillar mining comprises a cyclical operation using a variety of specialized mobile equipment that moves from one working mine face to another in a prescribed sequence (Figure 47). To ensure optimum use of equipment, these stages are pursued at adjacent working faces. In theory, only five working faces are required. However, to insure flexibility and smooth operation, additional working faces are usually maintained. The production cycle for this mining method consists of six operations (i.e. cutting, drilling, blasting, bolting, loading, hauling, and hoisting) (Figure 44). Five of the operations are conducted at the active mine face. Cutting consists of opening a slot (15-20 centimeter (6-8 inches) high) at the base of the seam to provide a free space into which the coal can expand when the explosive is detonated (Figure 47a). The cutting machine has a large cutting bar similar to that of a chain saw, but much larger. During the drilling stage, a pattern of holes are drilled into the face of the seam (Figure 47b). Each hole is 3 meters (10 feet) deep and spaced about 0.6 meters (2 feet) apart. The explosive is loaded into the holes and wired with blasting caps. When ready, the explosives are detonated electronically and remotely thereby blasting the face and fracturing the coal (Figure 47c). The innermost holes are detonated first with detonation proceeding

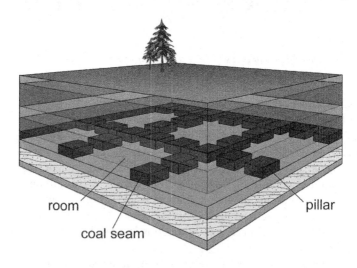

Figure 46. Block diagram illustrating the major features of the room and pillar mining methods. Source: J.D. Myers, used with permission.

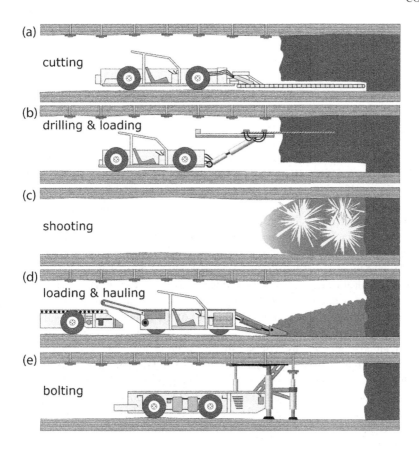

(a) cutting

(b) drilling & loading

(c) shooting

(d) loading & hauling

(e) bolting

Figure 47. Four stages in conventional room-and-pillar mining. Source: J.D. Myers, used with permission.

outward. Whereas in surface mining this operation is referred to as blasting, underground it is called *shooting*. The mined coal is loaded onto shuttle cars by a loading machine or loader that has two arms that operate in a crab-like manner to scoop the coal onto a conveyor belt on the loader (Figure 47d). The loader dumps the coal onto a shuttle car or conveyor system for transport. If the active face is a long distance from the shaft, the shuttle cars transfer the coal to an in-mine transport system (conveyor or rail). When the distance to the shaft is short, the shuttle car may move the coal to the hoist system. Once at the shaft, the coal is loaded into a cage and hoisted out of the mine to the surface. With the fractured coal cleared, the newly exposed roof section is bolted to provide additional support (Figure 47e). Rock bolts, which are nearly 2 meters (6 feet) long, are inserted in a one meter (4 foot) grid pattern into the roof to bind the different strata above the seam together and strengthen the roof. The bolts are either expansion versions which expand or press against the rock as they are drilled in or set in resin that when set bonds them to the rock. Clearly, conventional cycle room and pillar mining requires significant numbers of specialized machines and a large, trained workforce. It also results in multiple rehandling of the mined coal. This type of mining requires a 6-8 person crew and produces on average 6 tonnes (6.5 tons) of coal per day per person. For these reasons, the use of conventional for room-and-pillar mining operations has declined drastically in recent years and it now produces less than 5% of U.S. coal.

An alternative mining method for room-and-pillar mining is the *continuous mining method*. This method uses a specialized mining machine, the *continuous miner* (Figure 48), that combines the operations of drilling, blasting and loading into one single operation. Thus, it replaces three mining machines and their operators. A continuous miner consists of a cutting drum on an arm capable of being raised or lowered, a loading shovel, a conveyor system, a discharge system, and a track drive system. The cutting drum is 0.6 meters (2 feet) in diameter and 2.4-5 meters (8-16 feet) long. Mounted on the drum are replaceable cutting bits tipped with silicon carbide. The drum rotates at 60 rpm and is slowly advanced into the seam chewing it up. Cutting starts at 0.6 meters (2 feet) from the top of the seam and moves into the seam until it has cut its way the full diameter of the drum. The drum is then moved downward shattering the coal. Simultaneous with cutting, two crab-like arms scoop the broken coal onto a conveyor belt that runs the length of the continuous miner. It conveys the coal away from the active mine face and discharges it onto a shuttle car, which moves the coal to a transport system like in the conventional mining cycle. The continuous miner is operated remotely from a safe position away from the active mine face. They are called continuous miners because they do not need to interrupt mining to load the coal. A continuous miner can mine 34 tonnes (38 short tons) of coal per hour.

Haulage of the mined coal from the active mining face to the hoist point can be either batch or continuous. Batch systems use shuttle cars to move the coal. Shuttle cars are electric powered, rubber-tired vehicles with a large bin for carrying coal. They are manually operated by a driver. Power for the car is supplied by either a trailing cable that reels off a cable reel opposite the driver's position or by a battery pack. Shuttle cars are loaded using feeder/breaker cars, which load the coal and move it to the shuttle car by an on-board conveyor. It too has an operator who sits on board the car to operate it. Shuttle cars although providing great flexibility are limited in the amount of coal they can move at any one time. In some mines, they are being replaced by chain haulers or flexible train conveyors. Both are variants of a power unit with multiple attached cars that can all be loaded and unloaded from the front power unit (Figure 49). Continuous haulage is achieved using either a rail system or a conveyor belt. Although both can move more coal in a given time interval than shuttle cars, they are much less flexible.

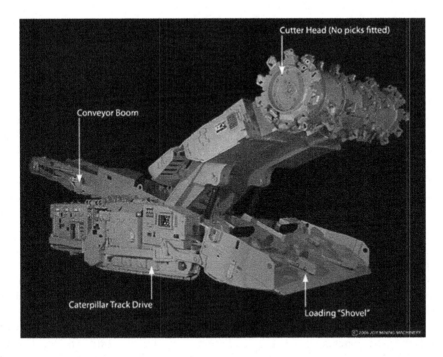

Figure 48. A continuous miner combines several stages of the room-and-pillar mining method thereby reducing labor and capital costs while increasing productivity. Source: Joy Mining Machinery.

Despite its name, continuous room-and-pillar mining is still a cyclic process. It reduces the conventional mining cycle considerably because cutting, drilling, blasting, and loading are all combined into a single step. After advancing about 6 meters (20 feet), the continuous miner is moved to another face and a roof bolter moved in to bolt the roof. After bolting, the face is cleaned to remove dust, which is a potential explosion hazard. This type of mining can produce 6,000 tons of coal per day per person, a much greater production rate than for conventional room-and-pillar. In the U.S., approximately 45% of coal mined underground is extracted using the continuous room-and-pillar mining method.

Retreat mining is done in the last stages of room and pillar mining. It recovers some of the coal that has been left in the pillars to support the mine's roof. During retreat mining, mining starts at the furthest point in the mine from the entry way and successively removes some of the pillars as personnel and equipment retreat toward the shaft. Obviously, retreat mining is very dangerous. To be accomplished safely, the mining team must have a good understanding of the stresses acting on the mining cavity. They also have to know which pillars can be removed safely. In some mines, remotely-controlled, hydraulic roof support systems are used as scaffolding for the roof to protect miners during retreat mining. After the scaffolded area is cleared, the system is lowered and moved to a new location.

A form of caving mining that is well suited for horizontal or very nearly horizontal coal seams of uniform thickness is *longwall mining* (Figure 49). It involves the removal of coal in a continuous operation. A longwall mining unit, or longwaller, consists of a cutter, an armoured face conveyor and a series of hydraulic roof supports. The cutter can be either a shearer or plow. A shearer, which consists of a rotating drum with cutting teeth, takes a deeper cut and is suitable for moderate to thick seams. A plow cuts a shallower swath and works only in seams that are thin or moderately thick. In either case, the cutting unit moves back and forth along the mine face breaking off chunks of coal. The coal falls onto the face conveyor and is transported along the mine face to the mine conveyor system that moves it toward the mine shaft for hoisting. The shearer, conveyor, and their operators are protected by hydraulic supports that press against the mine roof. Although each hydraulic roof unit operates independently, together they provide a long safe working environment. After the cutter passes, a support, which is about a meter wide, automatically lowers, advances forward, rises up, and wedges against the roof. The area behind the roof supports is allowed to collapse. This jumbled area of collapsed coal and roof rock is called the 'gob' or 'goaf'.

Before longwall mining can begin a large amount of underground development work must be conducted. It begins with continuous miners cutting the coal seam to define the mining panels, roadways, and other openings. Panels are separated by unmined pillars of coal that provide roof support. Once the openings are cut, ventilation systems and conveyor systems are installed. With the development work accomplished, the longwaller itself is installed, which can take a year or more of

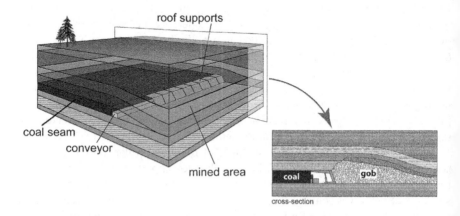

Figure 49. Block diagram of a longwall mining setup showing the hydraulic supports and the conveyor system. The cross-section shows the area where the roof collapses after mining producing the gob or goaf. Source: J.D. Myers, used with permission.

work. Advancing at 50-60 meters (164-196 feet) per week, it can take 1-2 years to mine an entire coal panel.

There are two major variants of longwall mining (Figure 50). In *longwall advance*, mining proceeds from near the main development headings and moves outward. Roadways defining the panel are constructed adjacent to the caved area, the gob, and driven outward as mining progresses. In this set-up, the power supply and secondary conveyor belt are run down one of the parallel roadways. In *longwall retreat*, two gateways 100-250 meters (320-520 feet) apart are driven away from the main development. When the desired length of the panel is reached (1-2 kilometers (0.6-1.2 miles)), the gateways are connected by a cross-cut. The longwall unit is installed at the far end of this panel and mining proceeds back toward the main development. The mined out area is allowed to collapse behind the longwall. In this case, the secondary conveyor and power and logistics are run through the main gate to the panel.

The longwaller has a very simplified production cycle that consists simply of mining. All of the operations of the room-and-pillar mining are combined into a single operation. Coal is mined in panels that may be as big as 1,000 meters (3,280 feet) wide (the shear face) and 4,000 meters (13,000 feet) long. Longwall mining is very efficient recovering nearly 80% of the coal in a panel quite rapidly. Shortwall mining is a variation of longwall mining, but where the panels mined are only 40-60 meters (196 feet) wide and 1,000 meters (3,280 feet) long. A single shift of 12 hours has produced 21,951 tons of coal from a seam 3 meter (9.5 feet) tall and a 152 meter (550 foot) long panel. Modern larger longwall units operating with bigger panels can produced 36,287 tonnes (40,000 short tons) of coal per day per person. The disadvantages of a longwall miner are high capital costs, long development

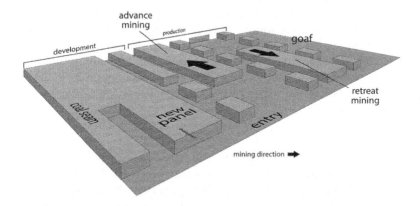

Figure 50. Longwall layout and mining direction. Advance longwall mining progresses or advances away from the entry. In contrast, retreat mining moves toward the entry. Source: J.D. Myers, used with permission.

times, and an inflexible mining operation. For example, if the longwall unit goes down for mechanical reasons all production halts until it is fixed. If the mining is close enough to the surface to cause subsidence, it is uniform over the area mined. Most subsidence occurs within six weeks of mining and it is pretty much complete within a year.

Underground Mine Development Sequence

Underground mines have a fairly set development sequence. It involves sinking a shaft or slope, installing the hoisting equipment, opening development levels in the mine, preparing the mine faces for extraction, ensuring a strong roof by adding supports if necessary, developing in-mine transportation and haulage systems, and installing all necessary support and auxiliary systems . Although all of these are critical, perhaps the two primary activities are the sinking of a shaft or driving of the decline and the development necessary to open the coal seam for mining.

Mine shafts are about 6 meters (20 feet) in diameter and are produced in one of two ways. One method is by drilling and blasting to break up the rock over the coal seam. The fragmented rock is removed by hoisting it to the surface in a temporary skip or cage. Alternatively, the shaft can be bored using a large-diameter boring machine to cut a continuous shaft. Material is pumped to the surface as a slurry after boring. This method is faster than the drill and blast technique. A shaft is normally lined with either steel or concrete to prevent collapse and protect shallow aquifers. Once the shaft reaches the coal seam, the hoisting equipment is installed and utility connections run down the shaft to the workings.

The other major task for underground mine development is creating the tunnels (drifts) that are necessary to access the coal seam. These are often cut into the seam itself. In addition, spaces must be created for personnel, machine shops, and storage. Secondary ventilation and escape shafts also have to be drilled to the surface. A sump (i.e. a chamber at the lowest point in the mine) is created and a pumping system installed. As the lowest point in the mine, water entering the mine drains to the sump where it collects. From here, the water is pumped out of the mine. Most of the openings and drifts developed are created using continuous miners. Driving the shaft and completing all the underground development work can take several years and is very expensive.

Machinery

Drilling, loading, hauling, and bolting are the primary operations in an underground coal mine. Each requires a different type of machinery. Unlike for surface mines, nearly all of this equipment is purposely designed and built for mining. These include a variety of machines for cutting and transporting coal. Some of the mobile types of underground mining equipment are roof bolters, continuous miners, loaders, and shuttle cars (Figure 51). Stationary equipment includes longwall units (i.e. shearer, roof supports, conveyors, secondary conveyor units, and crushers).

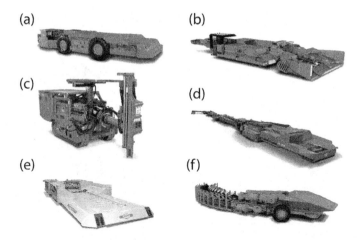

Figure 51. A few examples of underground mining machinery. (a) shuttle car, (b) loader, (c) bolter, (d) chain hauler, (e) feeder-breaker, and (f) a flexible conveyor train. The short height of all the machines testifes to the confined space in which underground ocal mining is carried out. Source: Joy Mining Machinery.

Preparation

In most cases, coal directly out of the mine or run-of-mine (ROM) coal is not ready for shipment to the market. It is a heterogeneous mixture of coal, rock, and mining debris. The latter consists of material introduced during mining and consists of machine parts, tools and other debris lost during mining operations. ROM coal also consists of a large range of particle sizes, the largest of which may be too big for subsequent handling. Thus, ROM coal is generally sent to a coal preparation plant (CPP) to prepare it for market (Figure 52). Coal preparation uses mechanical means to separate the components of ROM coal based on physical characteristics alone. There are no chemical changes in the coal during preparation. This process increases the market value of the coal and lowers transportation costs by removing material with no heat value. The processes of coal preparation consist of coal sampling, washing, crushing, screening, gravity separation, treatment of fine coal particles, and dewatering. The CPP must also handle contaminated water and solid waste products produced by the coal processing.

Crushers are used to reduce the size of coal fragments to a specified size range. Coal is separated into size fractions (grades) using screens that allow certain size fragments to fall through but pass larger ones on for further processing or screening. Gravity separation is used to separate coal from rock and metal fragments. Since coal has a low density, it will float in gravity separation devices whereas the rock and metal will sink. Separation devices used to clean coal are jibs (mechanical shaking

Figure 52. Photograph of a coal preparation plant where coal is screened, sized, crushed, and dried in preparation for shipment. Source: Kentucky Coal Education (http://www. coaleducation.org/technology/Transportation_Coal_Prep/Coal_Preparation.htm).

in water) and dense media separation (separation in suspension of magnetite and water). Because gravity separation relies on particles of a certain minimum size to settle, fine coal cannot be cleaned of contaminants by gravity separation. Hence, they are separated by froth flotation where they are introduced in a tank with rising air bubbles. The coal, which is water phobic, attaches to the bubbles and rises to the top where it is skimmed off. The non-coal material sinks to the bottom of the tank. To reduce transportation costs, coal is dewatered using centrifuges, cyclones, and filters. Soil and fine organic material is removed from coal by washing the coal in water.

At nearly all stages of coal preparation, water contaminated with a variety of fine solid particles is produced. These solids are separated from the water in thickeners (i.e. large tanks of standing water in which the solid particles slowly sink to the floor). Clean water at the top of the tank flows over the tank lip and is collected and recycled back through the CPP. The solid material at the bottom of the thickeners is collected and disposed of in secure containment structures. The contaminated slurry is placed in slurry storage facilities (Figure 53).

Figure 53. Coal preparation plant (blue structure in left middle ground) and coal slurry retention pond. Source: Kentucky Coal Education (http://www.coaleducation.org/technology/Transportation_Coal_Prep/Coal_Preparation.htm).

Transport

Once prepared, coal is ready for transportation to market. The key characteristic that determines potential transportation methods is the solid nature of the coal. Transport distances may be only a few tens of kilometres or it may be thousands of kilometres from one continent to another. In addition to distance travelled, the volume of coal to be moved is another important parameter in determining the method of transportation. Basically, there are two types of transport, either over land or by water.

For land transport, there are three basic options: conveyor, truck, and rail. Conveyors are good for short distances (<30 kilometers (18 miles)) and can move large amounts of coal in a continuous manner. They are good for feeding mine mouth power plants. Occasionally, they are used to move coal to railheads or to and within shipping terminals. Truck transport can move coal further than conveyor systems, but is still limited in a practical sense to 150 kilometers (93 miles) or less. In addition, they can move only moderate amounts of coal. Because of increased traffic, noise, and road damage, many communities oppose transport of coal on public roads by truck.

The most inexpensive means of moving large amounts of coal long distances on land is by rail. In the U.S., *unit trains* (i.e. trains carrying only coal and operating between a single mine and utility) consisting of upwards of 100 cars or more transport coal from the western U.S. mines to power plants in the eastern part of the country (Figure 54). These trains are typically loaded automatically from coal bins. The trains pass under the bin and coal is loaded in the cars as the train advances. Cars are weighed after loading. In this manner, a single unit train can be loaded in several hours and some of the large western mines can dispatch multiple unit trains a day. Large unit trains are also commonly unloaded automatically as well. The cars, which are made of either aluminium or steel, can be either bottom or top discharge. A typical car is about 15 meters (50 feet) long, 3-3.3 meters (10-11 feet) wide and approximately 4 meters (13 feet) tall. For bottom-discharge cars, the train simply moves over a grate or grizzly for unloading. The bottom gates automatically open and the coal is discharged without decoupling the cars. When the car is empty, the train moves forward and the doors automatically close. For top discharge cars, the cars are turned upside down by a rotary dumper to discharge their load. Because of special couplings, unit trains with top discharge cars also do not have to be uncoupled for unloading. In Wyoming, 53-70 unit trains a day leave the state (Figure 54). Each train carries 15,000 to 20,000 tons of coal in 115-140 coal cars. An individual train can stretch for 2.4 kilometres (1.5 miles). In less developed parts of the world, rail cars are still loaded and unloaded by front loaders or even by hand. In some areas of the world where discharge is done manually, rail cars may have side discharge doors for unloading.

Figure 54. A coal unit train is used to move coal from mine to power plant or coal terminal. These trains may be over a mile long with 100 or more coal cars. Photo by J.D. Myers.

Water transport of coal is primarily used for regional or international destinations. The two primary methods are by barge and bulk carrier. Barges are non-powered vessels that are designed for sheltered waters like rivers, bays, lakes, etc. They rely on a tug boat for power. Bulk carriers are ocean-going vessels designed to hold dry, bulk, solid, unpackaged goods that are directly loaded into the ship's cargo holds. They have multiple open holds with large hatches to facilitate rapid loading and unloading and travel at average speeds of 10-15 knots. These ships are classified by the mass of cargo they can carry measured in deadweight tons (dwt), International coal bulk carriers are typically in the range of 40,000 to 80,000 dwt. Large bulk carriers typically rely on port facilities for loading or unloading, whereas smaller ships often have their own loading/unloading capabilities.

Coal terminals represent the transhipment point between rail and water transport (Figure 56). These facilities receive coal, stack it for storage, blend coal to meet contract requirements, reclaim coal for loading, and load coastal barges and ocean-going bulk carriers. Unit trains arriving at a coal terminal are unloaded using rotary dumpers and the coal moved by conveyor to a stockpile area. In this area of the terminal, stackers pile and blend coal into long stockpiles using a boom-supported conveyor that continuously tips (pours) coal onto a stack. Once blended and ready for shipment, the stockpiled coal is removed by reclaimers. A common type of reclaimer employs a large rotating bucket wheel mounted on the end of a long boom (40-80 meters (130-360 feet)) to scoop up the stacked coal. The bucket wheel of a reclaimer

Figure 55. A coal bulk carrier loading Powder River Basin coal at a port on the Great Lakes. Source: International Mining (http://www.im-mining.com/2010/12/23/engineered-coal-chutes-reduce-maintenance-extend-conveyor-belt-life/).

391

Figure 56. Aerial photograph of the Port of Hay Point in eastern Australia. The Dalrymple Bay Coal Terminal stockyard with stacker/reclaimers is seen in the center of the photo. The pier to the offshore loading berths extends from the center to the left edge of the photo. Source: North Queensland Bulk Ports Corporation.

has numerous, large capacity buckets mounted around its perimeter. Both stackers and reclaimers are typically rail mounted for movement within the stockpile area. A system of interconnected conveyor belts is used to move coal from the unloading facility, between various points in the stockpile area, and to the loading pier. These systems can handle 7,250-9,000 tonnes (8,000-10,000 short tons) of coal per hour. Specially designed stackers and reclaimers are capable of moving 18,000 tonnes (20,000 short tons) of coal in an hour. After reclaiming, coal is moved by conveyor to a berth or pier where a shiploader loads it into the holds of a bulk carrier. The shiploader, which can be as tall as 20 m (65 feet)), moves along the pier on rails or tires so it can reach all parts of a ship's holds. Loading booms typically are 20-40 meters (65-130 feet) long and can extend forwards and backwards as well as swivel from side to side thereby allowing it to access all corners of a hold. Some terminals, particularly those in Australia (Figure 56), have piers a kilometer or more long that extend offshore for loading in deep water. This ability eliminates the need to have a deep water port for ships to enter. It can, however, result in lost operational time when storms approach. As the global trade in coal grows, siting coal terminals has become increasingly difficult because of growing opposition from local communities.

GENERATING ELECTRICITY FROM COAL

Electricity impacts our everyday lives to a degree we can hardly imagine. The number of electronic and electrical devices in our homes, offices, and stores is amazing. Commercial amounts of electricity have reduced workloads, spawned new industries, and altered old ones. Electricity is an energy carrier like fuel, heat and hydrogen, but electricity has many benefits that set it apart from other energy carriers. For this reason, many commentators describe electricity as higher quality energy than say coal. Some of electricity's benefits include constant and effortless consumer access; readily convertible to motion, heat, light and chemical potential; capacity to transmit electronic information with unmatched control, precision, and speed; easily converted to other energy forms silently and cleanly; reliable, individualized delivery; producible from a wide variety of fuels (many of them inferior in quality); virtually perfect conversion to heat; ability to provide temperatures higher than those obtained by fossil fuel combustion (important in a lot of industrial applications); and the absence of inventory. Because of these characteristics, electricity has revolutionized industry, communication, and virtually every other aspect of modern, industrialized society. Not surprisingly, electricity is the fastest growing of the various energy carriers (Figure 57). In 1950, the dominant U.S. energy carriers were fuels derived from fossil fuels. By 2010, electricity had surpassed coal as an energy carrier and nearly 20% of all end use energy in the U.S. was delivered as electricity.

There are several different ways of creating electricity. These include: electromagnetic induction (moving a conductor through a magnetic field); photoelectric conversion (converting light into electrical energy (e.g. solar cells)); thermoelectric effect (use of temperature differences to generate electricity (e.g. thermocouples, thermopiles)); piezoelectric effect (flexing a solid to create mechanical strain, which produces electricity); and nuclear transformation (accelerating charged particles created by nuclear decay to produce electricity). With current technology, only one of these methods of electricity generation (electromagnetic induction) is capable of producing commercial quantities of electricity at low prices.

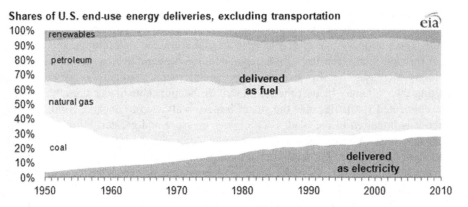

Figure 57. Electricity has grown steadily as an energy carrier in the U.S. over the past six decades. Its use is projected to grow even more in the future. Source: U.S. Energy Information Administration, Annual Energy Review 2012.

To produce electricity by electromagnetic induction, a source of kinetic energy is needed to spin the shaft of a turbine-generator unit. This can be accomplished in a number of ways. For example, the motion of a moving fluid (e.g. wind or water) can be harnessed. Alternatively, heat can be used to make steam and the kinetic energy of the steam captured. There are four basic ways of using thermal energy to produce steam for electricity generation. One is to use concentrated sunlight (i.e. thermal solar power plants). A more common way is to burn a combustible material to produce thermal energy. The fuel can be a fossil fuel, including coal, or biomass. The third method is to use the heat produced by nuclear fission. In certain favorable locations, electricity can be generated by tapping into steam produced in the subsurface by geothermal energy.

Thermal Electricity Generation

Globally the most commonly used thermal electricity generation method is coal combustion. A coal-fired power plant converts the chemical energy stored in coal to heat in a boiler or furnace. The heat converts water circulating through tubes in a boiler to steam. The steam enters a turbine commonly at 600°C (1,112°F) and pressures of 130 kg/cm² (1,849 lb/in²). When the steam impinges on the blades of a turbine, it causes the blades and the shaft they are attached to spin rapidly thereby converting some of the steam's kinetic energy to rotational mechanical energy. The rotating shaft is attached to the rotor of a generator, which it turns thereby producing electricity using electromagnetic induction.

The steam turbine has been used to generate electricity since Charles Parson first introduced it in 1885. Although major refinements to the steam turbine have been made since, the basic design is still the same. To extract as much kinetic energy as possible, modern steam turbines typically consist of multiple stages (Figure 58). Each state consists of alternating fixed and moveable, angled blades attached to a common shaft. The stationary blades acts as nozzles and allow the steam to expand as they pass through them. Because of the expansion, the pressure decreases but the steam velocity increases thereby increasing its kinetic energy (remember ½mv²). Upon exiting the stationary blades, the steam strikes the moveable blades thereby turning the connected shaft. Because the steam has been allowed to expand, more kinetic energy is imparted to the blades. The lower pressure and greater volume steam is next sent to the intermediate stage. Here it encounters another set of alternating fixed and stationary blades, however they are longer than those in the first stage and the turbine housing bigger. Again the steam is allowed to expand as it passes through the fixed intermediate stage blades and strikes the moveable blades. With steam pressure further reduced and volume increased, it finally enters the low-pressure stage, which has even larger diameter blades housed in a correspondingly larger turbine cavity. The shaft of a turbine can rotate at up to 3,600 rpm. After exiting the last turbine stage, the steam goes to a condenser where it is cooled and converted back to liquid to be recycled back through the process again.

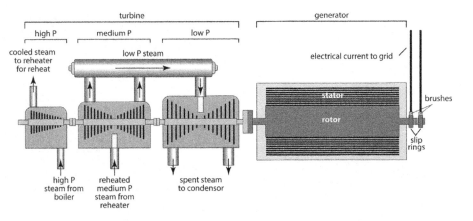

Figure 58. A schematic diagram of a typical modern, multi-stage steam turbine-generator unit. Steam impinging on the turbine blades turns a shaft which rotates the rotor within the stator in the generator thereby producing electricity by electromagnetic induction. High pressure-temperature steam enters the high-pressure stage of the turbine and expands as it passes through the blades. After it exits the high-P stage, the steam is sent back to the boiler for reheating. The reheated steam enters the medium P turbine at the center and flows outward. The lower P steam exits at both ends of the medium P turbine. It is collected and piped to the low pressure stage. In some systems, there may be a second reheat stage between the medium and low P units. To increase the kinetic energy of the steam, its volume is allowed to expand at each stage in the turbine. Contact between slip rings on the rotor and external brushes tap the electrical current that is ultimately feed to the grid. Source: J.D. Myers, used with permission.

The steam turbine is connected to a generator, the other component of a turbine-generator unit (Figure 59). The electrical generator consists of two major parts, a rotor and a stator. The rotator is moveable and consists of copper wire wrapped tightly around the shaft. It sits within a large magnet. The spinning of the rotor, a big conductor, in a magnetic field exerts an electromagnetic force on the electrons of the rotor. By connecting the rotor to an electrical load (i.e. the electrical grid) an electrical current is produced. Slip rings tap the current from the rotor and send it to a transformer that steps the voltage up for transmission. This is the basic principle behind *electromagnetic induction,* the primary means of generating commercial amounts of electricity.

Thus, a coal-fired power station involves four energy conversions (Figure 60). The energy stored in the chemical bonds of the coal macerals is converted to thermal energy by combustion. This thermal energy is expressed macroscopically as heat. The heat produces steam, which is moving, creating a transition from thermal to kinetic energy. Upon impinging on the blades of the turbine, the kinetic energy of motion is changed to rotational mechanical energy. Finally, this rotation is converted

Figure 59. A turbine-generator on the turbine deck of a coal-fired power plant. The tube on top of the turbine moves steam between the different stages. The generator part is located at the far end of the unit. The overhead crane in the background is used for disassembling the units during maintenance. Source: Photo by J.D. Myers, used with permission.

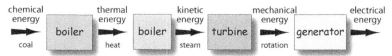

coal-fired thermal electricity generation

Figure 60. The successive energy conversions in the thermal generation of electricity. The conversions are (from left to right): 1) chemical energy to thermal energy; 2) thermal energy to kinetic energy of moving steam; 3) kinetic energy to mechanical energy of rotation; and 4) finally mechanical energy to electricity. Source: J.D. Myers, used with permission.

to electricity through electromagnetic induction occurring in the generator. Because of the laws of thermodynamics, some fraction of the energy released initially when the coal was burned is rendered unusable at each conversion step.

Coal Combustion

To power a thermal electrical power plant, a source of thermal energy is needed. Historically, this has been supplied by a variety of fossil fuels (Figure 61). Fossil

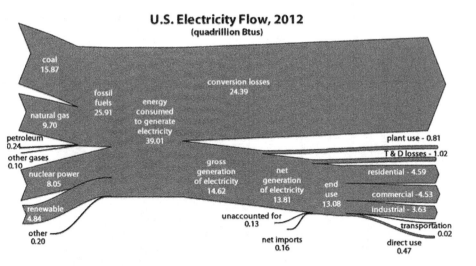

Figure 61. Sankey diagram depicting the flow of electricity in the U.S. economy in 2012. Historically, a primary source of thermal energy for electricity generation has been coal. Source U.S. Energy Information Administration, Monthly Energy Review (January, 2014 (http://www.eia.gov/totalenergy/data/monthly/#electricity).

fuels, including coal, release the chemical energy in their bonds by combustion (i.e. chemical reaction combining oxygen with the hydrogen and carbon of the fuel). For natural gas and petroleum, these are straightforward reactions as both consist almost exclusively of hydrocarbon molecules with only hydrogen and carbon.

In contrast, the combustion of coal is much more complex. Coal almost always contains some amount of moisture, which in some coals may be as much as 20-60%. It also has volatile material and elements such as nitrogen, oxygen, and sulphur (Figure 62). This complexity makes coal combustion a very complex process.

Because of its complexity, coal undergoes a series of complex physical changes and chemical reactions as it burns. During the early stages of combustion, as the temperature initially rises, moisture is evaporated. This evaporation requires energy, which is supplied by the energy released from the burning of coal itself. This decreases the amount of energy available to do work. At even higher temperatures, gases are given off (carbon monoxide, methane, light hydrocarbons, etc.). These gases are the volatile matter of coal and some of them actually have value as a fuel source, if they can be captured. Fixed carbon (and hydrogen) remains at the highest temperatures (Figure 62) and combusts with oxygen to release heat and produce carbon dioxide. Even at the highest possible temperatures not all the coal will combust. This incombustible fraction is ash and it has no heat or economic value. Ash often contains as many as fourteen trace elements. Some of these elements are toxic (As, Se), whereas others are radioactive (U, Th). It can also have dioxins

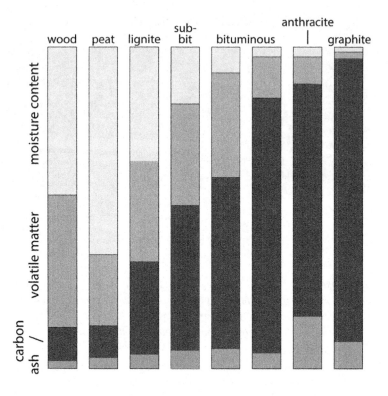

Figure 62. Comparison of the different components in different ranks of coal precursors and coal. As rank increases, carbon content increases and volatile matter and moisture content decrease. Because of these changes, the heat value of coal also increases with rank. For most of these fuels, ash content is very low.

and polycyclic aromatic hydrocarbon (PAH) compounds. Since it contains so many harmful elements, ash must be disposed of in a safe and environmentally friendly manner.

Types of Coal-fired Power Plants

Although all coal-fired power plants involve the same basic steps to generate electricity, there are many different ways in which this can be accomplished. Each of these designs results in different efficiencies and emissions. These different designs are important because they determine how much of coal's chemical energy is converted to electricity and how much escapes as heat to the environment. Higher conversion factors also mean less coal must be burned to produce the same amount of electricity. Burning less coal, decreases carbon dioxide and other atmospheric emissions as well as solid waste streams.

Pulverized coal (PC) and supercritical pulverized coal (SCPC)
Globally, most electricity is generated by pulverized coal (PC) combustion. Crushing and pulverizing coal ensures that all particles of coal will contact air in the firebox and be burned. This makes the combustion process more like that of a gas and hence more efficient. To achieve this behaviour, coal is crushed and pulverized to the consistency of face powder (Figure 64a). The pulverized coal is mixed with preheated air and injected into the boiler where it forms a flame that juts out a meter or more from the boiler walls (Figure 64b). Before it is injected into the furnace, secondary air is injected around the coal stream to ensure adequate combustion. Additional ports in the boiler are used to inject tertiary air and sorbents into the combustion chamber. A typical boiler at a large power plant may be several stories

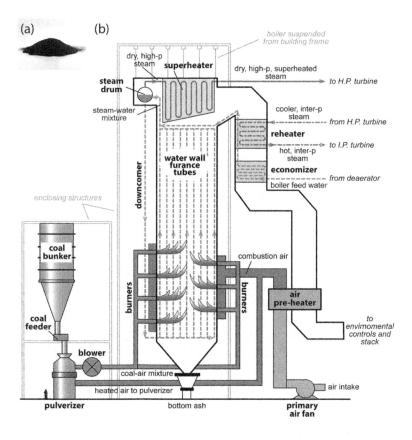

Figure 63. (a) In pulverized coal (PC) power plants, coal is pulverized to the consistency of powder before combustion. (b) The pulverized coal is mixed with air and injected into the furnace/boiler where it combusts almost immediately. Source: J.D. Myers, used with permission.

tall with multiple coal ports on different levels. Tubes running just inside the boiler walls in a water wall carry water that is converted to steam by the heat released from the coal combustion. Ash behaves in two ways in the boiler. Ash with fusion temperatures greater that the firebox temperature remains solid and is entrained in the flue gas as it exits the boiler. This is fly ash. Ash that melts falls to the bottom of the boiler where is collected either as molten liquid (liquid bottom boiler) or as solid, individual particles (dry bottom).

PC plants are divided into three subclasses based on whether or not the steam produced is a supercritical fluid (DOE, 2007). A supercritical fluid is one that shares properties of both a gas and a liquid and exists only at elevated temperatures (373°C (> 705°F)) and pressures (22 Mpa (3,208 psi)). Subcritical PC plants produce steam at 538°C (1,000°F) and 168 kg/cm^2 (2,400 lbs/in^2). Supercritical PC plants produce much hotter steam (593°C [1,000°F]) at higher pressures (253 kg/cm^2 (3,600 lbs/in^2)). An ultra-supercritical PC plant operates at temperatures above 600°C (1,115°F) and pressures of 267 kg/cm^2 (3,800 lbs/in^2). The first ultra-supercritical power plant in the U.S. cost $1.8 billion and took four years to build (SEPC, unknown). DOE (2007) envisions future ultra-supercritical power plants operating at temperatures greater the 700°C (1292°F) and steam pressures of 351 kg/cm^2 (5,000 lbs/in^2). Such operating conditions will, however, require the development of new materials. The higher steam temperature results in an increase in the thermodynamic efficiency of the plant. For example, the thermal efficiency of a subcritical plant is around 35%, a supercritical is approximately 40% and an ultra-supercritical in the range of 42-45%. A 550 MW$_e$ pulverized coal power plant, whether sub or supercritical, burns about 190,508 kilograms (420,000 pounds) of subbituminous coal per hour. Because of their proven technology, PC power plants normally run 85 % of the time (DOE, 2007).

Fluidized bed combustion (FBC)
Fluidized bed combustion plants burn coal with a sorbent, such as limestone or dolomite. The sorbent combines chemically with sulfur released during coal combustion to tie up nearly 90% of the sulfur that would be released as SO$_2$ in a pulverized coal plant. Jets of air mix the coal-sorbent mixture until it is a suspension of red-hot particles that flow like a fluid (i.e. the fluidized part in the name of the plant design). The hot combustion gases enclose steam-generator tubes in and above the fluidized bed. At the same time, the fluidized nature of the bed promotes the burning of the coal as well as more efficient transfer of heat to the steam tubes. Consequently, the boiler can be run at a lower combustion temperature thereby reducing the amount of thermal nitrogen oxides (NOx) produced.

An atmospheric fluidized-bed combustor (AFBC) operates at standard atmospheric pressure like conventional steam boilers. They are the most widely deployed FBC systems and have thermal efficiencies of 30-40% (i.e. similar to pulverized coal combustion). A pressurized fluidized-bed combustor (PFBC), burns coal at six to sixteen times atmospheric pressure. By using the hot pressurized, combustion gases to power a gas-driven turbine in addition to the primary steam turbine extra thermodynamic efficiency is obtained.

Integrated gasification combined cycle (IGCC)
Integrated gasification combined cycle or IGCC represents the melding of two different technologies: coal gasification to produce a syngas; and combined-cycle that employs the capture of waste heat to power a second turbine and generator pair (Figure 64). This type of plant emits fewer pollutants and less carbon dioxide than a conventional pulverized coal plant. In the gasification part of the plant, coal is converted from a solid to a gas in a pressurized reactor known as a gasifer. In this oxygen-poor environment, coal is heated to high temperatures where it breaks down chemically and physically. This decomposition produces a synthetic gas (syngas) consisting mostly of hydrogen (H_2) and carbon monoxide (CO) with lesser amounts of methane (CH_4), carbon dioxide (CO_2), and hydrogen sulfide (H_2S). The syngas is cooled and cleaned in a gas clean-up process that removes impurities such as sulfur. Up to 99% of hydrogen sulfide produced is removed before combustion thereby eliminating the need for post-combustion scrubbers. After clean-up, the syngas is sent to a combustion turbine/generator.

The combined cycle consists of a combustion turbine/generator unit, a heat recovery/steam generator unit, and a steam turbine/generator unit. First, the syngas from the gasifer is burned in a combustion turbine, which drives an associated combustion turbine-generator to produce electricity. The hot gas exhausted from this turbine is run through a heat recovery system. The heat from the exhaust gas is captured via a heat exchanger and used to create steam, which, in turn, drives a

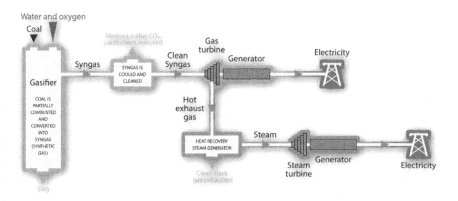

Figure 64. Schematic diagram of the main systems of an integrated gasification combined cycle (IGCC) power plant. The various stages of an IGGC plant are gasification, hot gas clean-up, integrated high pressure air separation, and combined cycle power generation. Source: Wolfe and Wickstrom (2008).

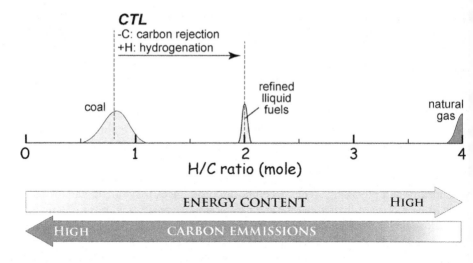

Figure 65. The hydrogen-carbon (H/C) ratio of coal is less than half that of refined liquid fuels. Production of transportation fuels from coal requires doubling the H/C ratio. A large number of chemical processes have been developed to produce this chemical change via carbon rejection and/or hydrogen addition (i.e. hydrogenation). Source: J.D. Myers, used with permission.

conventional steam turbine-generator unit. By combining the combustion and steam turbines in series, this type of plant recovers heat that would otherwise be wasted, thereby increasing thermodynamic efficiency.

An IGCC power plant has some advantages over other types of coal-fired power plants. Its SO_2, NOx, and particulate emissions are lower and the same is true for mercury and volatile organic compounds (VOC). In addition, it emits 20% less CO_2 than more conventional coal plants. In an era of changing water patterns, it also uses 20-30% less water for cooling. Because of higher efficiencies (presently 42% with 60% expected), it requires less fuel to produce the same amount of electricity. With the initial gasification stage, CO_2 can be captured for sequestration more easily with this type of a plant. Hydrogen can also be captured from the syngas stream for use as a transportation fuel. Despite their many advantages, not many IGCC power plants have been built in the United States. The primary reason for lack of adoption of these plants is they are much more complex and hence expensive to build than a simple pulverized coal combustion plant. Thus, the electricity they generate is 20% more expensive than that from standard coal power plants. DOE funded the construction of three pilot IGCC plants. Two of these plants (Wabash River, Polk) are still operational, but the one constructed in New Mexico never ran continuously for more than 24 hours at a time and operation ceased in 2001 (DOE, 2002).

COAL AS A SOURCE OF ALTERNATIVE FUELS

Despite powering the Industrial Revolution, coal is now used almost exclusively for electricity generation. However, the increasing concern about the high environmental impact of burning coal is threatening its viability as an energy source. Because of its low H/C ratio (Figure 65), coal has a lower energy density than either petroleum or natural gas thereby producing a larger carbon footprint. In addition, solid coal presents a greater fuel handling problem than hydrocarbon-based liquid fuels. In the past, coal has been successfully converted chemically to a variety of gaseous and liquid fuels (i.e. coal gas, coke, diesel, and gasoline). In light of the impact of its current use on carbon dioxide emissions and the looming peak of crude oil production, the future of coal may rest on the ability to convert it to these more high-value, liquid or gaseous fuels on a massive scale.

Coal Gas and Tar

Coal gas is produced by the destructive distillation of coal, a thermochemical process that heats a feedstock, typically organic, in a retort to high temperatures in an atmosphere with little or no oxygen. The process may or may not involve a catalyst. The resultant chemical reactions breakdown (i.e. crack) the larger organic molecules of the feedstock into smaller ones. In addition, to the production of useful products, destructive distillation also produces solid wastes, such as char or tar. Because this process requires heat (i.e. it is endothermic), it is very energy intensive and hence costly.

Around the end of the 19th century, coal gas produced by destructive distillation, called *town gas*, was used to light street lamps and homes. Coal gas consists of a combination of carbon monoxide (CO), hydrogen (H_2), methane (CH_4), and other hydrocarbon as well as non-hydrocarbon gases. Destructive distillation of coal also produces coal tar, a black to brown viscous, carcinogenic liquid that can be used as a fuel or a feedstock for making dyes and pharmaceuticals. Despite the widespread production and use of coal gas at the end of the 1800s, the discovery of large reservoirs of natural gas and the development of electricity as a source of illumination doomed the coal gas industry. It is highly unlikely that this industry will ever return on a large commercial scale.

Coke

Coke is a solid, gray, hard, porous, carbonaceous fuel made from coal. Chemically, it is almost pure carbon and produced by heating coal to high temperature in an oxygen-deficient or oxygen-free furnace. As a fuel, coke burns smokeless and at a higher temperature than coal, which also produces significantly more smoke when burned. Despite its potential as a fuel, the primary use of coke today is as a reducing agent in iron and steel production. It reduces the iron-rich, oxidized mineral hematite

(Fe_2O_3), a major component of iron ore, to elemental iron (Fe) according to the reactions:

$$\underbrace{C_{(s)}}_{coke} + 0.5O_{2(g)} \rightarrow CO_{(g)}$$

$$\underbrace{Fe_2O_{3(s)}}_{hematitie} + 3CO_{(g)} \rightarrow \underbrace{3Fe_{(l)}}_{\substack{molten\ metallic \\ iron}} + 3CO_{2\ (g)}$$

Coke can also be used to make syngas, a combination of carbon monoxide and hydrogen, by reacting it with steam:

$$\underbrace{C_{(s)}}_{coke} + \underbrace{H_2O_{(g)}}_{steam} \rightarrow \underbrace{CO_{2(g)} + H_{2(g)}}_{synthetic\ gas}$$

Although coke could be used as a solid fuel or a source of syngas, neither option offers any significant advantages over simply burning coal itself as a fuel. Thus, it is unlikely that coke will be used for anything other than a reducing agent in the near future.

Liquid Fuels

The most valuable fuels are liquid hydrocarbons (e.g. gasoline, diesel, jet fuel, etc.) used for transportation and derived from the refining of petroleum. However as mentioned previously, crude oil is a finite, non-renewable resource that will probably experience peak production in the next three or four decades. A potential means of replacing crude oil is through coal-to-liquid (CTL) conversion (Hirsch et al., 2005). Although itself a non-renewable resource, coal is much more abundant than petroleum and offers the potential of being a substitute for crude oil because of its carbon rich nature.

Historically, coal-to-liquid conversion has been investigated extensively. Research interest typically peaks when oil prices are high (e.g. after the Arab Oil Embargo) or when there is concern about a nation's access to crude oil or refined transportation fuels. During World War II, Germany, which has little domestic crude oil, was ultimately cut off from imports of crude oil. However using its abundant domestic supply of coal, it developed an extensive CTL industry using a variety of different chemical processes (Stranges, 2001). Toward the end of World War II, the German army and air force were almost entirely dependent upon synthetic transportation fuel produced by these plants. During the apartheid era, South Africa was also denied imports of crude oil. Since it has significant coal reserves, the nation developed an extensive CTL program, which today supplies a significant amount of South Africa's liquid fuels. All of the chemical reactions that are employed in CTL processes occur at high temperature and pressure; hence they require significant energy inputs to proceed. In addition, many of the liquid products produced have to be further processed before they can be used as transportation fuel. Both of these factors plus the cost of the feedstock for the process makes CTL-derived fuels expensive, especially compared to fuels produced from conventional crude oil. Because of its high cost, interest in pursuing industrial scale CTL production wanes when crude oil prices fall.

Coal has an atomic H/C less than half that of refined liquid fuels (Figure 66). To create synthetic liquid hydrocarbons from coal, the H/C ratio must be adjusted by adding hydrogen (hydrogenation) or removing carbon (carbon rejection). Extensive research in the last 75 years has identified a large number of chemical processes that can be used to convert coal to liquid fuels. These processes can be divided into two classes (i.e. direct liquefaction and indirect liquefaction) (Figure 66). *Direct coal liquefaction* converts coal directly to liquids. *Indirect coal liquefaction* first gasifies coal to produce a synthetic gas consisting of carbon monoxide and hydrogen. A secondary process then converts this gas to a liquid.

Direct Coal Liquefaction (DCL)
Direct liquefaction is those chemical processes that convert solid coal directly to liquid. Within this class are two different types of chemical reactions. Hydrogenation is the addition of hydrogen to increase the H/C ratio, whereas

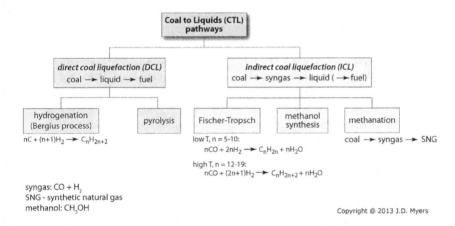

Figure 66. Potential coal-to-liquid conversion pathways. Many of these processes have been extensively investigated and specific variations patented. Some are used to produce liquid fuels today, but their contribution to global liquid fuels is highly limited. They are commonly pursued when oil prices are high, but soon abandoned if oil prices fall significantly. Source: J.D. Myers, used with permission.

pyrolysis involves the destructive distillation of the feedstock to produce a liquid with hydrocarbon molecules that have higher H/C ratios. Both have their advantages and disadvantages.

Pyrolysis is accomplished by heating coal to a high temperature in a low air pressure or oxygen-poor environment. The process produces condensable coal tar, oil, water vapour, and non-condensable syngas as well as char, a solid residual. Because they contain contaminants, coal tar and oil are hydrotreated (a common refinery process – see petroleum chapter) to remove sulphur and nitrogen. These cleaned liquids must be subsequently refined to produce suitable liquid transportation fuels.

Developed by Friedrick Bergius in 1913, the Bergius process is a hydrogenation process that breaks down coal's chemical and physical structure. Dry coal is mixed with heavy oil, recycled from the process itself, and a catalyst and injected into a reactor vessel. Inside the reactor, the temperature is 400°C (752°F) to 500°C (932°F) and the hydrogen pressure between 204 and 713 kg/cm^2 (2,901 to 10,141 lb/in^2). The chemical reactions in the vessel produce a low quality oil. The molecular components produced in the liquid are defined by the chemical reaction for the process:

$$nC + (n+1)H_2 \rightarrow C_nH_{(2n+2)}$$

where n is a positive integer. The liquid fractions are separated by distillation, but at this stage are unsuitable for use as transportation fuels. They must be hydrogenated, which uses a catalyst to add hydrogen to the molecular structure thereby increasing the H/C ratio. Chemically, the process is quite effective with 70% (by weight) of the coal converted to liquid, has 60-70% thermal efficiency, and the resultant liquid can be used directly as a stationary power generation fuel. The major drawback is the need to further upgrade the liquid for transportation use. During World War II, Germany operated several CTL plants using the Bergius process. Despite some attempts since WWII to run the process on a commercial scale, there are no plants operating commercially today.

Indirect Coal Liquefaction (ICL)
All indirect liquefaction processes involve two stages. In the first stage, the feedstock, which can be any H-C rich source, is gasified to produce a synthetic gas. The gas is processed in a second stage to convert it into a liquid. There are three options for the second stage of the process: Fischer-Tropsch (F-T), methanol synthesis, and methanation. The methanation process produces a synthetic natural gas (SNG) that must be further refined to produce a transportation fuel (Figure 67). In contrast, the methanol pathway produces a carbohydrate-based (CH$_3$OH) fuel that can be used in suitably modified vehicles. Because it is a carbohydrate, it is partially oxidized and has an energy content less than conventional petroleum-based fuels. Given these constraints, the common choice for an indirect CTL-based transportation fuel production facility is to use the Fischer-Tropsch (F-T) process.

The F-T process, developed by two German chemists between the world wars, adjusts the hydrogen-carbon ratio of a variety of H-C rich sources to produce liquid fuels (Figure 67). The process utilizes a synthesis gas (CO + H_2) that has been purified of contaminants such as sulfur and nitrogen. The process uses a reactor-catalyst combination. The catalyst is often metallic cobalt in a slurry. Because the fuel produced is expensive, interest, development, and use of the F-T process is generally correlated with global high oil prices or with some local shortage of petroleum often due to political factors. Historically, there have been three principal time periods when interest in this process was particularly high (i.e. 1920s-1950s, 1970s and 1980s-present).

The general F-T chemical reaction is:

$$nCO + (2n+1)H_2 \rightarrow nH_2O + C_nH_{(2n+2)}$$

where n is a positive integer. There are many process variables in the Fischer Tropsch process that must be controlled to produce the required liquid fuel. Some of these variables include the catalyst used, the reaction pressure and temperature, the reactor design, process flow, and the nature of the feedstock. Adjusting the temperature of the process, alters the nature of the chemical reaction that occurs (Höök and Aleklett, 2010). At higher temperatures, the reaction simplifies to:

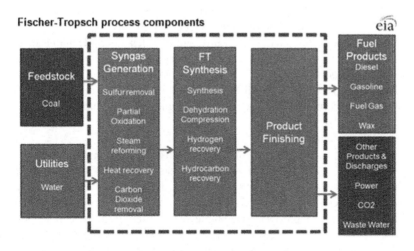

Figure 67. Schematic diagram showing the two stages of an indirection liquefaction process employing Fischer-Tropsch for the second stage. The first stage in the process breaks coal down into a syngas (CO + H_2) and is followed by a second stage F-T process that increases the H/C ratio thereby producing a liquid fuel. This fuel must be further processed to produce a liquid transportation fuel. Source: Modified from U.S. Energy Information Administration graphic, http://www.eia.gov/todayinenergy/detail.cfm?id=15071.

$$nCO + 2nH_2 \rightarrow nH_2O + C_nH_{2n}$$

Hydrocarbons with the chemical formula C_nH_{2n} are olefins. With n in the range of 5 to 10, these molecules are liquid at ordinary temperature and pressure. Olefins of this type can be used to make synthetic gasoline. If they have n between 2 and 4 (ethylene, propylene, and butane), the olefins are gaseous at ordinary temperature and pressure and used extensively in the petrochemical industry.

At lower temperatures, the F-T reaction has the general form:

$$nCO + (2n+1)H_2 \rightarrow nH_2O + C_nH_{2n+2}$$

This reaction produces paraffins, which are hydrocarbon molecules with the general chemical formula of C_nH_{2n+2}. This class of hydrocarbon is a major component of natural gas and petroleum. Gaseous paraffins have n less than 5, whereas an n of 5 to 10 produces liquids. If the process conditions are adjusted such that the reaction n varies from 12 to 19, the resultant paraffin-rich liquids are suitable for creating synthetic diesel.

Products of the Fischer-Tropsch process include completely synthetic materials as well as feedstocks for fuel blending. Totally synthetic products include very high viscosity lubricants and ultra-cetane diesel fuel. The cetane number (CN) of a fuel is a measure of its ignition delay (i.e. the time between the start of injection and the first identifiable pressure increase due to combustion of the fuel). In a given diesel engine, higher cetane fuels will have shorter ignition delay periods than lower cetane fuels. In short, the higher the cetane number, the more easily a fuel combusts during compression. This characteristic is beneficial for diesel fuels. Cetane numbers are only used for the relatively light distillate diesel oils. Blending feedstocks are mixed with other hydrocarbons to produce different liquid fuels and lubricants.

Coal to Liquid's Future

As an industrial process, both of the CTL approaches require a number of inputs. These include energy (generally thermal), catalysts, chemicals, and water (Höök and Aleklett, 2010). Water is used for steam, as a hydrogen feedstock, and for cooling. The water requirements between DCL and ICL are about the same. Any upgrading that must be done to produce acceptable transportation fuels will also require additional heat, energy, water, and hydrogen. Another concern with expanded CTL production is the significant CO_2 emissions, which are much higher than for conventional crude oil refining. On the plus side, CTL fuels are far cleaner than conventional petroleum-based fuels. The many obstacles to large-scale replacement of a significant fraction of conventional oil with CTL-derived fuels led Höök and Aleklett (2010) to conclude "…it is unrealistic to claim that CTL provides a feasible solution to liquid fuels shortages created by peak oil. For the most part, it can only be a minor contributor and must be combined with other strategies." Alternatively, coal can be used as a feedstock for gaseous fuels by simply modifying process conditions of the F-T reaction thereby producing not liquid fuel, but synthetic natural gas (SNG). Thus, coal may be the source of gaseous fuel in the future. Indeed, China is engaged in creating an SNG industry with nine plants with an output capacity of 37.1 billion m^3 (1,300 billion ft^3) of natural gas already approved and another 30 or more projects in the planning stage (Yang and Jackson, 2013).

ENVIRONMENTAL CONCERNS OF USING COAL

Whether justified or not, coal as an energy source has a poor reputation with the general public. It invokes an image of devastated landscapes, polluted streams, and air pollution. Historic images of city skylines obscured by belching smokestacks re-enforce this perception. Indeed, its production and use has been marred by many unfortunate episodes: the deadly London fogs of the 1950s, the catastrophic and oftentimes fatal failures of waste piles in the U.S. and Wales, a legacy of black lung disease, and horrific mining accidents (e.g. explosions, fires, collapses, etc.). All of these have contributed to the poor reputation of coal. Although the coal and power industries have alleviated many of these negative impacts, the use of coal still has some serious environmental impacts. It disturbs large areas of the Earth's surface and can be a major pollutant of air, water, and soil. Other problems associated with coal use revolve around miner health and safety, surface disturbance and subsidence, ground and surface water impacts, habitat disruption, wildlife displacement, biodiversity loss, and issues of slurry disposal. Some of the concerns about atmospheric emissions include acid precipitation, greenhouse gases, mercury, heavy metals, and particulate matter. In addition, the solid waste products of coal combustion (e.g. fly and bottom ash) must be disposed of safely and efficiently.

The magnitudes of the environmental impacts of the unregulated use of coal are readily illustrated by the London fog event. Starting in December 1952 and lasting until March 1953, there was an unusual episode of heavy smog in London. Light winds and high atmospheric moisture content created ideal conditions for smog formation. That winter was also extremely cold, which caused an increase in coal combustion and car travel. Both factors produced a deadly combination of black soot (i.e. sticky particles of tar) and gaseous sulphur dioxide. This freak occurrence lead to the heaviest winter smog episode recorded. The smog was so thick that moving around the city was dangerous (Figure 68). The smog episode killed almost 12,000 people, mainly children, the elderly, and people with chronic respiratory diseases. The number of deaths during the smog episode was three to four times more than that of a normal day and was attributed to lung disease, tuberculosis, and heart failure. Mortality from bronchitis and pneumonia increased more than sevenfold. Most deaths occurred due to the breathing in of acid aerosols, which irritate and inflame bronchial tubes. The acidity of the air was not measured at the time, but estimates suggest that pH levels could have fallen as low as 2 at the peak

Figure 68. Nelson's tower during the Great London Fog of 1952. The fog was caused by a combination of black soot and high levels of SO_2 from, in part, coal combustion.

of the smog episode. The highest death rate recorded was between December 8th and 9th, with an average of 900 deaths a day. In some of the poorer parts of the city, death rates were nine times their normal number. The heavy pollution and the resulting death toll increased awareness of the seriousness of air pollution. The London smog disaster and other events like it eventually lead to the passage of the first environmental laws.

Historically, environmental impacts were not considered when extracting or using coal. They were costs (externalities) passed on to others or even later generations. With the advent of the environmental movement and enactment of relevant laws, many of these activities or impacts have been dealt with explicitly. In a bipartisan effort, a series of ground-breaking environmental laws were passed in the U.S. in the late 1970s and early 1980s (Figure 69). Many of these important federal laws apply to various stages of the coal life-cycle. Environmental laws relevant to the coal industry in the U.S. include the: Clean Air Act (CAA); Clean Water Act (CWA); National Environmental Policy Act (NEPA); Endangered Species Act (EAS); Safe Drinking Water Act (SDWA); Resource Conservation and Recovery Act (RCRA); Surface Mining Control and Reclamation Act (SMCRA); and Comprehensive Environmental Response, Compensation and Liability Act (CERCLA) or "superfund". Passage of the CWA during Richard Nixon's administration led to the establishment of the U.S. Environmental Protection Agency (EPA), which enforces the majority of these laws.

Environmental Laws

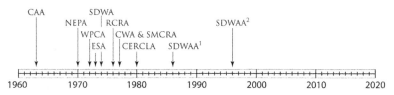

CAA: Clean Air Act (1963); NEPA: National Environmental Policy Act (1970); WPCA: Water Pollution Control Act (1972);
ESA: Endangered Speices Act (1973); SWDA: Safe Drinking Water Act (1974); RCRA: Resource Conservation and
Recovery Act (1976); CWA: Clean Water Act (1977); SMCRA: Surface Mining Control and Reclamation Act (1977);
CERCLA: Comprehensive Environmental Response, Compensation, and Liability Act (1980); SDWAA[1]: Safe Drinking
Water Act Amendments of 1986; SDWAA[2]: Safe Drinking Water Act Amendments of 1996

Figure 69. Timeline of the major U.S. environmental laws impacting coal industry activities.
These laws were passed with bipartisan support. Source: J.D. Myers, used with permission.

Mitigating the Impacts of Surface Coal Mining: U.S. Approach

Surface mining has a profound impact on the land. It completely destroys pre-existing vegetation, eliminates the original soil profile, displaces wildlife, destroys habitat, disrupts surface hydrology, impacts air quality, changes groundwater systems, and alters surface topography. Mine spoils dumps can produce acid drainage if the mined material originally contained sulfides and water is allowed to filter through them. This can damage drinking water supplies and adversely impact aquatic ecosystems.

However with the growing demand for coal during World War II and immediately after, surface mining of coal quickly expanded in the U.S. As surface mining expanded, individual states responded with their own laws regulating this industry. Despite this legislation, surface mines of the 1940s, 50s, and 60s were rarely reclaimed after mining ceased. Rather operators simply stopped mining and moved to new areas thereby abandoning the mine site and all of its potential hazards. Thus, surface mining left a scarred landscape marked by hummocky topography (the ungraded overburden spoils piles), a lack of vegetation, streams fouled by acid mine drainage, and open cuts. These regions were also susceptible to enhanced erosion typically resulting in increased stream sediment load and turbidity. Prior to 1977, an estimated 1.1 million coal mines in the U.S. had been abandoned by their owner/operators (Kenney, 2007).

The growing environmental problems associated with surface coal mining were finally addressed on the federal level with the passage of the Surface Mining Control and Reclamation Act (SMCRA) of 1977. This bill was signed into law on August 3, 1977 by President Jimmy Carter. SMCRA regulates the surface mining of coal including exploration activities and those operations of underground coal mines that occur at the surface. It also is responsible for regulating the reclamation of lands that have been mined for coal. In addition to these mining activities, the law covers coal preparation and processing facilities, coal waste piles, and coal loading facilities if these activities occur at or near a mine. The law has jurisdiction over these activities on both federal and state land. Coal mining operations that produce less than 250 t/y as well as some other types of mining are except from the act (Title VI). Under SMCRA, a mine operator must minimize surface disturbances and adverse impacts on fish and wildlife as well as other environmental values. The law also seeks to ensure that any land mined for coal is adequately reclaimed such that the land and water resources of the site are restored to a state comparable to or better than that before mining. SMCRA has two major parts. Title IV addresses mines abandoned prior to the law's passage and that pose a hazard to public health and/or the environment. The regulating of new surface coal mining activities is carried out under the authority of Title V of SMCRA.

Under the act's Title II, the Office of Surface Mining Reclamation and Enforcement (OSMRE or OSM for short) was established in the Department of Interior to enforce the law. As with many of the other U.S. environmental laws, the original intention of the law was to have the individual states administer SMCRA rules and regulations themselves. The OSMRE would oversee these programs for compliance with federal rules. Any state could be given the authority, called *primacy*, to administer SMCRA programs if they could show that state laws were as strict as the federal law and that the relevant state agency had the authority to enforce civil and criminal penalties for non-compliance. States, if they wish, could also enact rules and regulations more strict than those of the federal government. If a state chose not to apply for primacy, OSMRE would enforce SMCRA in that state. Presently, thirty-six states have SMCRA primacy (Figure 70). In addition, two tribes in the western U.S. have primacy over SMCRA enforcement on their lands. To oversee these state programs, OSMRE has divided the nation into three administrative regions (i.e. Appalachian, Mid-Continent, and Western) each with a regional office.

There are four major components that regulate all surface coal mining activities under SMCRA's Title V. These components are: permitting; bonding and insurance; performance standards; and inspection and enforcement. Before mining can begin, an operator must submit an application for a permit to mine. The application must describe the mining plan, the operator's background and history of SMCRA compliance, and the plans for reclamation. Once a permit is issued, the operator must follow its conditions. Major changes to any part of the plan require approval from the relevant state or tribal agency or OSMRE.

As part of the permit, a mine operator must have adequate bonding and insurance. Operators post reclamation bonds to ensure that there are sufficient funds for the regulatory agency to complete site reclamation in the event that the permittee does not complete the approved reclamation plan. There are three types of financial instruments that can be used as bonds. Once the reclamation has been completed according to the mining permit and regulatory statutes, OSMRE can release the bond. The bond may be released in phases as different stages of reclamation are achieved. The end of Phase I coincides with completion of all backfilling, regrading, and drainage control. Topsoil replacement and re-establishment of vegetation

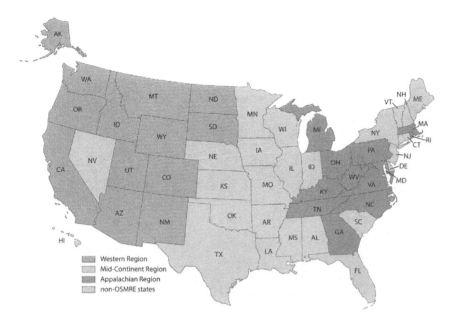

Figure 70. U.S. map showing the non-coal states and the states and tribes in the three OSMRE regions. Source: EPA.

constitute Phase II completion. Phase III is the final reclamation stage and requires demonstrating that revegetation has been successful for various prescribed periods of time. In addition to bonding, a mine operator must also have insurance to cover personal injuries or property damage that might result from mining.

Under SMCRA, all coal mining activities such as blasting, road construction and maintenance, wildlife protection, spoils disposal, etc. are regulated by performance standards that are part of the original mine permit. These standards are intended to ensure the impacted land is restored to a state where it can support the uses it did before mining occurred. One of the most significant performance standards for accomplishing this goal is reclamation. To accomplish this task, reclamation must accomplish a number of different tasks. One primary task is to restore through backfilling, grading, and compacting the land to approximate original contour (AOC) (Figure 71). Reclamation must also minimize impact to the hydrologic system disturbed by mining. For surface water systems, this entails preventing acid mine and/or acid rock drainage and increased sediment load in impacted streams. Reclamation activities are required by law to commence as soon as possible after mining is complete. In many instances, one part of a large surface coal mine maybe undergoing reclamation while another part is still being actively mined. Finally, a permanent vegetative cover must be re-established as the final stage of reclamation. In arid climates (63.5 cm/y (<25 in/y)), the vegetative must remain viable without

Figure 71. A mined out portion of a surface coal mine undergoing reclamation. This portion of the mine has been backfilled, graded, and compacted to restore approximate original contour and is almost ready for revegetation. Source: Photo by J.D. Myers, used with permission.

intervention for ten years after final seeding, fertilizing, and irrigating. In wetter climates, the waiting period is only five years.

The last major Title V component of the SMCRA is inspection and enforcement of compliance with mining permit conditions. On-site inspections by state and federal regulators are the major means by which compliance with the conditions of a mine permit are ensured. For any operating mine, a complete on-site inspection must be conducted every quarter. In addition, a partial inspection is required each month. These inspections are conducted without prior notification. Inspections are also performed when a citizen complaint about possible hazards or non-compliance is received by the appropriate agency. When inspectors discover permit violations, they must take action. The nature of their actions is determined by the severity of the violation. In extreme cases where there is an immediate threat to the public or environment, the inspector has the authority to shut down the mine immediately. For less severe violations, a notice of violation (NOV) is issued noting the problem and setting a timeline by which it must be rectified. If the problem is not addressed in the allotted time period, a cessation order (CO) can be issued forcing the mine to halt operations until the problem is resolved.

The biggest program OSMRE administers under SMCRA is the Abandoned Mine Land (ABL) fund, a part of Title IV. This fund is designed to provide the resources necessary to reclaim mines abandoned prior to the passage of the act. In 1990, the program was amended to also allow for addressing mine sites that were abandoned after 1977. Monies from the fund are collected by assessing a tax on all the coal produced in the U.S. In 2014, these fees were $0.315/t for coal mined from the surface, $0.15/t for underground mined coal, and $0.10/t for lignite. The majority of the fund (80%) is disbursed to states with approved mine reclamation plans. OSMRE uses the remaining fees to address emergencies associated with mining activities.

The major result of SMCRA is that coal mines in the U.S., unlike other types of non-coal mines, are now reclaimed after mining ceases. Since 1977, the ABL fund has collected over $10.1 billion in fees from the coal mining industry. Of this amount, $7.6 billion has been awarded in grants to states and tribes for enforcing SMCRA and reclaiming abandoned mine sites.

Mountaintop Removal: SMCRA & CWA

In recent decades as the demand for eastern bituminous coal with the lowest possible sulfur content grew and draglines increased dramatically in size, mountaintop removal (MTR) mining became an important method of extracting coal from the steep and rugged topography of Appalachia (Humphries, 2003). The depletion of near surface coal in this region also contributed to the expansion of this mining method. Yet, as MTR operations expanded in number and scale, the problem of spoil disposal grew. With the development of valley fill disposal and subsequent burial of kilometers of streams (Figure 72), new environmental and regulatory issues emerged that have contributed to making MTR mining highly controversial and led to extended legal actions.

As a form of surface coal mining, MTR mining is covered by the provisions of SMCRA. Thus, various state agencies issue permits for mining operations and conduct inspection and enforcement. They also oversee mine reclamation, including AOC requirements, and certify when it is complete and performance bonds can be released. Thus, MTR mining with regards to SMCRA enforcement raises no new regulatory issues. However, because valley fills result in the discharge of mining spoils to the nation's surface waters, MTR mining operations are also regulated by the Clean Water Act. This automatically involves additional agencies in the regulatory process.

Clean Water Act (CWA)
Water quality in the U.S. is protected by the Clean Water Act, which was passed in 1977, and its amendments (Figure 69). The CWA is intended to restore and protect the quality of the surface waters of the U.S. As such, it applies to rivers, lakes, streams, intermittent streams, and wetlands. Under the law, it is illegal to discharge effluents to a stream unless the provisions of the CWA are followed and a discharge permit has been obtained. The law regulates a number of different classes of pollutants including: conventional pollutants, priority pollutants, and non-conventional

Figure 72. A valley fill with re-constructed stream and sediment retention ponds at its base. The edge of the active mine can be seen in the upper right corner of the photograph. Source: Ohio Valley Environmental Coalition Flyover courtesy SouthWings.org (http://ohvec.org/galleries/mountaintop_removal/013/).

pollutants. Conventional pollutants include organic material, total suspended solids, fecal coliform, oil and grease, and acid producing material. Priority contaminants include those effluents that are toxic. Any material not falling into the first two contaminant categories are deemed non-conventional pollutants.

Although the law has four major programs, only two are relevant to mountaintop removal mining. CWA Section 402 established The National Pollutant Discharge Elimination System, which is a permitting program for discharge of pollutants to the nation's surface waters (Humphries, 2003). Under this program, anyone discharging a pollutant must obtain a permit from EPA, relevant state agency, or designated tribal government. 402 permits cover discharge from point sources (e.g. industrial facilities, sewage treatment plants, etc.) and place limits on the types and amounts of pollutants that can be discharged. This program is mainly focused on maintaining water quality and limiting the amount of pollutants discharged to U.S. surface water. 402 permits also require the use of pollution control technology to minimize effluents (Copeland, 2008).

Dredge-and-fill activities are exempt from the NPSES permitting program by CWA Section 404. Thus, activities such as dam construction, flow regulation, water diversion, irrigation system development, streambed modification and stabilization, real estate development, and stream crossings all require a dredge and fill permit not a discharge permit (i.e. Section 402). Accordingly, these activities are regulated by 404 permits issued by the U.S. Army Corps of Engineers (COE) not EPA. The Corps in consultation with EPA establishes environmental guidelines for issuing such permits (Humphries, 2003). If the proposed activity results in significant degradation in water quality it is expressly forbidden (Copeland, 2008). In addition, a 404 permit application must be denied if there is an environmentally less damaging alternative to the proposed activity. When evaluating an application for a 404 permit, the COE evaluates the balance between the negative and positive outcomes of the proposed activity. There are two types of 404 permits. Nationwide or general permits can be issued for certain classes of dredge and fill activities that have minimal adverse impacts on surface waters. Conversely, individual permits are issued for individual projects. The COE has permitted the discharge of spoils from mountaintop removal mining to streams under Nationwide Permit 21 (Humphries, 2003). This 404 permit allows discharges from surface coal mining operations that result in minimal impact on the aquatic environment. Under this ruling, individual MTR operations in Appalachia do not have to apply for separate 404 permits. Rather, they are covered by the Nationwide Permit 21.

MTR Regulatory Controversy

Not surprisingly, different groups have taken different views on the merit of MTR mining and the regulatory stance different U.S. administrations have taken toward such operations. The mining industry and its supporters argue that the use of valley fills for disposing of spoils produced during MTR operations is an integral part of the mining process. Without these disposal mechanisms, they argue MTR would be uneconomical and that there are no viable options for spoils disposal in such rugged topography. Thus, a regulatory shift from Section 404 to Section 402 permits for MTR mining would essentially end a class of mining activity that has long been permitted (Humphries, 2003). Conversely, MTR critics maintain that valley fills destroy streams and aquatic communities while displacing wildlife. Because the activity results in the degradation of water quality, they argue that it is unlawful regardless of whether a Section 404 or 402 permit is deemed most appropriate. Contributing to the controversy over MTR permitting is the redefinition of fill material by COE and EPA (Copeland, 2013). The revised rule was intended to replace two distinct but different definitions of fill material in CWA Section 404 with a single consistent definition. The revised rule expanded the types of discharge activities permitted by Section 404 to include mining overburden. This decision angered environmental groups who believe MTR disposal activities should be regulated under the more environmentally restrictive Section 402. Not surprisingly, the revised wording was welcomed by the mining industry and its supporters. Other impacts cited as reasons for banning or severely restricting MTR mining include damage done to adjacent structures, noise, dust, and vibrations produced by blasting, collapse of water

417

wells, destruction of streams, loss of hunting, hiking, and fishing areas, and forced movement of communities (Rosenberg, 2000). Terrestrial impacts of MTR mining include loss and fragmentation of forest, soil losses, loss of biological carbon sinks, and alteration of biodiversity among other things (Wickham et al., 2013).

Atmospheric emissions

Because of its heterogeneous nature, the combustion of coal is a complex process that results in the production of a number of different reaction products, (e.g. NOx, SO_2, particulate matter (PM), mercury, heavy metals, etc.). Before the Clean Air Act, these products were simply emitted with the flue gas out of exhaust stacks. Not surprisingly, these materials damaged both human health and ecosystems downwind of any facility burning coal. With passage of the Clean Air Act, the emission of flue gas from coal-fired electrical power stations became a regulated activity, which required discharge permits and carry hefty fines for non-compliance.

Clean Air Act
In the U.S., the first major federal clean air law was the Air Pollution Control Act of 1955 (Figure 69). It was followed by three successive clean air laws (i.e. Clean Air Act of 1963; Clean Air Act of 1970; and the Clean Air Act of 1990). The law has not been modified since 1990 and is the primary federal environmental law regulating atmospheric emissions in the U.S. Some of the important programs of the Clean Air Act of 1990 include:

* *National Ambient Air Quality Standards (NAAQS)*: authorizes EPA to set outdoor (ambient air) quality standards for six criteria pollutants (i.e. ozone, carbon monoxide, sulfur dioxide, lead, nitrogen oxides, and suspended particulates). EPA is required every five years to review the scientific data on the health impact of each criteria pollutant and revised the standards when necessary.
* *National Emissions Standards for Hazardous Air Pollutants*: emissions standards for toxic air pollutants not covered by NAAQS. EPA must establish Maximum Achievable Control Technology emission standards for 188 hazardous air pollutants These standards are to be reviewed and, if necessary, revised every eight years.
* *New Source Performance Standards*: as new types of industrial facilities are developed EPA must set emission standards for these new categories of industrial activity.
* *Prevention of Significant Deterioration*: In those parts of the country where outdoor air quality exceeds the NAAQS criteria, the Prevention of Significant Deterioration program prevents deterioration in air quality by establishing standards for pollutant emissions. To achieve this goal, EPA established three different types of attainment zones and set limits on how much pollutant emissions can increase in each of these zones. Of the six criteria pollutants, only SO_2, NOx,

and particulate matter are currently covered by the PSD program. Regardless of the standards set by the PSD program, ambient air quality in these zones cannot fall below NAAQS criteria.

- *Control of Ozone-Depleting Chemicals*: places limitations on production and consumption of particular ozone-depleting substances with timelines for the eventual phasing out of these substances. This section of the CAA implements U.S. obligations under the U.N *London Protocol on Substances that Deplete the Ozone Layer*.

- *Operating Permit Program*: under Title V of CAA any source that emits or has the potential to emit 90 tonnes (100 short tons) of any regulated pollutant must obtain a discharge permit. HAPs are also covered by a discharge permit, but the triggering emission level is higher. This program, which is run by the states, collects a fee for permits to offset the administrative costs of the program. Excluding carbon monoxide, permits must cost at least $25/ton. Permits specify how much of a pollutant can be emitted and are valid for five years after which a new permit application must be submitted.

Under CAA, EPA must set ambient air standards for substances considered harmful to public health and the environment. There are two types of standards. *Primary standards* protect the health of the public, including asthmatics, children, and the elderly (sensitive populations). In contrast, public welfare protection is provided by *secondary standards*, which protect against decreases in visibility and damage to animals, crops, vegetation, and buildings. The current standards for the criteria pollutants are listed in Table 3 (EPA, 2014b).

Table 3. EPA primary and secondary standards for the six criteria pollutants regulated by the Clean Air Act

pollutant	final rule date	primary/secondary	averaging time	level
carbon monoxide	31-Aug-11	primary	8 hour	9 ppm
			1 hour	35 ppm
lead	12-Nov-08	primary/secondary	rolling 3 month	0.15 µg/m^3
nitrogen dioxide	9-Feb-10	primary	1 hour	100 ppb
		primary/secondary	annual	53 ppb
ozone	27-Mar-08	primary/secondary	8 hour	0.074 ppm
particulate matter	14-Dec-12	primary	annual	12 µg/m^3
		secondary	annual	15 µg/m^3
		primary/secondary	24 hour	35 µg/m^3
sulfur dioxide	22-Jun-10	primary	1 hour	75 ppb
		secondary	3 hour	0.5 ppm

Of the six criteria air pollutants for which EPA sets National Ambient Air Quality Standards, three are produced by the combustion of coal. Thus, the electrical power industry is regulated by the EPA under the CAA, among other environmental laws. The three air pollutants the power industry must deal with include particulate matter, nitrogen oxides, and sulfur dioxide. Short-term (5 minutes to 24 hours) exposure to SO_2 causes an array of adverse respiratory effects including bronchoconstriction and increased asthma symptoms. Exposure also leads to increased hospital visits and admission for respiratory illness, especially among children, the elderly, and asthmatics. NOx exposures lasting 30 minutes to 24 hours produce airway inflammation in healthy people and aggravate symptoms for people with respiratory problems. Particulate matter exposure has been linked by studies to premature death for people with heart or lung disease, nonfatal heart attacks, irregular heartbeat, aggravated asthma, decreased lung function, and respiratory distress (e.g. airway irritation, coughing, and difficulty breathing).

To compile with CAA, coal-fired power plants in the U.S. have installed a variety of pollution control devices (Figure 73). These include selective catalytic reduction (SCR) reactors to deal with nitrogen oxides, flue gas desulfurization (FGD) units

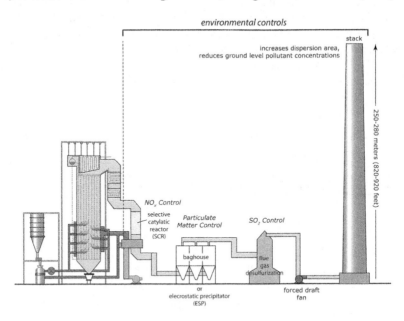

Figure 73. Schematic diagram of air pollution control devices installed on coal-fired power plants to compile with CAA emission requirements. Selective catalytic reduction (SCR) reactors are used to control nitrogen oxides, electrostatic precipitators (ESP) or baghouses remove particulate matter, and scrubbers or more formally flue gas desulfurization (FGD) units remove sulfur dioxide. Each type of control system is placed at a different position along the path flue gas takes from boiler to stack. Source: J.D. Myers, used with permission.

to capture SO_2, and baghouses or electrostatic precipitators to capture fly ash, a major source of particulate matter. Other developed nations have also required the deployment of similar air pollution control devices.

Particulate Matter

Particulates or particulate matter (PM) are fine particles and soot suspended in a gas. Because they are small enough to be respired, particulates have respiratory health impacts when inhaled in large quantities. PM with diameters less than 10 micrometers can reach the deepest regions of the lungs and cannot be ejected during exhaling (Figure 74). Some of the health consequences of particulate pollution include asthma, difficult or painful breathing, and chronic bronchitis, especially in children and the elderly.

EPA classifies particulate pollution into two categories. Inhalable coarse particles are larger than 2.5 micrometers and smaller than 10 micrometers in diameter and consist of solids found near roadways and dusty industries. Fine particles, such as those found in smoke and haze, are 2.5 micrometers in diameter and smaller. These particles can be directly emitted from sources such as forest fires, or they can form indirectly when gases emitted from power plants, industries, and automobiles react in the air. Because of their health hazards, EPA regulates the amount of these particulates a power plant can emit.

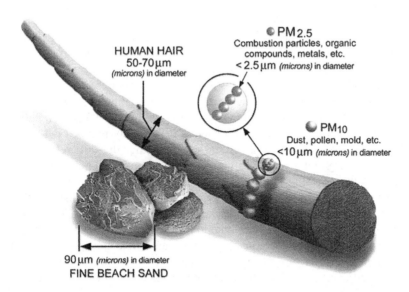

Figure 74. Inhalable particulate matter (PM) has diameters smaller than that of a human hair. These particles can reach the deepest parts of the lung when inhaled and are not ejected when a person exhales. EPA classifies particulate matter into two size classes (i.e. PM_{10} and $PM_{2.5}$). Source: U.S. EPA.

421

There are two primary ways of removing particulates from the flue gas stream of a coal-fired power plant. Electrostatic precipitators remove particles from a flowing gas (such as flue gas) using the force of an induced electrostatic charge. In contrast, baghouses use fabric filters to remove particulates through mechanical filtration.

Electrostatic precipitators (ESP)

ESPs use electromotive forces to separate and collect particulates thereby employing a capture and disposal approach to pollution control. They are 99 to 99.99% effective in removing PM from a flue gas stream. Electrodes in the ESP create an electric field that ionizes gas molecules and charges the dust particles. The charged particles are captured on collector surfaces. The efficiency of the separation process increases with the length of time the gas spends in the unit and the strength of the electrical field. There are two main variations in ESP design: pipe vs. plate and wet vs. dry.

The first variation determines the physical form of the collectors and hence how gas flows through the unit. In pipe ESPs, the collectors are pipes of circular, square or hexagonal cross-sections arranged vertically (EPA, 2003a; EPA, 2003h). The pipes are 7-30 centimeter (3-15 inches) in diameter, 1-4 meters (3-12 feet) tall, and arranged in parallel. An electrode extends down through the center of each pipe creating a corona that charges the particulates and forces them to the walls of the pipe. Dusty gas enters a pipe at the base, flows upward through the pipe, and exits out of the unit at the top. Plate ESPs use sheet metal plates hung vertically and spaced 19-38 centimeters (9-18 inches) apart. The area between adjacent plates are referred to as ducts and are 6-14 meters (20-45 feet) long. A series of electrodes is hung in the center of the ducts (Figure 75). In a plate ESP, gas flow is horizontal and parallel the plates (EPA, 2003b; EPA, 2003i).

The second variant in ESP design is the manner in which the dust is cleaned from collector surfaces. Wet ESPs periodically inject or continuously spray water onto the collectors thereby washing off the dust particles (EPA, 2003h; EPA, 2003i). The wash slurry is collected in a sump, which is periodically pumped out. The slurry is either dewatered or sent to a settling pond whether the dust settles out under the influence of gravity. Dry ESPs use mechanical motion to physically knock the particles off the collectors (EPA, 2003a; EPA, 2003b). In these systems, the electric field is turned off and a mechanical system raps the collectors to dislodge the dust.

ESPs do not produce a decrease in the pressure of the flue gas so their use does not require the installation of additional induction fans in the ductwork. They have low energy demands and operational costs and can handle large gas flows routinely. In addition, ESPs can operate in both high pressures and vacuums. Their high initial capital costs, higher maintenance (electrode replacement), and large spatial footprints are their main disadvantages.

Baghouses

PM can also be removed from flue gas mechanically by passing the flue gas through fabric filter bags (Figure 76). In these systems, dirty flue gas is passed through

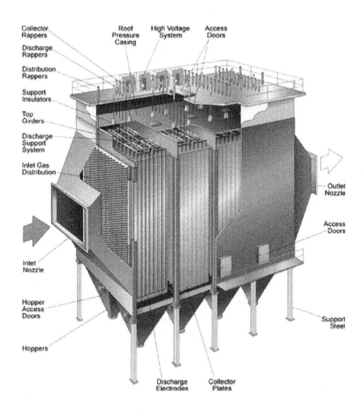

Figure 75. Schematic diagram of a dry, wire-plate electrostatic precipitator. The plates are charged electrically, which attracts the PM to them thereby removing them from the flue gas stream. Gas flow is horizontal and parallel the plates. Source: The Babcock & Wilcox Company, http://www.babcock.com/products/Pages/Dry-Electrostatic-Precipitator.aspx.

tightly woven or felted fabric which traps and removes PM through a variety of physical processes (EPA, 2003c; EPA, 2003d; EPA, 2003e). The fabric can be deployed as sheets, cartridges or bags. The most common scheme is cylindrical bags 13-31 centimeters (5-12 inches) in diameter and 6-9 meters (20-30 feet) long. To facilitate cleaning and replacement, the bags are often distributed among a series of compartments. Because the flow of gas is restricted by the fabric, baghouses produce a drop in flue gas pressure. To minimize this pressure drop, large surface areas of fabric are needed. A 250 MW power plant requires a baghouse with 5,000 bags providing a total surface area of 46,500 square meters (500,000 square feet). Baghouse configurations vary in the manner in which the bags are cleaned and how air flows through the bags.

Perhaps the simplest design uses mechanical shaking to clean the bags (EPA, 2003c). Bags with open bases and closed tops are hung vertically in the baghouse. Gas enters the bag at its base, moves upward, and out through the fabric

423

(Figure 76a). Dust accumulates on the inside of the bag in a filter cake. The presence of the filter cake improves the efficiency of particle removal especially at the smaller size ranges. To clean a bag, a shaker bar attached at the top of the bag physically shakes it by moving it back and forth horizontally thereby dislodging the filter cake. Alternative systems actually vibrate the bag. In a reversed air design (EPA, 2003e), dirty flue gas enters the bag from the base and exits out to the dust chamber leaving the PM coated on the inside surface of the bag as with the shaker design (Figure 76b). When the bags are fully loaded, the flue gas is shut off to the bag and clean air pumped into the bag chamber. The increased pressure in the chamber causes the bags to partially collapse thereby knocking off the dust cake. To prevent complete collapse of the bags, they are supported by rings spaced evenly along their length. Restoring the flue gas flow to the bags inflates them again and restarts the flue gas cleaning process. For the pulse-jet configuration, the bags are stretched over a supporting frame. Dirty air flows through the fabric into the bag building the filter cake on the outside of the bag with the clean air exiting out the top of the bag (Figure 76c). To clean the bag, a pulse of high pressure air is injected into the bag creating a shock wave that travels the length of the bag (EPA, 2003d). As the wave passes, it forces the bag outward off the frame. After the shock wave passes, the bag snaps back onto the frame causing the filter cake to be dislodged and the dust falls under the influence of gravity the length of the bag where it is discharged out hopper at the base. In all cases, the dust is collected in hoppers at the base of the baghouse.

Acid Deposition
Acid deposition comprises those physical and chemical processes that remove acidic material (i.e. material with lower than normal pH values) from the atmosphere and deposit them on animals, vegetation, buildings, land, water bodies, etc. It generally results from higher than normal levels of sufluric and nitric acid in the atmosphere. These acids are produced from chemical and physical precursors that react with water, oxygen, and other chemicals in the air to produce various acids of nitrogen and sulfur (Figure 77). The sources of these precursors can be natural (e.g. volcanoes, decaying vegetation) or anthropogenic (e.g. fossil fuel combustion).

There are two primary mechanisms for acid deposition (Figure 77). *Wet deposition* or *acid precipitation* occurs when various forms of precipitation (e.g. rain, snow, sleet, fog, mist, etc.) wash acids from the air and carry them to the ground. Upon contact, this acidic water impacts plants and animals as well as buildings, soils, and bodies of water in a variety of ways. *Dry deposition* occurs when acidic components are incorporated into smoke or dust and carried to the ground in a dry form. They coat any surface on which they land. Later precipitation can wash off these acidic compounds thereby producing acidic run-off.

In the U.S., two thirds of SO_2 and a fourth of NOx emissions comes from electricity generation. To reduce the negative impacts of acid precipitation, EPA established the Acid Rain Program under Title IV of the Clean Air Act. The program was deployed in two phases. Phase I began in 1995 and covered primarily large,

(a) shaker

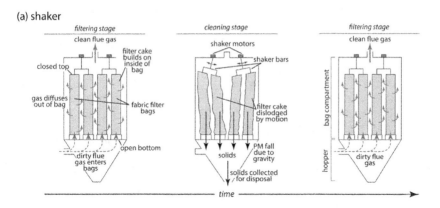

(b) reverse air

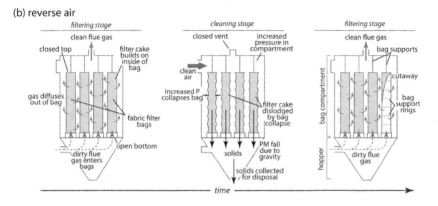

(c) pulse jet

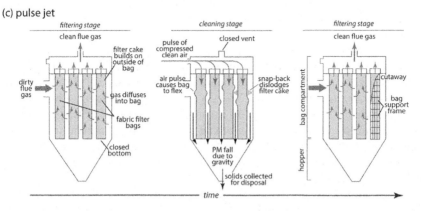

Figure 76. The three possible configurations for fabric filter baghouses (a) shaker type; (b) reverse air; and (c) pulse-jet. For all three types, particulate matter is collected as a solid in hoppers at the bottom of the structure. Source: J.D. Myers, used with permission.

425

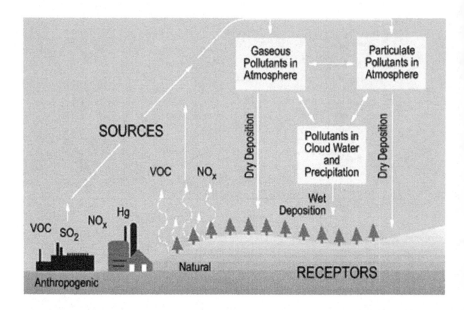

Figure 77. Acid is removed from the atmosphere by dry and wet deposition. The major anthropogenic precursors to acid precipitation are gaseous emissions (e.g. VOC, NOx, SO₂, and particulate matter) mostly from fossil fuel combustion. Source: EPA.

coal-fired power plants in the East and Midwest. Phase II, starting in 2000, tightened emissions standards and added all plants with greater than 25 MW output to the program. The program allows for trading of emission allowances for NOx and SO_2, requires emission monitoring and reporting, mandates plants to have allowances to cover the acid gases they emit, and have permits for their discharges.

NOx: Selective Catalytic Reduction
An important class of gaseous precursors to acid deposition is the nitrogen oxides or NOxs. As N_2, nitrogen makes up approximately 80% of the Earth's atmosphere and is relatively inert chemically. However as an element, nitrogen is highly reactive and can assume a wide variety of chemical forms (EPA, 1999). Consequently, when chemically bonded to oxygen it can produce many different nitrogen oxides including N_2O, NO, N_2O_2, N_2O_3, NO_2, N_2O_4, and N_2O_5. All of these are produced in the process of combustion, although the most common form produced by a power plant boiler is NO.

Unlike sulfuric oxides which are produced only from sulfur in the fuel, there are two sources of nitrogen oxides during coal combustion. *Fuel NOx* is produced during burning when nitrogen in the fossil fuel combines with oxygen in the air to generate NOx. In contrast, *thermal NOx* is produced when nitrogen and oxygen in air interact with each other at high temperatures (> 900°F) in a furnace or boiler. The higher the combustion temperature, the more thermal NOx produced. Because of thermal nitrogen, even a fuel with no nitrogen will produce NOxs upon combustion.

There are two ways to lower nitrogen oxides emissions from power plants. During the combustion process, low-NOx burners can be used to control fuel and air mixtures and temperature to limit thermal NOx production. Alternatively, post-combustion selective catalytic reduction (SCR) reactors can be installed to reduce the nitrogen oxides in the flue gas stream.

Selective catalytic reduction of NOxs in flue gas is achieved by injecting a reducing agent into the flue gas stream. The reducing agent can be ammonia (NH_3), either anhydrous (i.e. dry) or aqueous, or urea ((NH_2)$_2$CO) and is introduced using sprayers deployed in a grid-like pattern in the flue-gas ductwork. Downstream of the injection point, the flue gas passes through a series of porous layers where a catalyst causes the nitrogen oxides in the flue gas to react with the reducing agent thereby producing diatomic molecular nitrogen and water vapour (EPA, 2003g). The dominant SCR chemical reactions for ammonia-based SCR systems are (EPA, 2001):

$$\underbrace{4NO}_{\substack{nitrogen\\oxide}} + O_2 + \underbrace{4NH_3}_{ammonia} \rightleftharpoons 4N_2 + 6H_2O$$

$$\underbrace{2NO_2}_{\substack{nitrogen\\dioxide}} + O_2 + \underbrace{4NH_3}_{ammonia} \rightleftharpoons 3N_2 + 6H_2O$$

$$\underbrace{NO}_{\substack{nitrogen\\oxide}} + \underbrace{NO_2}_{\substack{nitrogen\\dioxide}} + \underbrace{2NH_3}_{ammonia} \rightleftharpoons 2N_2 + 3H_2O$$

In addition to N_2 and H_2O, carbon dioxide is produced by systems using urea as a reducing agent. Because these reactions work best at high temperatures (315-400°C (600-750°F)), the reactant is injected soon after the flue gas leaves the boiler. In the SCR reactor unit, a series of layers consisting of replaceable units housing a porous ceramic structure embedded with base metal, zeolite, or precious metal catalysts are positioned in the flue gas pathway. As the reactant and flue gas pass through the catalyst layers, the nitrogen reduction reaction occurs. When the catalyst in a unit is consumed, it must be replaced. Reductions of 90 % can be achieved with this method of pollution control (EPA, 2003g). The disadvantages of a SCR unit are high capital and operating costs and the large volumes of reagent and catalyst that must be used. In addition, high levels of dust and fly ash tend to clog the catalyst layers thereby impeding gas flow. Reaction of ammonia with sulfur in the flue gas produces ammonium sulfur reaction products thereby consuming both reducing agent and catalyst. Because of these problems, SCR catalysts typically have an operational lifetime of between 16,000 and 40,000 hours in coal-fired power plants.

SO₂ Removal: Flue Gas Desulfurization (FGD)

Suflur is a reactive element that readily combines with oxygen to form sulfur oxides or the SOxs. The two most important of these oxides are sulfur dioxide (SO_2) and sulfur trioxide (SO_3). SO_2, which is much more abundant, is a colorless gas with a strong and irritating odour and taste. In the atmosphere, SO_2 combines with oxygen to create SO_3. This oxide in turn combines with atmospheric water to produce sulfric acid, a major cause of acid deposition. The sulfur oxides have an atmospheric lifetime of 4 to 10 days. Because coal invariably contains some amount of sulfur, its combustion produces sulfur dioxide (SO_2) that unless captured is emitted to the atmosphere.

Flue-gas desulfurization (FGD) is a group of technologies that capture sulfur dioxide (SO_2) from exhaust flue gases of fossil-fuel power plants, as well as other sulfur oxide emitting industrial processes. FGD is implemented using scrubber systems, which are a diverse group of air pollution control devices that can be used to remove some particulates and/or acid gases from industrial exhaust streams. They use an alkaline reagent to absorb, neutralize, and/or oxidize the SO_2 and produce a solid compound. Depending upon the type, FSD scrubbers typically remove 50-98% of SO_2 from the exhaust gas stream (EPA, 2003f). FGD scrubbers use inexpensive and readily available reagents, but have high capital and operating and maintenance costs.

There are three different types of scrubbers: wet, semi-wet, and dry. Wet scrubbers use an aqueous slurry of sorbent to remove acidic pollutants from flue gases. In these types of scrubbers, the slurry and flue gas are reacted in a spray tower (Figure 78). Using a series of nozzles at the top of the tower to disperse the slurry, a mist of droplets is created from the aqueous slurry. Under the influence of gravity, the droplets fall toward the base of the tower. At the same time, flue gas at temperatures of 150-370°C (300-700°F) enters the base of the tower and rises upward through the falling mist. The SO_2 in the flue gas reacts with the sorbent to form solid crystals that fall to the bottom of the tower where they are collected. Any droplets entrained in the flue gas stream are removed before the flue gas exits the tower by a mist eliminator positioned at the top of the tower (Figure 78). The collected solids are dewatered and disposed of in an environmentally safe manner. Web scrubbers have a capture efficiency of over 90% and comprise 85% of the FGD units installed in the U.S. (EPA, 2003f). Power plants store large volumes of reagent on site, which they use to make the slurry for the FGD scrubber.

Semi-dry FGD systems also use an aqueous slurry, but it has a much higher concentration of sorbent than in wet systems. In this case, the solid produced is dry and is collected using an ESP or baghouse. Dry systems employ a sorbent that is solid and is injected into the boiler, downstream heat exchangers (economizers), or duct work. These systems have recovery rates of less than 80%.

Because they must be alkaline, the reagents used in FGD systems are generally Na or Ca based. The primary Ca-based sorbents are either lime (CaO) or limestone ($CaCO_3$) whereas ammonia (NH_3) is the main sodium reagent. In the United States,

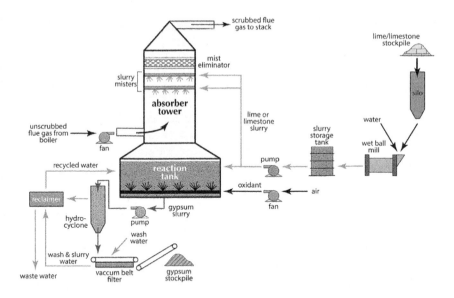

Figure 78. One of the main types of FGD scrubbers is the mist tower. A mist of sorbent slurry is produced at the top of the tower by sprayers. As the mist falls, SO₂ diffuses into the droplets and reacts with the sorbent to form a solid compound. The solid falls to the bottom of the tower for collection and disposal. A mist eliminator at the top of the tower removes any residual droplets from the flue gas before it exits the tower. Source: J.D. Myers, used with permission.

nearly all systems use either lime or limestone, because they are inexpensive and easy to obtain. A limestone reagent produces calcium sulphite according to the reaction:

$$\underbrace{CaCO_{3(s)}}_{\text{limestone}} + SO_{2(g)} \rightarrow \underbrace{CaSO_{3(s)}}_{\text{calcium sulfite}} + CO_{2(g)}$$

By introducing an oxidizing gas and water (Figure 78), calcium sulphite can be converted to gypsum:

$$\underbrace{CaSO_{3(s)}}_{\text{calcium sulfite}} + 0.5O_{2(g)} + H_2O \rightarrow + \underbrace{CaSO_4 \cdot 2H_2O_{(s)}}_{\text{gypsum}}$$

Because it is often marketable, the additional step to create gypsum can partially offset the cost of scrubbing the flue gas. The corresponding neutralization reaction for lime is:

$$CaOH_{2_{(s)}} + SO_{2_{(g)}} \rightarrow CaSO_{3(s)} + H_2O_{(l)}$$

$\underbrace{\qquad\qquad}_{\text{lime}}$ $\underbrace{\qquad\qquad}_{\text{calcium sulfite}}$

Systems employing ammonia as a reducing agent produce ammonium sulfate $[(NH_4)_2SO_4]$. In all three systems, the sludges must be disposed of as solid waste, which may have high concentrations of trace elements. FGD material can be used for a variety of products including: raw material for wallboard; fill for structural applications and embankments; feed stock for cement production; raw material for concrete products and grout; and material for waste stabilization and/or solidification.

SO_2 and NOx Emissions: Cross-State Air Pollution Rule (CSAPR)
Since 1986, emissions of NOx have decreased by 54% and SO_2 by 42% in the United States (Figure 79). These decreases have come despite increases of 85% and 64% in GDP and electricity use. In 2010, coal-fired plants with FGD scrubbers generated 57% of the total electricity, but emitted only 27% of the total sulfur dioxide emissions. The direct result of these changes has been dramatic improvement in the health of ecosystems downwind of coal-fired power plants.

Despite the Clean Air Act, many of U.S. coal-fired power plants still do not have environmental controls to reduce SO_2 and NOx emissions because they were grandfathered out of the program when it was initially established (Figure 80). Thus, these plants are still the largest source of sulfur dioxide (SO_2) emissions across the

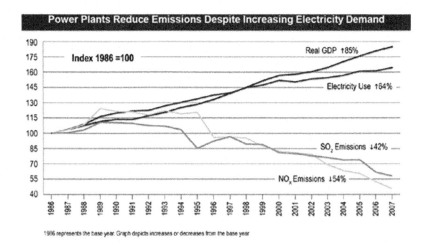

Figure 79. Changes in NOx and SO_2 emissions from 1986 to 2007. Sources: U.S. Department of Energy, Energy Information Administration (EIA), U.S. Environmental Protection Agency (EPA), and U.S. Bureau of Economic Analysis.

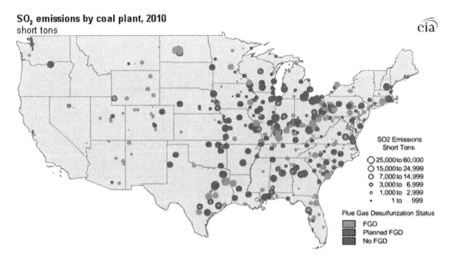

SO₂ emissions by coal plant, 2010
short tons

Note: Circles denotes plants with capacity greater than 25 megawatts. Red circles are unscrubbed coal plants, green circles indicate coal plants with scrubbers, and blue circles indicate coal plants that plan to add scrubbers.

Figure 80. Coal-fired power plants (> 25 MW) with and without flue gas desulfuization (FGD) scrubbers. Source: U.S. Energy Information Administration, based on Form EIA-860, EPA Continuous Emissions Monitoring System, Ventyz Energy Velocity. http://www.eia. gov/todayinenergy/detail.cfm?id=4410.

nation. Because they commonly cross state lines, acid gas emissions from power plants can cause ground level ozone and particulate matter pollution in downwind states making it hard for these states to attain their NAAQS requirements of the Clean Air Act.

To improve air quality in these downwind states, EPA issued its new Cross-State Air Pollution Rule (CSAPR) in July, 2011. This rule requires 28 states in the middle and eastern part of the country (Figure 81) to reduce annual SO_2 and NOx emissions from the electrical power sector. Under the new rule, power plant SO_2 emissions will drop 73% compared to 2005 levels and 54% for NOx by 2014. Reductions can be accomplished by: 1) use of lower sulfur coal; 2) retirement of plants without emission controls; 3) installation of emission control equipment (e.g. FGD and/or SCR units) on existing plants; and/or 4) some combination of these strategies.

COAL, STEM, QUANTITATIVE SKILLS AND PERFORMANCE TASKS

Like petroleum, coal is an energy resource that is critical to modern, industrialized society. For most of the world, it produces much of the electricity used in most nations. It also figures prominently in the question of anthropogenic climate change and how to decarbonize the world's energy supply. Take coal away and cities go

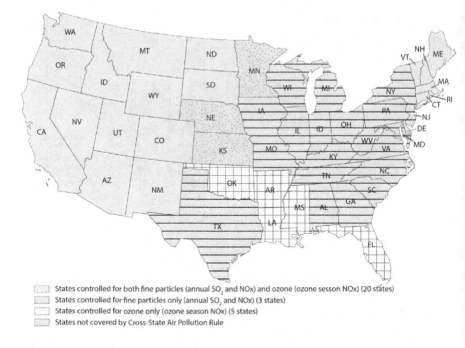

Figure 81. States covered by the Cross-State Air Pollution Rule (CSAPR). Under the new rule, SO_2 emissions in affected states will be cut by 6.4 million tons per year (73%) and NOx by 1.4 million tons per year (54%). Source: (EPA, 2014a).

dark, industry comes to a standstill, and commerce is negatively impacted. Despite coal's importance in producing the electricity modern society needs, there are individuals and groups who argue that, in an effort to combat global climate change, coal should be abandoned as an energy source no matter the social and/or economic consequences. These groups care little about the role coal can play in reducing energy poverty in developing nations and improving the lives of countless millions in the third world. Clearly, we, as citizens, need to make some hard choices about the future role of coal in our energy mix. However, we should make those choices based on more than a celebrity's sound bite about the evil of coal. We need to understand the science behind coal use as well as the numbers that provide a sense of the scale of the energy problem we face if we are to replace coal in the current energy mix.

The topic of coal provides an excellent context within which to introduce our students to an important but controversial energy source. By preparing them to move beyond mere sound bites and engage in the discussion in a meaningful manner, it is possible to teach many of the concepts and principles that are at the foundation of STEM. For example, coal combustion, the products produced, and how they impact atmospheric quality are all closely related to many STEM principles and concepts highlighted in both national and international educational standards. At the same time, the physical and geological processes that form coal allow us to introduce our students to Earth systems, energy flows, and the influence of time on natural processes. As with petroleum, the topic also encompasses big numbers and quantitative reasoning. How much carbon dioxide does a coal-fired power plant emit? How does that compare to carbon emissions from other thermal means of producing electricity? How much coal do we consume to generate electricity? When will the world run out of coal? How much will it cost to retrofit current power plants with carbon capture and storage technology? Once the science, engineering, and technology of these subjects are broached, the next logical step is to look at how quantitative data can inform the political debate surrounding coal and its future role as an energy source.

In the remaining pages of this chapter, we describe three performance tasks that revolve around humanity's use of coal as an energy source. They include: 1) a look at the costs of building power plants and their annual fuel needs; 2) an examination of the magnitude of harmful atmospheric emissions produced by electricity; and 3) an investigation of the magnitude of CO_2 emissions as related to coal-fired electricity generation. On a global, societal scale, this information is critical in understanding our potential options for decarbonizing the world's energy mix while meeting the growing global demand for electricity. These performance tasks represent only a small sample of how the energy topic of coal can be used to create performance tasks that span the entire STEM and QR spectrums.

Building and Powering a coal-fired Power Plant: How Much Coal?

The predominant technology used to produce electricity for residential, commercial, and industrial use is thermal power conversion. This process involves burning a fuel and, via a series of energy transformations (Figure 60), converting the heat released into electricity. The type of fuel used may be oil, natural gas, coal, biomass, or even municipal waste. In addition, it can be uranium in a nuclear power plant. A wide variety of technologies are available for thermal power conversion. Each process has different conversion efficiencies and emission characteristics as well as construction costs. This performance task (see Appendix A) examines the different types of thermal conversion technologies available and their economic and environmental advantages and disadvantages.

Heat Engine
Regardless of their heat source, thermal power plants are simply large, complex heat engines. A heat engine is a thermodynamic device that takes heat from a heat source at high temperature, produces some work (i.e. the electricity in our power plant example) and exhausts some heat to a heat sink at a lower temperature (Figure 82). Because heat engines were the driving force behind the Industrial Revolution, their study created the new science of thermodynamics (i.e. the study of the interaction of heat and matter).

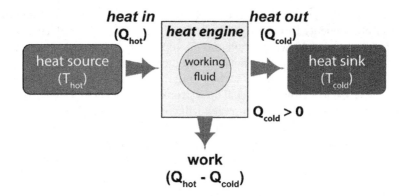

Figure 82. A heat engine is any machine that takes heat from a hot source and uses it to do useful work while exhausting unused heat to the environment. Our modern society is critically dependent upon heat engines to power almost all of its activities. Source: J.D. Myers, used with permission.

The real power of the heat engine concept is not its ability to explain how heat is converted to work, but in defining the maximum amount of work a heat engine can generate. Through the concept of thermal efficiency, thermodynamics defines how much work can be extracted from a given amount of heat. This limit is expressed in the concept of thermal or thermodynamic efficiency (i.e. the ratio of work out to heat in). The French engineer Sadi Carnot showed that the thermodynamic efficiency of an ideal heat engine (i.e. one with no extraneous energy losses) is equal to the ratio of the heat source and sink temperatures:

$$h = \left(1 - \frac{T_{cold}}{T_{not}}\right) \times 100\%$$

Based on this expression, thermodynamics clearly states that no matter how efficient our power plant, some of the energy in will be lost to the surroundings as waste heat.

Power Plant Capacity
Power plant electricity generating capacity is generally expressed in units of power (i.e. how much energy it can produce in a period of time). The unit for power is the watt (W) that is a Joule/second (J/s). Power plant electrical generating capacity is indicated in megawatts (1 MW = 10^6 W). Typical power plant capacities range from a few tens of a MW to several thousands of MW (1 GW = 1000 MW). Quite simply, thermal energy goes into a thermal power plant and electricity comes out. However, the laws of thermodynamics indicate that it is impossible to convert all of the heat input into an equivalent amount of electricity. Thus, power plants are described by

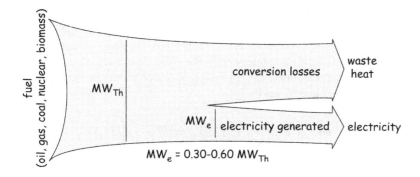

Figure 83. Schematic representation of the relation between the thermal input (MW$_{th}$) of a thermal electrical power station (left side) and its electrical output (MW$_e$) (right side). Much of the thermal input ends up as waste heat lost to the environment. Source: J.D. Myers used with permission.

the amount of energy they consume (MW$_{th}$ or megawatts thermal) and the amount of electricity they generate (MW$_e$ or megawatts electric) (Figure 83). Knowing the electrical generating capacity of the power plant (MW$_e$) and its efficiency (amount of thermal energy it converts to electricity), MW$_{th}$ can be calculated according to the equation:

$$MW_{th} = \frac{MW_e}{efficiency}$$

where plant efficiency is expressed as a decimal.

Powering an Electrical Power Plant
For a power plant to produce electricity, it must convert a specific amount of thermal energy into electrical energy. The energy a plant needs during a year is the product of the energy it uses per unit of time and the amount of time it is in operation during the year. From this knowledge, we can write the general expression for a power plant's annual energy need as:

$$annual\ energy\ demand = \left(\frac{energy\ used}{time}\right) \times \left(operating\ time\right)$$

Because W is a measure of power (i.e. energy/time), the thermal capacity (MW$_{Th}$) of a plant states how much energy it uses per second. Thus, the first term in the general expression is known. The second term is the amount of time a plant is actually producing electricity during the year. Because Watts are J/s, it is necessary to express operational time in s. When expressed in this form, the product of the two terms on the right yields J/y (i.e. the thermal energy converted in a year). For simplicity sake, it can be assumed that the plant operates 100% of the time. Since there are 3.17×10^7 seconds in a year, substitution into the relation above produces the equation for a power plant's annual energy needs:

$$annual\ energy\ demand = \left([MW_{Th}] \times 10^6 \frac{J}{s} \right) \times \left(3.15 \times 10^7 \frac{s}{y} \right)$$

Because power plants will be down some portion of the year for maintenance and repair, the energy demand calculated with this equation will be a maximum.

Fuel Needs

Once the energy used during a year by a power plant is known, it is a simple matter to calculate the amount of fuel necessary to supply this energy. The answer is found by dividing the energy demand by the energy content of the fuel that will be consumed:

$$annual\ fuel\ consumption = \frac{annual\ energy\ demand}{fuel\ energy\ content}$$

Perhaps the only real problem with using this expression is keeping the units straight. Typically, the annual energy demand will be in J/s. Unfortunately, the units of the fuel energy content will vary depending upon the type of fuel. Typically, coal will be expressed in Btu/lb whereas natural gas is Btu/ft^3. Thus, the energy units of one of two quantities must be converted to the other. If Btus are used, the final answer is in pounds, a rather small unit to be using for the annual fuel needs of a power plant. Thus, this quantity would have to be converted to the more useful tons.

How Much Does it Cost to Build and Fuel an Electrical Power Station?

Using the data in the handout, for each plant type calculate: MW_{Th}; total construction cost; Joules (J) and Btu required to run each plant for a year assuming the plant runs 24/7 for 365 days; annual fuel requirements; how much coal is consumed over a 30 year lifetime; and the amount of ash (in tons) each plant must dispose of annually and over its operational lifetime.

Atmospheric Emissions: SO_2 and NOx

Coal combustion is an important source of SO_2 and NOx emissions. To provide a sense of scale for these emissions and how effective the various pollution control devices that are available are, we are going to calculate the emissions for a single coal-fired power plant.

Using the data in Appendix B and your results from the performance task for Appendix A, for each plant type calculate: amount of SO_2 (in tons) emitted yearly over an operational lifetime (e.g. 30 years); tons of SO_2 that must be disposed of yearly. Although you will find these are large numbers, remember they represent the SO_2 emissions from a single power plant. Think about the magnitude of this environmental issue when all the power plants in the nation or world are included.

We can do the same exercise for nitrogen oxides. Thus, over a 30 year period; calculate the amount of NO_2 (in tons) emitted yearly over an operational lifetime (e.g. 30 years); and tons of NO_2 that must be disposed of yearly and over a 30 year period. Notice how the numbers are large, but not as large as for sulfur dioxide.

Once these values have been calculated, there are many follow-up activities that could be used to teach additional QR skills and highlight the complexity of energy use. For example, there could be a discussion of the factors that will change the magnitude of the emissions (e.g. change in fuel used), installation of different pollution control technologies, etc. To bring in an economic viewpoint while still working with QR skills, students could be asked to calculate how much installation of the pollution devices cost and how that impacts the price of electricity.

Coal's Greenhouse Gas (GHG) Emissions and Carbon Footprint

Since the start of the Industrial Revolution, there has been an ever increasing growth in the amount of carbon dioxide in the Earth's atmosphere (Figure 84). Because it is a greenhouse gas, many scientific models of the atmosphere project that the growth in CO_2 will negatively impact future climate. To slow or stop this increase, there have been national, regional, and international efforts to limit the emission of carbon dioxide from fossil fuel combustion. Although many proponents point to the success in lowering sulfur dioxide and nitrogen oxide emissions as evidence that CO_2 emissions can be readily controlled, the emission of carbon dioxide is on a much larger scale than either SO_2 or NOx. These acid gases are present in flue streams in only trace amounts. In contrast, CO_2 makes up a much larger portion of the exhaust gas of a fossil fuel combustion chamber.

The CAA and GHG Emissions

Currently, there is no law limiting emissions of CO_2 in the United States. The Clean Air Act does not list carbon dioxide as one of the atmospheric pollutants that EPA was required to set emission standards for. There have been, however, attempts to legislation a 'price' on carbon at the federal level. The American Clean Energy and Security Act of 2009 (H.R. 2454) would have placed a limit on carbon emission. It was introduced into the House on May 15, 2009 and passed in the House of Representatives on June 26, 2009 (219 yea/212 nay/3 present-not voting). The bill was introduced into the Senate on July 7, 2009, but never voted on. It has not been re-

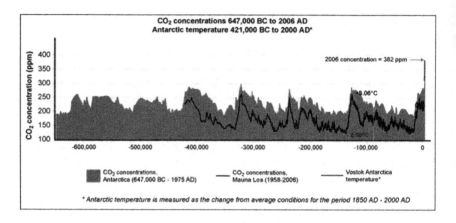

Figure 84. Atmospheric CO_2 for the last 700,000 years. The increase in CO_2 since the start of the Industrial Revolution is the fast change recorded in the last seven millennium and has attained the highest level in this time span. Source: EPA.

introduced in subsequent Congressional sessions. There have been, however, efforts at the state and even municipal levels to limit the emission of carbon dioxide. Given the lack of legislative movement on reducing carbon dioxide emissions, some groups have pursued a legal approach to carbon dioxide emission reductions in the U.S.

In 1999, EPA was petitioned by a number of parties to regulate greenhouse gas (GHG) emissions from new motor vehicles under provisions of the Clean Air Act (CAA). After review, EPA concluded that the CAA did not give them authority to regulate CO_2 as an air pollutant. Furthermore, they stated that even if it did, the agency would not propose such regulation because of policy reasons (Meltz, 2007).

Several years later, Massachusetts brought legal suit against EPA to force them to regulate GHGs as pollutants under the CAA. Numerous states, cities, and NGOs joined the suit as co-complainants whereas other states, industry groups as well as business organizations sided with the EPA. This litigation worked its way through the federal court system all the way to the U.S. Supreme Court. In April, 2007, the court decided 5-4 in favour of Massachusetts and ordered EPA to conduct a review of carbon dioxide emissions under the authority of the CAA to determine if CO_2 emissions are a threat to human welfare and health. On April 17, 2009, EPA issued a finding that six GHGs "in the atmosphere may reasonably be anticipated to endanger public health and ... public welfare". With this finding, EPA has the statutory authority to regulate carbon emissions. However, the original CAA was designed for a different class of pollutants and had set threshold levels for emissions of regulated pollutants at 100-250 tons/year. At this level, virtually anyone in the U.S. who used fossil fuels would be deemed a polluter and subject to regulation. To adjust the CO_2 emission threshold level, EPA has created the Greenhouse Gas Tailoring Rule, which set the standard for regulation at 50,000 tons of CO_2 per year.

EPA has now issued standards for new power plants and is working on rules for existing installations.

At first glance it may seem that the application of the CAA to the problem of acid precipitation and smog provides a hopeful precedent for dealing with carbon emissions and global climate change. However, the magnitude of CO_2 emissions is far greater than for either SO_2 or NOx. Indeed, the former are present in flue gas streams at only trace element abundances. In contrast, the exhaust gas from a coal-fired power plant may contain several percent carbon dioxide. Mitigating carbon dioxide emissions from electricity generation is going to be a far more difficult task than it was for sulfur dioxide or nitrogen oxides. Illustrating the magnitude of this task provides a unique and powerful opportunity to teach students the power of quantitative reasoning.

How Big Are CO_2 Emissions?
Using the data from Appendix C and your results from the first performance task, for each plant type calculate: the yearly CO_2 emissions; and the carbon dioxide emitted by a plant over its 30-year operational lifetime. Compare these results to those for SO_2 and NOx. Do you think the regulatory framework for these latter air pollutants will work effectively for carbon dioxide emissions?

SUMMARY

The widespread and extensive use of coal as an energy source changed the world forever. As the primary energy source for the Industrial Revolution, it completely altered industry, transportation became cheaper, faster and available to a wider segment of society, and whole new economic sectors emerged. With its ascendance as the primary energy source for electricity, it again had a profound impact on the world. Electricity has transformed nearly every aspect of modern life. It is hard to imagine modern society without it. Likewise, it is difficult to envision the global spread of electricity access without cheap and abundant coal supplies. Coal has done much to improve the lives of many of the world's peoples. Because it is widely distributed and easy to extract, coal has the potential to lift millions in the developing world out of energy poverty and improve their lives in numerous ways. As the demand for energy grows in the developing world, the use of coal to meet this demand is likely to grow as well. Coal is cheap to produce and there are proven and tested technologies to harness its energy.

Yet, there is a dark side to coal use as well. Coal mining has devastated landscapes, polluted streams, and cost countless lives in mining accidents across the world. It is a major contributor to air pollution through the emission of oxides of sulfur and nitrogen as well as particulate matter. Likewise, mercury emissions have had a negative impact on ecosystems across the globe. However, in much of the developed world, these impacts have been minimized and even mitigated with the passage of environmental laws regulating how coal is used. The deployment of air pollution control devices has dramatically improved air quality by lowering the emission of a range of air pollutants. At the same time, regulations have reduced the adverse impacts of coal mining on the landscape, wildlife, and ecosystems. As these technologies and legal frameworks migrate to developing nations, the impacts of these environmental consequences of coal are also likely to decrease.

While coal has changed the world for the better in many ways, it is facing an increasingly uncertain future. As a fossil fuel, it emits carbon dioxide, a potent and persistent greenhouse gas. Because it is the most carbon-rich of the fossil fuels, coal produces more carbon dioxide per unit of energy than any other fossil fuel. With the growth in energy demand and the desire for the services electricity provides, the combustion of coal threatens the stability of the world's climate. These factors all suggest humanity should replace coal in our global energy mix with other less carbon intense primary energy sources. However at present, these sources cannot provide the reliable, cheap, and consistent source of energy the world needs. Coal offers the billions of energy-poor people around the world with a quick and relatively cheap path to energy security and wealth, while maintaining living standards for billions of others. In the past, a combination of regulation and scientific, technological, and engineering innovations have reduced coal's negative externalities. Can it be done again? Given our need to protect the global climate and to meet the growing global demand for energy, humanity faces two important and interrelated questions. First, can we find a way to replace the vast energy extracted with coal with an equally large, reliable, and cheap low-carbon energy source? Second, can we devise a way to keep using coal while reducing its carbon footprint? How humanity answers these two questions will determine the energy future of millions. Preparing our students adequately to engage in this important debate about the future of coal is an important and critical educational task that also allows educators to introduce students to STEM and QR principles in an engaging, relevant, and meaningful manner. Providing students with the QR and STEM skills necessary to address this and other energy questions aligns well with the goals of a liberal education.

NOTES

[1]   A quad is an energy unit equal to a quadrillion (10^{15}) Btus or 1.055×10^{18} Joules and used extensively by the U.S. Department of Energy.

[2]   A short ton is a unit of mass equal to 2,000 pounds (907 kg). It is commonly used in the U.S where it is simply referred to as the ton. A long ton equals 2,200 pounds and is equivalent to the metric ton or tonne.

[3]   The toe or tonnes of oil equivalent is an energy unit equivalent to the burning of 1 tonne of crude oil (i.e. by convention 42 GJ of energy) and is a means of comparing the energy content of different types of primary energy. Mtoe is a multiple of toe equalling one million toe. A Gtoe is one billion toe. Mtoe and Gtoe are used for very large amounts of energy.

[4]   The other mine class for surface mining is aqueous mining.

[5]   The coal mining industry refers to this type of mining as highwall mining. However, since both auger and 'cutter' mining begin operations at a highwall, the term highwall is used for both variants here.

REFERENCES

Baer, A. (1998). *Down the common: A year in the life of a medieval woman.* M. Evans & Company.

BP. (2013). *Statistical Review of World Energy 2013.*

Copeland, C. (2008). *Mountaintop mining: Background on current controversies* (9 pp). Washington, DC: Congressional Research Service.

Copeland, C. (2013). *Controversies over redefining "fill material" under the Clean Water Act* (10 pp), Congressional Research Service.

DOE. (2002). *Pinon pine IGCC power project—A DOE assessment* (39 pp). Morgantown, WV: Department of Energy.

DOE. (2007). *Cost and performance baseline for fossil energy plants—Volume 1: Bituminous coal and natural gas to electicity final report* (516 pp). Morgantown, WV: Department of Energy.

EIA. (2011). *Wyoming produces almost as much coal as the next seven states combined.* Washington, DC: Today in Energy, Energy Information Administration. Retrieved March 1, 2014, from http://www.eia. gov/todayinenergy/detail.cfm?id=2770

EIA. (2012). *Annual energy review 2011.* Energy Information Administration: Washington, DC.

EPA. (1999). *Nitrogen oxides (NOx), why and how they are controlled* (57 pp). Washington, DC: Environmental Protection Agency.

EPA. (2001). *Cost of selective catayltic reduction (SCR) application for NOx control on coal-fired boilers* (23 pp). Washington, DC: Environmental Protection Agency.

EPA. (2003a). *Dry electrostatic precipitator (ESP)—Wire-pipe type* (5 pp). Washington, DC: Environmental Protection Agency.

EPA. (2003b). *Dry electrostatic precipitator (ESP)—Wire-plate type* (6 pp). Washington, DC: Environmental Protection Agency.

EPA. (2003c). *Fabric filter—Mechanical shaker cleaned type* (6 pp). Washington, DC: Environmental Protection Agency.

EPA. (2003d). *Fabric filter—Pulse-jet cleaned type* (6 pp). Washington, DC: Environmental Protection Agency.

EPA. (2003e). *Fabric filter—Reverse-air cleaned type* (7 pp). Washington, DC: Environmental Protection Agency.

EPA. (2003f). *Flue gas desulfurization (FGD)—Wet, spray dry, and dry scrubbers* (6 pp). Washington, DC: Environmental Protection Agency.

EPA. (2003g). *Selective catalytic reduction (SCR)* (5 pp). Washington, DC: Environmental Protection Agency.

EPA. (2003h). *Wet electrostatic precipitator (DSP)—Wire-pipe type* (4 pp). Washington, DC: Environmental Protection Agency.

EPA. (2003i). *Wet electrostatic precipitator (ESP)—Wire-plate type* (6 pp). Washington, DC: Environmental Protection Agency.

EPA. (2011). *The effects of mountaintop mines and valley fills on aquatic ecosystems of the central appalachian coalfields* (153 pp). Washington, DC: Environmental Protection Agency.

EPA. (2014a). *Cross-state air pollution rule (CSAPR).* Washington, DC: Environmental Protection Agency. Retrieved March 6, 2014, from http://www.epa.gov/airtransport/CSAPR/

EPA. (2014b). *National ambient air quality standards (NAAQS).* Washington, DC: Environmental Protection Agency. Retrieved March 4, 2014, from http://epa.gov/air/criteria.html

GEA. (2012). *Global energy assessment—Toward a sustainable future,* Cambridge University Press, Cambridge, UK and New York, NY, USA and the International Institute for Applied Systems Analysis, Laxenburg, Austria, 1865 pp.

Hirsch, R. L., Bezdek, R., & Wendling, R. (2005). *Peaking of world oil production: Impacts, mitigation, and risk management.* Pittsburgh, PA: National Energy Technology Laboratory, Department of Energy.

Höök, M., & Aleklett, K. (2010). A review on coal-to-liquid fuels and its coal consumption. *International Journal of Energy Research, 34*(10), 848–864.

Humphries, M. (2003). *U.S. coal: A primer on the major issues* (40 pp). Washington, DC: Congressional Research Service.

Jaireth, S., & Huleatt, M. (2012). *Australian coal resources* (2012 ed.). Canberra, ACT: Geoscience Australia.

Jones, N. R. (2010). *Genesis of thick coal deposits and their unique angular relationships: Powder River Basin* (55 pp). Wyoming State Geological Survey. Report of Investigations No. 60.

Kenney, R. (2007). Surface Mining Control and Reclamation Act of 1977, United States.

McClurg, J. E. (1988). *Peat forming wetlands and the thick Powder River Basin coals.* Casper, WY: Wyoming Geological Association. 39th Field Conference Guidebook, 229–236.

Meltz, R. (2007). *The supreme court's climate change decision: Massachusetts v. EPA* (6 pp). Washington, DC: Congressional Research Service.

Mohr, S., Höök, M., Mudd, G., & Evans, G. (2011). Projection of long-term paths for Australian coal production—Comparisons of four models. *International Journal of Coal Geology, 86*(4), 329–341.

Rhodes, R. (2007). *Energy transitions: A curious history* (17 pp). Stanford, CA: Stanford University.

Rosenberg, D. L. (2000). Mountaintop mining and proposed rule change will waste Clean Water Act. *National Wetlands Newsletter, 22*(4), 12.

Schimm, B. (2001). Efficiency with surface miners. *World Coal, 10,* 15–18.

Schweinfurth, S. P. (2003). Coal—A complex natural resource. *U.S. Geological Survey Circular 1143* (51 pp). Reston, VA: U.S. Geological Survey.

Schweinfurth, S. P. (2009a). *Chapter C: An introduction to coal quality* (20 pp). U.S.G.S. Professional Paper 1625-F: The National Coal Resource Assessment Overview. U.S. Geological Survey, Washington, DC.

Schweinfurth, S. P. (Ed.). (2009b). *Chapter C: An introduction to coal quality* (20 pp). U.S.G.S. Professional Paper 1625-F: The National Coal Resource Assessment Overview. U.S. Geological Survey, Reston, Virginia.

SEPC. (n.d.). John W. Turk, Jr. Power Plant, pp. 1.

Shen, B., & Fama, M. D. (2001). Geomechanics and highwall mining. *World Coal, 10*(2), 35–38.

Stranges, A. N. (2001). Germany's synthetic fuel industry 19-27-1945. *Energeia, 12*(5), 1–2, 6.

Tao, Z., & Li, M. (2007). What is the limit of Chinese coal supplies—A STELLA model of Hubbert Peak. *Energy Policy, 35*(6), 3145–3154.

Thomas, L. (2002). *Coal geology* (384 pp). Hoboken, NJ: John Wiley & Sons, Ltd.

Vasireddy, S., Morreale, B., Cugini, A., Song, C., & Spivey, J. J. (2011). Clean liquid fuels from direct coal liquefaction: Chemistry, catalysis, technological status and challenges. *Energy & Environmental Science, 4*(2), 311–345.

Walker, S. (2001). Highwall miners keep the coal flowing. *World Coal, 10*(12), 20–26.

WCA. (2013a). *Coal market & transportation.* World Coal Association.

WCA. (2013b). *Coal statistics.* World Coal Association.

Wickham, J., Wood, P. B., Nicholson, M. C., Jenkins, W., Druckenbrod, D., Suter, G. W., … Amos, J., 2013. The overlooked terrestrial impacts of mountaintop mining. *BioScience, 63*(5), 335–348.

Wolfe, M. E., & Wickstrom, L. (2008). Coal (9 pp). *Educational Leaflet No. 8.* Ohio Geological Survey. Retrieved October 28, 2014 from http://minerals.ohiodnr.gov/portals/minerals/pdf/coal/el08.pdf

Yang, C. -J., & Jackson, R. B. (2013). China's synthetic natural gas revolution. *Nature Climate Change, 3*(10), 852–854.

APPENDIX A: FUEL CONSUMPTION AND PLANT DESIGN

To gain a feeling for the environmental impact of coal-fired electrical power, we need to calculate how much fuel a plant uses on an annual basis as well as the amount it will consume over its operational lifetime. The amount of fuel a coal-fired power plant uses to generate electricity is dependent upon: 1) the size of the plant; 2) the technology used by the plant; and 3) the type of coal being burned. In this activity, we will compare how these factors influence fuel consumption.

The characteristics of the power plants we will investigate are given in the table below:

Plant Type	Capacity (MW$_e$)	Efficiency (%)	Capital Costs ($/kW$_e$)	Sulfur Reduction %
pulverized coal (PC) w/o scrubbers	850	36	$1,100	-
pulverized coal (PC) w/ scrubbers	850	36	$1,100	90
pressurized fluidized bed combustor (PFBC)	850	42	$1,700	90
super-critical pulverized coal (SCPC)	850	38.5	$2,500	90
SCPC w/ CC	850	29.3	$4,205	90

Type	Energy Content (Btu/lb)	Ash (%)	S (%)	C (%)	H (%)	O (%)	N (%)	Hg (%)	Price ($/ton)
subbituminous	8,350	0.1	1.5	75	0.2	0.3	0.3		$13

Using the data above, for each plant type calculate:

1. MW$_{Th}$
2. Total construction cost
3. Joules (J) and British thermal units (Btu) required to run each plant for a year assuming the plant runs 24/7 for 365 days
4. Annual fuel requirements
5. How much coal is consumed over a 30 year lifetime?
6. The amount of ash (in tons) each plant must dispose annually and over its operational lifetime.

APPENDIX B: SOX AND NOX EMISSIONS

Coal contains small amounts of trace constituents (e.g. sulfur (S), nitrogen (N), mercury (Hg)) as well as a variety of heavy metals. Prior to the Clean Air Act (CAA), these combustion products were simply vented to the atmosphere. During combustion, sulfur combines with oxygen to form sulfur dioxide (SO_2), which when combined with water vapor in the atmosphere produces sulfuric acid. This contributes to acid precipitation, which harms plants and aquatic species. Nitrogen oxides in the atmosphere contribute to smog.

The CAA required power plants to control the amounts of these air pollutants they released. In most cases, this involved installing scrubbers on the plant. These scrubbers removed these gas components from the exhaust gas before it is sent up the smokestack. This activity will demonstrate the impact the CAA has had on limiting emissions of nitrogen and sulfur oxides from coal-fired power plants.

The following are the characteristics of the power plants we investigated in the first activity.

Plant Type	Capacity (MW$_e$)	Efficiency (%)	Capital Costs ($/kW$_e$)	S Reduction %	N Reduction %
pulverized coal (PC) w/o scrubbers	850	36	$1,100	-	-
pulverized coal (PC) w/ scrubbers	850	36	$1,100	90	95
pressurized fluidized bed combustor (PFBC)	850	42	$1,700	90	95
super-critical pulverized coal (SCPC)	850	38.5	$2,500	90	95
SCPC w/ CC	850	29.3	$4,205	90	95

Type	Energy Content (Btu/lb)	Ash (%)	S (%)	C (%)	H (%)	O (%)	N (%)	Hg (%)	Price ($/ton)
subbituminous	8,350	0.1	1.5	75	0.2	0.3	0.3		$13

Using the data above and your results from the first activity, for each plant type calculate:

1. Amount of SO_2 (in tons) emitted yearly over an operational lifetime (e.g. 30 years)
2. Tons of SO_2 that must be disposed of yearly and over a 30 year period
3. Amount of NO_2 (in tons) emitted yearly over an operational lifetime (e.g. 30 years)
4. Tons of NO_2 that must be disposed of yearly and over a 30 year period.

APPENDIX C: CARBON DIOXIDE (CO_2) EMISSIONS

The combustion of any fossil fuels results in the emission of carbon dioxide (CO_2). Because it is a greenhouse gas (GHG), concern has grown over the continued emission of CO_2 from expanding fossil fuel use. Given their large production of CO_2 and stationary position, coal-fired electrical power stations are a particular concern with regards to controlling carbon dioxide emissions. This activity will investigate the magnitude of carbon dioxide emitted by typical coal power stations.

Below are the characteristics of the power plants we investigated in the first activity.

Plant Type	Capacity (MW_e)	Efficiency (%)	Capital Costs ($/kW_e$)	C Reduction %
pulverized coal (PC) w/o scrubbers	850	36	$1,100	-
pulverized coal (PC) w/ scrubbers	850	36	$1,100	-
pressurized fluidized bed combustor (PFBC)	850	42	$1,700	-
super-critical pulverized coal (SCPC)	850	38.5	$2,500	-
SCPC w/ CC	850	29.3	$4,205	90

Type	Energy Content (Btu/lb)	Ash (%)	S (%)	C (%)	H (%)	O (%)	N (%)	Hg (%)	Price ($/ton)
subbituminous	8,350	0.1	1.5	75	0.2	0.3	0.3		$13

Using the data above and your results from the first activity, for each plant type calculate:

1. The yearly CO_2 emissions
2. The carbon dioxide emitted by a plant over its 30-year operational lifetime.

CPSIA information can be obtained at www.ICGtesting.com
Printed in the USA
LVOW03s0042310315

432670LV00004B/59/P